POSUKA DEMIZU

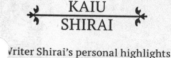

KAIU SHIRAI

Ev[...] libr[...] people ask me, "What [...] is Mr. Minerva?" And every time I evaded the question, I was looking forward to this day.

Isn't it nice to have something to look forward to?!

What I'm currently looking forward to is the second season of the anime in 2020! And what I'm going to eat tomorrow.

Next is volume 15! Please look forward to it!

Writer Shirai's personal highlights for *The Promised Neverland* fanatics, part 10!

1. Chris's name (Kurisu) and the Japanese word for medicine (kusuri) being similar was a coincidence. (I realized it later.)

2. Zazie is actually five years old.

3. Highlight #3 in volume 13 might make more sense after you read chapter 120 in this volume.

About the splash page for chapter 118… The remaining pages in their scripts represent their remaining life spans. Only Ray is holding two, but it's not clear which one is the script. Isn't that crazy? I love it!!

Please enjoy this volume!

Posuka Demizu debuted as a manga artist with the 2013 *CoroCoro* series *Oreca Monster Bouken Retsuden*. A collection of illustrations, *The Art of Posuka Demizu*, was released in 2016 by PIE International.

Kaiu Shirai debuted in 2015 with *Ashley Gate no Yukue* on the *Shonen Jump+* website. Shirai first worked with Posuka Demizu on the two-shot *Poppy no Negai*, which was released in February 2016.

THE PROMISED NEVERLAND

VOLUME 14
SHONEN JUMP Manga Edition

STORY BY KAIU SHIRAI
ART BY POSUKA DEMIZU

Translation/Satsuki Yamashita
Touch-Up Art & Lettering/Mark McMurray
Design/Julian [JR] Robinson
Editor/Alexis Kirsch

Printed in the U.S.A.

Published by VIZ Media, LLC
P.O. Box 77010
San Francisco, CA 94107

10 9 8 7 6 5 4 3 2 1
First printing, March 2020

VIZ MEDIA
viz.com

SHONEN JUMP
shonenjump.com

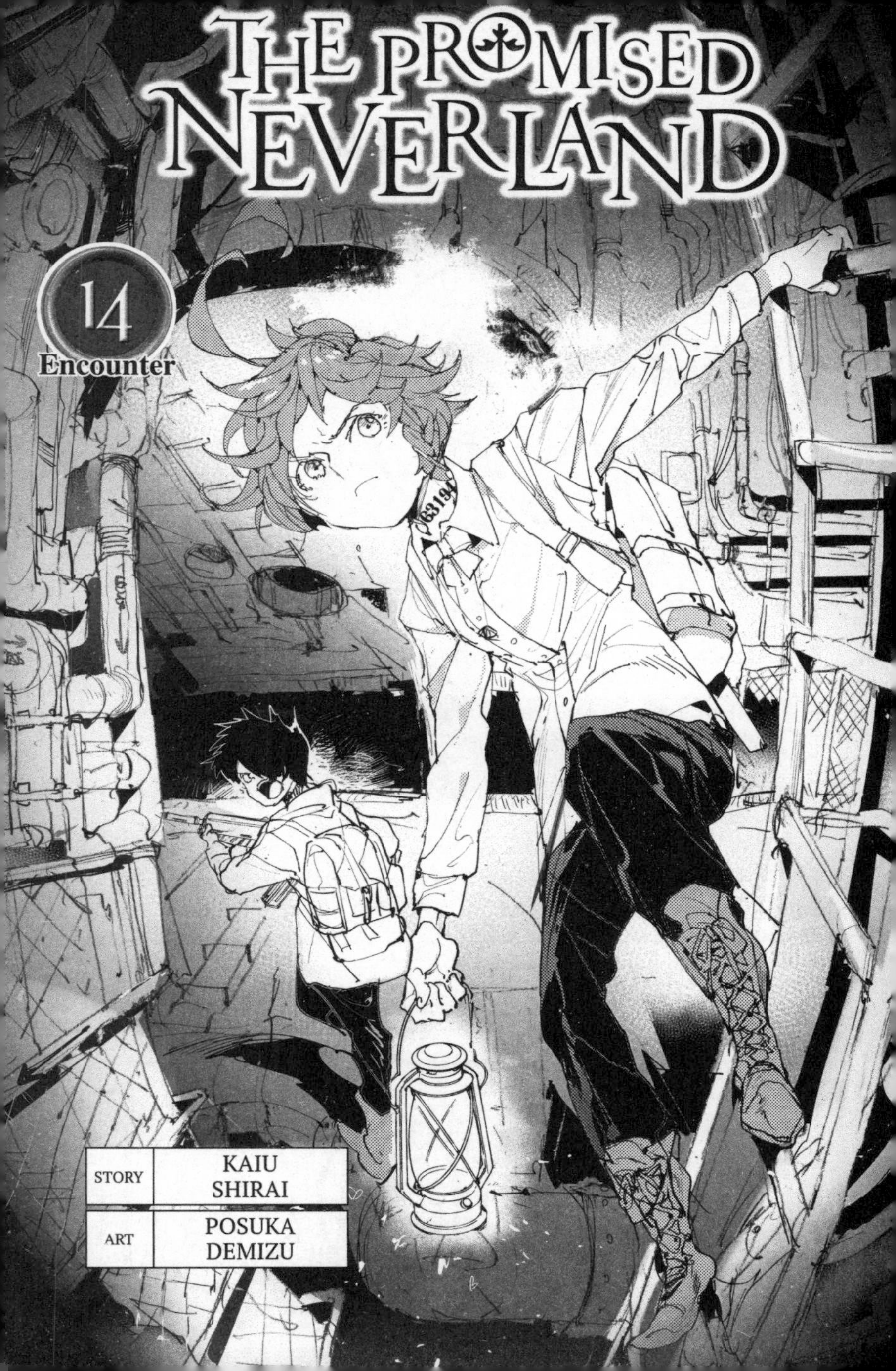
THE PROMISED NEVERLAND
14
Encounter
63194
STORY KAIU SHIRAI
ART POSUKA DEMIZU

CHARACTERS

The Children of Grace Field House

They aim to free all of the children who are trapped in Grace Field House within the next two months.

RAY

On the Run

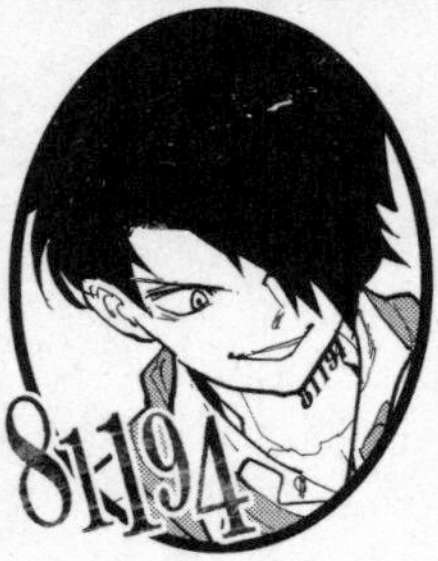
81194

The only one among the Grace Field House children who can match wits with Norman.

EMMA

On the Run

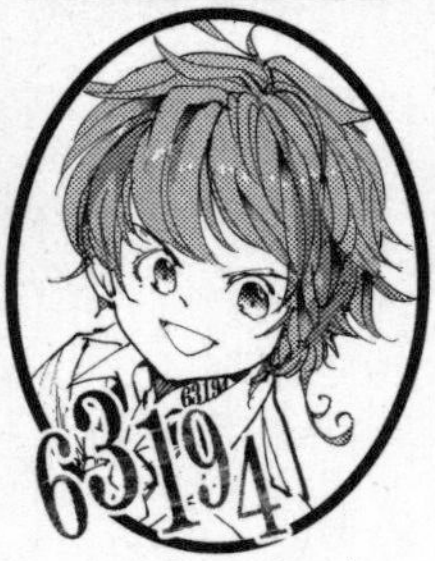
63194

An enthusiastic and optimistic girl with superb athletic and learning abilities.

NORMAN

In New Farm Lambda

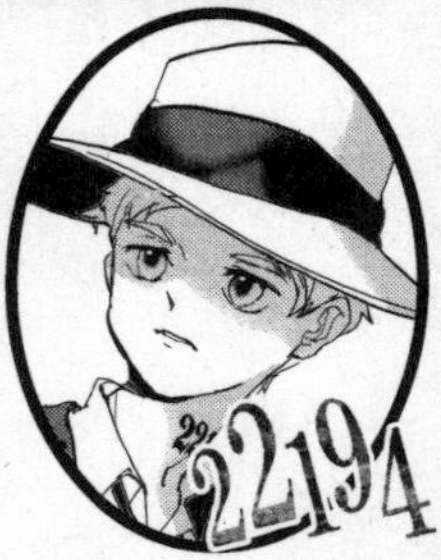
22194

A boy with excellent analytical and decision-making capabilities. He is the smartest of the children from Grace Field House.

CAROL

In Grace Field House

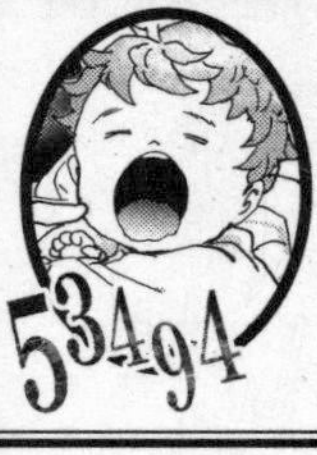
53494

PHIL

In Grace Field House

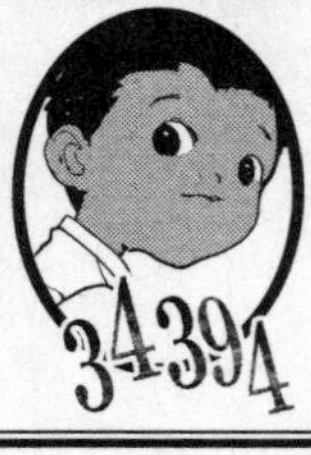
34394

GILDA

On the Run

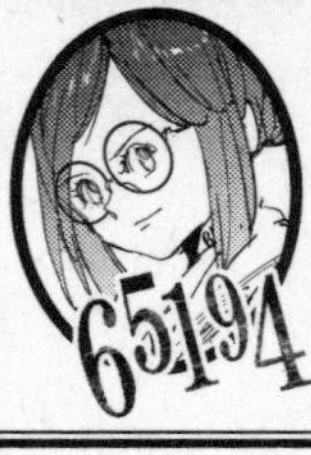
65194

DON

On the Run

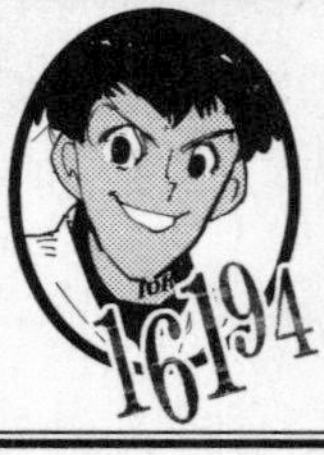
16194

The Children of Grand Valley

The children who were trapped in Goldy Pond, a hunting ground for demons. They started a rebellion and won the battle against the demons.

ZACK

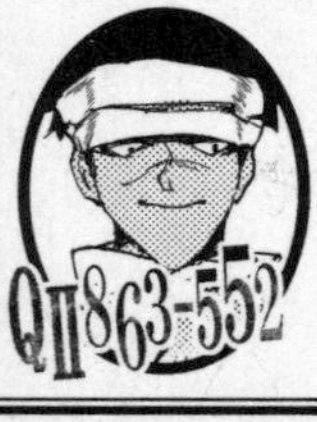
QII863-552

VIOLET

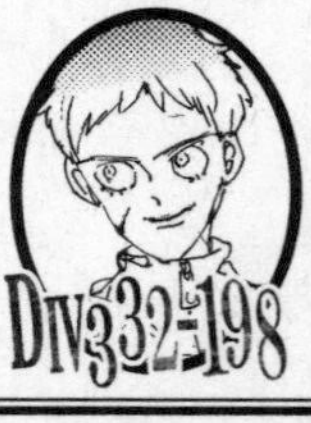
DIV332-198

SONYA

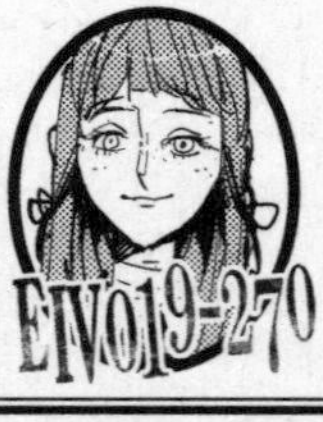
EIV019-270

OLIVER

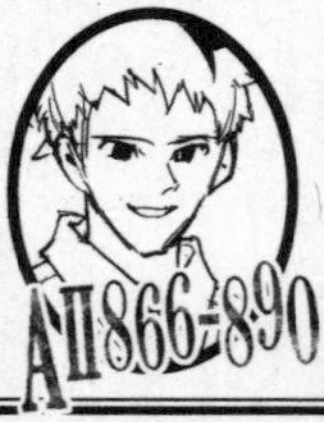
AII866-890

The Ratri Clan

They seek to kill the children who escaped the farms and Goldy Pond as well as the supporters who help them.

PETER RATRI   ANDREW

William Minerva's Group

They set out on a journey to protect Emma's group but were saved by them instead when they were attacked by a wild demon.

HAYATO   JIN

???

Said to be located in a mysterious space with a dragon.

???

???

Nomadic demons. They are forbidden by their religion to eat humans raised in farms.

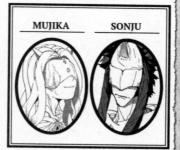

MUJIKA   SONJU

Supporters

They support children who escape by providing tools and facilities.

WILLIAM MINERVA (JAMES RATRI)

The Story So Far

Emma is living happily at Grace Field House with her foster siblings. One day, she realizes that they are being bred as food for demons and escapes with a group of other children. After meeting new friends and gaining further information, she decides to free all of the children raised in the farms. Her group takes action to achieve this goal and obtains a clue to overwrite the current promise that is the cause of the children being eaten. But suddenly they are attacked by the Ratri clan, and they lose their home and their means of contact with their supporters. With no time to mourn, the group heads to a new location, where they encounter Minerva's allies. They decide to head to Minerva's base, but then Chris's injuries take a turn for the worse.

THE PROMISED NEVERLAND 14

Encounter

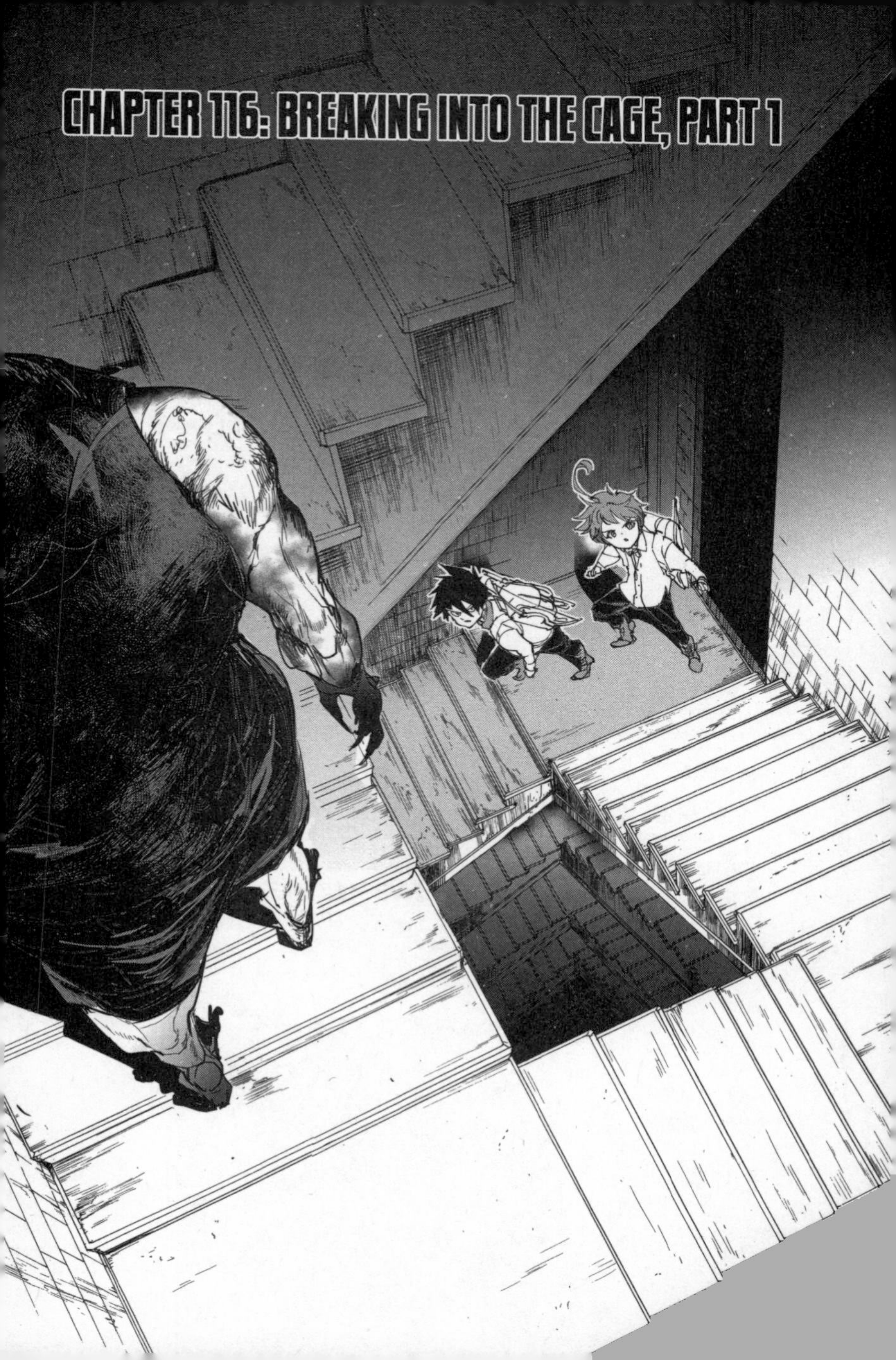
CHAPTER 116: BREAKING INTO THE CAGE, PART 1

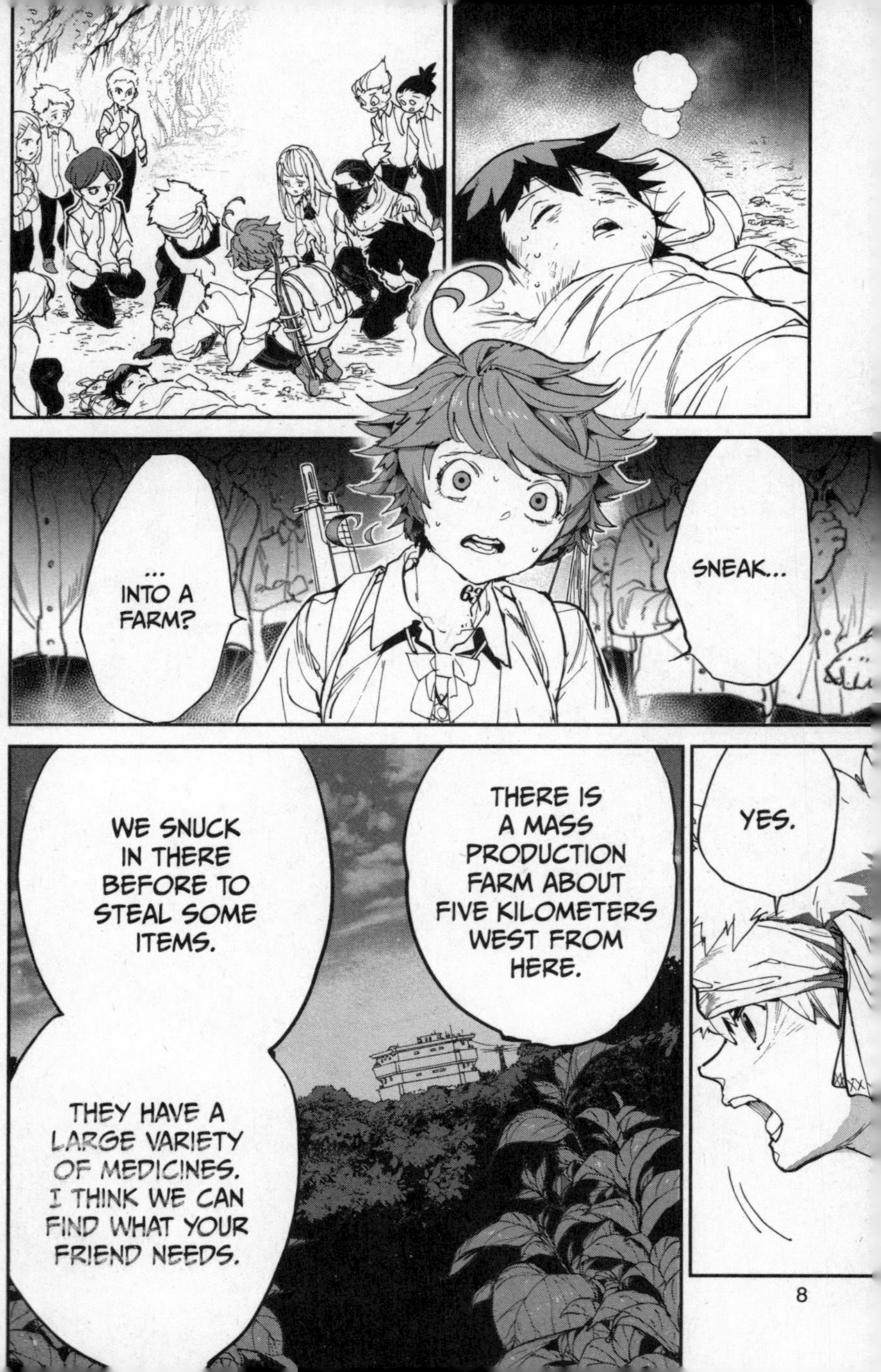
SNEAK...
... INTO A FARM?
YES.
THERE IS A MASS PRODUCTION FARM ABOUT FIVE KILOMETERS WEST FROM HERE.
WE SNUCK IN THERE BEFORE TO STEAL SOME ITEMS.
THEY HAVE A LARGE VARIETY OF MEDICINES. I THINK WE CAN FIND WHAT YOUR FRIEND NEEDS.

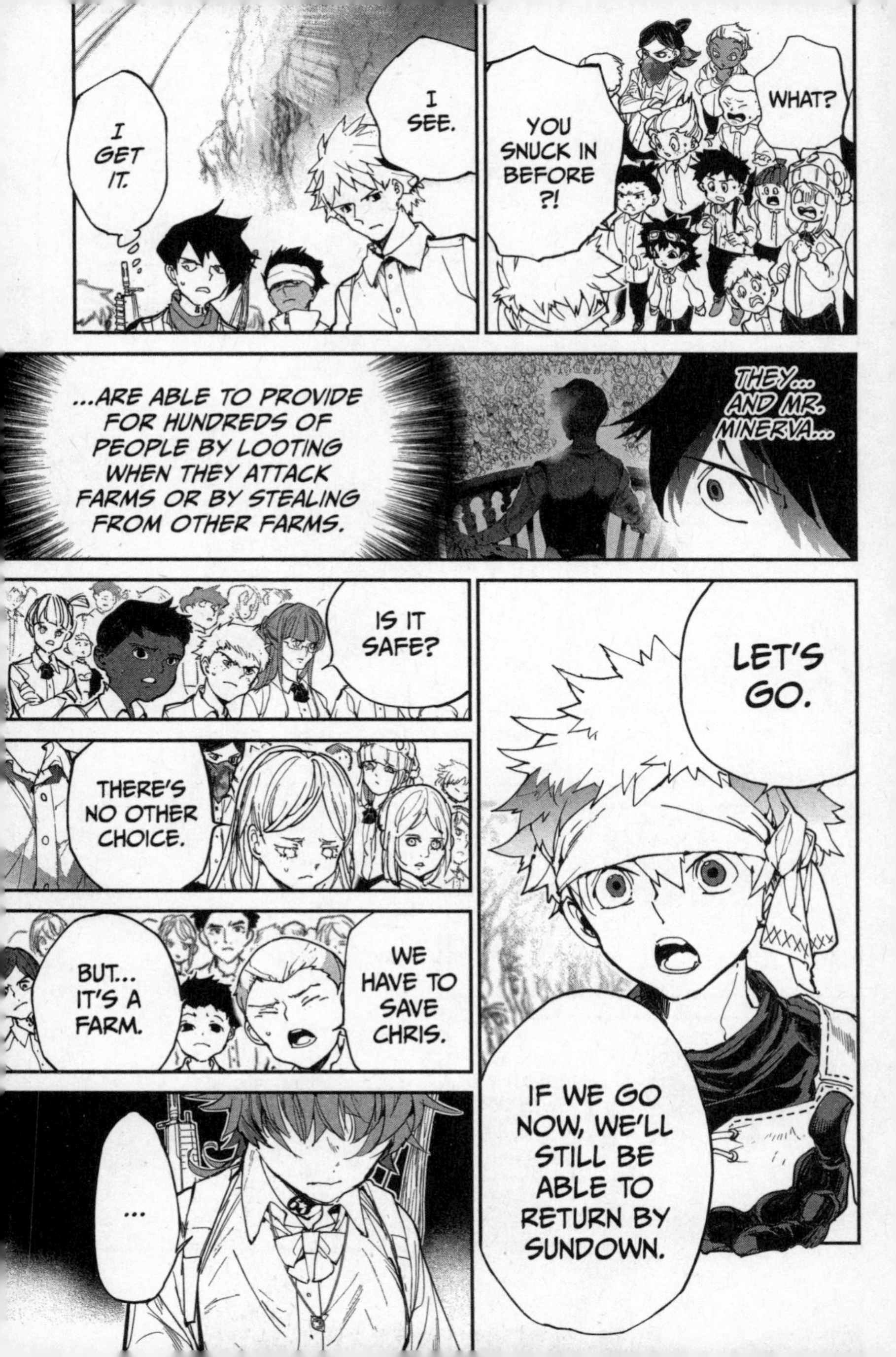
WHAT?
YOU SNUCK IN BEFORE ?!
I SEE.
I GET IT.
THEY... AND MR. MINERVA...
...ARE ABLE TO PROVIDE FOR HUNDREDS OF PEOPLE BY LOOTING WHEN THEY ATTACK FARMS OR BY STEALING FROM OTHER FARMS.
LET'S GO.
IF WE GO NOW, WE'LL STILL BE ABLE TO RETURN BY SUNDOWN.
IS IT SAFE?
THERE'S NO OTHER CHOICE.
WE HAVE TO SAVE CHRIS.
BUT... IT'S A FARM.
...

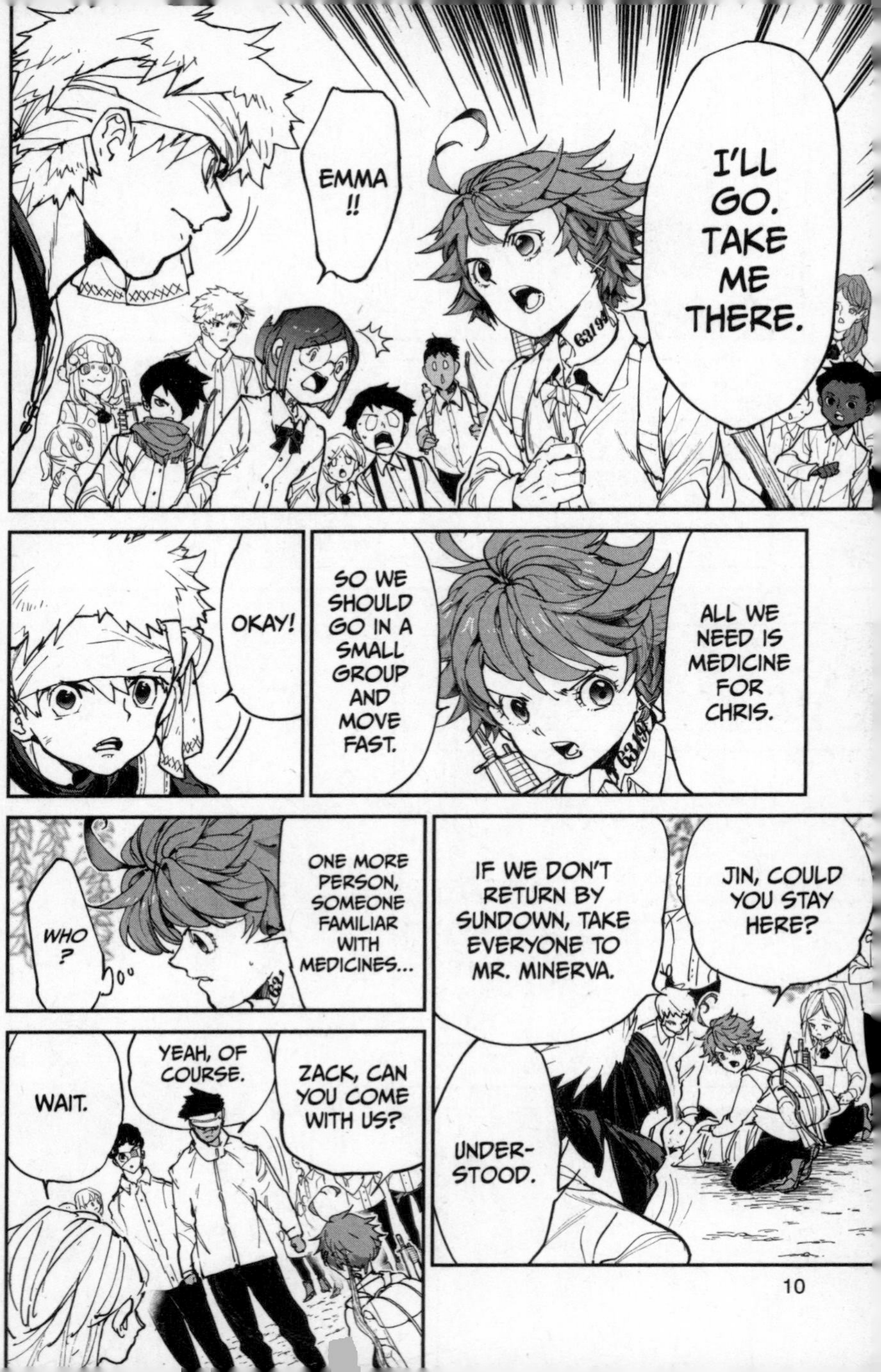

I'LL GO. TAKE ME THERE.
EMMA!!
ALL WE NEED IS MEDICINE FOR CHRIS.
SO WE SHOULD GO IN A SMALL GROUP AND MOVE FAST.
OKAY!
JIN, COULD YOU STAY HERE?
IF WE DON'T RETURN BY SUNDOWN, TAKE EVERYONE TO MR. MINERVA.
UNDER-STOOD.
ONE MORE PERSON, SOMEONE FAMILIAR WITH MEDICINES...
WHO?
ZACK, CAN YOU COME WITH US?
YEAH, OF COURSE.
WAIT.

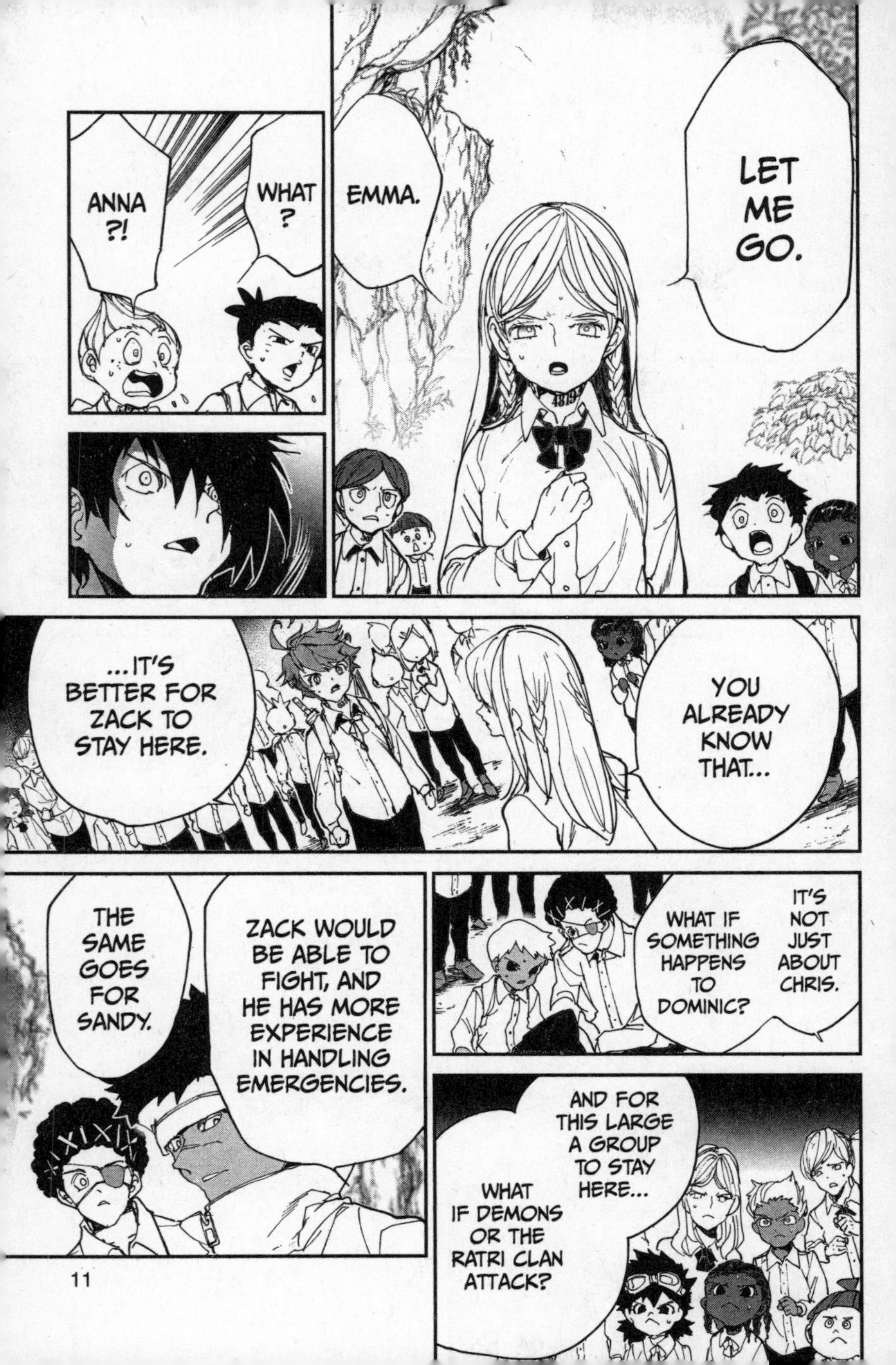
LET ME GO.
EMMA.
WHAT?
ANNA?!
YOU ALREADY KNOW THAT...
...IT'S BETTER FOR ZACK TO STAY HERE.
IT'S NOT JUST ABOUT CHRIS.
WHAT IF SOMETHING HAPPENS TO DOMINIC?
AND FOR THIS LARGE A GROUP TO STAY HERE...
WHAT IF DEMONS OR THE RATRI CLAN ATTACK?
ZACK WOULD BE ABLE TO FIGHT, AND HE HAS MORE EXPERIENCE IN HANDLING EMERGENCIES.
THE SAME GOES FOR SANDY.

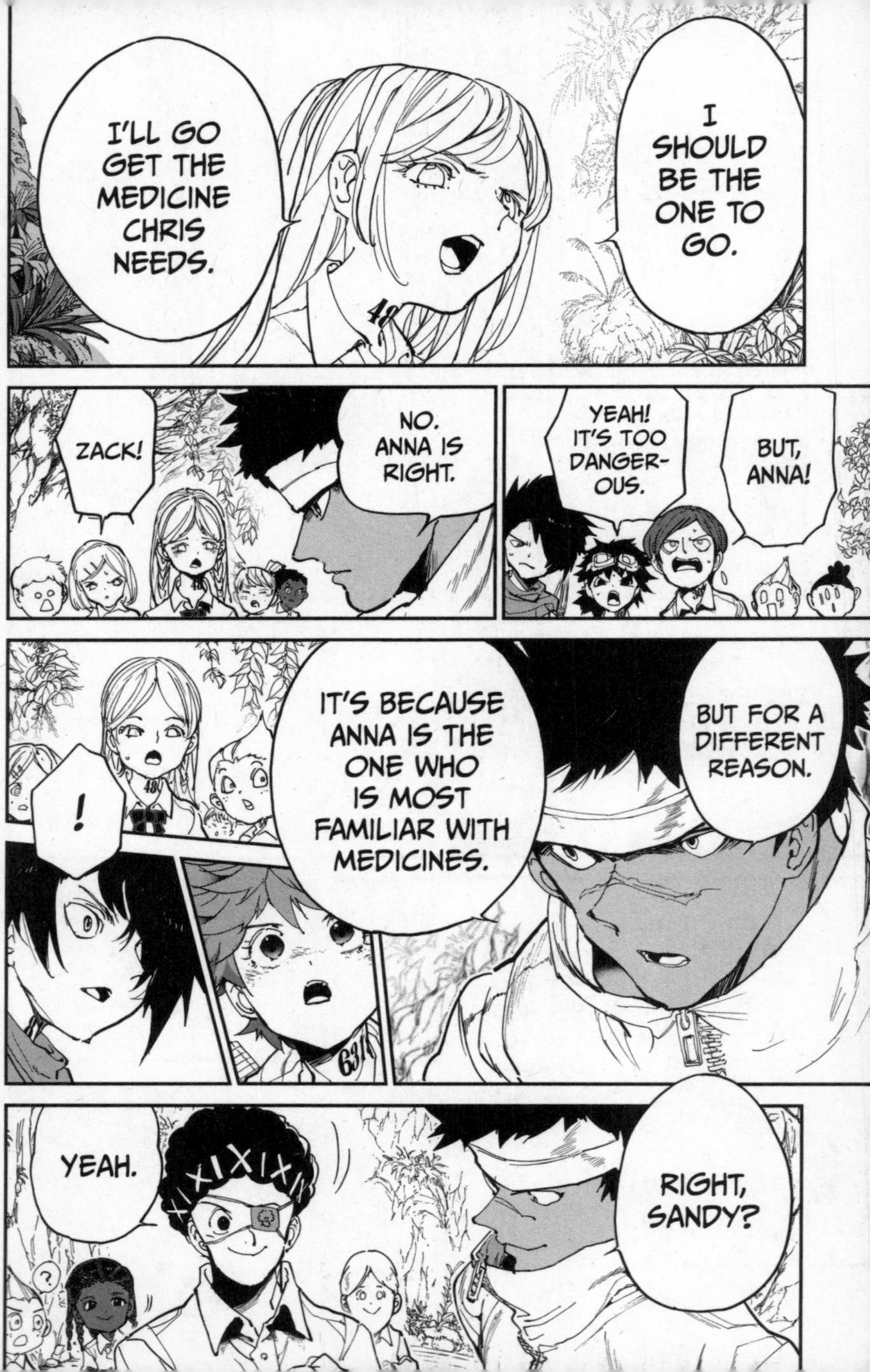
I SHOULD BE THE ONE TO GO.
I'LL GO GET THE MEDICINE CHRIS NEEDS.
BUT, ANNA!
YEAH! IT'S TOO DANGER-OUS.
NO. ANNA IS RIGHT.
ZACK!
BUT FOR A DIFFERENT REASON.
IT'S BECAUSE ANNA IS THE ONE WHO IS MOST FAMILIAR WITH MEDICINES.
!
RIGHT, SANDY?
YEAH.
?

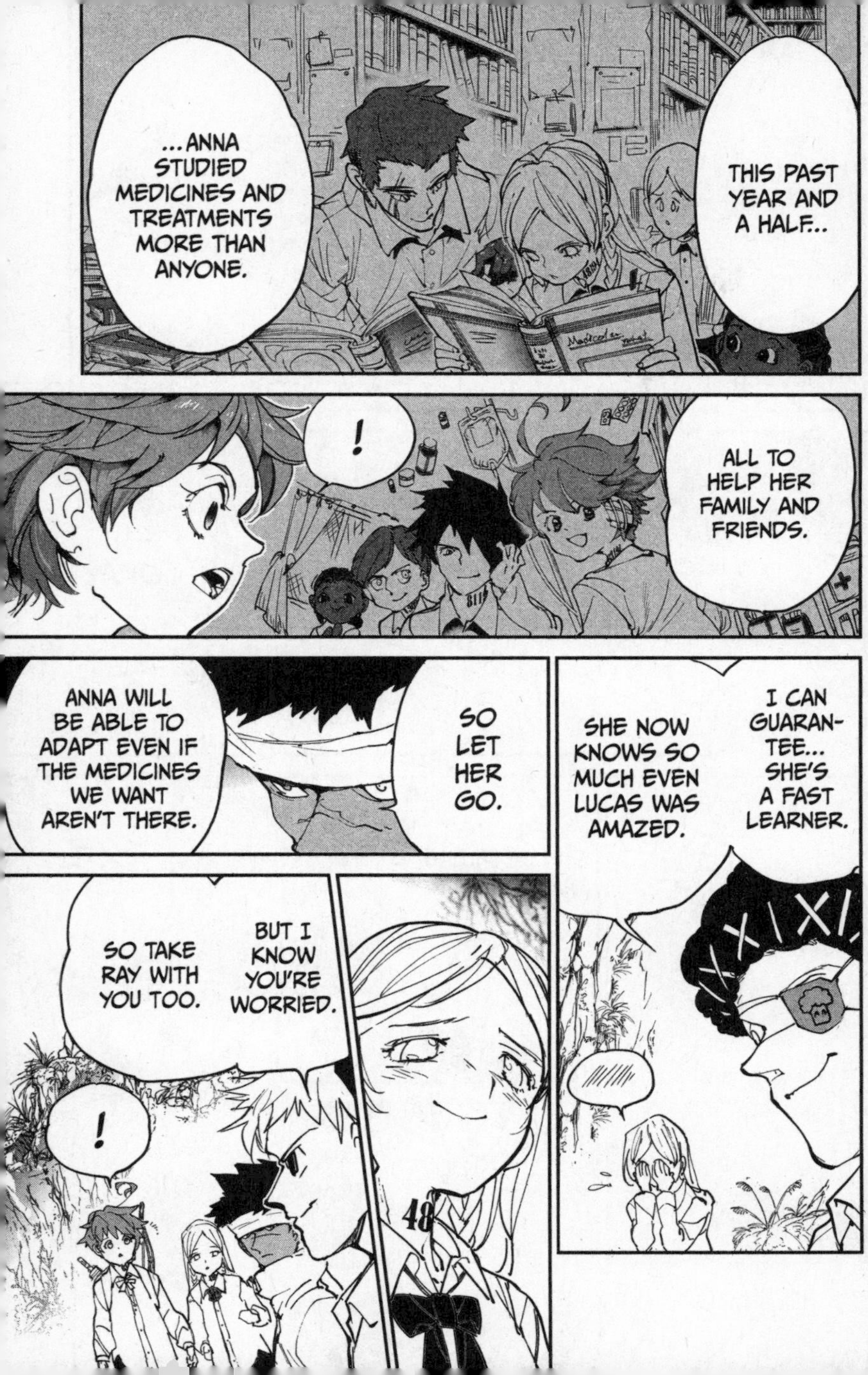
THIS PAST YEAR AND A HALF...
...ANNA STUDIED MEDICINES AND TREATMENTS MORE THAN ANYONE.
ALL TO HELP HER FAMILY AND FRIENDS.
!
I CAN GUARAN-TEE... SHE'S A FAST LEARNER.
SHE NOW KNOWS SO MUCH EVEN LUCAS WAS AMAZED.
SO LET HER GO.
ANNA WILL BE ABLE TO ADAPT EVEN IF THE MEDICINES WE WANT AREN'T THERE.
BUT I KNOW YOU'RE WORRIED.
SO TAKE RAY WITH YOU TOO.
!

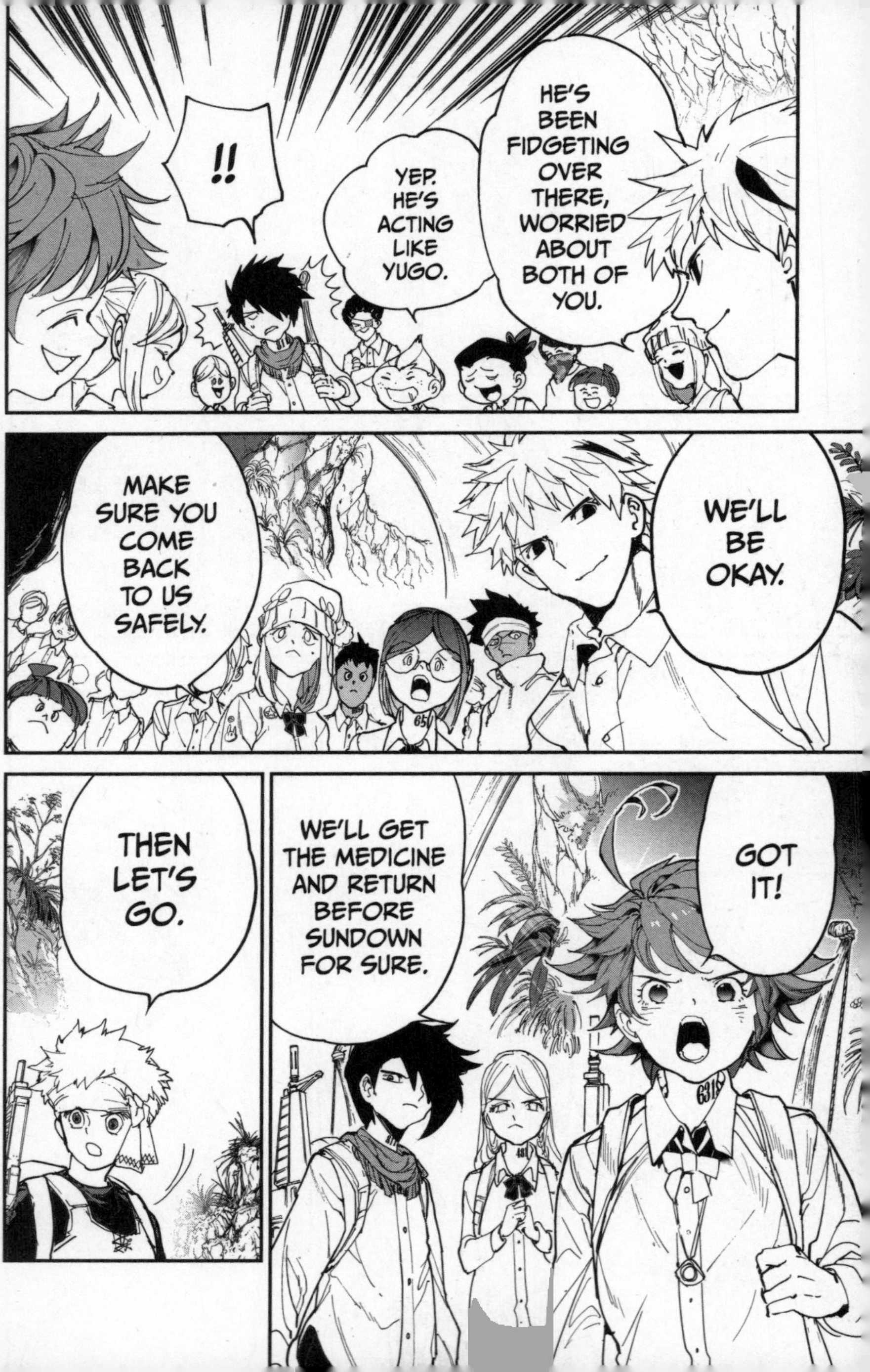
HE'S BEEN FIDGETING OVER THERE, WORRIED ABOUT BOTH OF YOU.
YEP. HE'S ACTING LIKE YUGO.
!!
WE'LL BE OKAY.
MAKE SURE YOU COME BACK TO US SAFELY.
GOT IT!
WE'LL GET THE MEDICINE AND RETURN BEFORE SUNDOWN FOR SURE.
THEN LET'S GO.

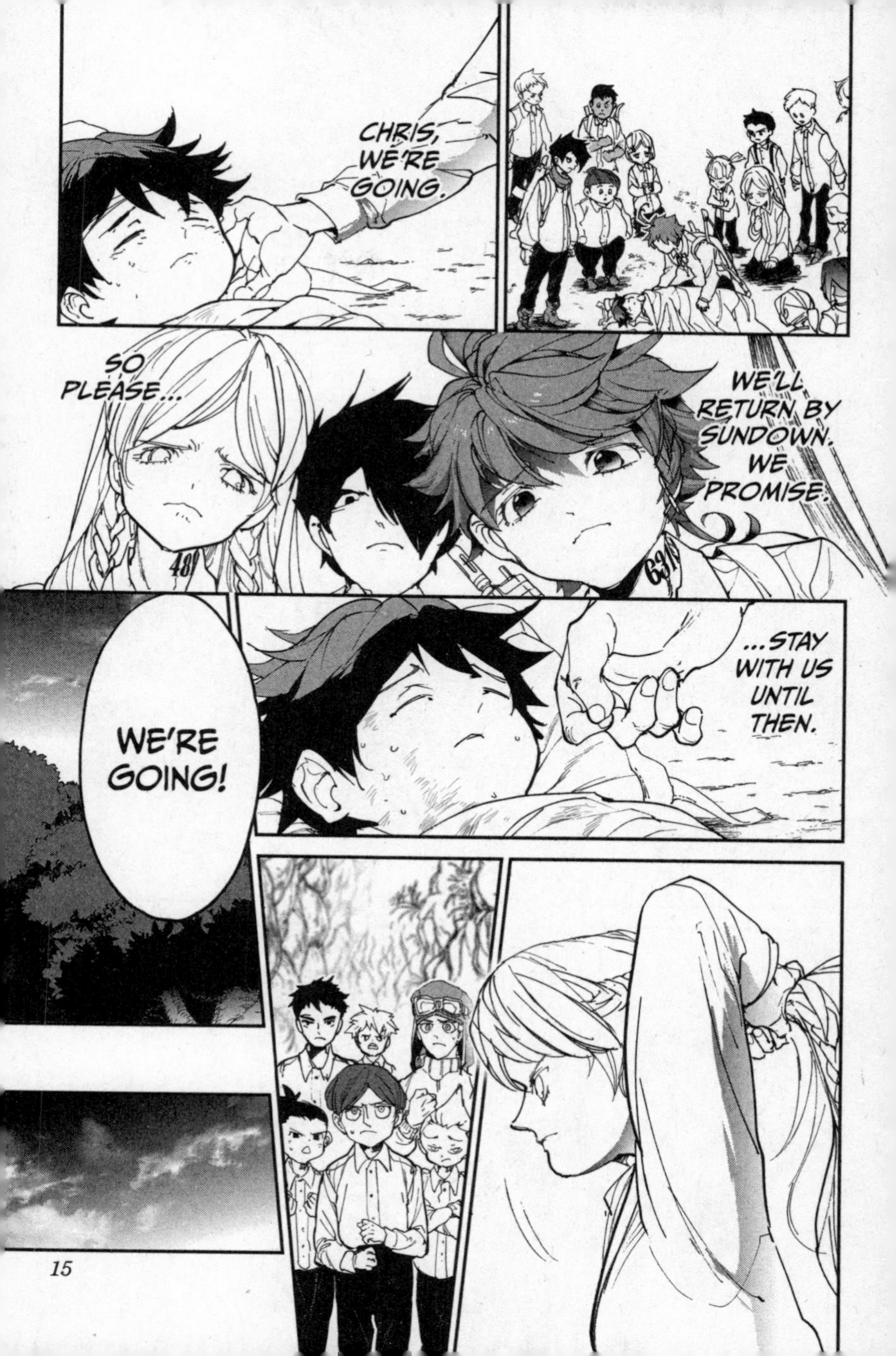
CHRIS, WE'RE GOING.
WE'LL RETURN BY SUNDOWN. WE PROMISE.
SO PLEASE...
...STAY WITH US UNTIL THEN.
WE'RE GOING!

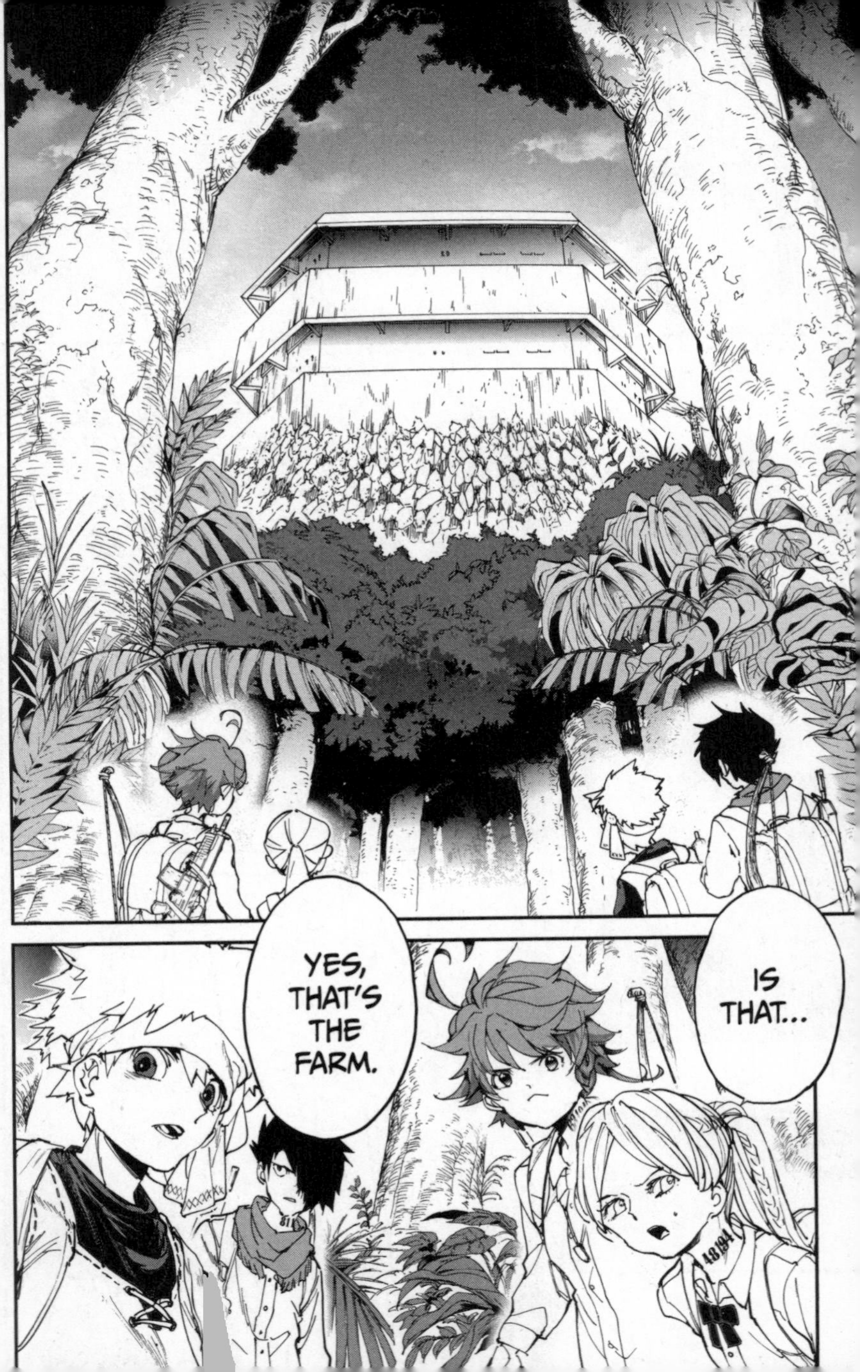
IS THAT...
YES, THAT'S THE FARM.

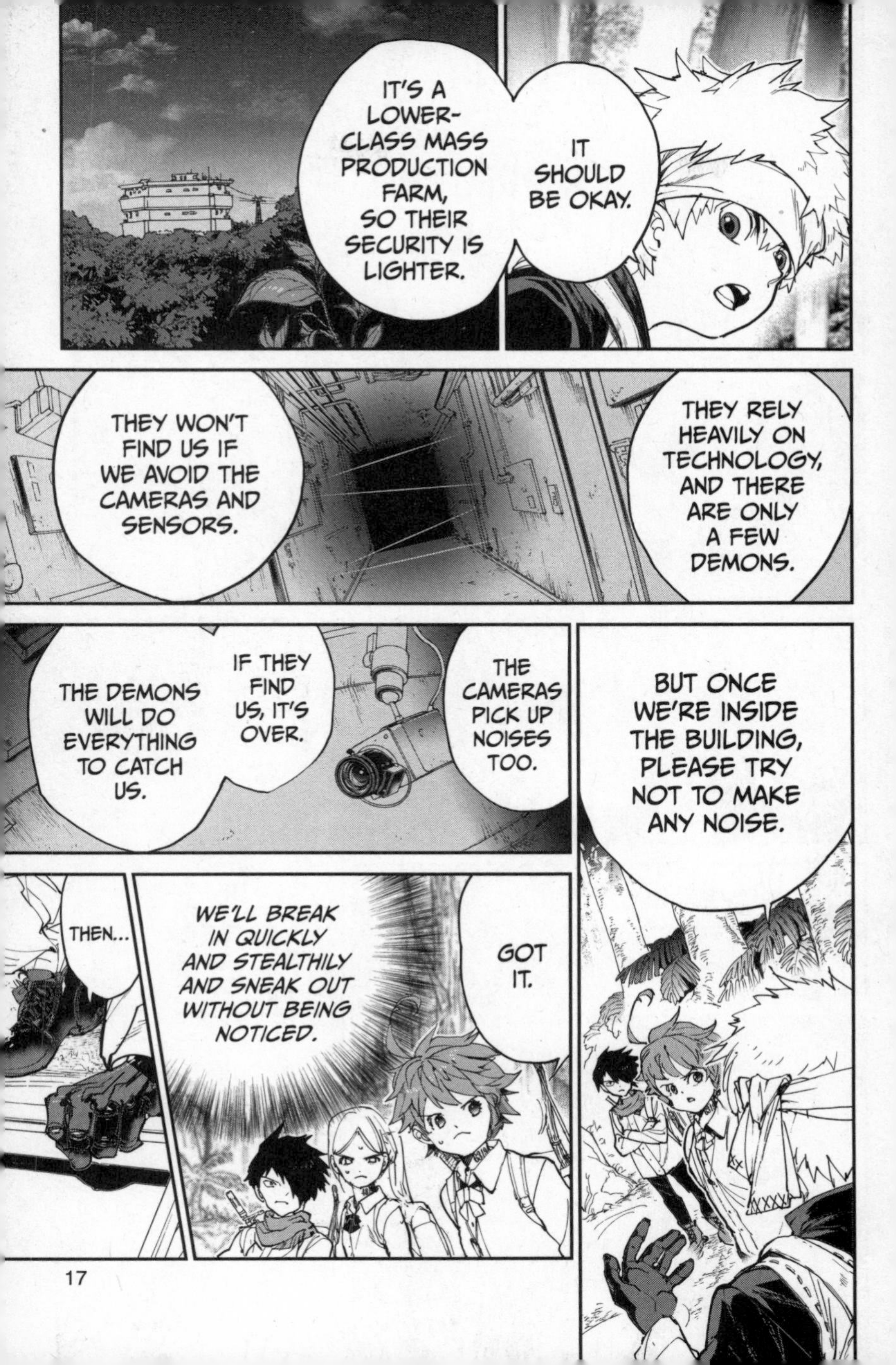
IT SHOULD BE OKAY.
IT'S A LOWER-CLASS MASS PRODUCTION FARM, SO THEIR SECURITY IS LIGHTER.
THEY RELY HEAVILY ON TECHNOLOGY, AND THERE ARE ONLY A FEW DEMONS.
THEY WON'T FIND US IF WE AVOID THE CAMERAS AND SENSORS.
BUT ONCE WE'RE INSIDE THE BUILDING, PLEASE TRY NOT TO MAKE ANY NOISE.
THE CAMERAS PICK UP NOISES TOO.
IF THEY FIND US, IT'S OVER.
THE DEMONS WILL DO EVERYTHING TO CATCH US.
GOT IT.
WE'LL BREAK IN QUICKLY AND STEALTHILY AND SNEAK OUT WITHOUT BEING NOTICED.
THEN...

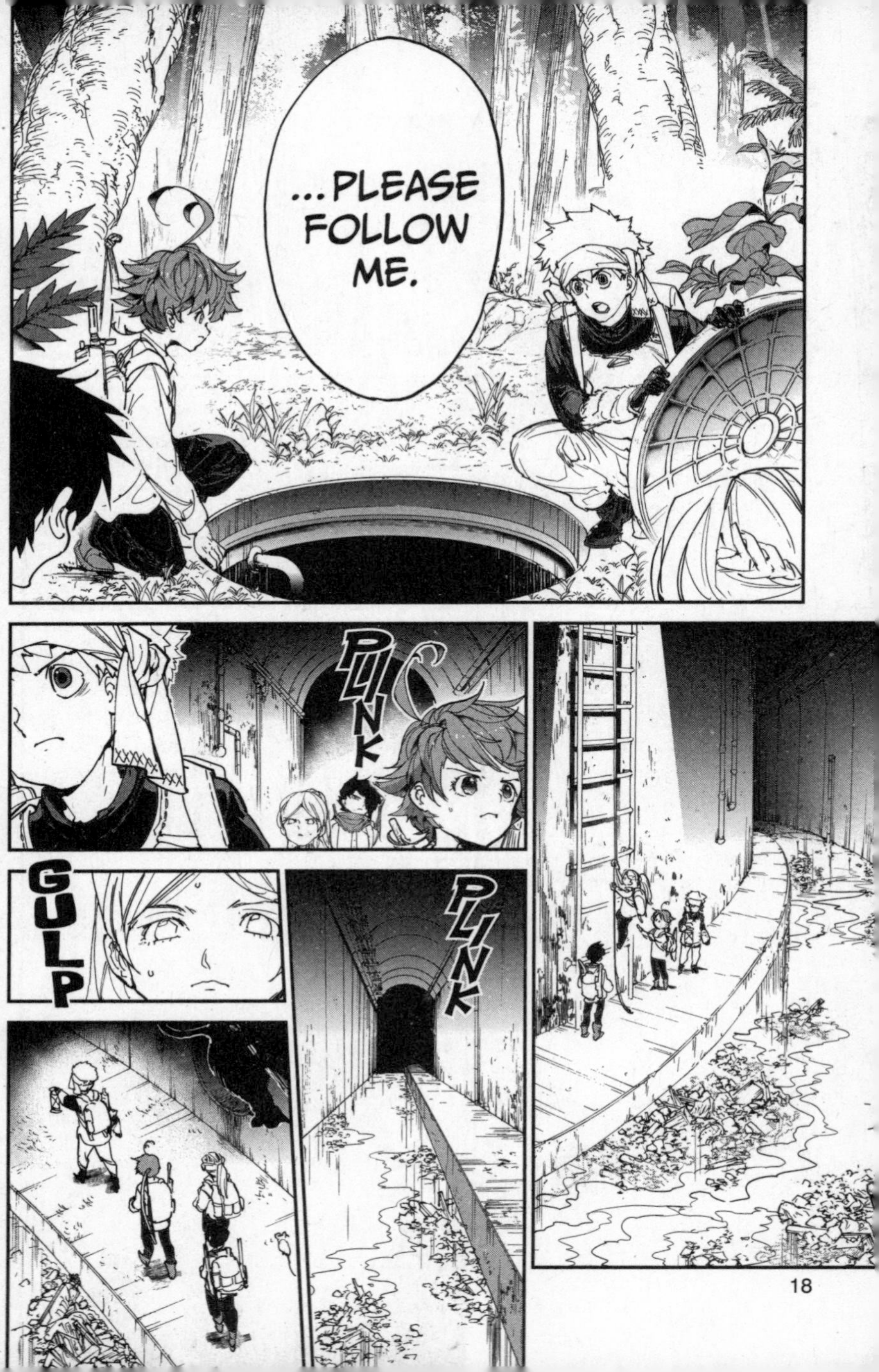
...PLEASE FOLLOW ME.
PLINK
PLINK
GULP

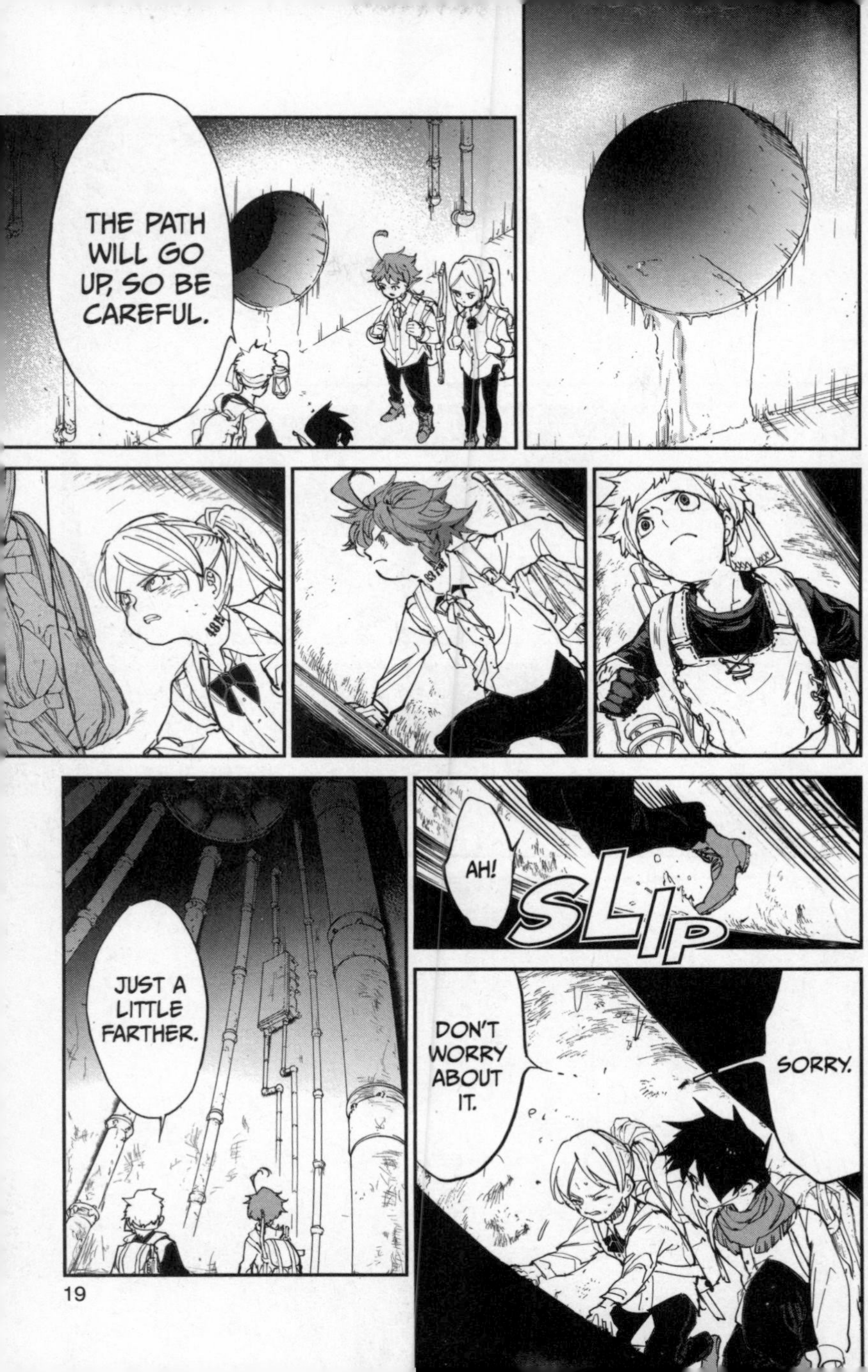
THE PATH WILL GO UP, SO BE CAREFUL.
AH!
SLIP
SORRY.
DON'T WORRY ABOUT IT.
JUST A LITTLE FARTHER.

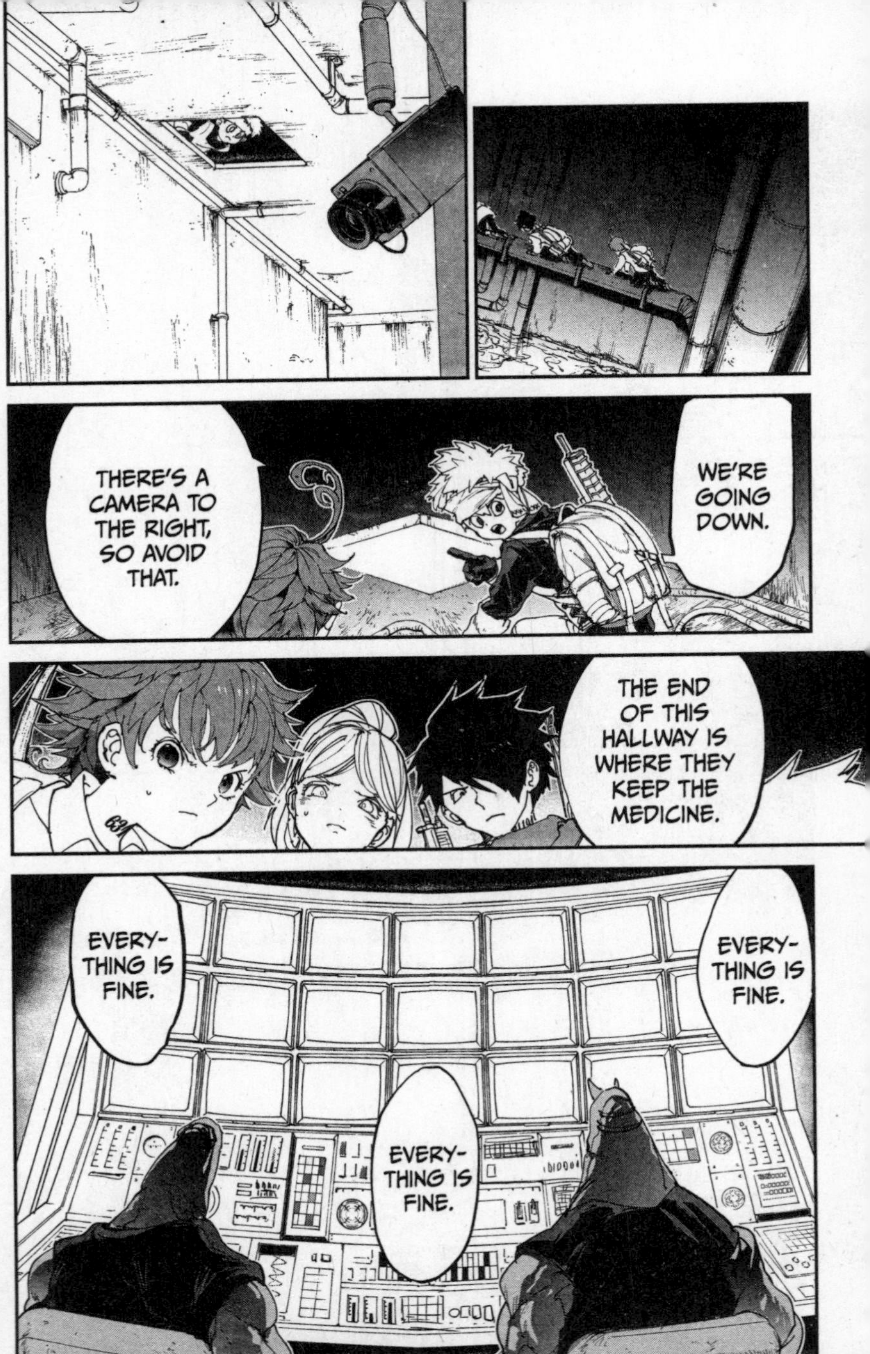
WE'RE GOING DOWN.
THERE'S A CAMERA TO THE RIGHT, SO AVOID THAT.
THE END OF THIS HALLWAY IS WHERE THEY KEEP THE MEDICINE.
EVERY-THING IS FINE.
EVERY-THING IS FINE.
EVERY-THING IS FINE.

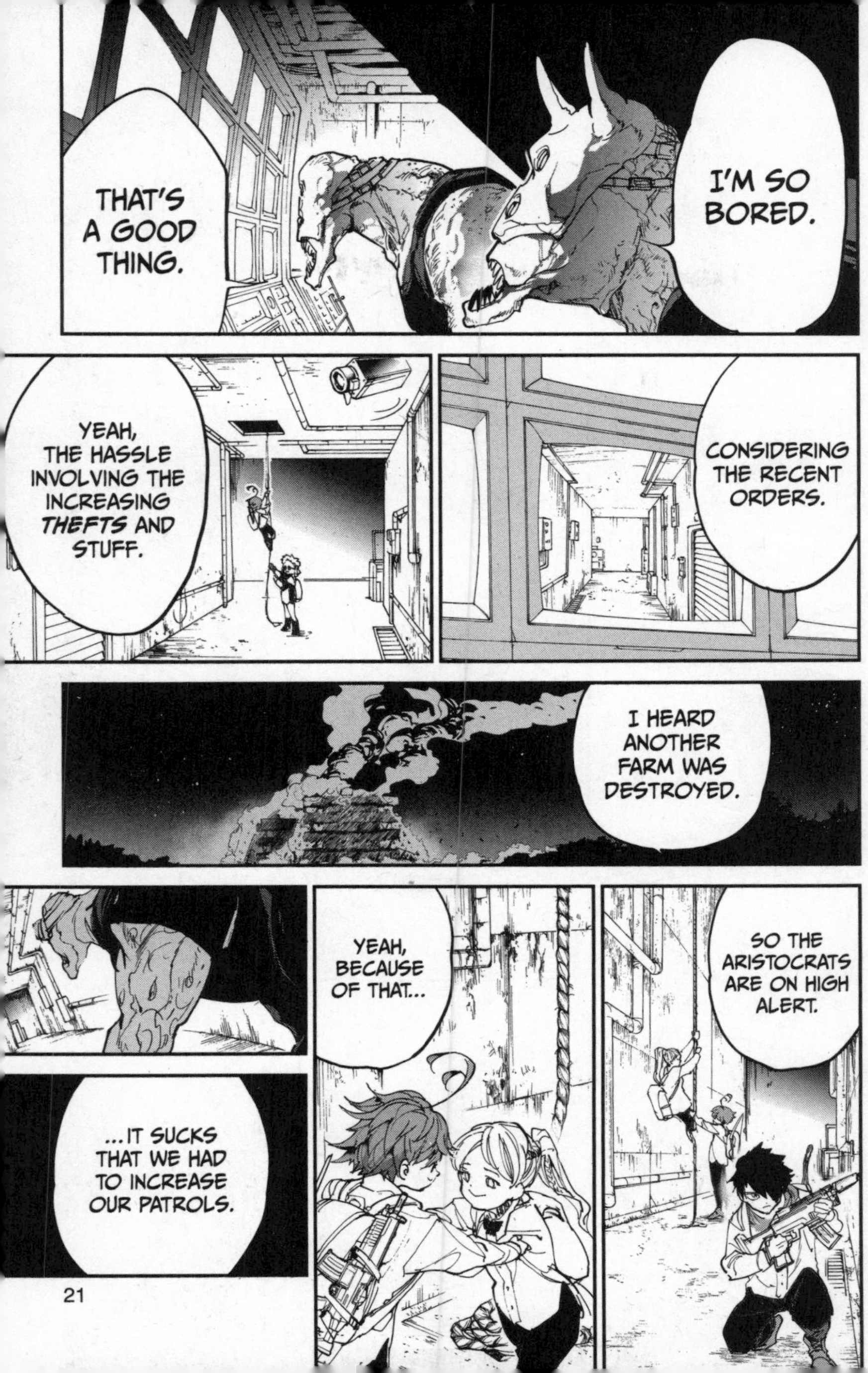
I'M SO BORED.
THAT'S A GOOD THING.
CONSIDERING THE RECENT ORDERS.
YEAH, THE HASSLE INVOLVING THE INCREASING *THEFTS* AND STUFF.
I HEARD ANOTHER FARM WAS DESTROYED.
SO THE ARISTOCRATS ARE ON HIGH ALERT.
YEAH, BECAUSE OF THAT...
...IT SUCKS THAT WE HAD TO INCREASE OUR PATROLS.

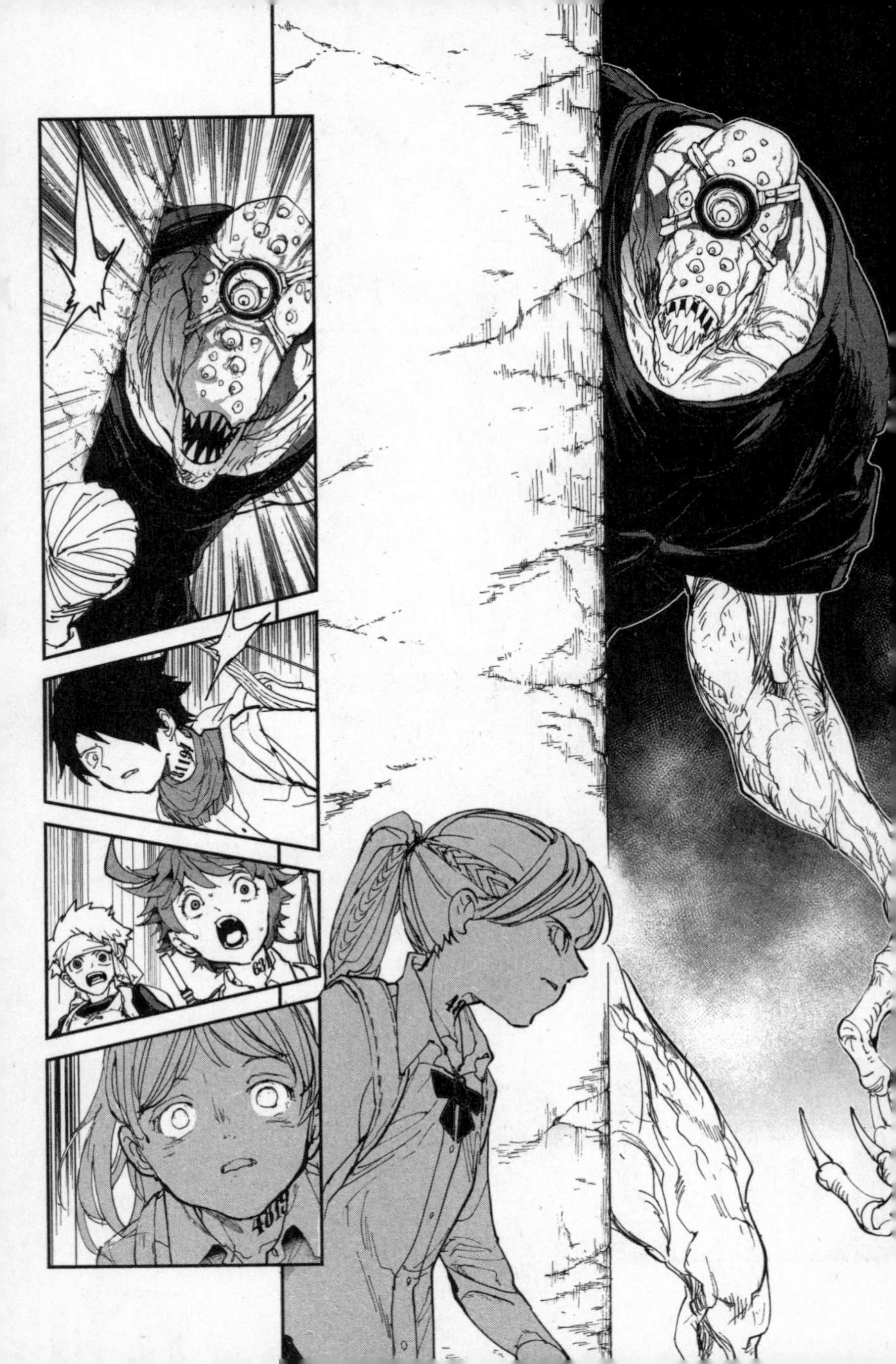

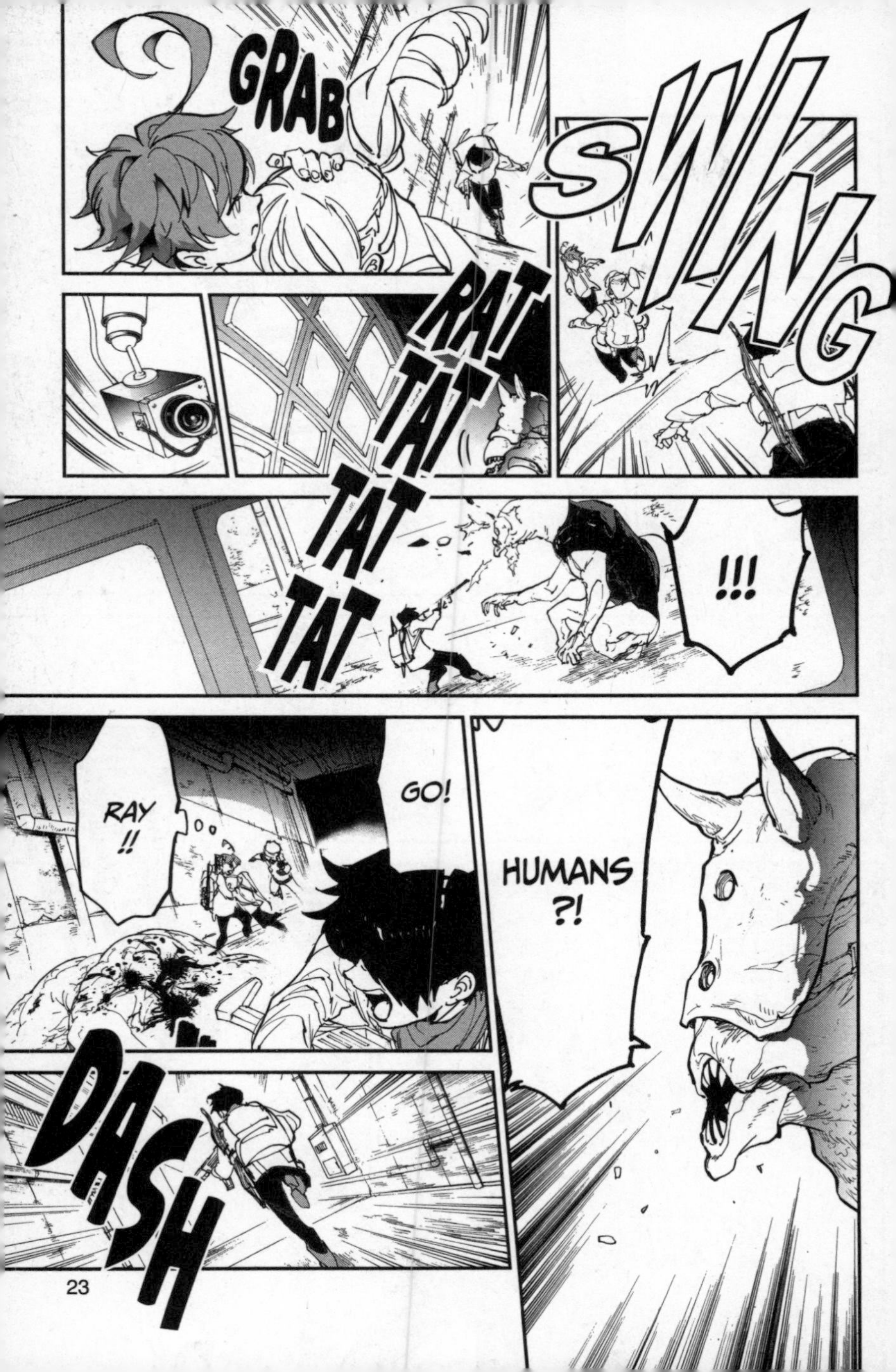

SWING
GRAB
RAT TAT TAT TAT
!!!
HUMANS ?!
GO!
RAY !!
DASH

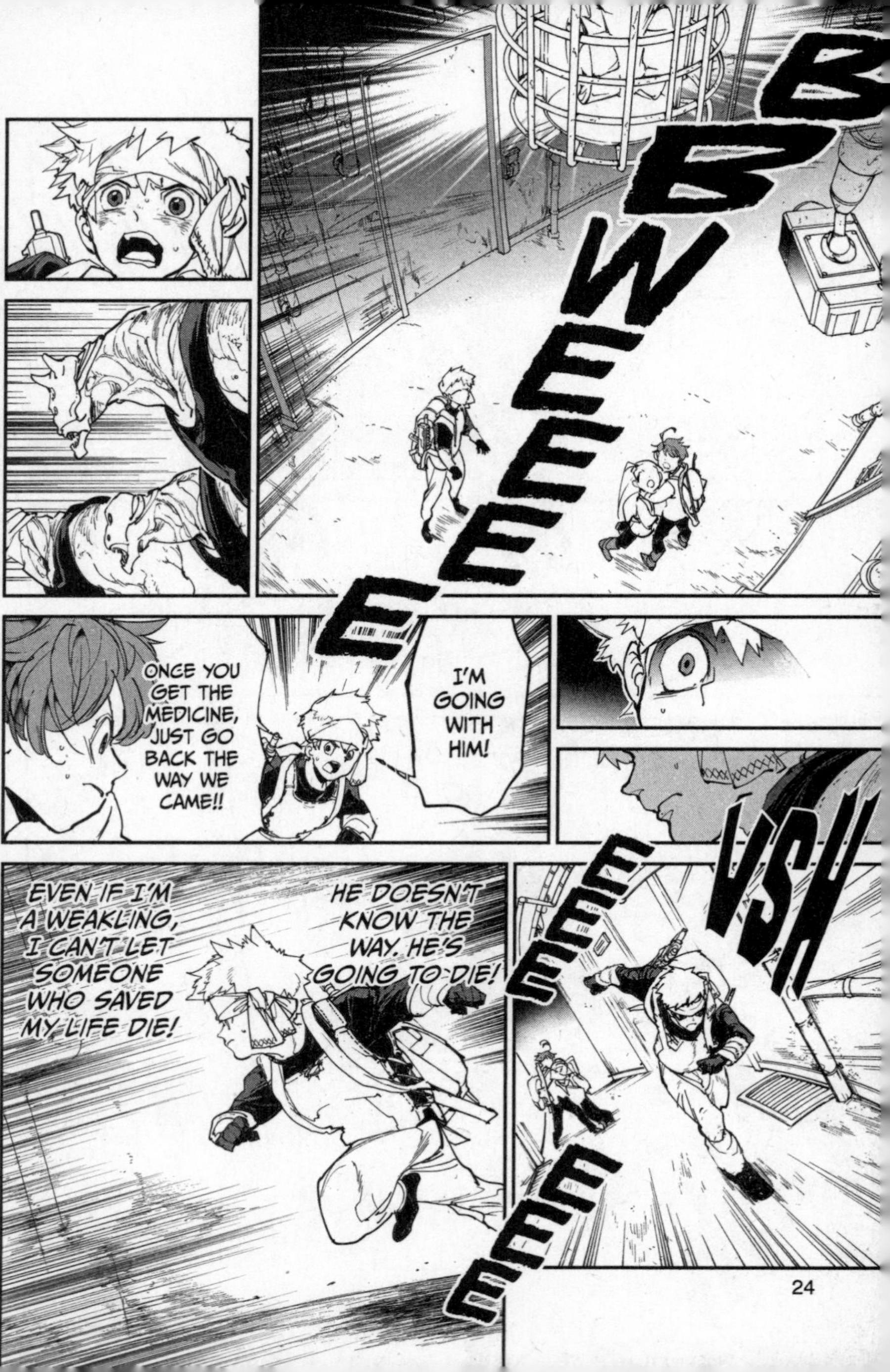
BBWEEEEEE
I'M GOING WITH HIM!
ONCE YOU GET THE MEDICINE, JUST GO BACK THE WAY WE CAME!!
VSH
EEEEEEEE
HE DOESN'T KNOW THE WAY. HE'S GOING TO DIE!
EVEN IF I'M A WEAKLING, I CAN'T LET SOMEONE WHO SAVED MY LIFE DIE!

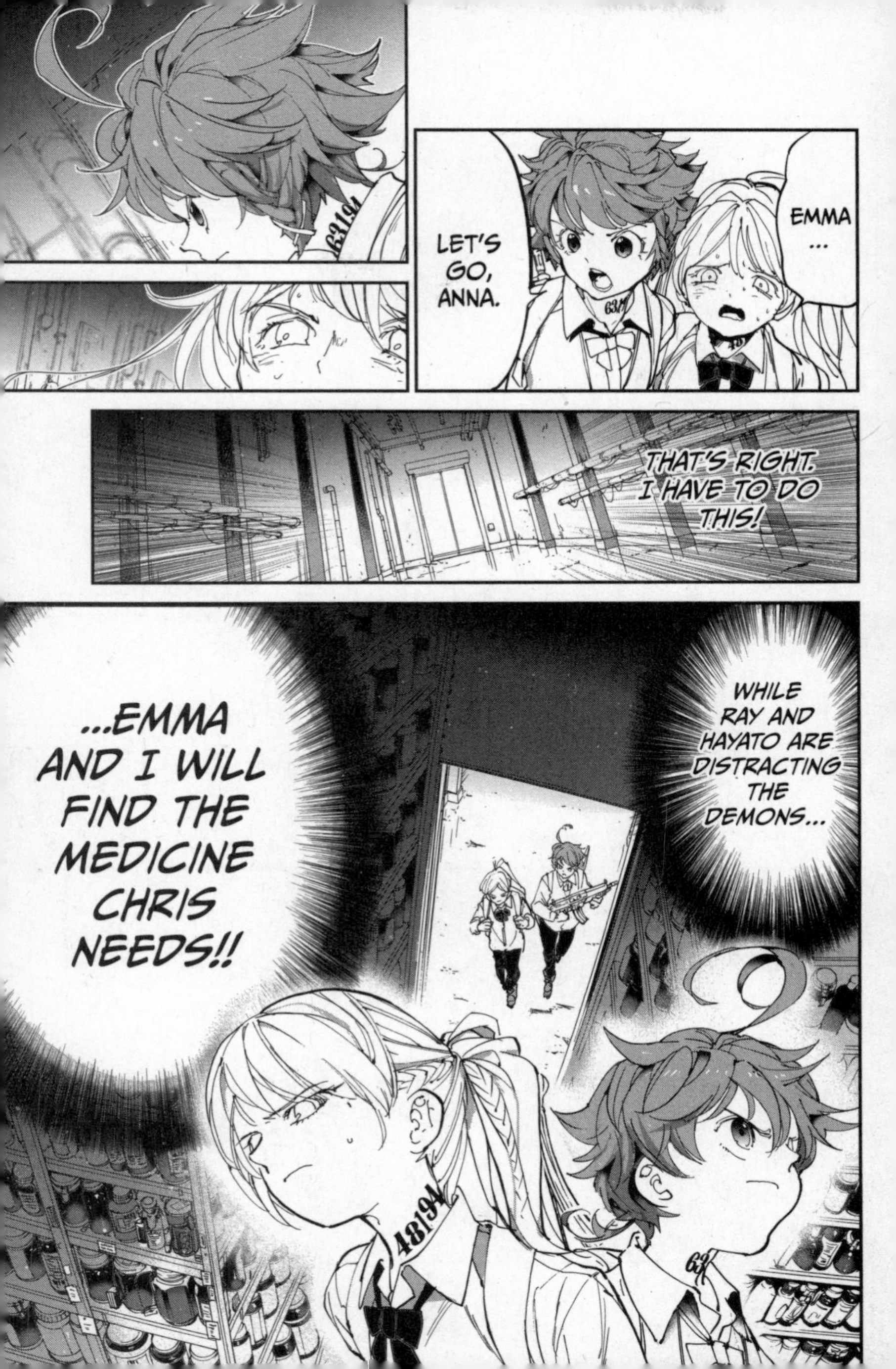
EMMA ...
LET'S GO, ANNA.
THAT'S RIGHT. I HAVE TO DO THIS!
WHILE RAY AND HAYATO ARE DISTRACTING THE DEMONS...
...EMMA AND I WILL FIND THE MEDICINE CHRIS NEEDS!!

HOW CUTE.
IT LOOKS GOOD ON HER.
SHE'S AN ANGEL.
I LIKE HER.
HOT!!
...IS WHAT YOU WERE THINKING, RIGHT? ☆
NO!!
I MEAN, IT IS, BUT IT ISN'T!!
WE WERE CON-CERNED!!

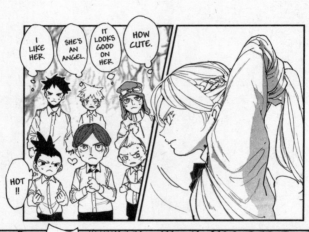

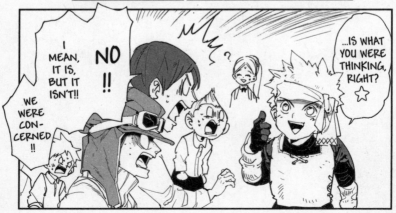

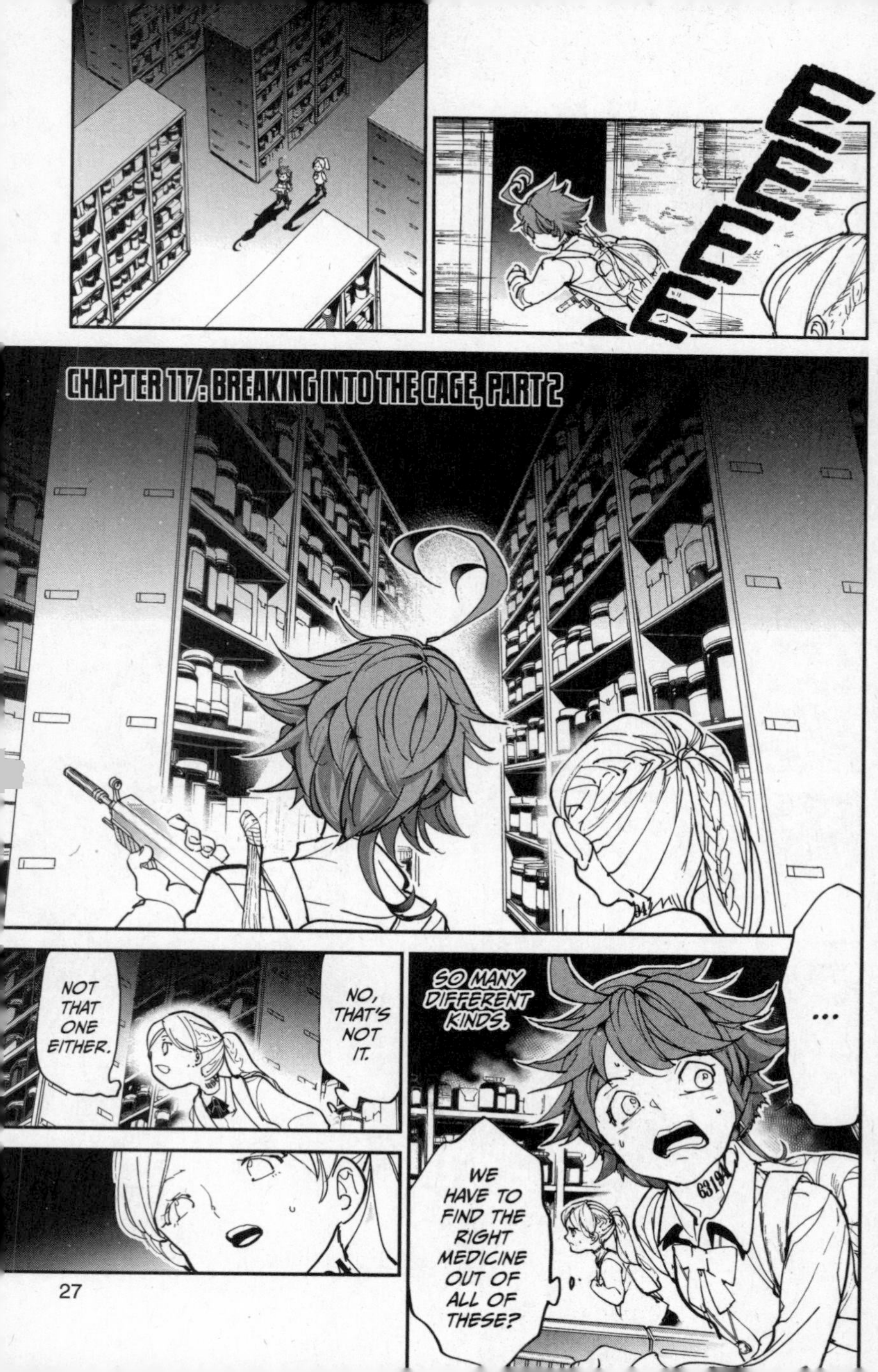
EEEEEE
CHAPTER 117: BREAKING INTO THE CAGE, PART 2
...
SO MANY DIFFERENT KINDS.
WE HAVE TO FIND THE RIGHT MEDICINE OUT OF ALL OF THESE?
NO, THAT'S NOT IT.
NOT THAT ONE EITHER.

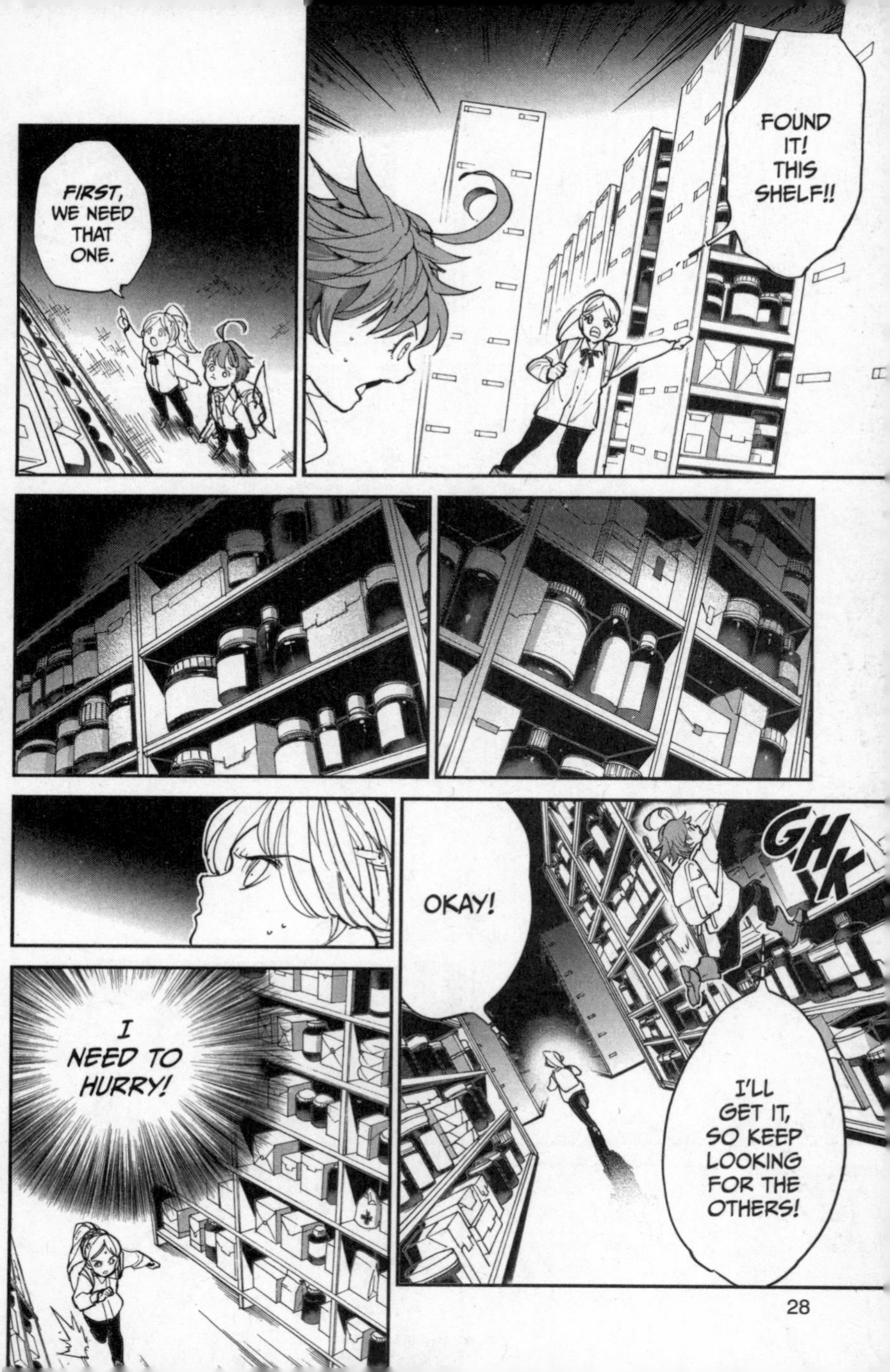
FOUND IT! THIS SHELF!!
FIRST, WE NEED THAT ONE.
GHK
OKAY!
I'LL GET IT, SO KEEP LOOKING FOR THE OTHERS!
I NEED TO HURRY!

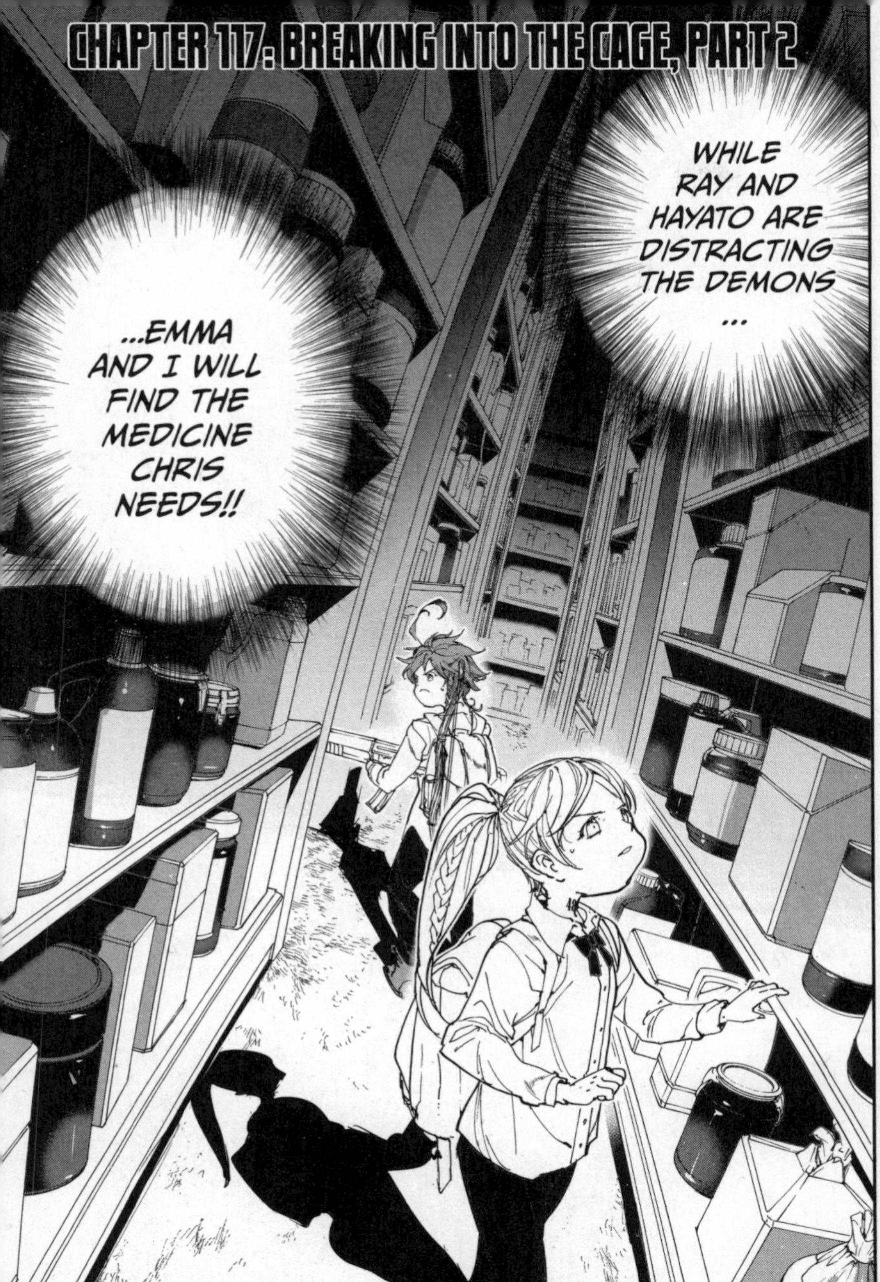
CHAPTER 117: BREAKING INTO THE CAGE, PART 2
WHILE RAY AND HAYATO ARE DISTRACTING THE DEMONS ...
...EMMA AND I WILL FIND THE MEDICINE CHRIS NEEDS!!

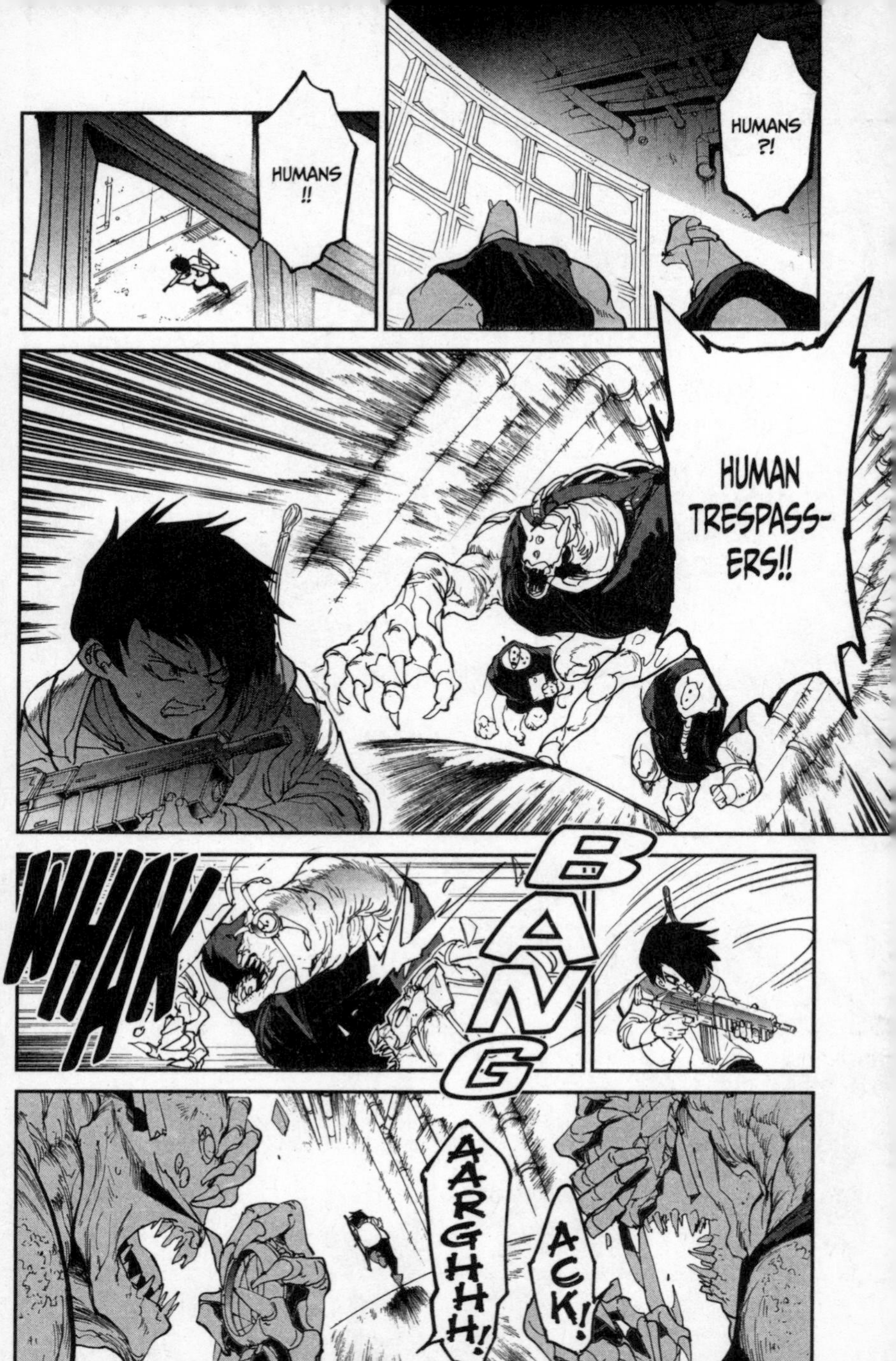
HUMANS ?!
HUMANS !!
HUMAN TRESPASS-ERS!!
BANG
WHAK
ACK!
AARGHHH!

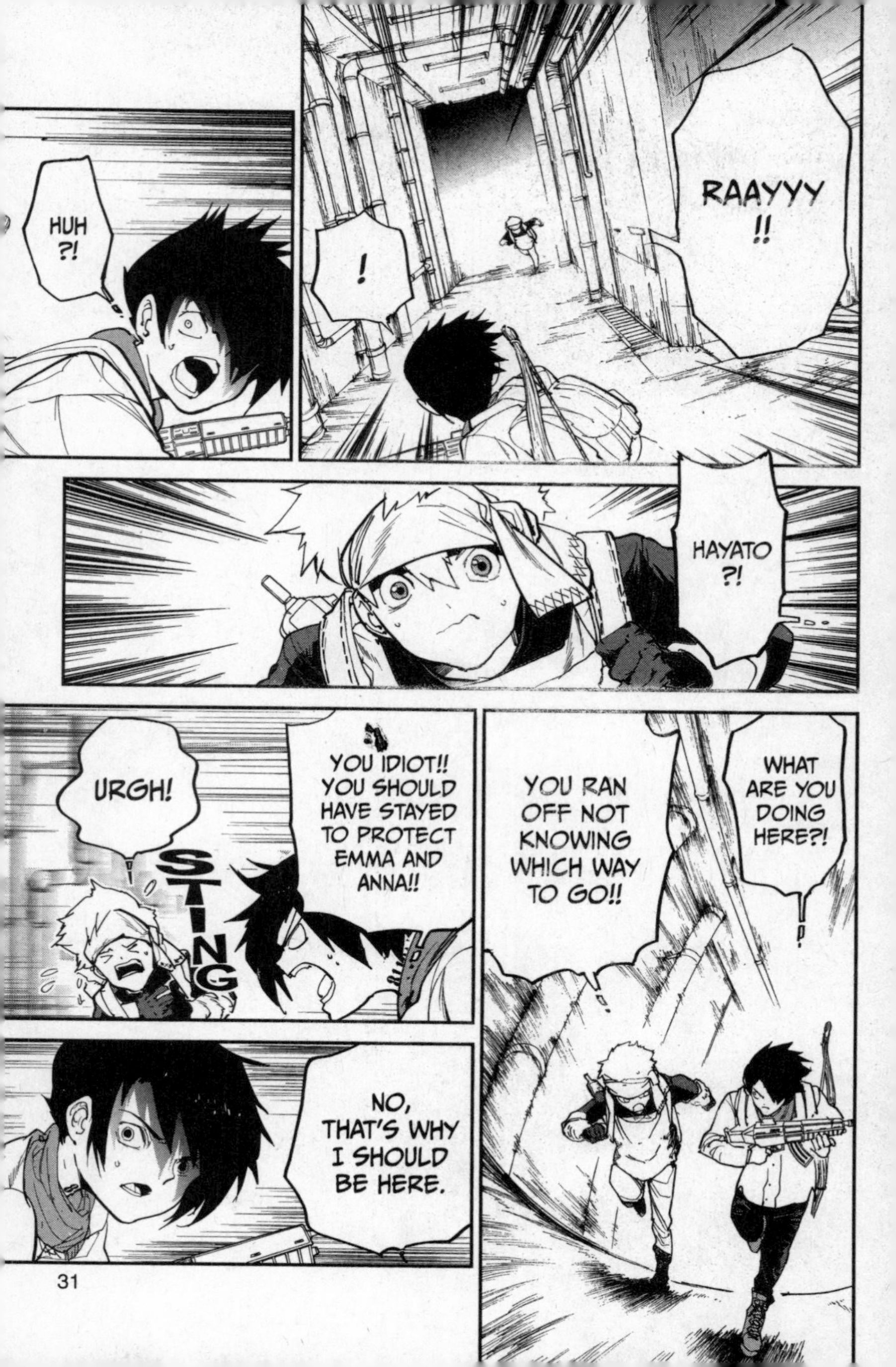

RAAYYY !!
!
HUH ?!
HAYATO ?!
WHAT ARE YOU DOING HERE?!
YOU RAN OFF NOT KNOWING WHICH WAY TO GO!!
YOU IDIOT!! YOU SHOULD HAVE STAYED TO PROTECT EMMA AND ANNA!!
STING
URGH!
NO, THAT'S WHY I SHOULD BE HERE.

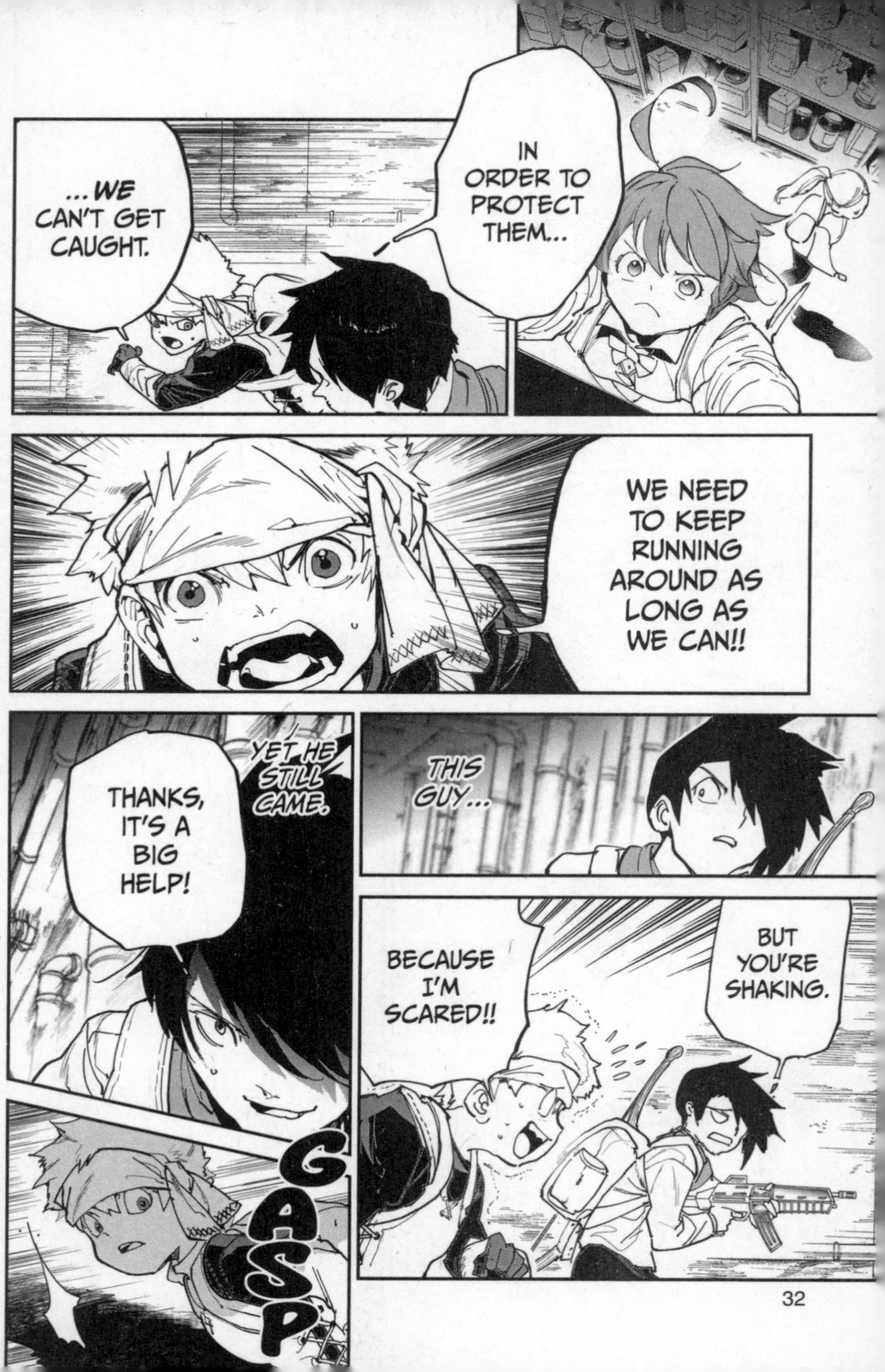
IN ORDER TO PROTECT THEM...
...WE CAN'T GET CAUGHT.
WE NEED TO KEEP RUNNING AROUND AS LONG AS WE CAN!!
THIS GUY...
BUT YOU'RE SHAKING.
BECAUSE I'M SCARED!!
YET HE STILL CAME.
THANKS, IT'S A BIG HELP!
GASP

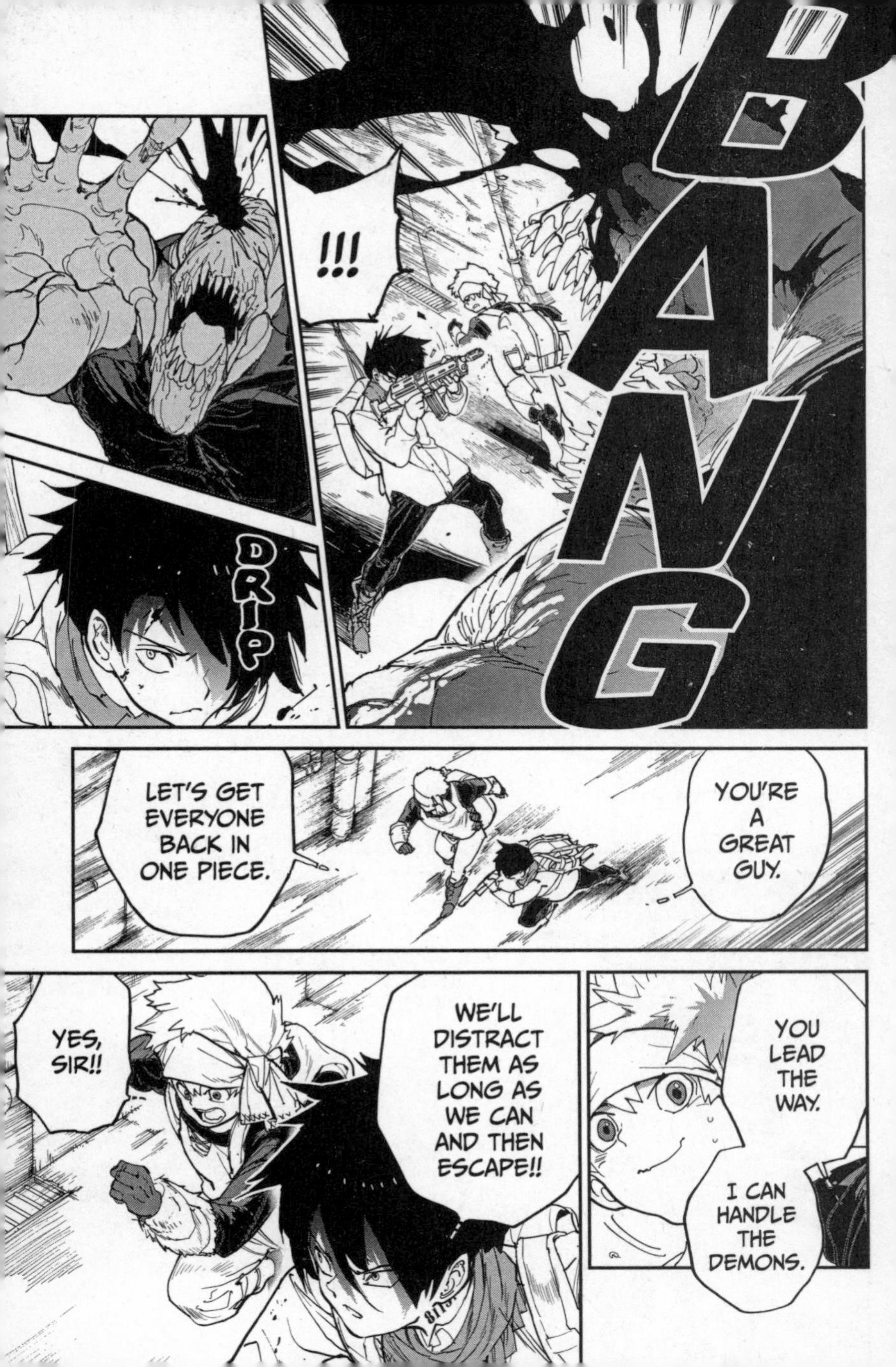
BANG
!!!
DRIP
YOU'RE A GREAT GUY.
LET'S GET EVERYONE BACK IN ONE PIECE.
YOU LEAD THE WAY.
I CAN HANDLE THE DEMONS.
WE'LL DISTRACT THEM AS LONG AS WE CAN AND THEN ESCAPE!!
YES, SIR!!

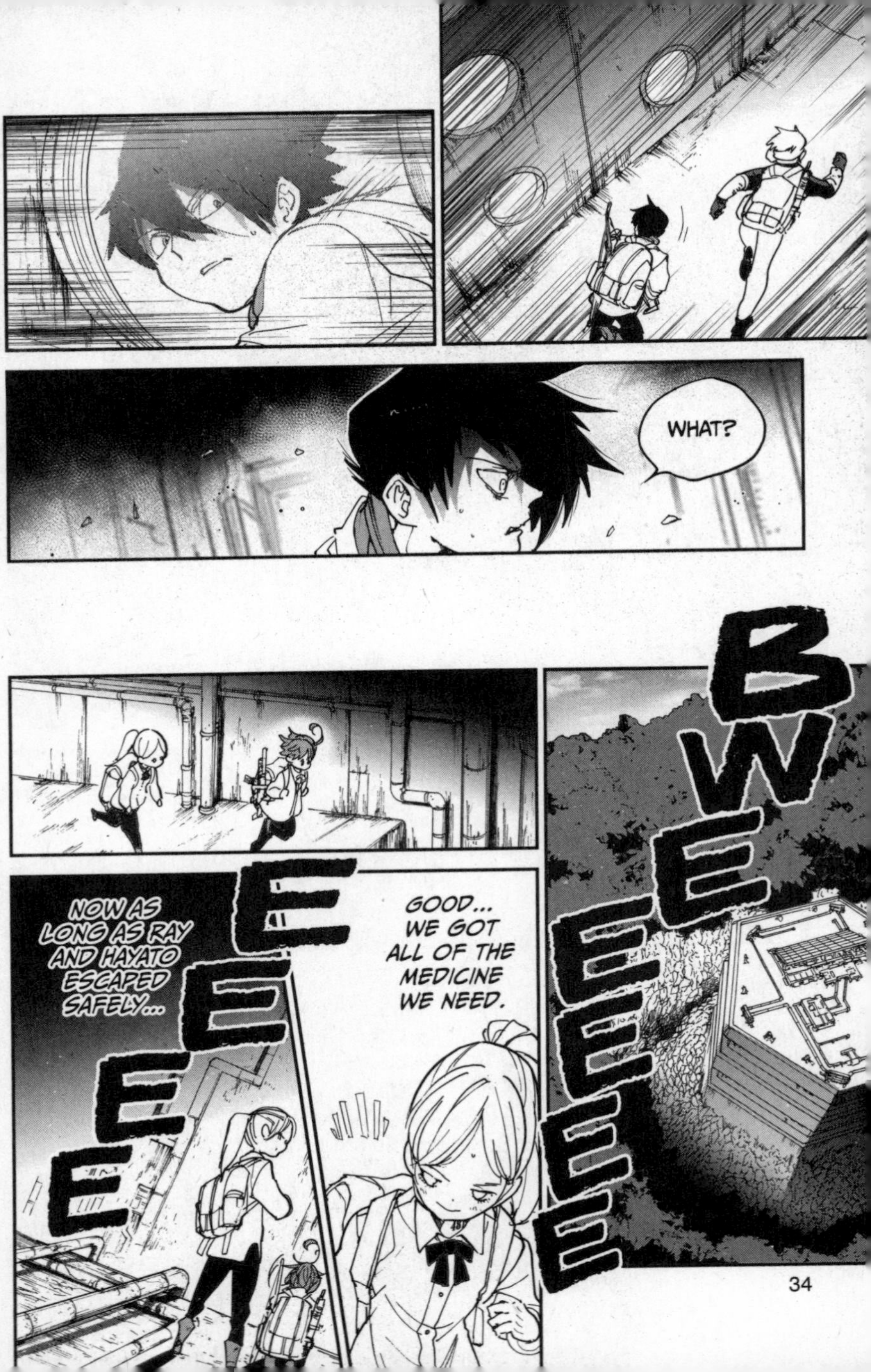
WHAT?
BWEEEEEEEEEE
GOOD... WE GOT ALL OF THE MEDICINE WE NEED.
NOW AS LONG AS RAY AND HAYATO ESCAPED SAFELY...
EEEEE

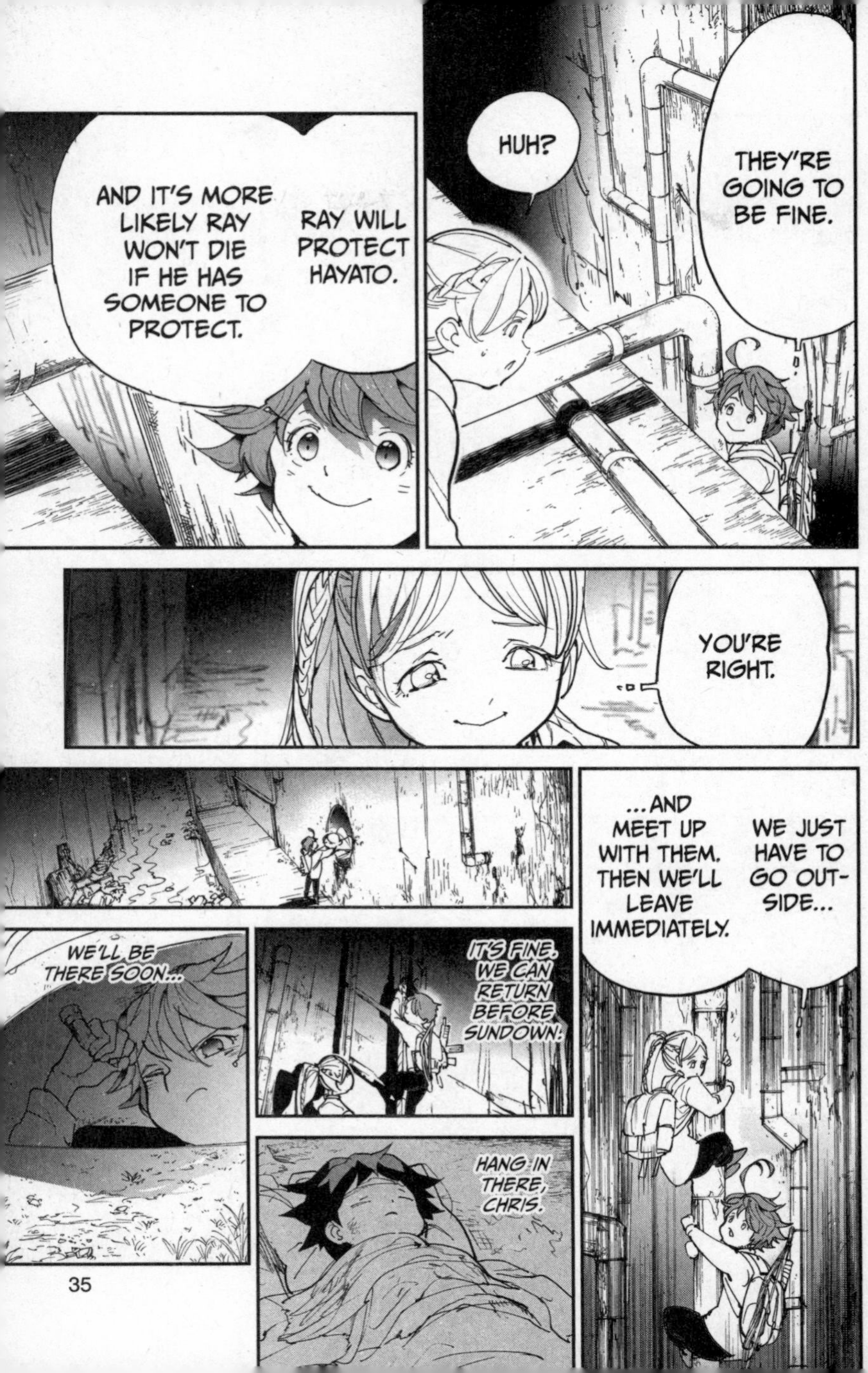
THEY'RE GOING TO BE FINE.
HUH?
RAY WILL PROTECT HAYATO.
AND IT'S MORE LIKELY RAY WON'T DIE IF HE HAS SOMEONE TO PROTECT.
YOU'RE RIGHT.
WE JUST HAVE TO GO OUT-SIDE...
...AND MEET UP WITH THEM. THEN WE'LL LEAVE IMMEDIATELY.
IT'S FINE. WE CAN RETURN BEFORE SUNDOWN.
HANG IN THERE, CHRIS.
WE'LL BE THERE SOON...

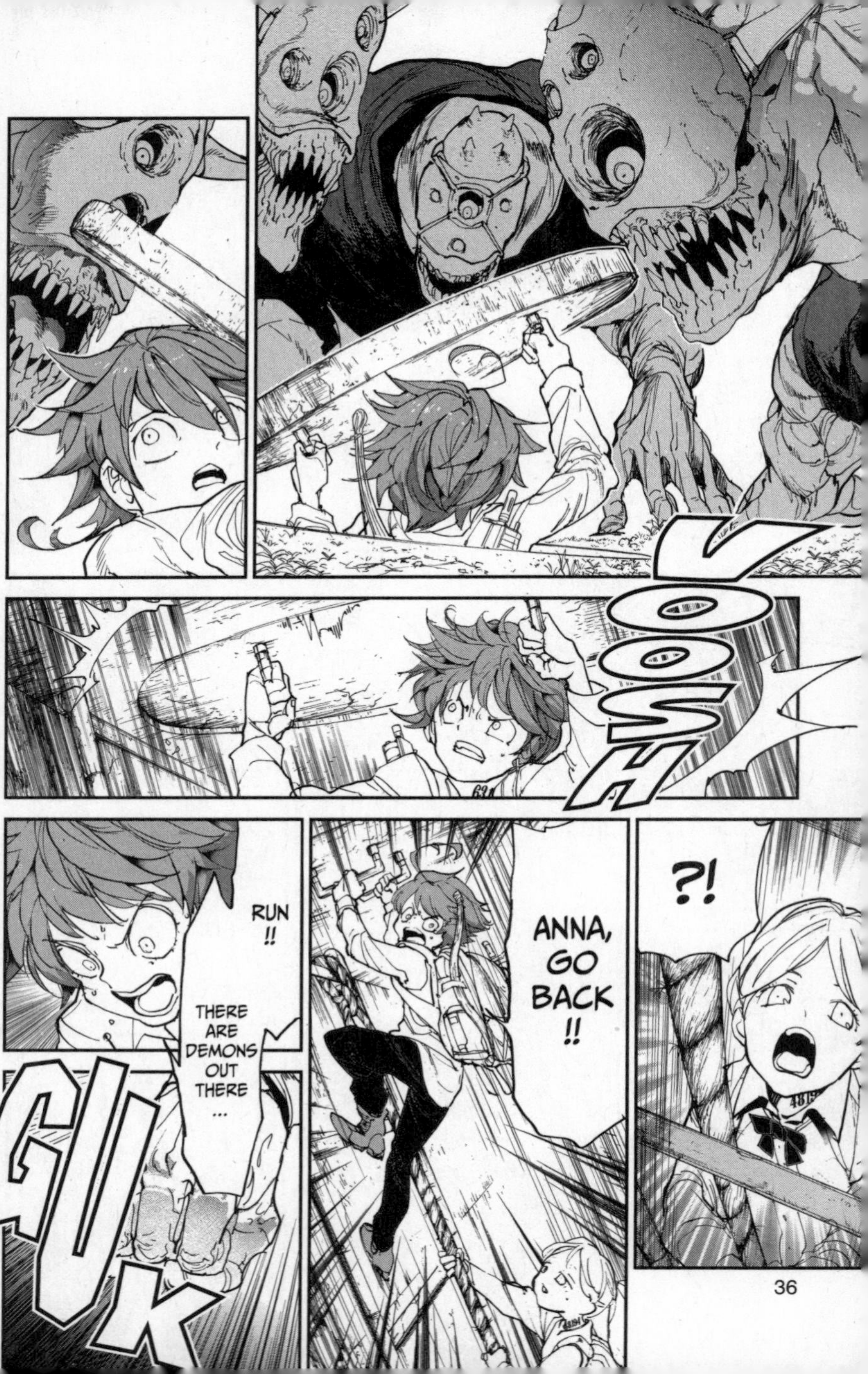
VOOOSH
?!
ANNA, GO BACK!!
RUN!!
THERE ARE DEMONS OUT THERE...
GUk

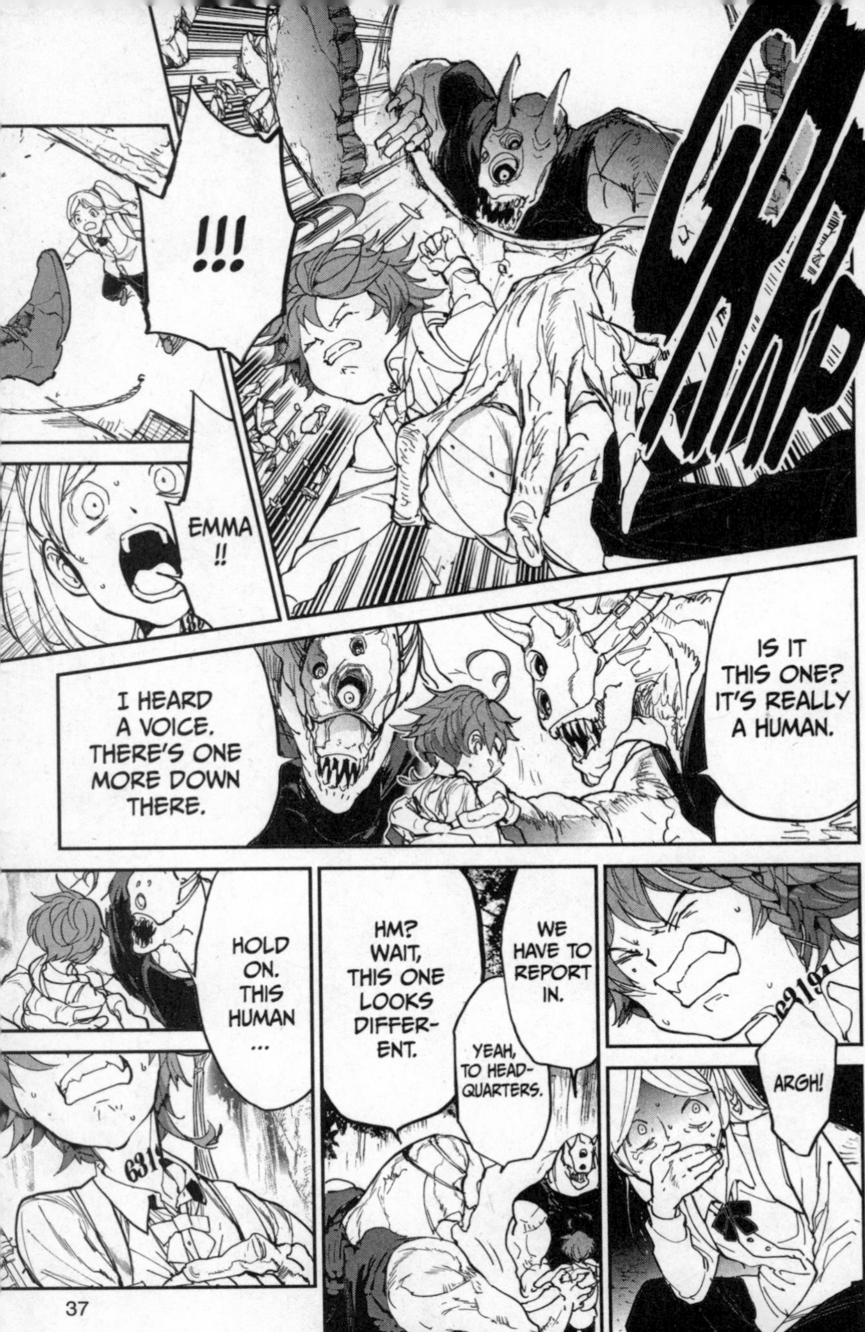
!!!
EMMA !!
IS IT THIS ONE? IT'S REALLY A HUMAN.
I HEARD A VOICE. THERE'S ONE MORE DOWN THERE.
ARGH!
WE HAVE TO REPORT IN.
YEAH, TO HEAD-QUARTERS.
HM? WAIT, THIS ONE LOOKS DIFFER-ENT.
HOLD ON. THIS HUMAN ...

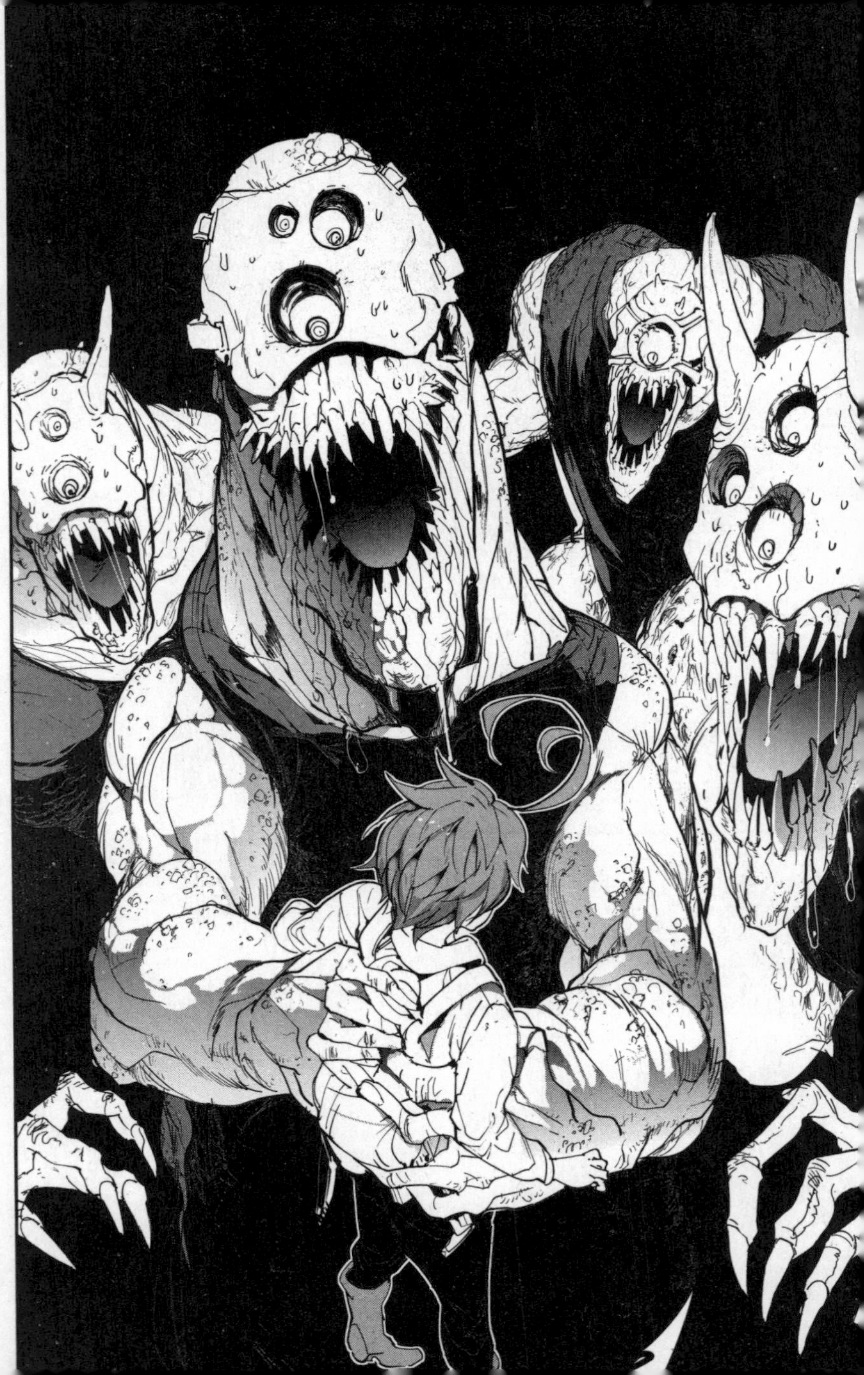

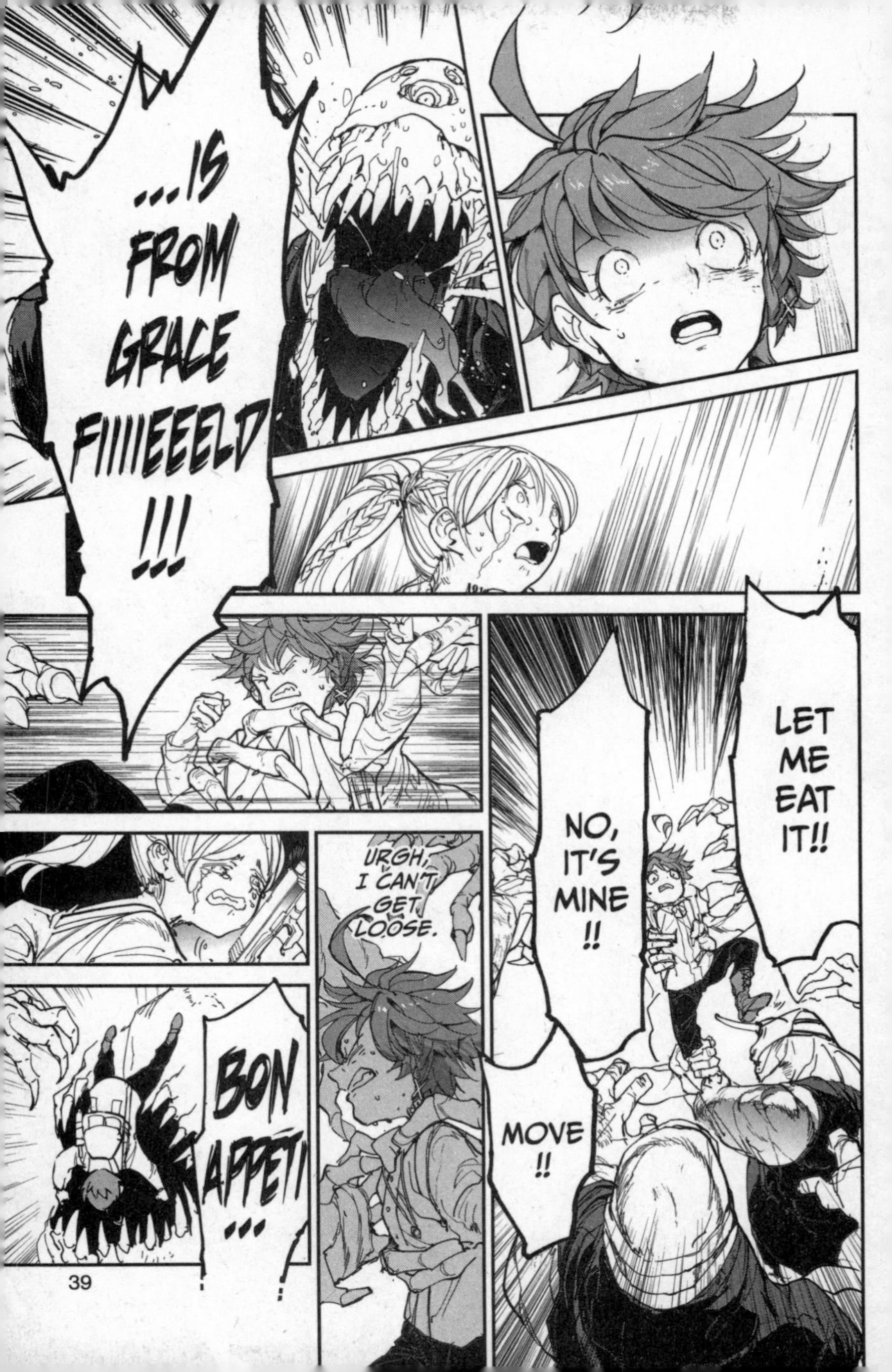

...IS FROM GRACE FIIIIEEELD !!!
LET ME EAT IT!!
NO, IT'S MINE !!
MOVE !!
URGH, I CAN'T GET LOOSE.
BON APPETI ...

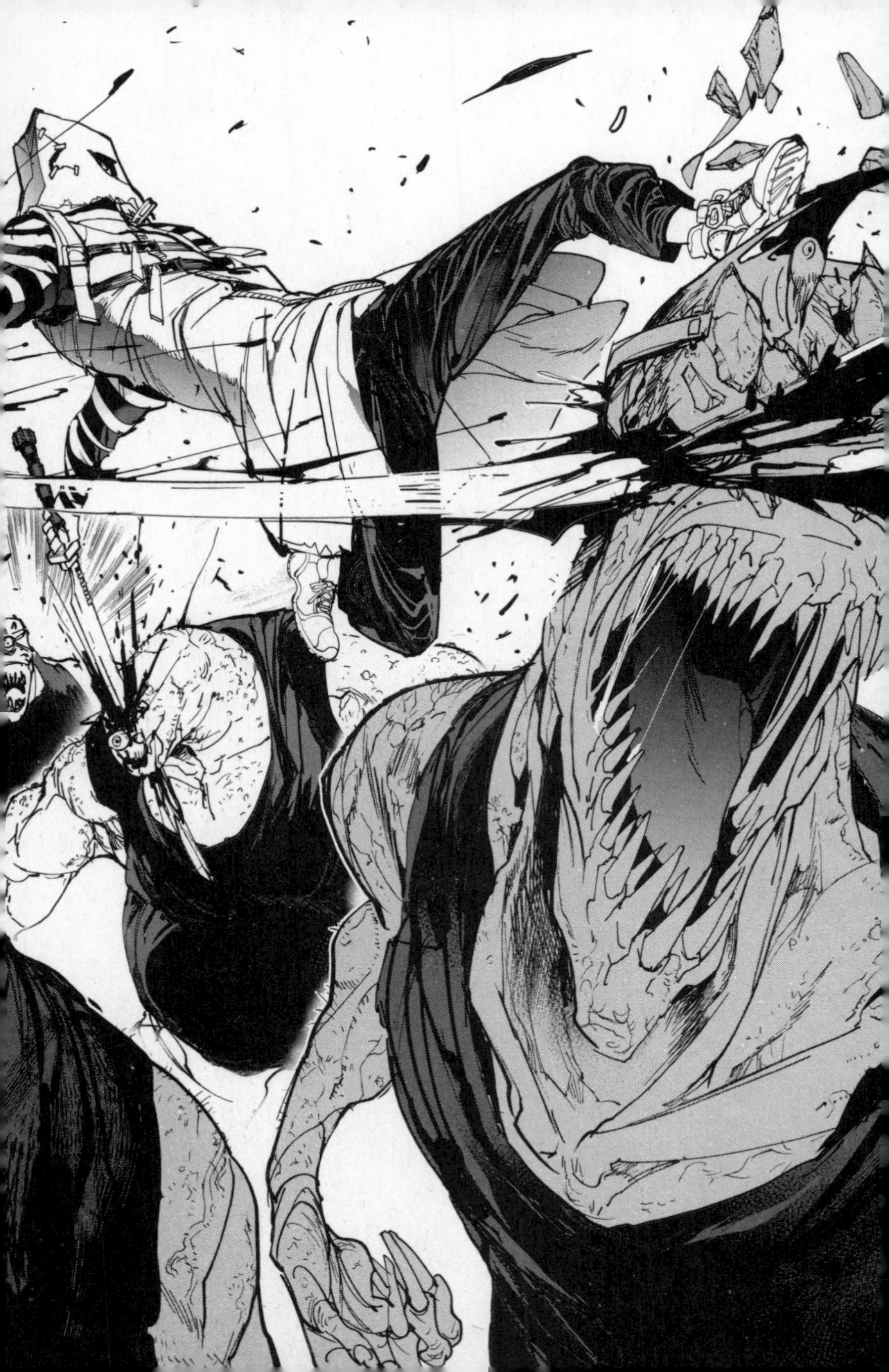

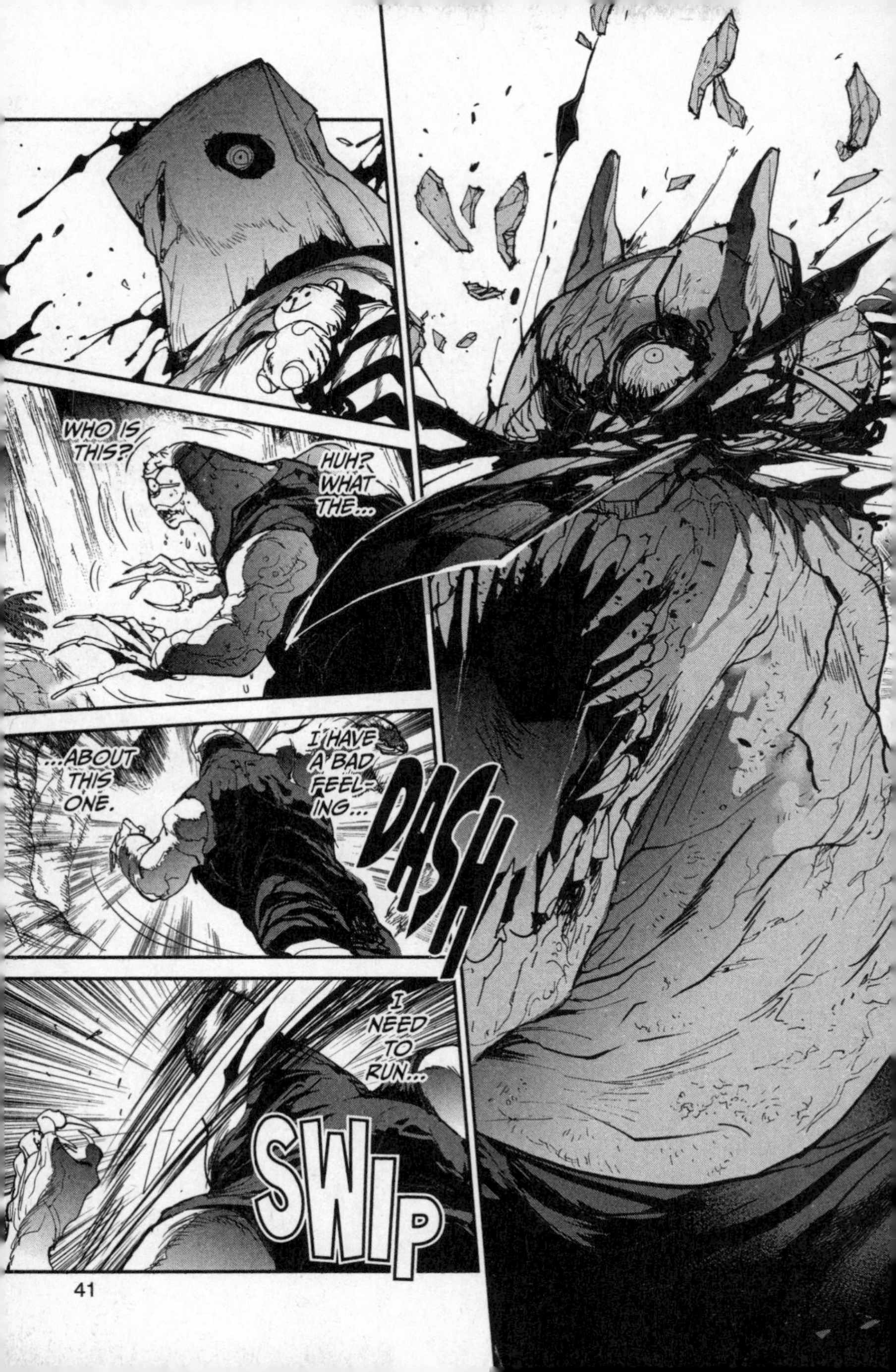
DASH
HUH? WHAT THE...
WHO IS THIS?
I HAVE A BAD FEEL-ING...
...ABOUT THIS ONE.
I NEED TO RUN...
SWIP

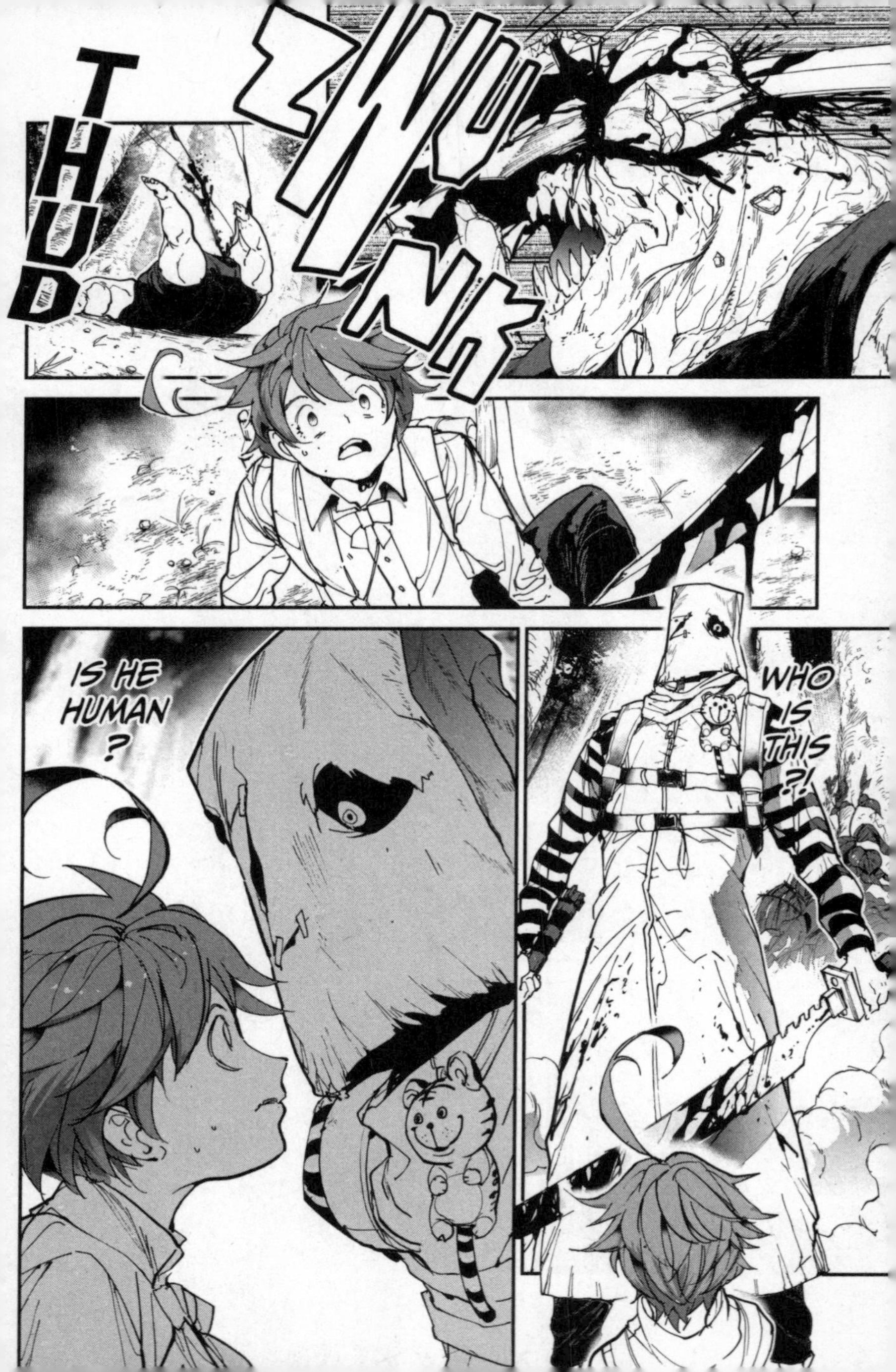
ZHUNK
THUD
WHO IS THIS ?!
IS HE HUMAN ?

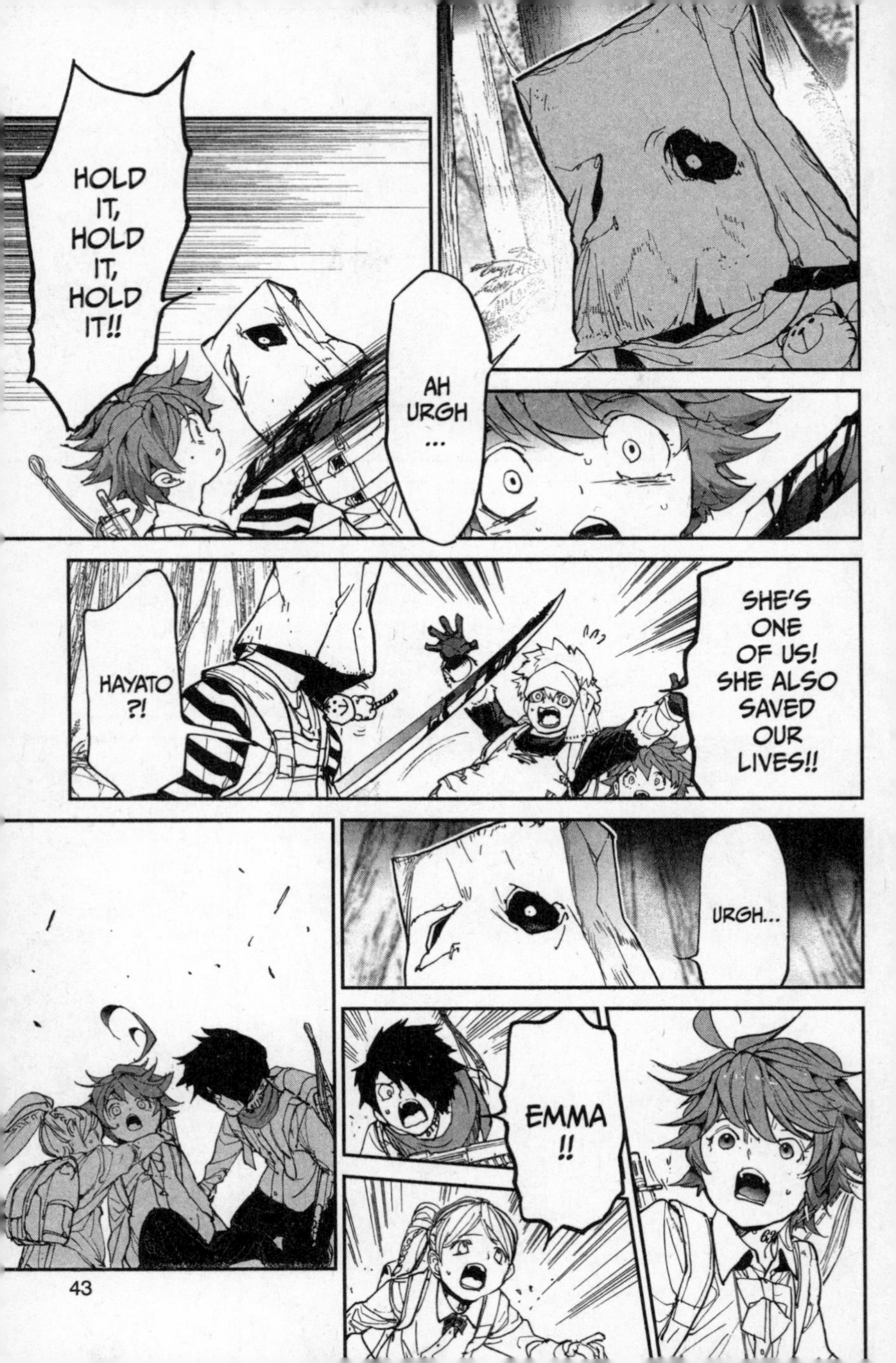
HOLD IT, HOLD IT, HOLD IT!!
AH URGH ...
SHE'S ONE OF US! SHE ALSO SAVED OUR LIVES!!
HAYATO ?!
URGH...
EMMA !!

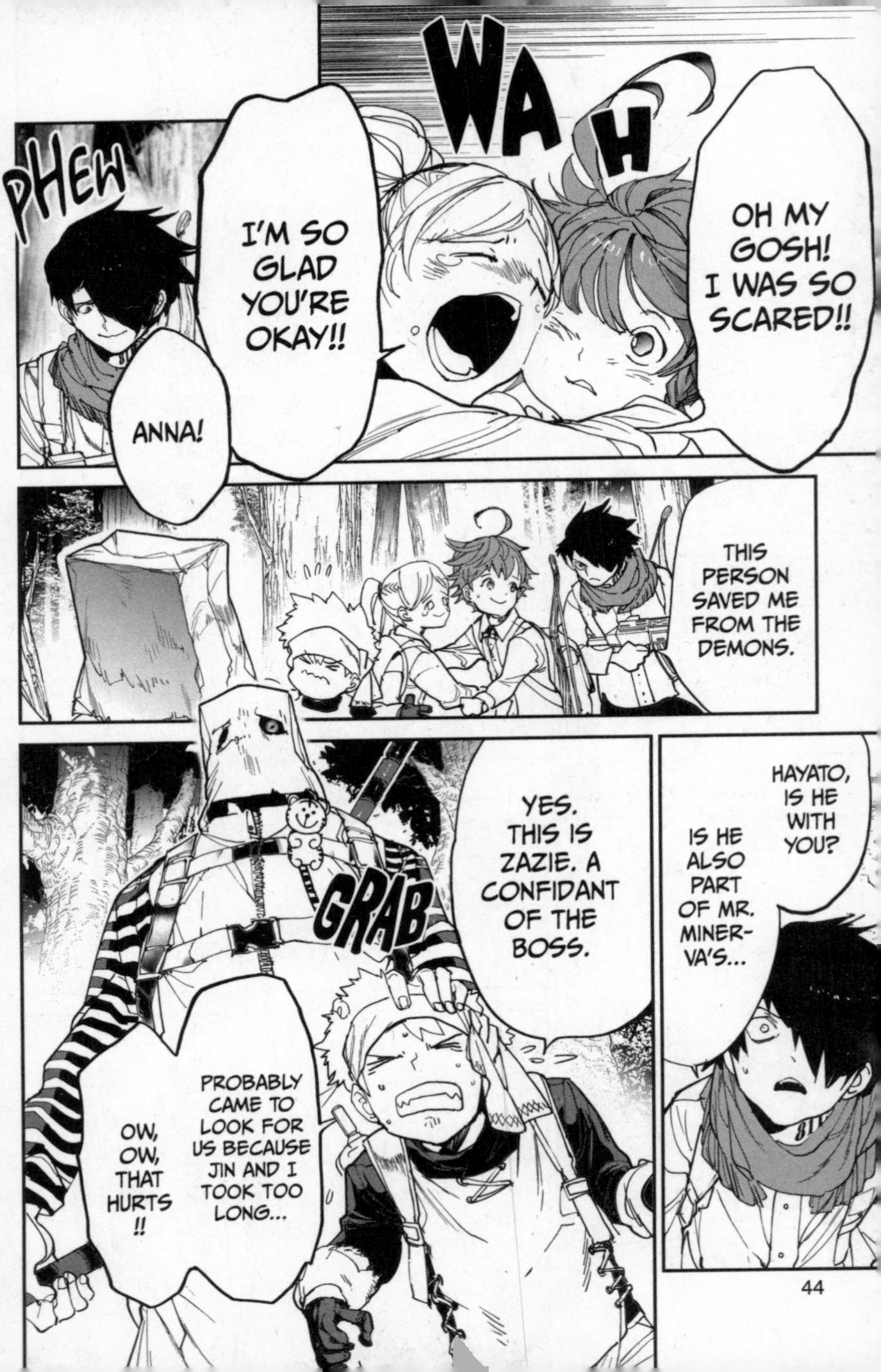
WAH
OH MY GOSH! I WAS SO SCARED!!
I'M SO GLAD YOU'RE OKAY!!
PHEW
ANNA!
THIS PERSON SAVED ME FROM THE DEMONS.
HAYATO, IS HE WITH YOU?
IS HE ALSO PART OF MR. MINER-VA'S...
YES. THIS IS ZAZIE. A CONFIDANT OF THE BOSS.
GRAB
PROBABLY CAME TO LOOK FOR US BECAUSE JIN AND I TOOK TOO LONG...
OW, OW, THAT HURTS!!

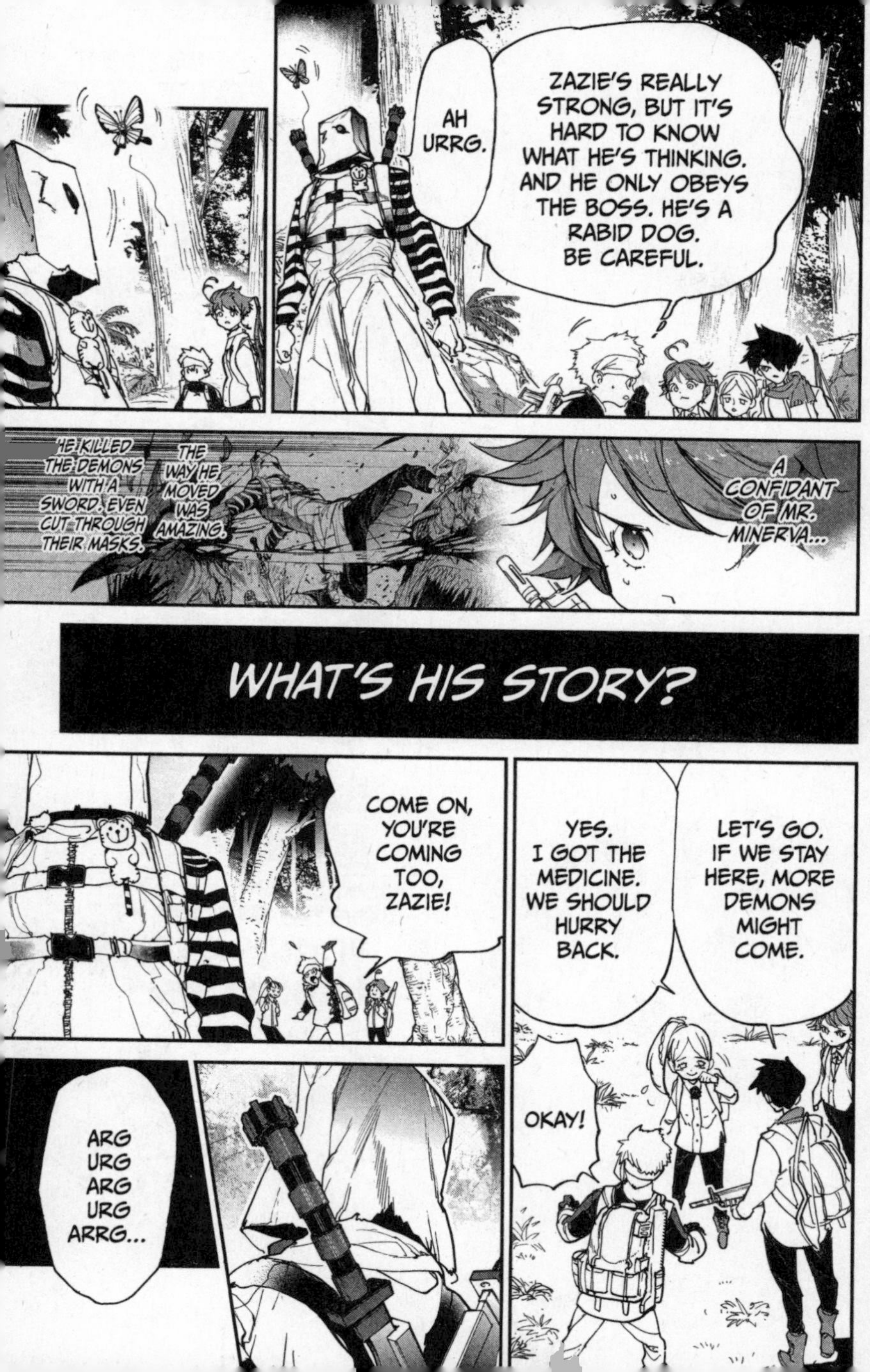
ZAZIE'S REALLY STRONG, BUT IT'S HARD TO KNOW WHAT HE'S THINKING. AND HE ONLY OBEYS THE BOSS. HE'S A RABID DOG. BE CAREFUL.
AH URRG.
A CONFIDANT OF MR. MINERVA...
THE WAY HE MOVED WAS AMAZING.
HE KILLED THE DEMONS WITH A SWORD. EVEN CUT THROUGH THEIR MASKS.
WHAT'S HIS STORY?
LET'S GO. IF WE STAY HERE, MORE DEMONS MIGHT COME.
YES. I GOT THE MEDICINE. WE SHOULD HURRY BACK.
OKAY!
COME ON, YOU'RE COMING TOO, ZAZIE!
ARG URG ARG URG ARRG...

FIVE YEARS OLD

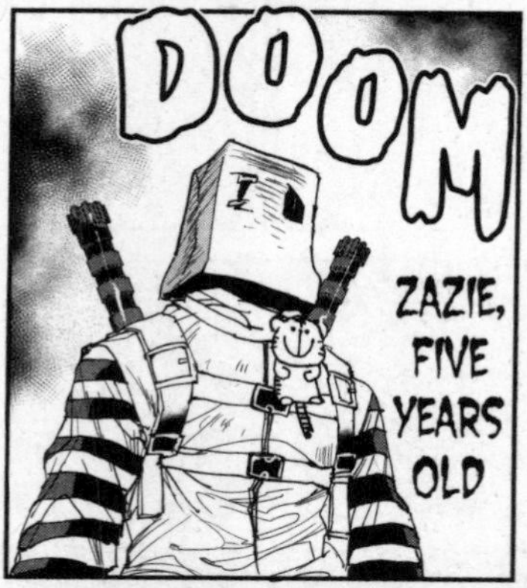
DOOM
ZAZIE, FIVE YEARS OLD

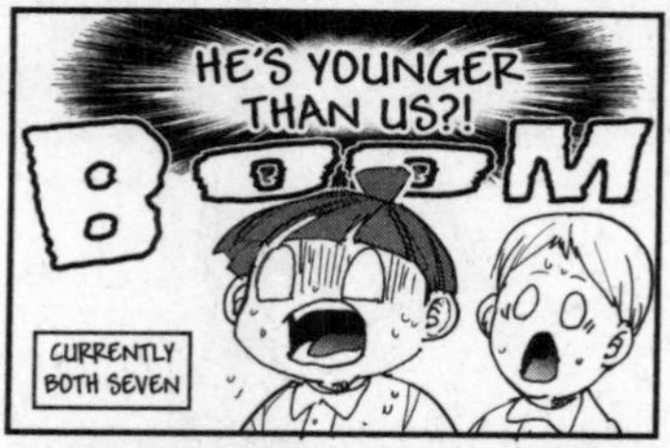
HE'S YOUNGER THAN US?!
BOOM
CURRENTLY BOTH SEVEN

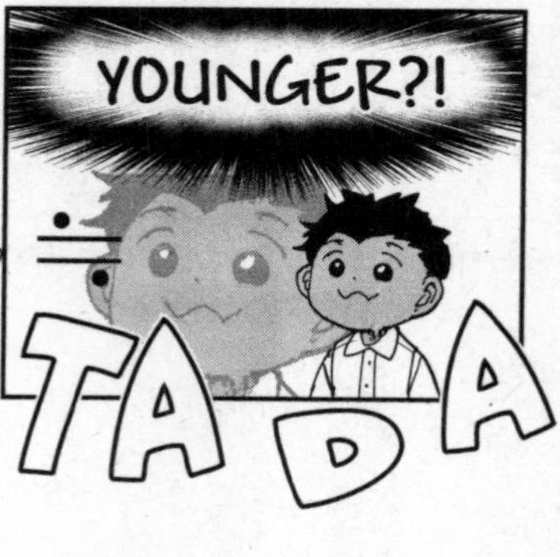
YOUNGER?!
TADA

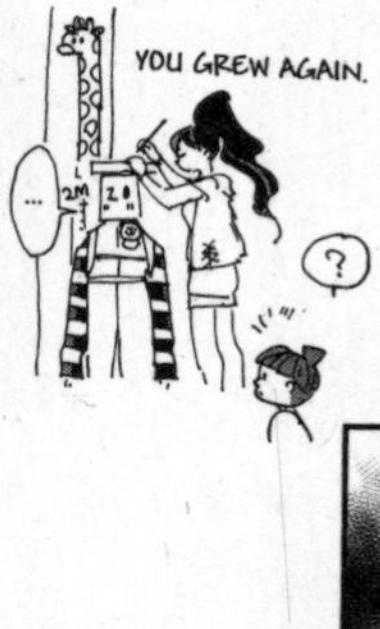
YOU GREW AGAIN.
...
2M
?

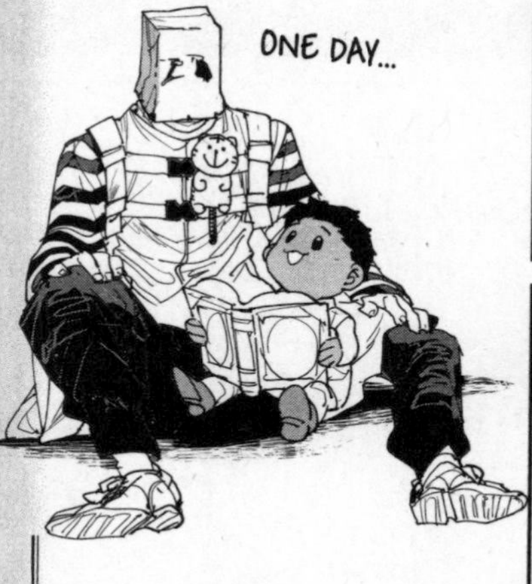
ONE DAY...

SIDE STORY 11...FIN

CHAPTER 118: MEETING

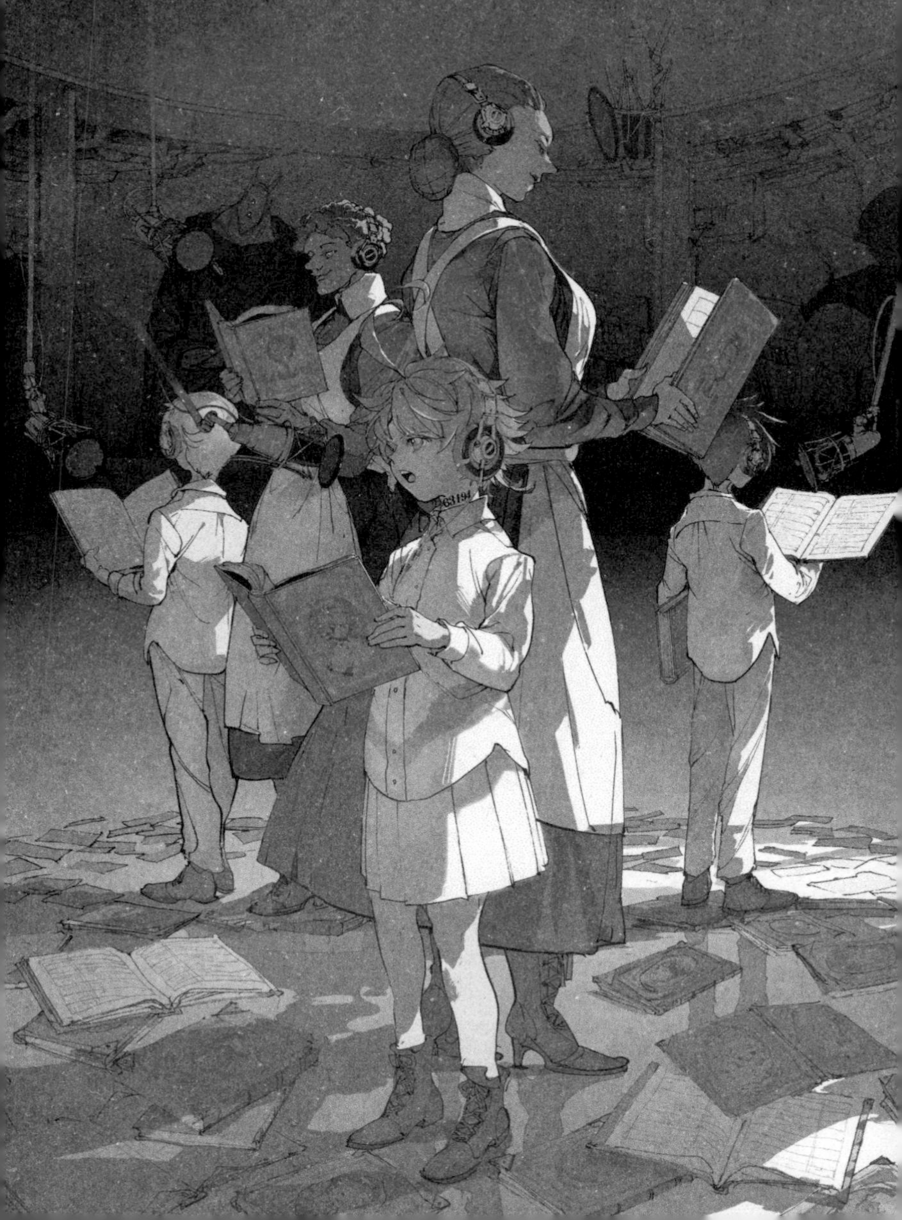
63194

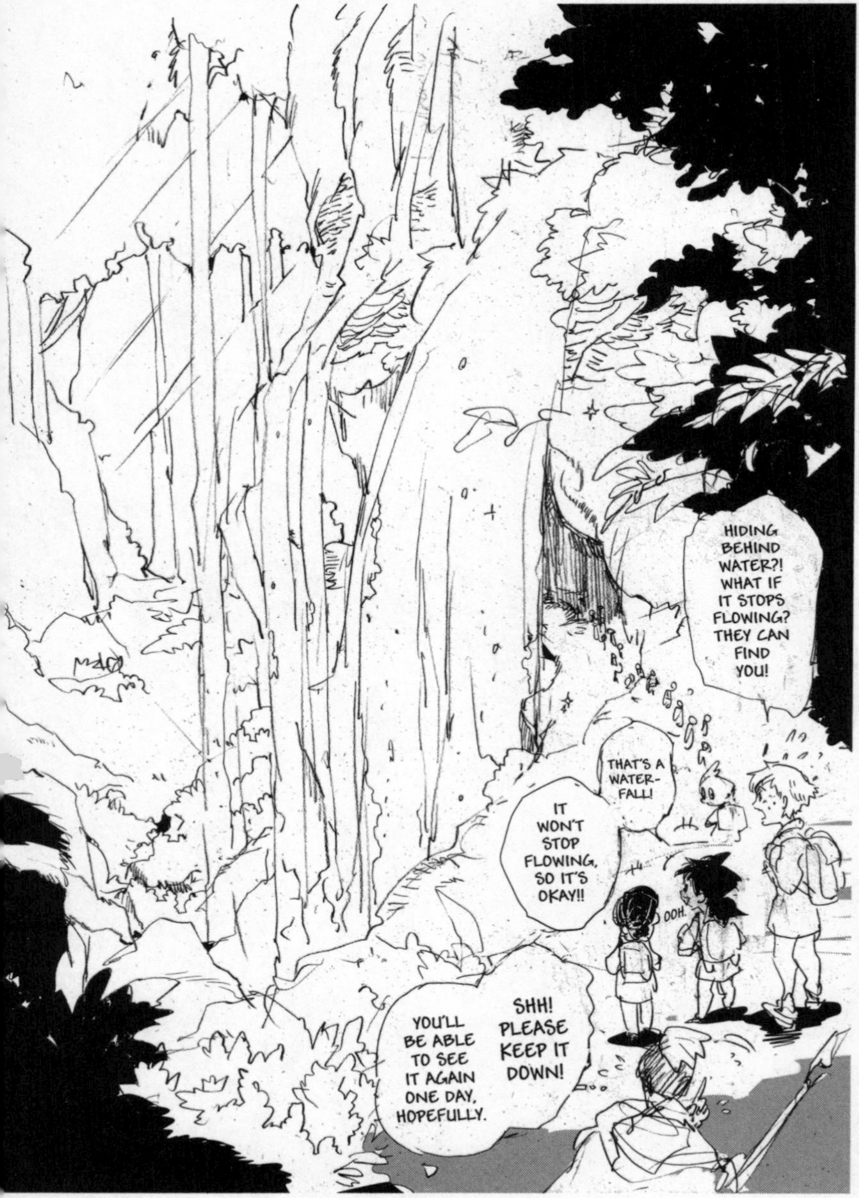
HIDING BEHIND WATER?! WHAT IF IT STOPS FLOWING? THEY CAN FIND YOU!
THAT'S A WATER-FALL!
IT WON'T STOP FLOWING, SO IT'S OKAY!!
OOH.
SHH! PLEASE KEEP IT DOWN!
YOU'LL BE ABLE TO SEE IT AGAIN ONE DAY, HOPEFULLY.

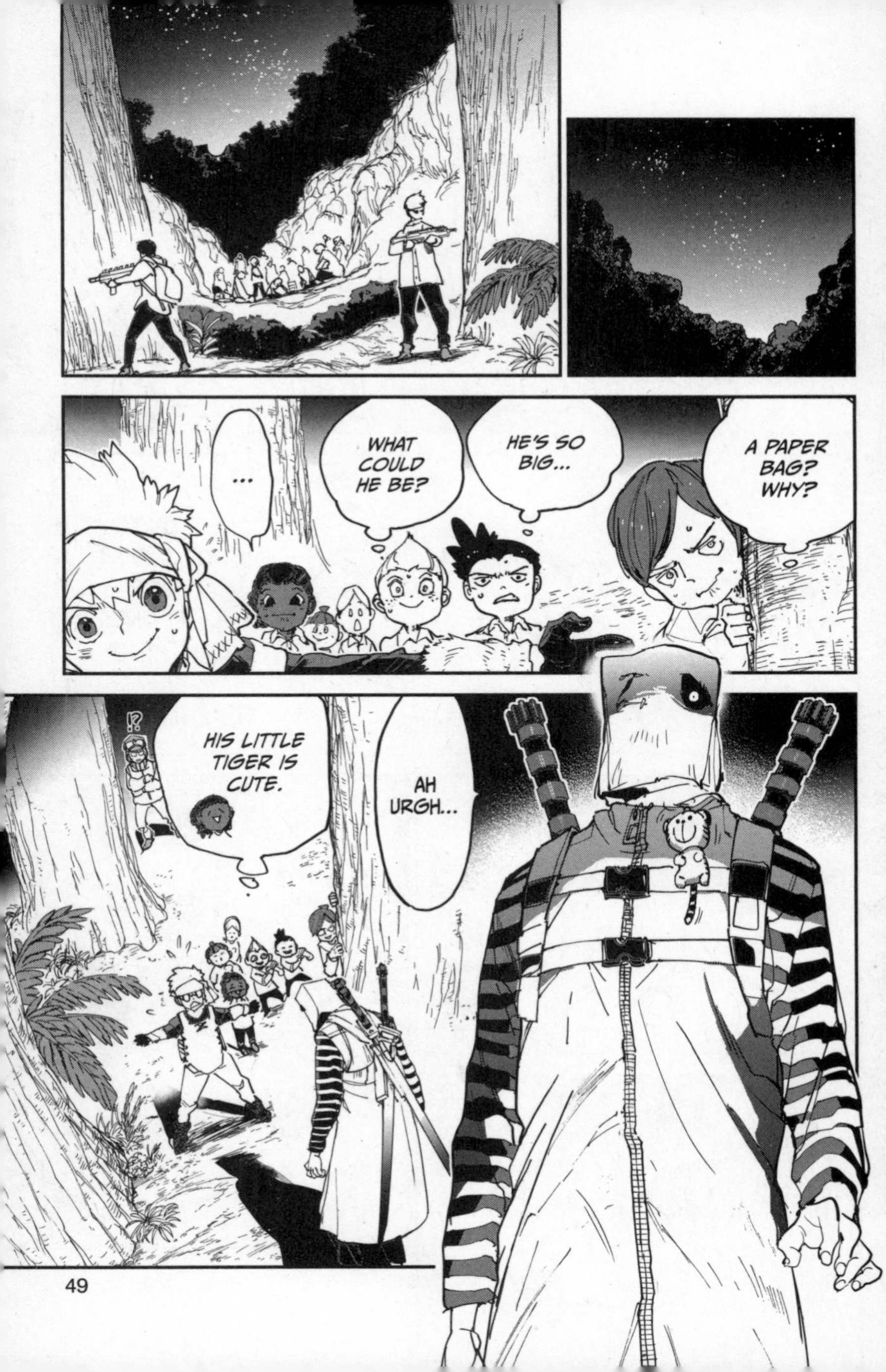
A PAPER BAG? WHY?
HE'S SO BIG...
WHAT COULD HE BE?
...
AH URGH...
HIS LITTLE TIGER IS CUTE.
!?

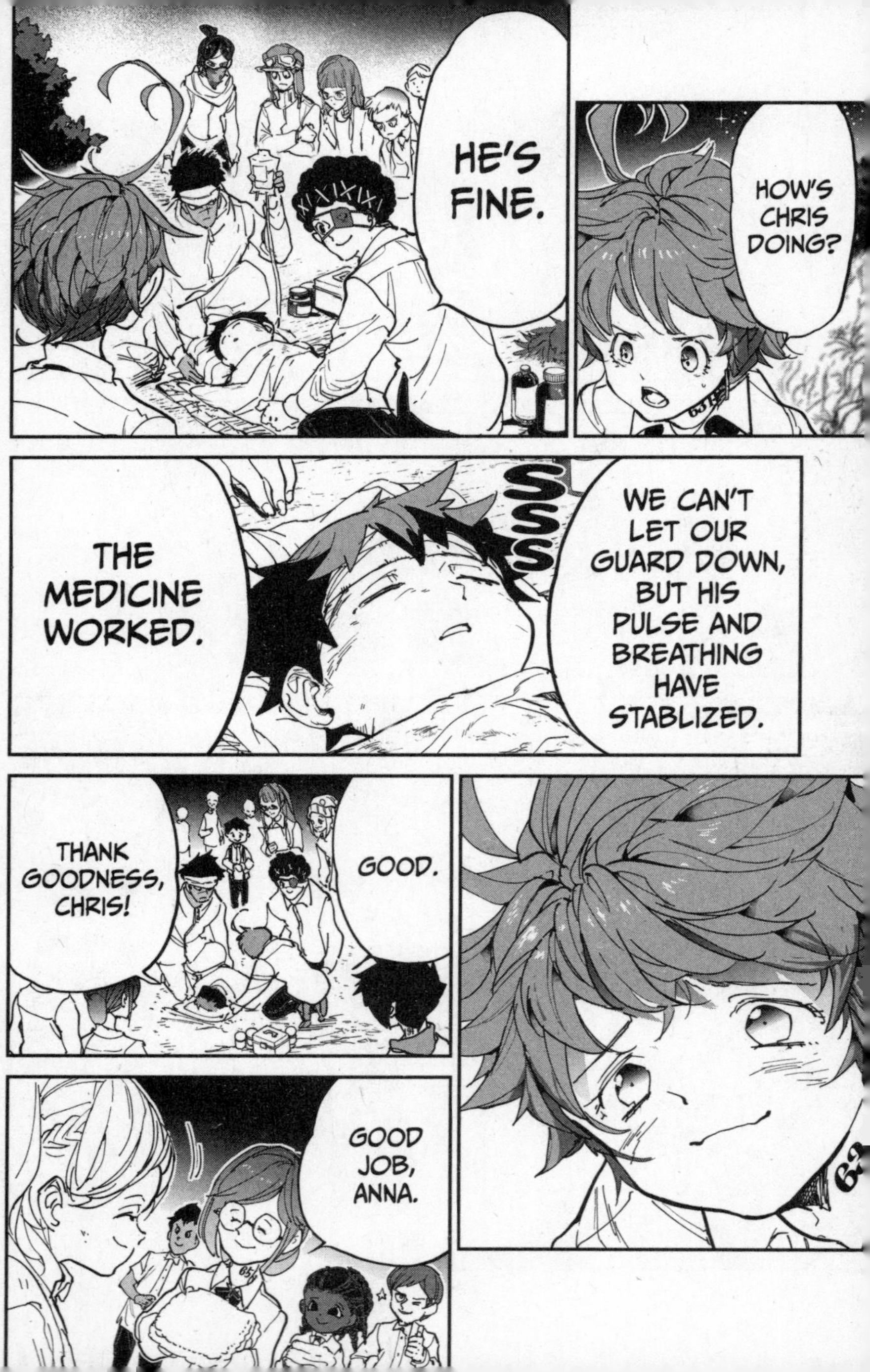
HOW'S CHRIS DOING?
HE'S FINE.
WE CAN'T LET OUR GUARD DOWN, BUT HIS PULSE AND BREATHING HAVE STABLIZED.
SSS
THE MEDICINE WORKED.
GOOD.
THANK GOODNESS, CHRIS!
GOOD JOB, ANNA.

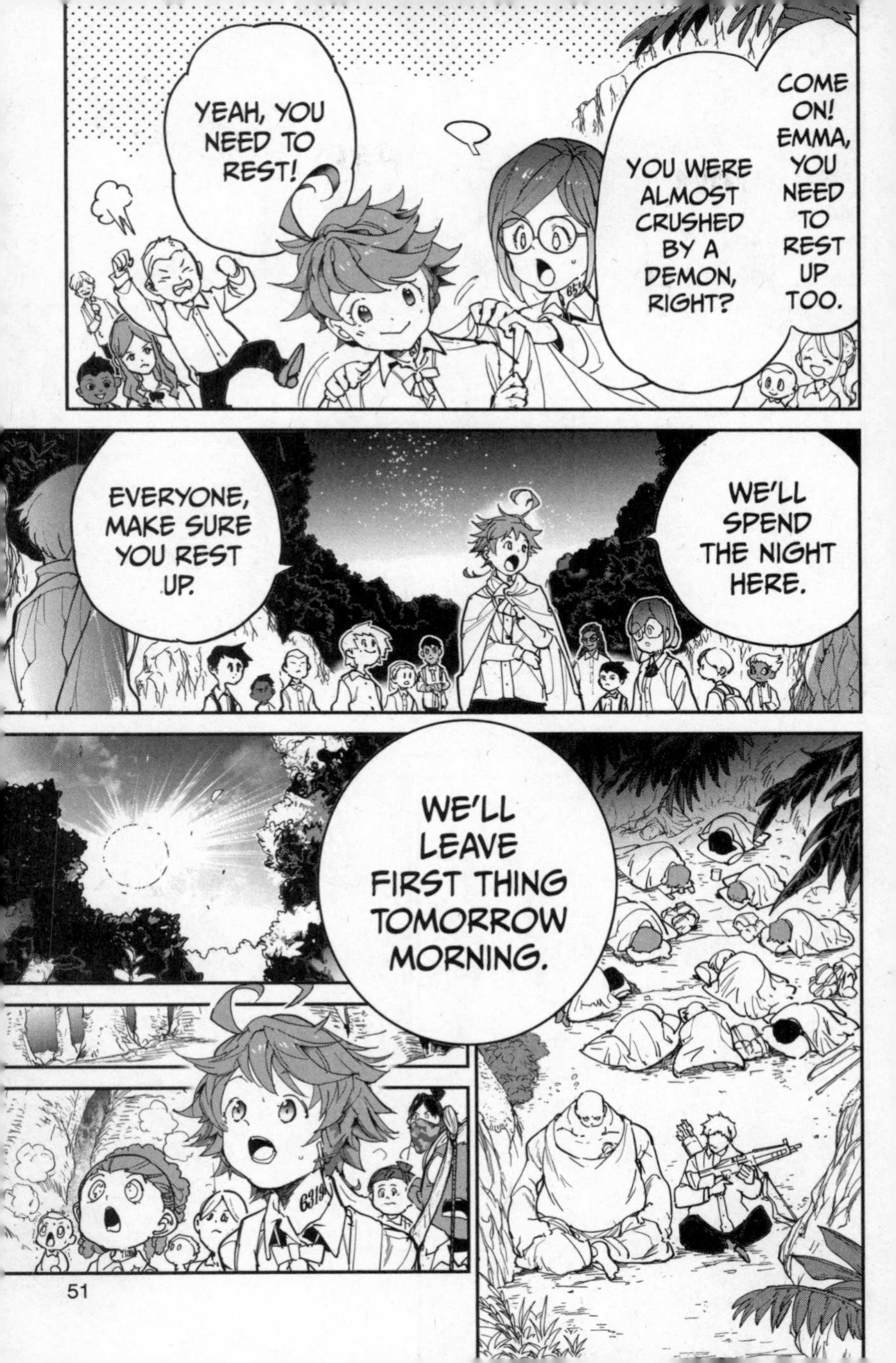
COME ON! EMMA, YOU NEED TO REST UP TOO.
YOU WERE ALMOST CRUSHED BY A DEMON, RIGHT?
YEAH, YOU NEED TO REST!
WE'LL SPEND THE NIGHT HERE.
EVERYONE, MAKE SURE YOU REST UP.
WE'LL LEAVE FIRST THING TOMORROW MORNING.

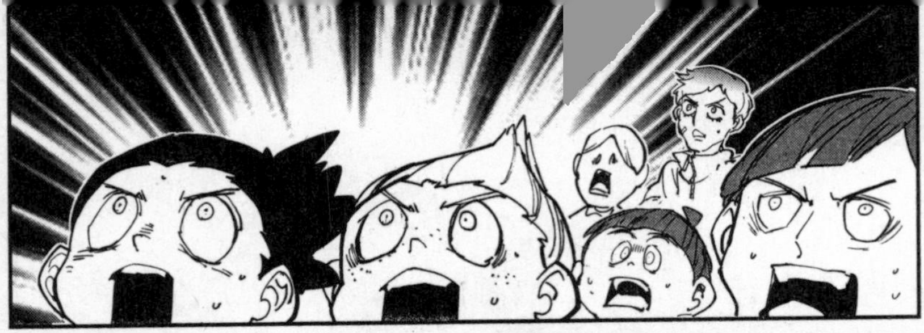

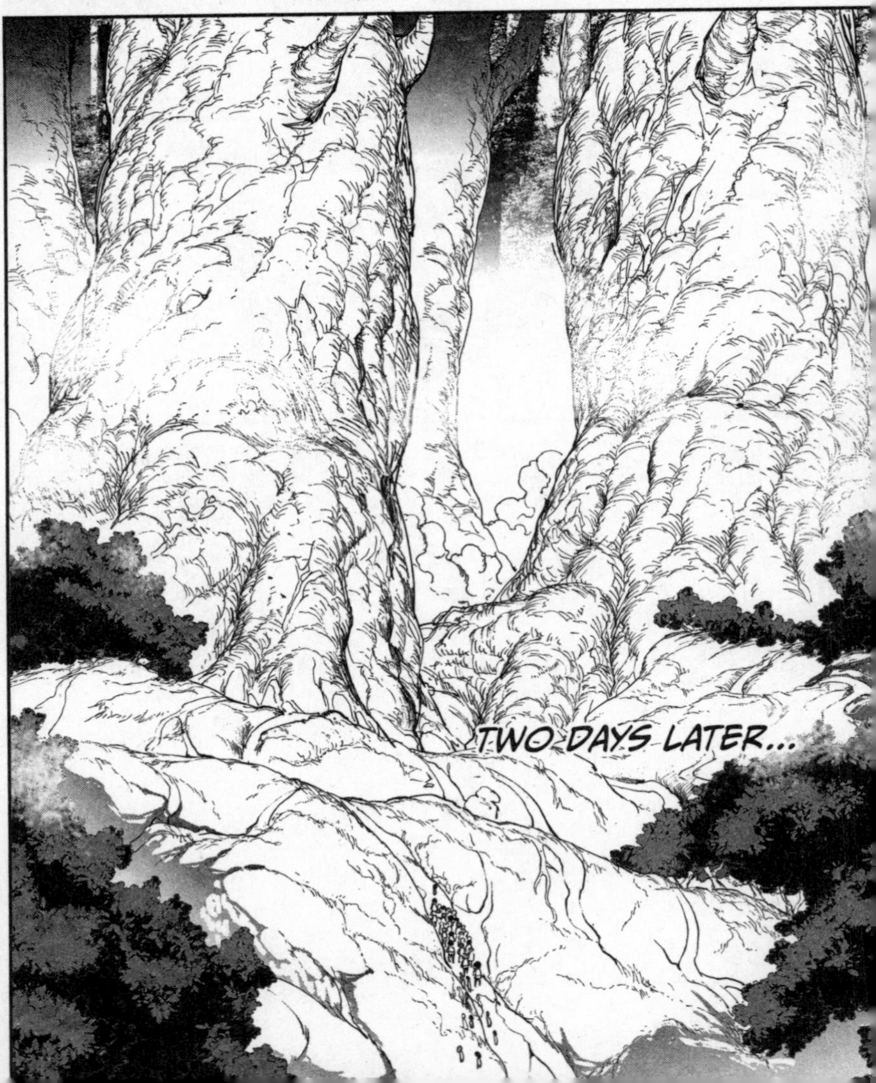
TWO DAYS LATER...

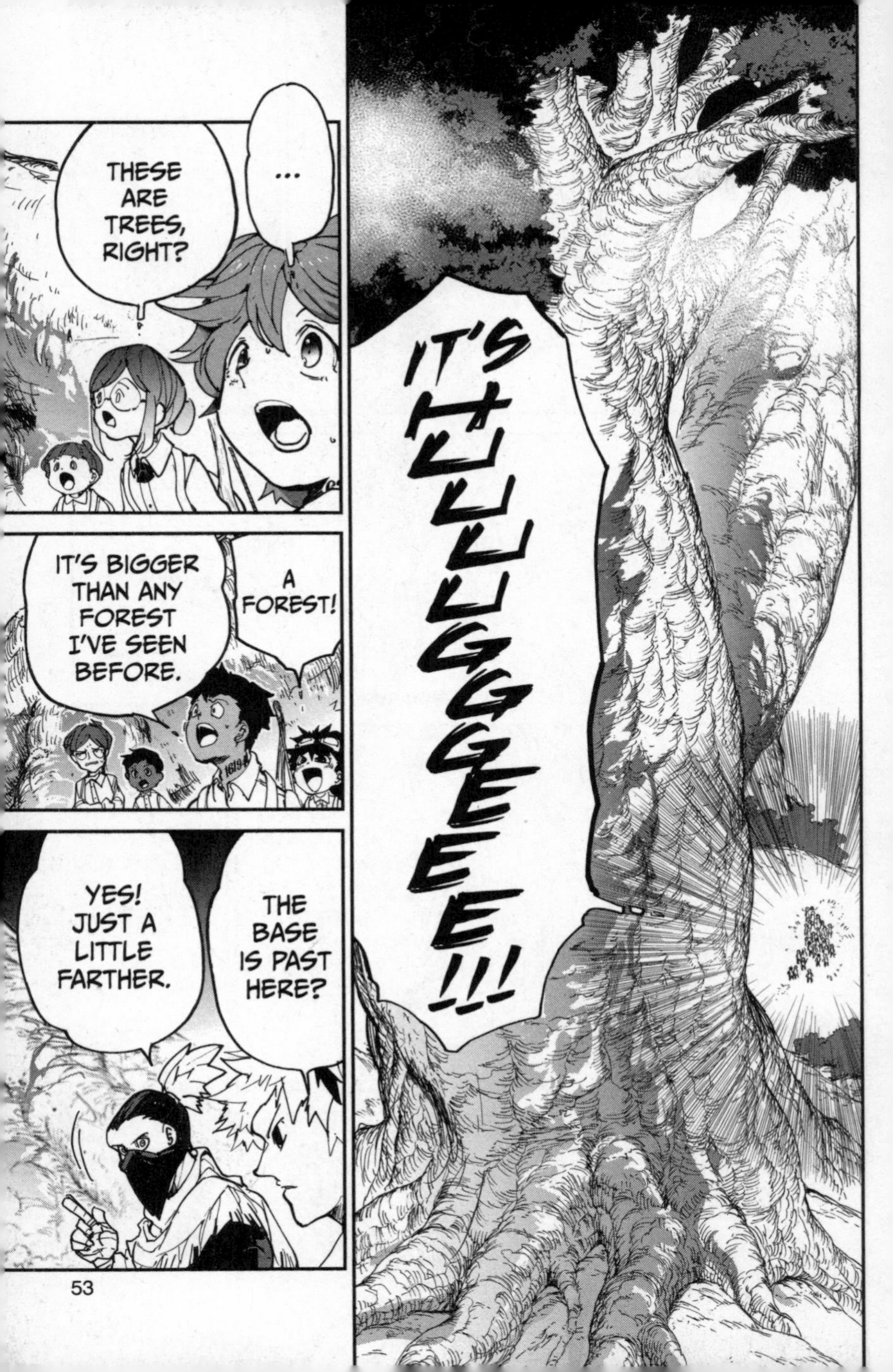
IT'S HUUUGGGEEE!!!
...
THESE ARE TREES, RIGHT?
A FOREST!
IT'S BIGGER THAN ANY FOREST I'VE SEEN BEFORE.
THE BASE IS PAST HERE?
YES! JUST A LITTLE FARTHER.

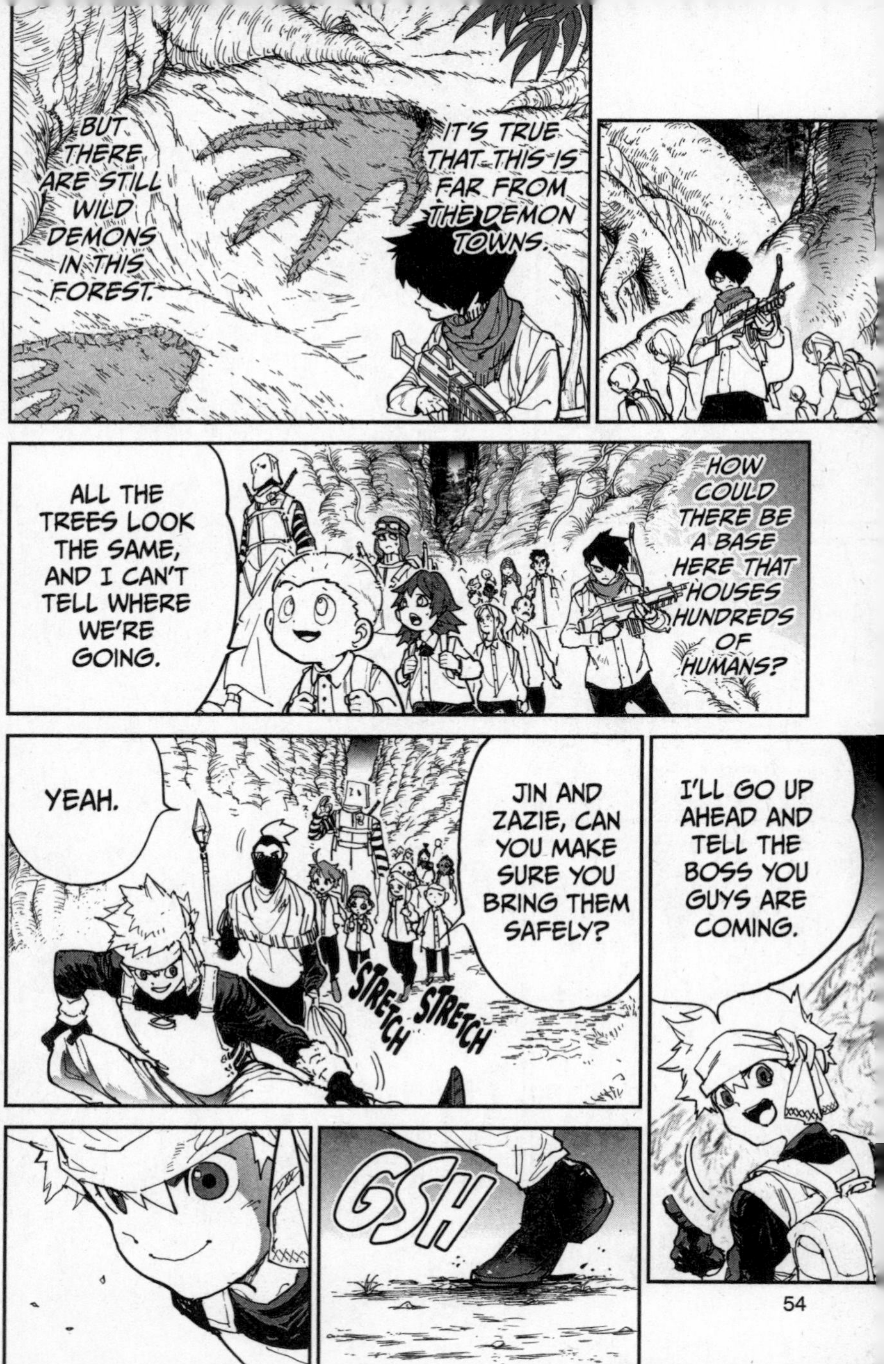
IT'S TRUE THAT THIS IS FAR FROM THE DEMON TOWNS.
BUT THERE ARE STILL WILD DEMONS IN THIS FOREST.
HOW COULD THERE BE A BASE HERE THAT HOUSES HUNDREDS OF HUMANS?
ALL THE TREES LOOK THE SAME, AND I CAN'T TELL WHERE WE'RE GOING.
I'LL GO UP AHEAD AND TELL THE BOSS YOU GUYS ARE COMING.
JIN AND ZAZIE, CAN YOU MAKE SURE YOU BRING THEM SAFELY?
YEAH.
STRETCH
STRETCH
GSH

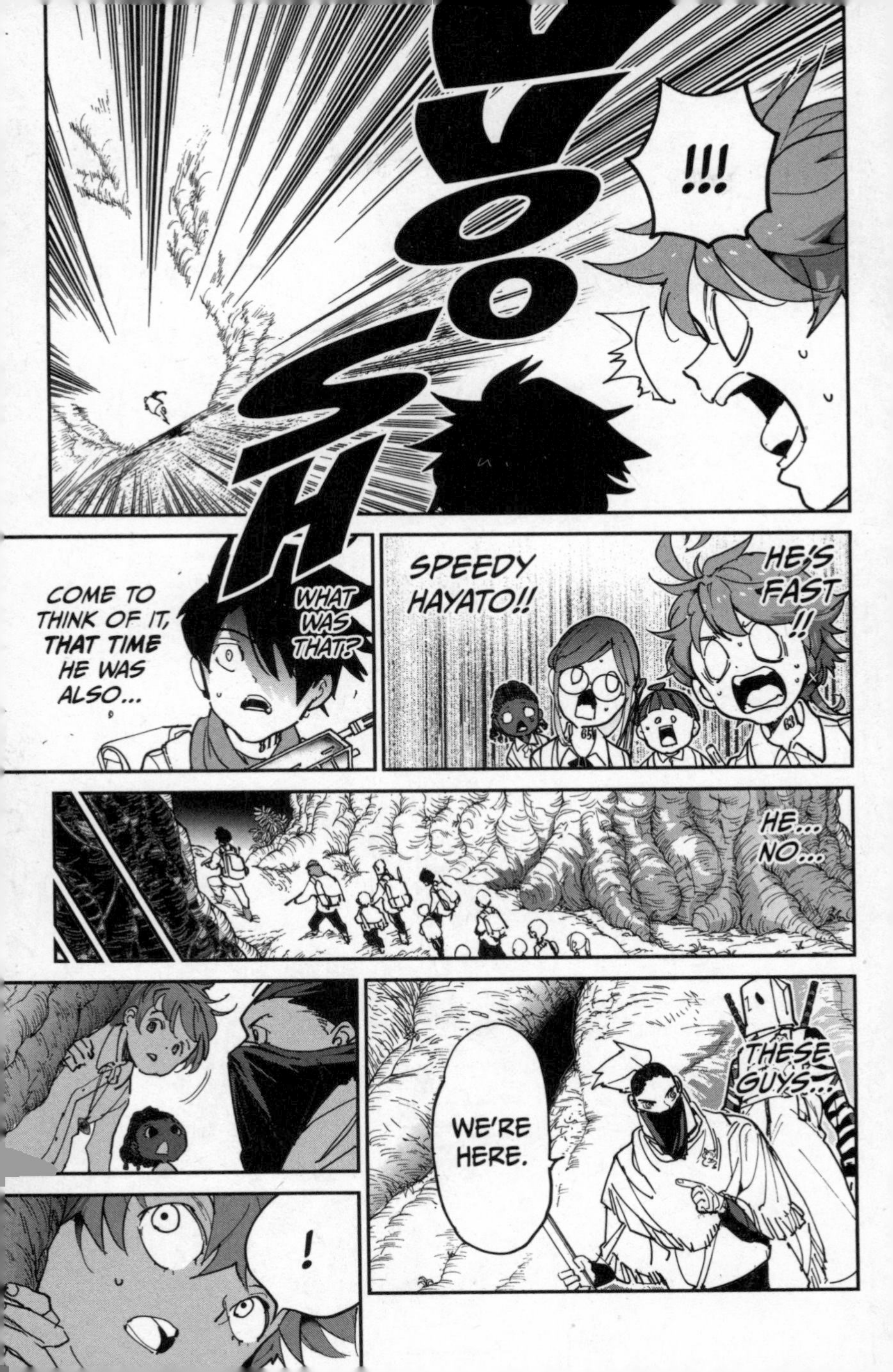
!!!
WHOOSH
HE'S FAST!!
SPEEDY HAYATO!!
WHAT WAS THAT?
COME TO THINK OF IT, THAT TIME HE WAS ALSO...
HE... NO...
THESE GUYS...
WE'RE HERE.
!

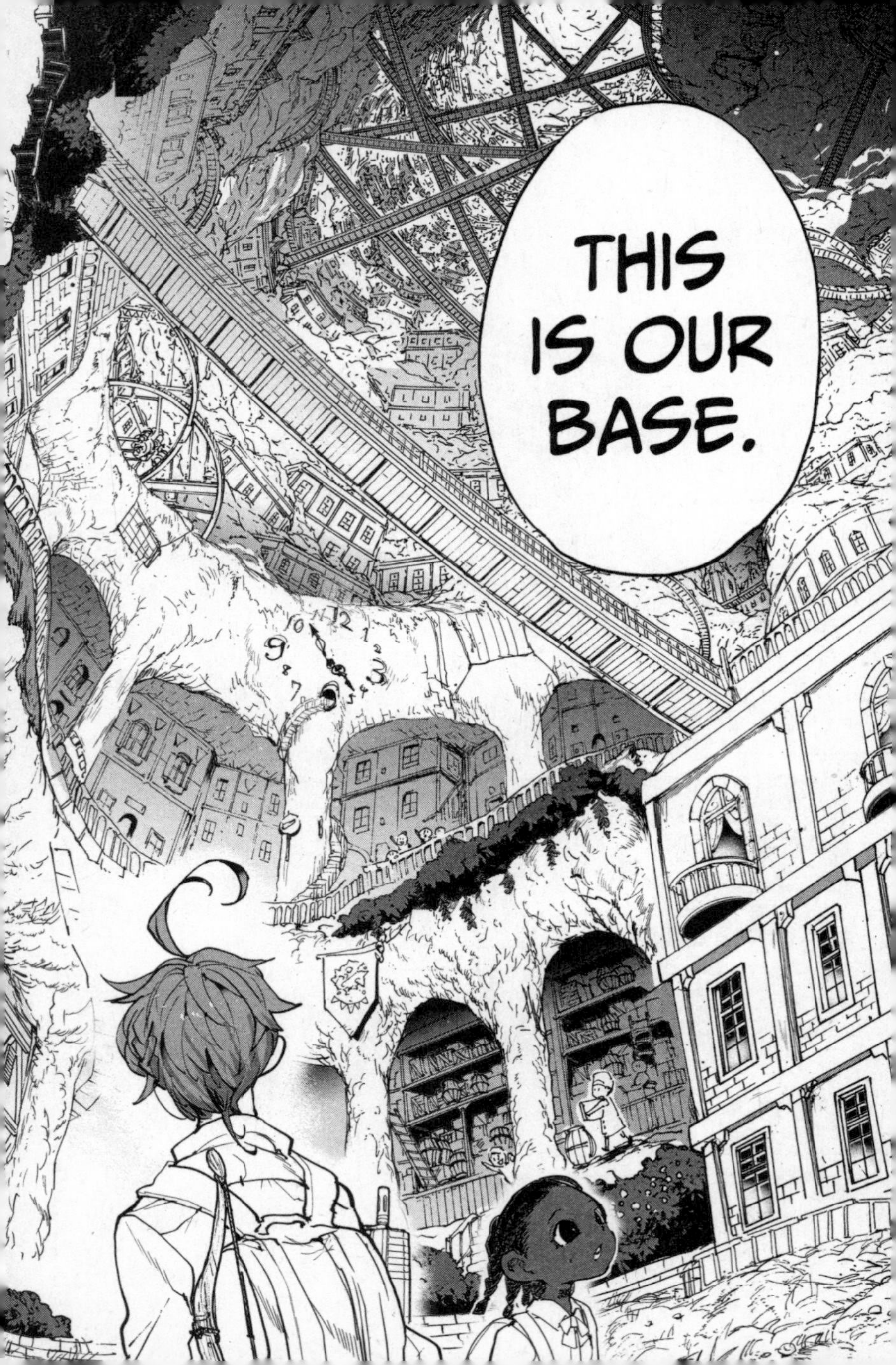
THIS IS OUR BASE.

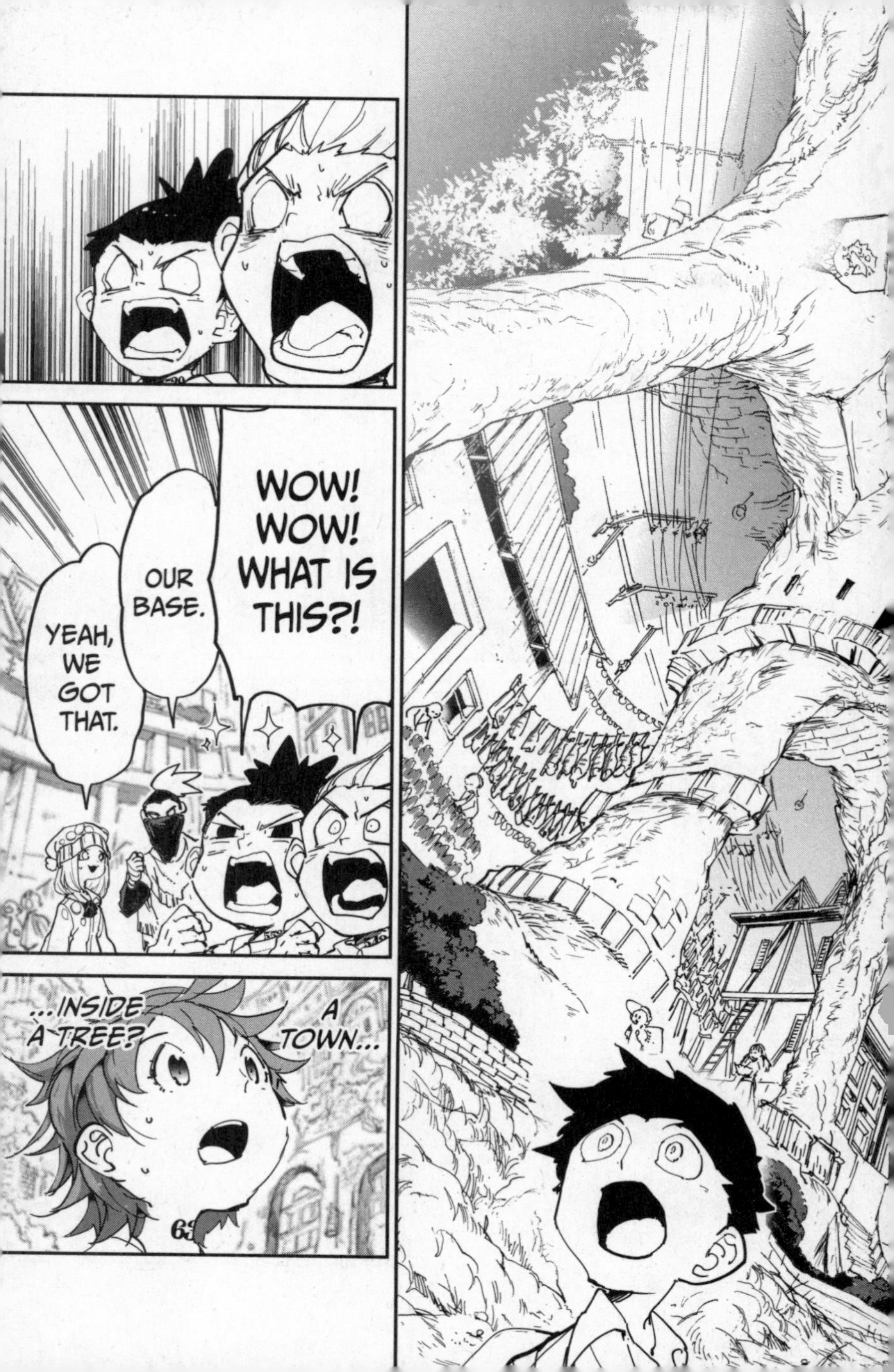
WOW! WOW! WHAT IS THIS?!
OUR BASE.
YEAH, WE GOT THAT.
A TOWN...
...INSIDE A TREE?

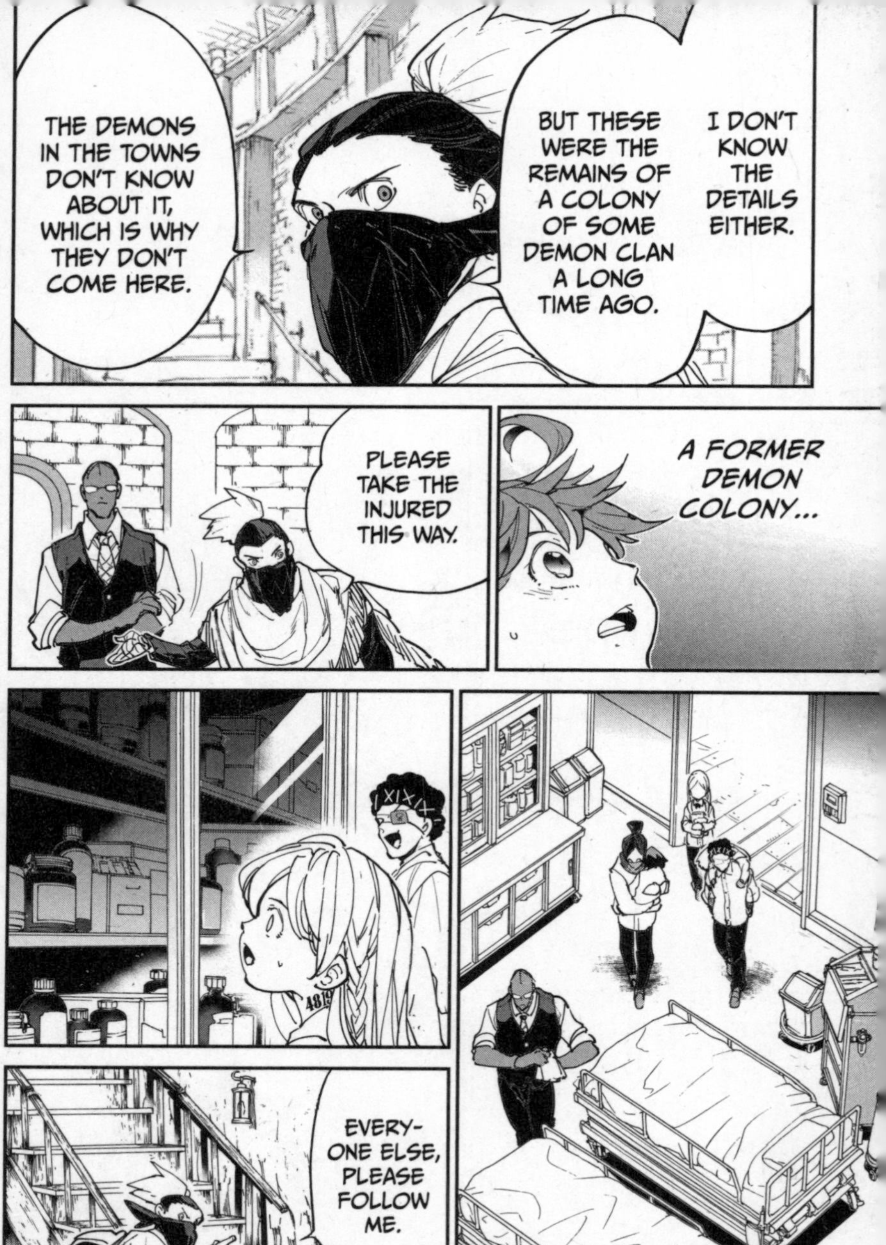
I DON'T KNOW THE DETAILS EITHER.
BUT THESE WERE THE REMAINS OF A COLONY OF SOME DEMON CLAN A LONG TIME AGO.
THE DEMONS IN THE TOWNS DON'T KNOW ABOUT IT, WHICH IS WHY THEY DON'T COME HERE.
A FORMER DEMON COLONY...
PLEASE TAKE THE INJURED THIS WAY.
EVERY-ONE ELSE, PLEASE FOLLOW ME.

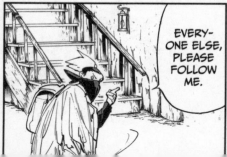

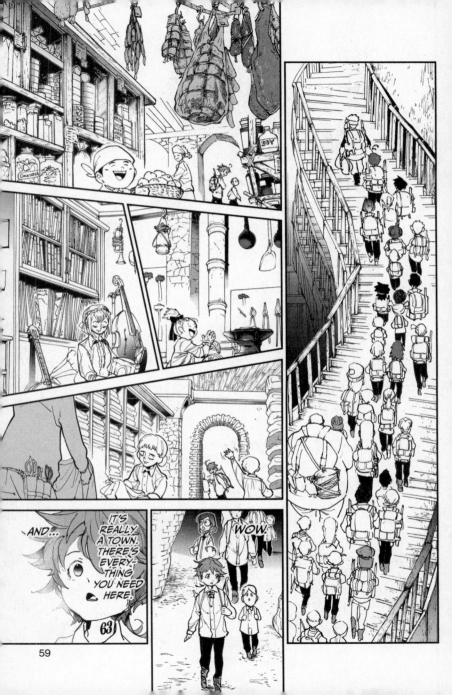

AND...

IT'S REALLY A TOWN. THERE'S EVERY-THING YOU NEED HERE!

WOW.

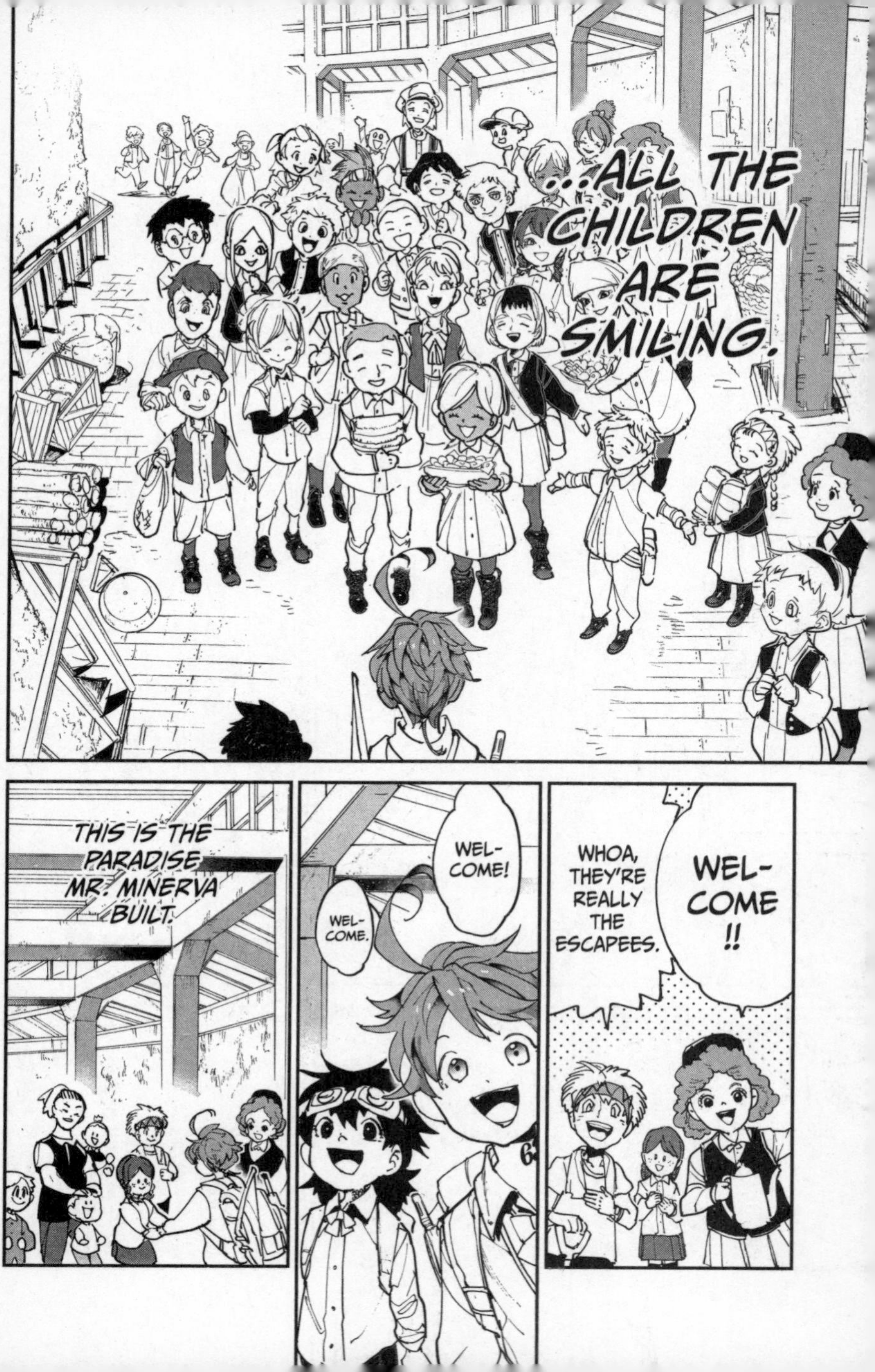
...ALL THE CHILDREN ARE SMILING.
WEL-COME!!
WHOA, THEY'RE REALLY THE ESCAPEES.
WEL-COME!
WEL-COME.
THIS IS THE PARADISE MR. MINERVA BUILT.

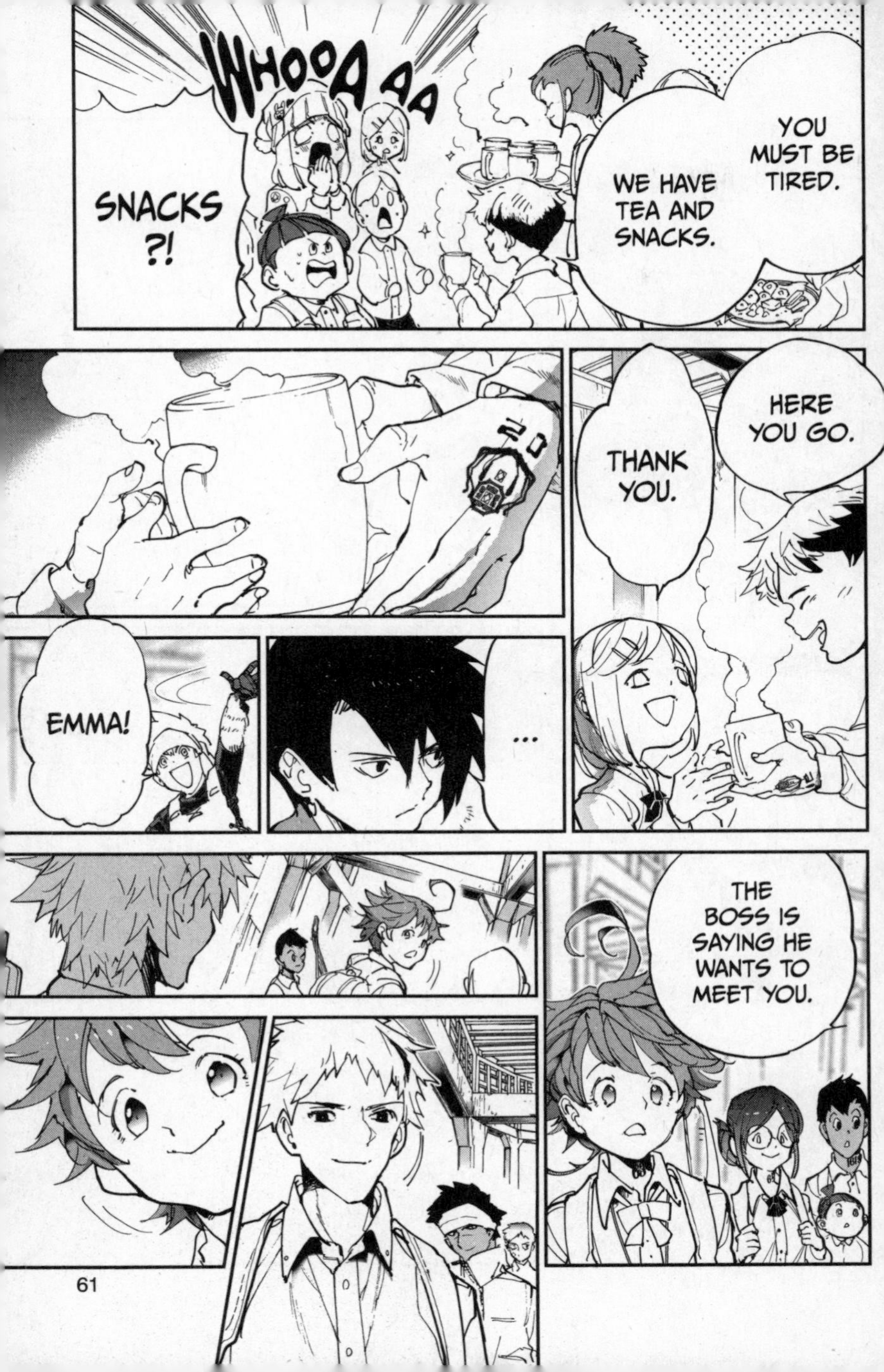
YOU MUST BE TIRED.
WE HAVE TEA AND SNACKS.
WHOOAAA
SNACKS ?!
HERE YOU GO.
THANK YOU.
...
EMMA!
THE BOSS IS SAYING HE WANTS TO MEET YOU.

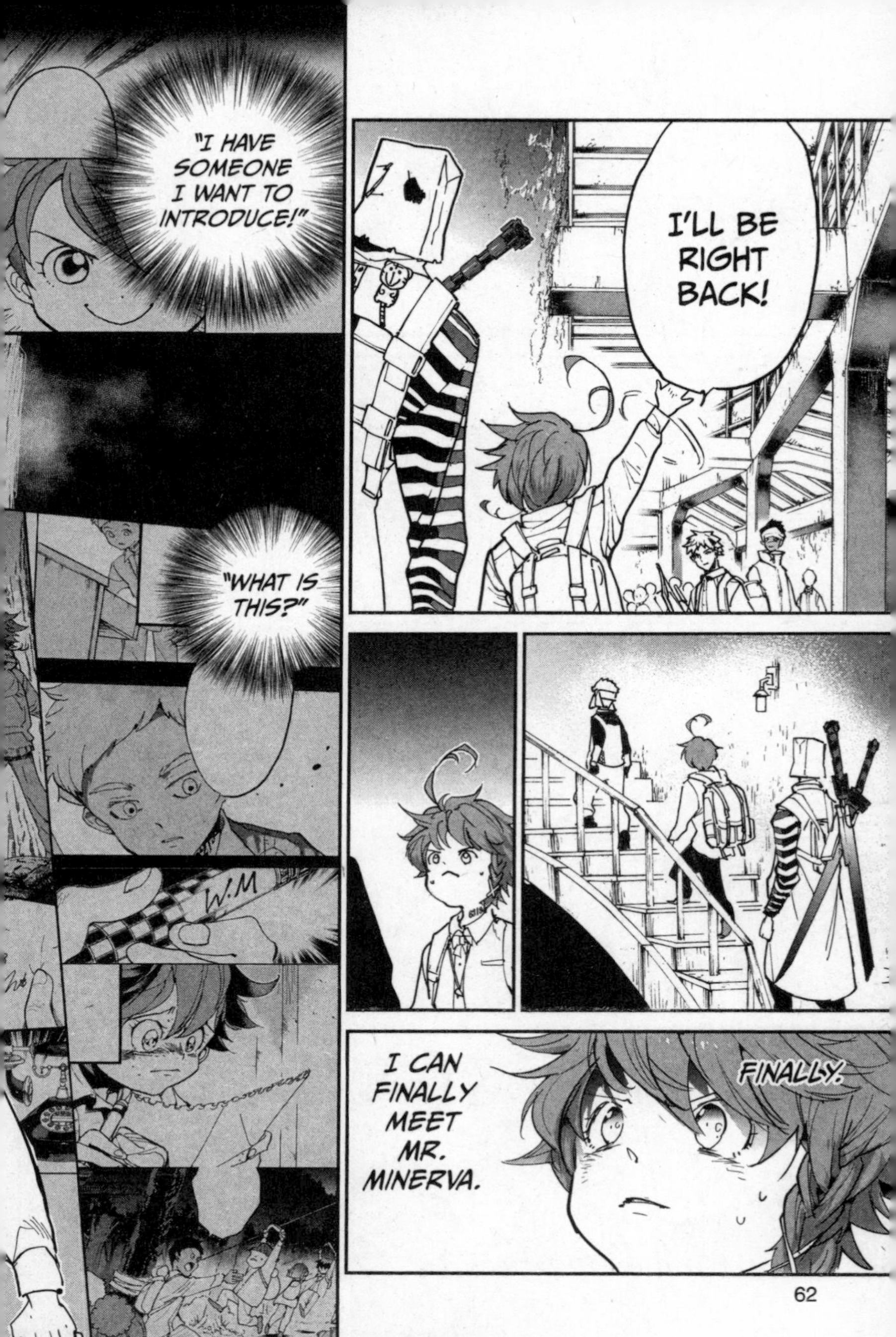
I'LL BE RIGHT BACK!
I CAN FINALLY MEET MR. MINERVA.
FINALLY.
"I HAVE SOMEONE I WANT TO INTRODUCE!"
"WHAT IS THIS?"
W.M

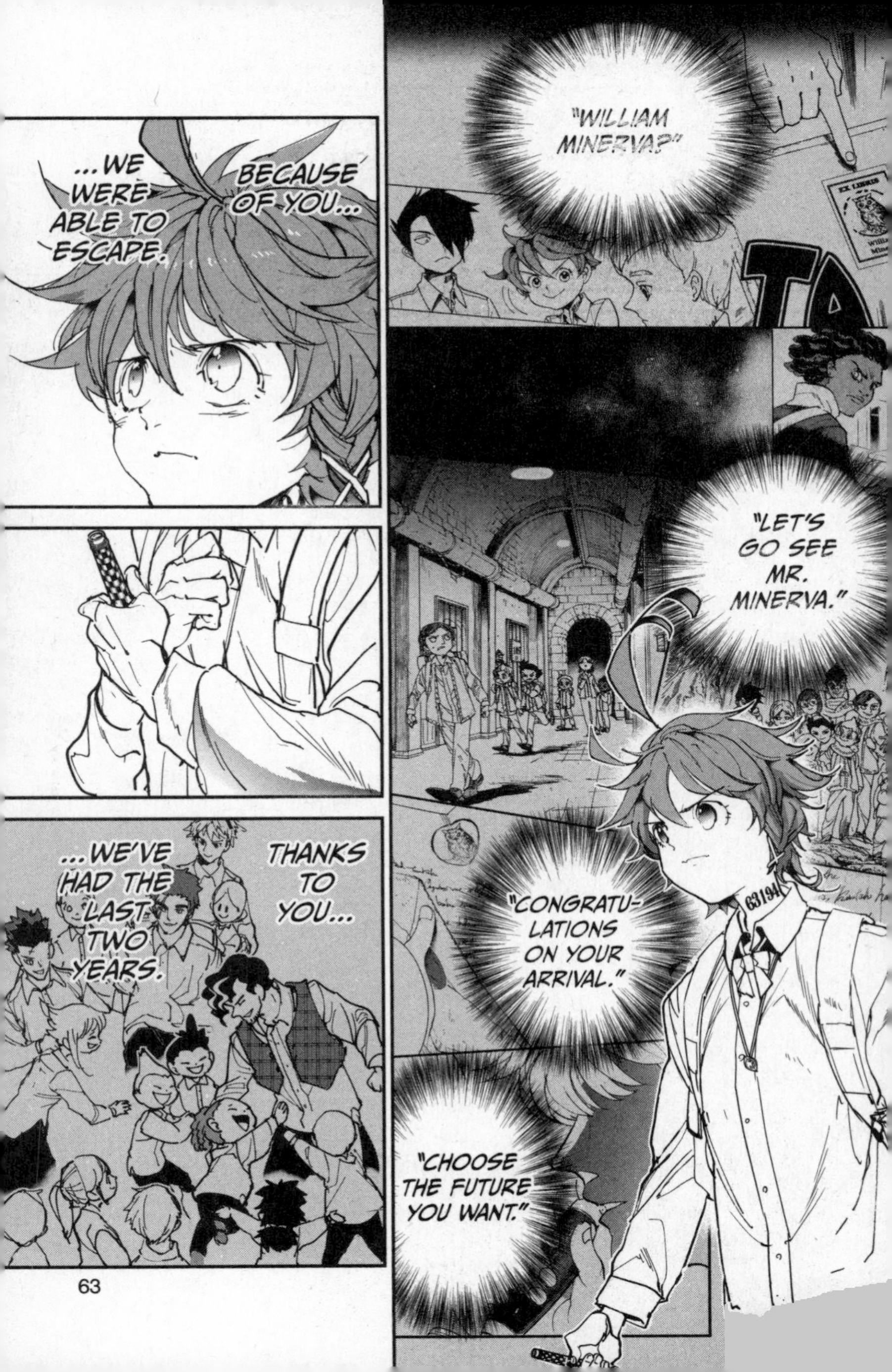
"WILLIAM MINERVA?"
"LET'S GO SEE MR. MINERVA."
"CONGRATU-LATIONS ON YOUR ARRIVAL."
"CHOOSE THE FUTURE YOU WANT."
BECAUSE OF YOU...
...WE WERE ABLE TO ESCAPE.
THANKS TO YOU...
...WE'VE HAD THE LAST TWO YEARS.

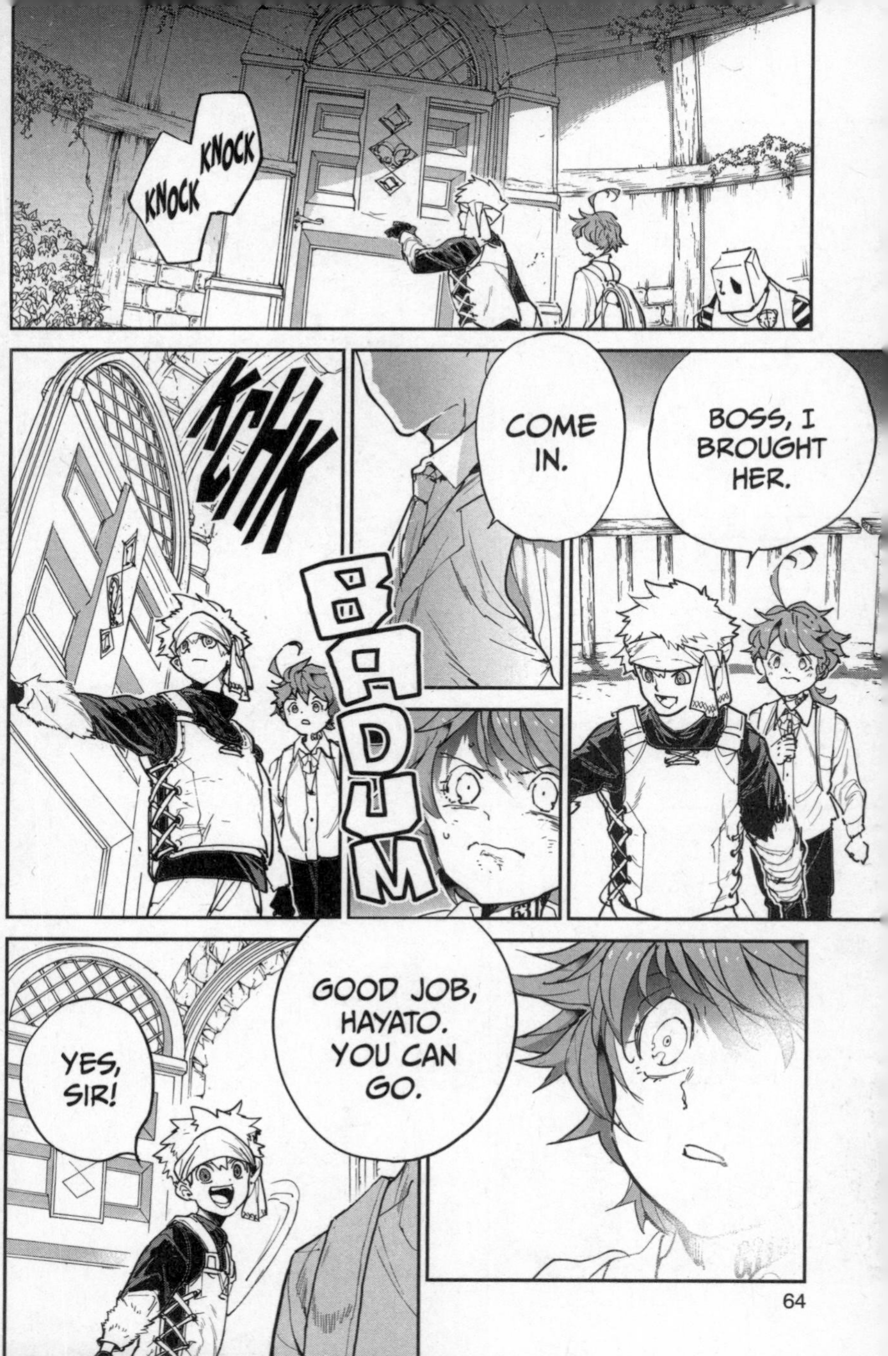
KNOCK KNOCK
BOSS, I BROUGHT HER.
COME IN.
BADUM
KCHK
GOOD JOB, HAYATO. YOU CAN GO.
YES, SIR!

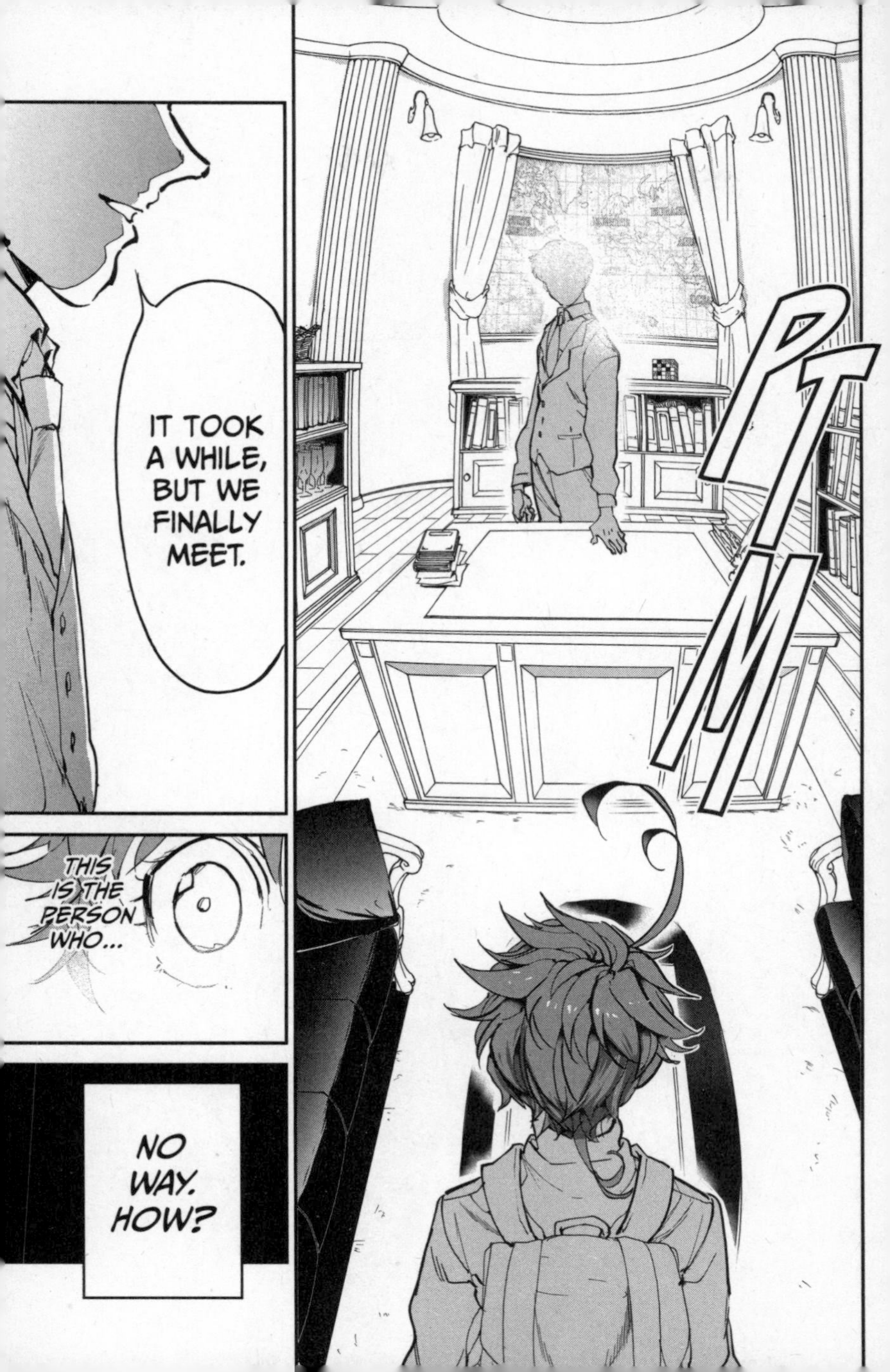
PTM
IT TOOK A WHILE, BUT WE FINALLY MEET.
THIS IS THE PERSON WHO...
NO WAY. HOW?

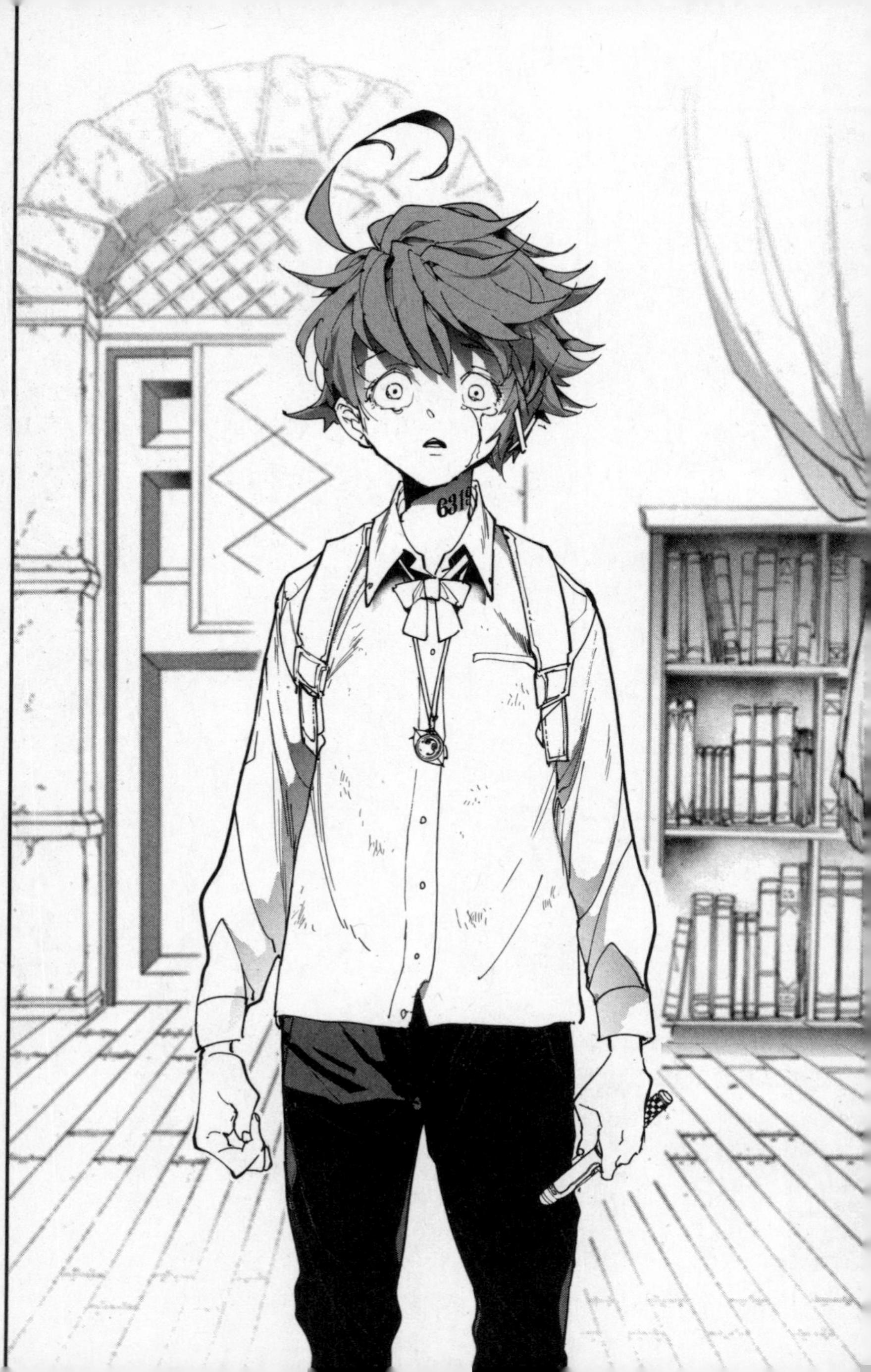

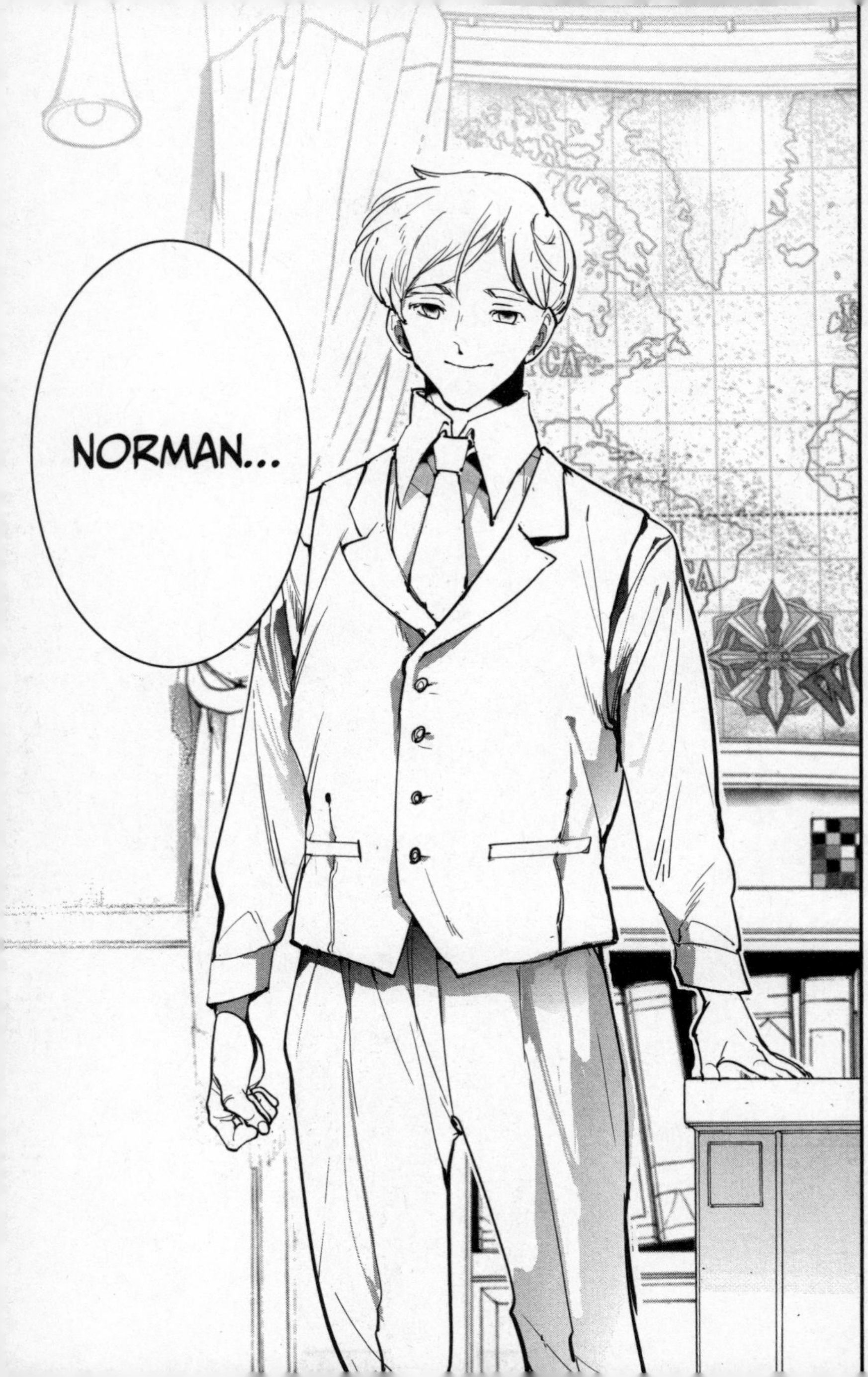
NORMAN...

CHAPTER 119: ENCOUNTER

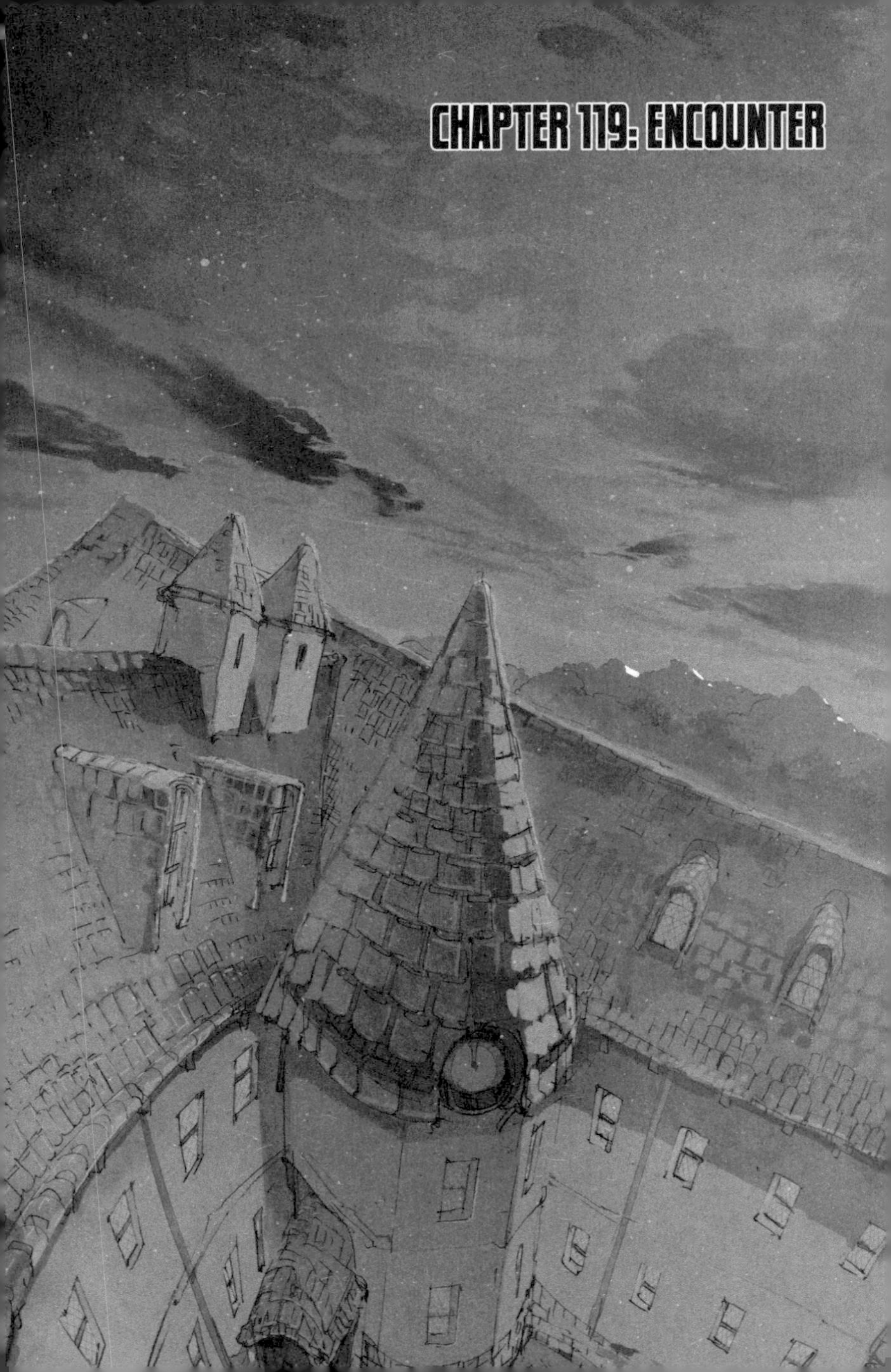

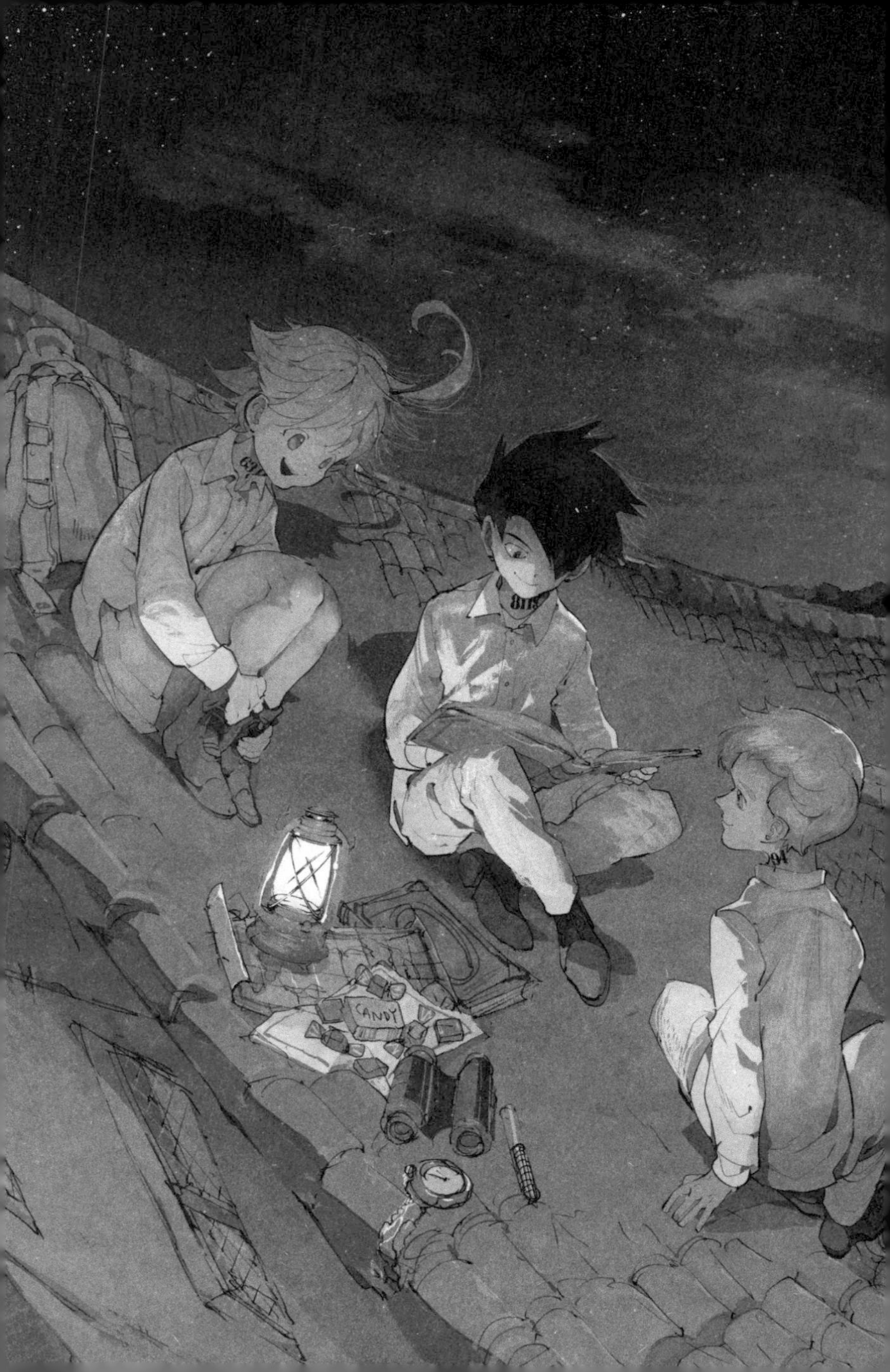
CANDY

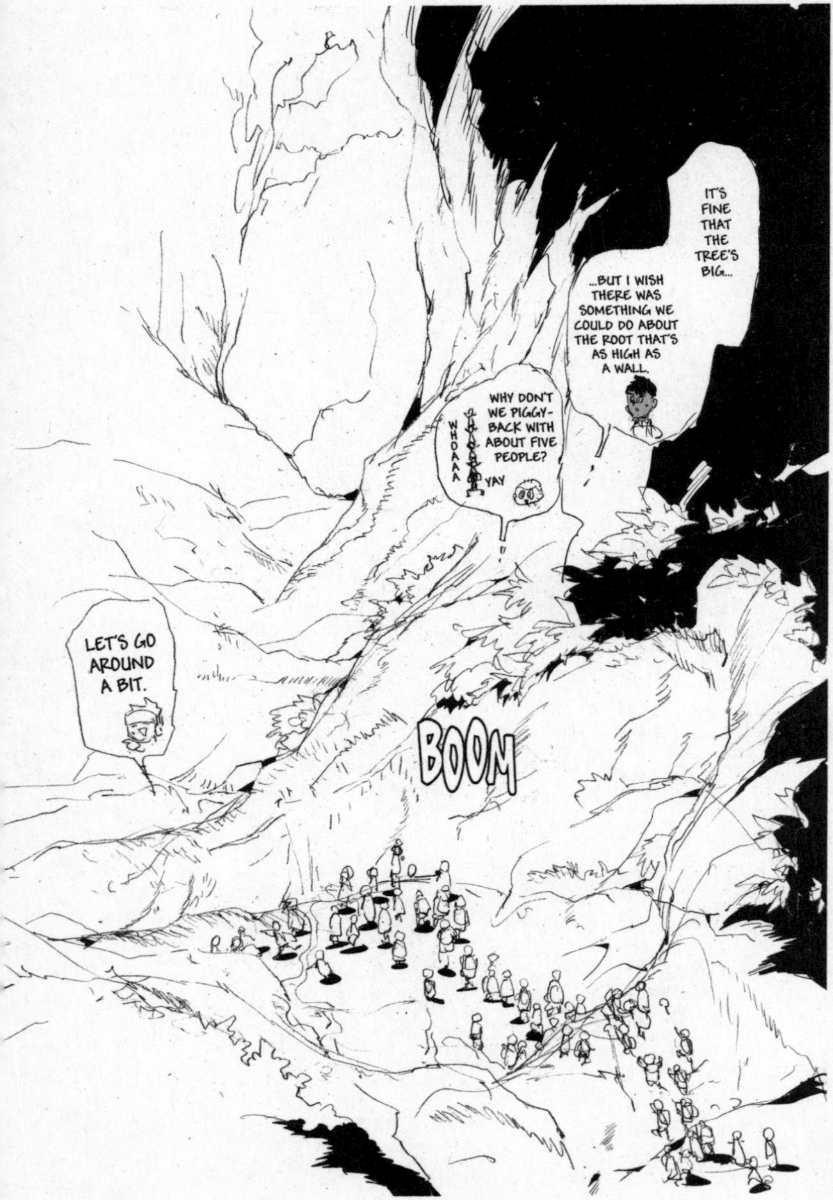
IT'S FINE THAT THE TREE'S BIG...
...BUT I WISH THERE WAS SOMETHING WE COULD DO ABOUT THE ROOT THAT'S AS HIGH AS A WALL.
WHY DON'T WE PIGGY-BACK WITH ABOUT FIVE PEOPLE?
WHOAAA
YAY
BOOM
LET'S GO AROUND A BIT.

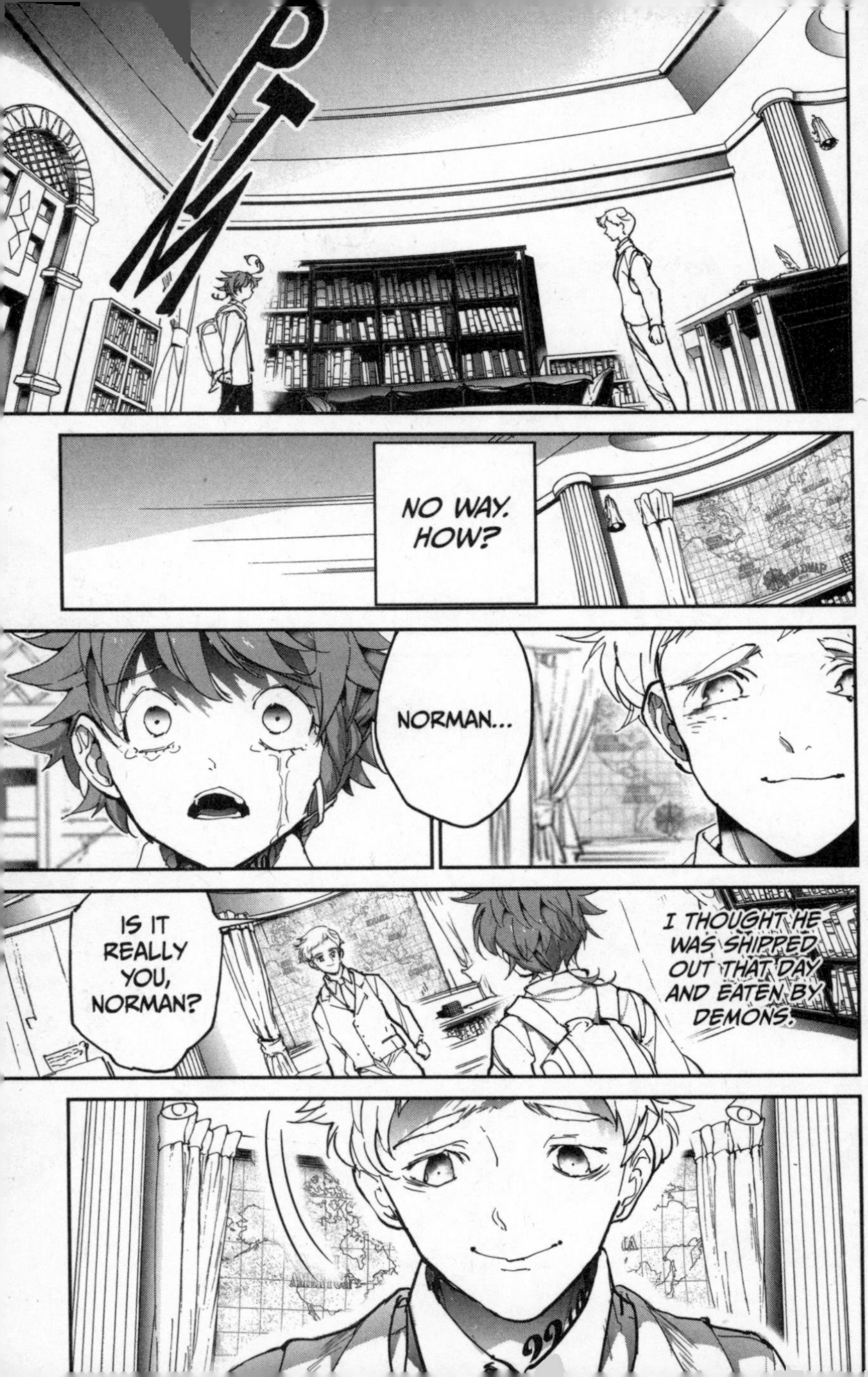
NO WAY. HOW?
NORMAN...
I THOUGHT HE WAS SHIPPED OUT THAT DAY AND EATEN BY DEMONS.
IS IT REALLY YOU, NORMAN?

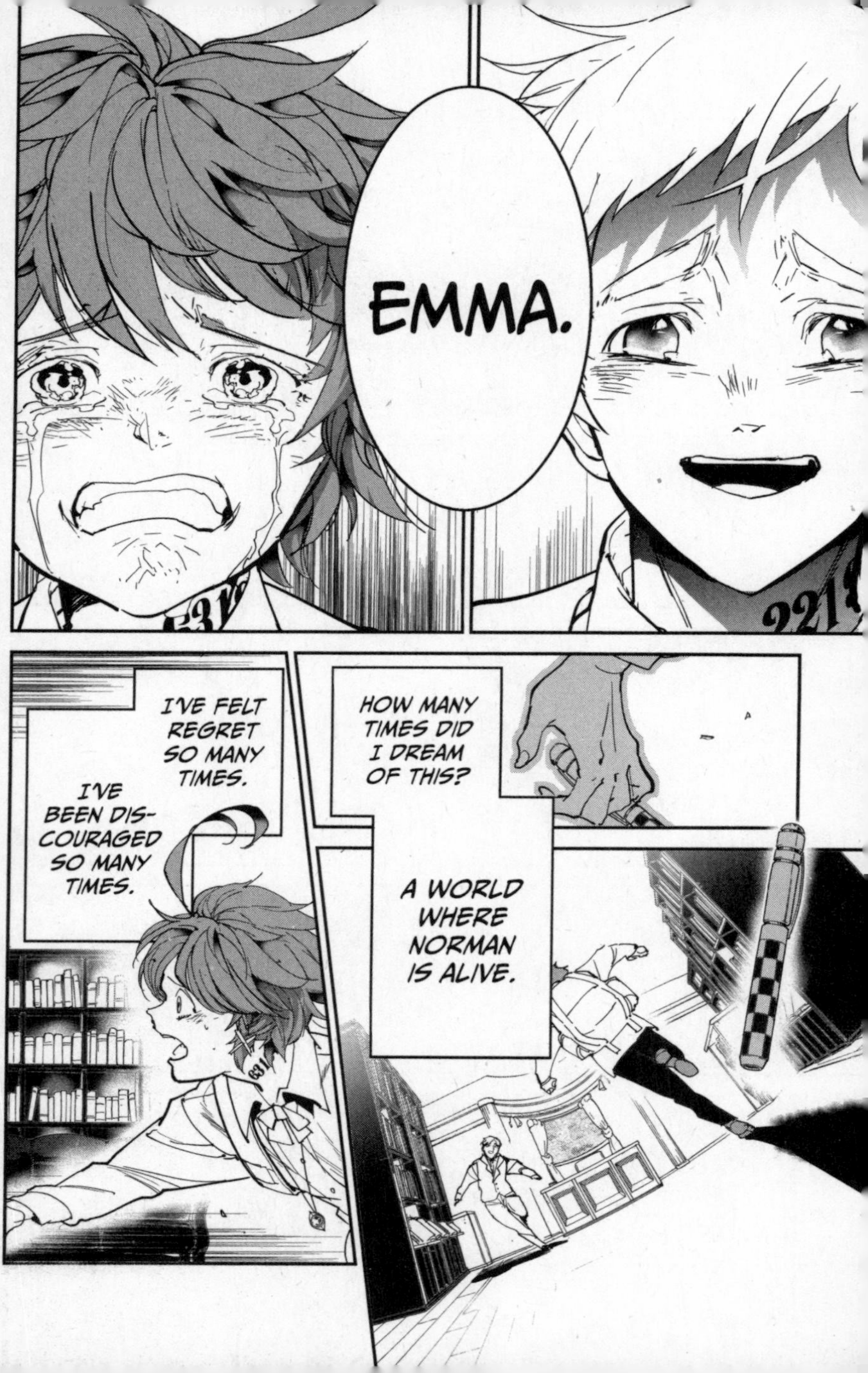

EMMA.
HOW MANY TIMES DID I DREAM OF THIS?
A WORLD WHERE NORMAN IS ALIVE.
I'VE FELT REGRET SO MANY TIMES.
I'VE BEEN DIS-COURAGED SO MANY TIMES.

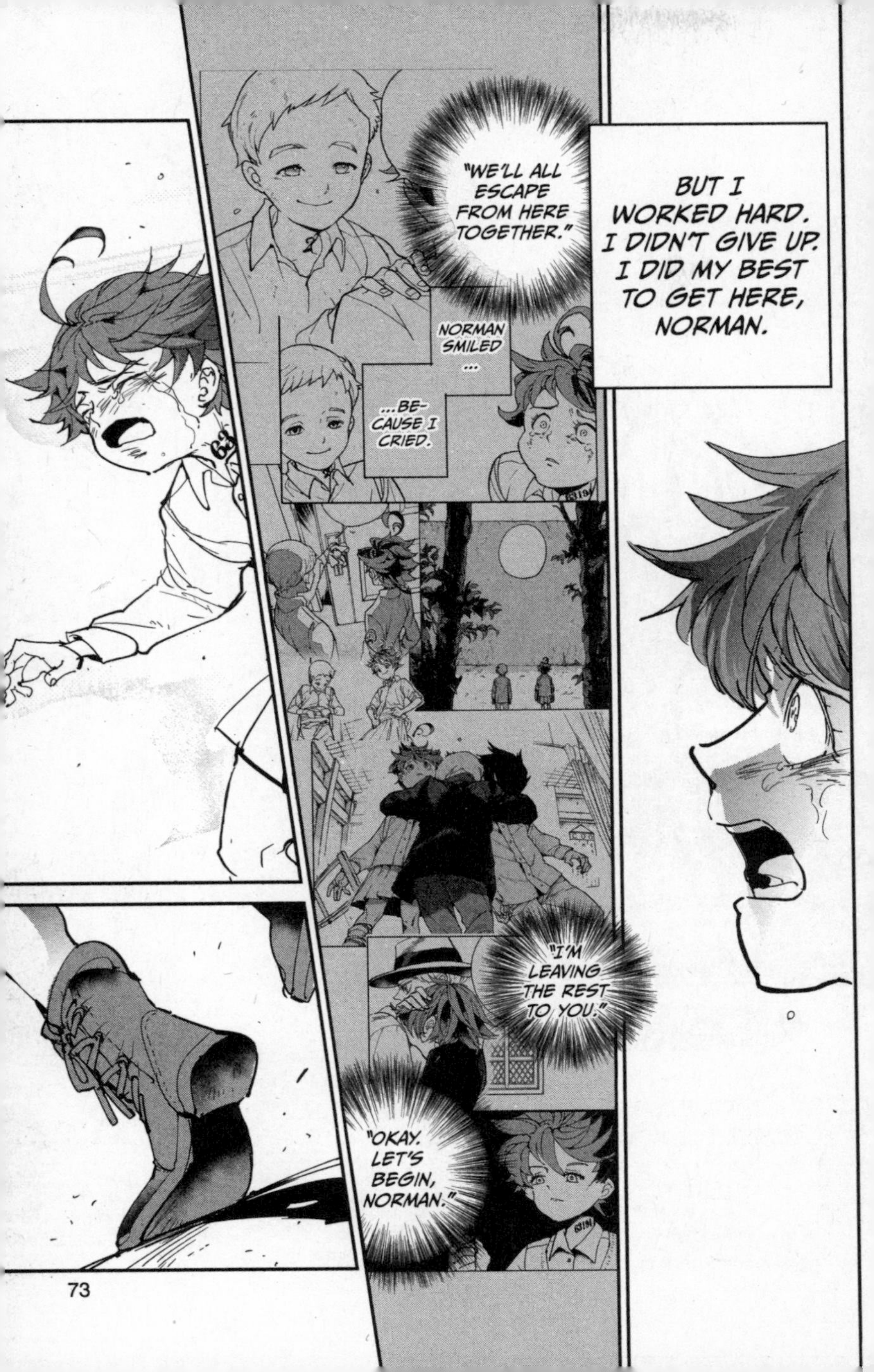
BUT I WORKED HARD. I DIDN'T GIVE UP. I DID MY BEST TO GET HERE, NORMAN.
"WE'LL ALL ESCAPE FROM HERE TOGETHER."
NORMAN SMILED ...
...BE-CAUSE I CRIED.
"I'M LEAVING THE REST TO YOU."
"OKAY. LET'S BEGIN, NORMAN."

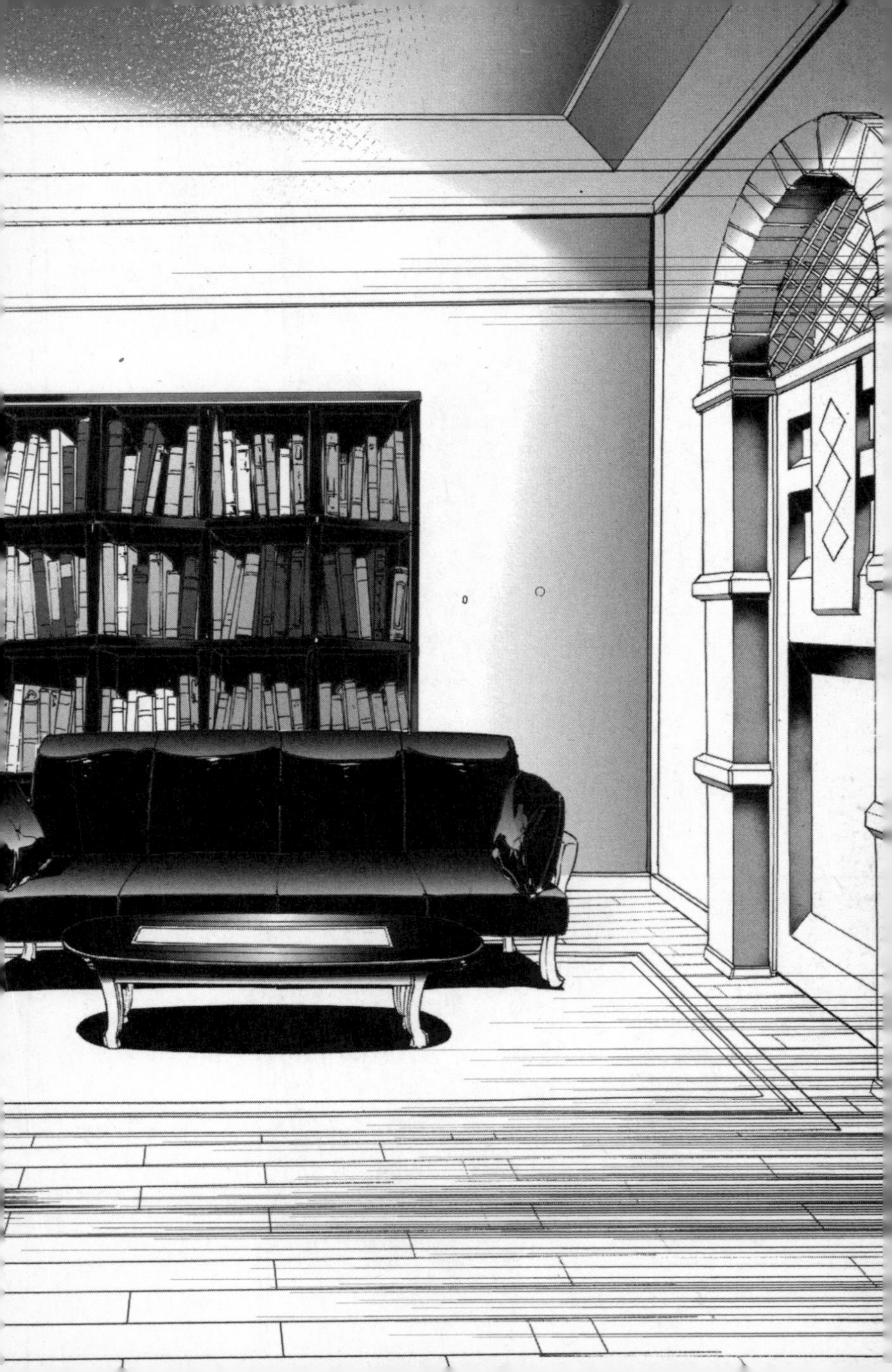

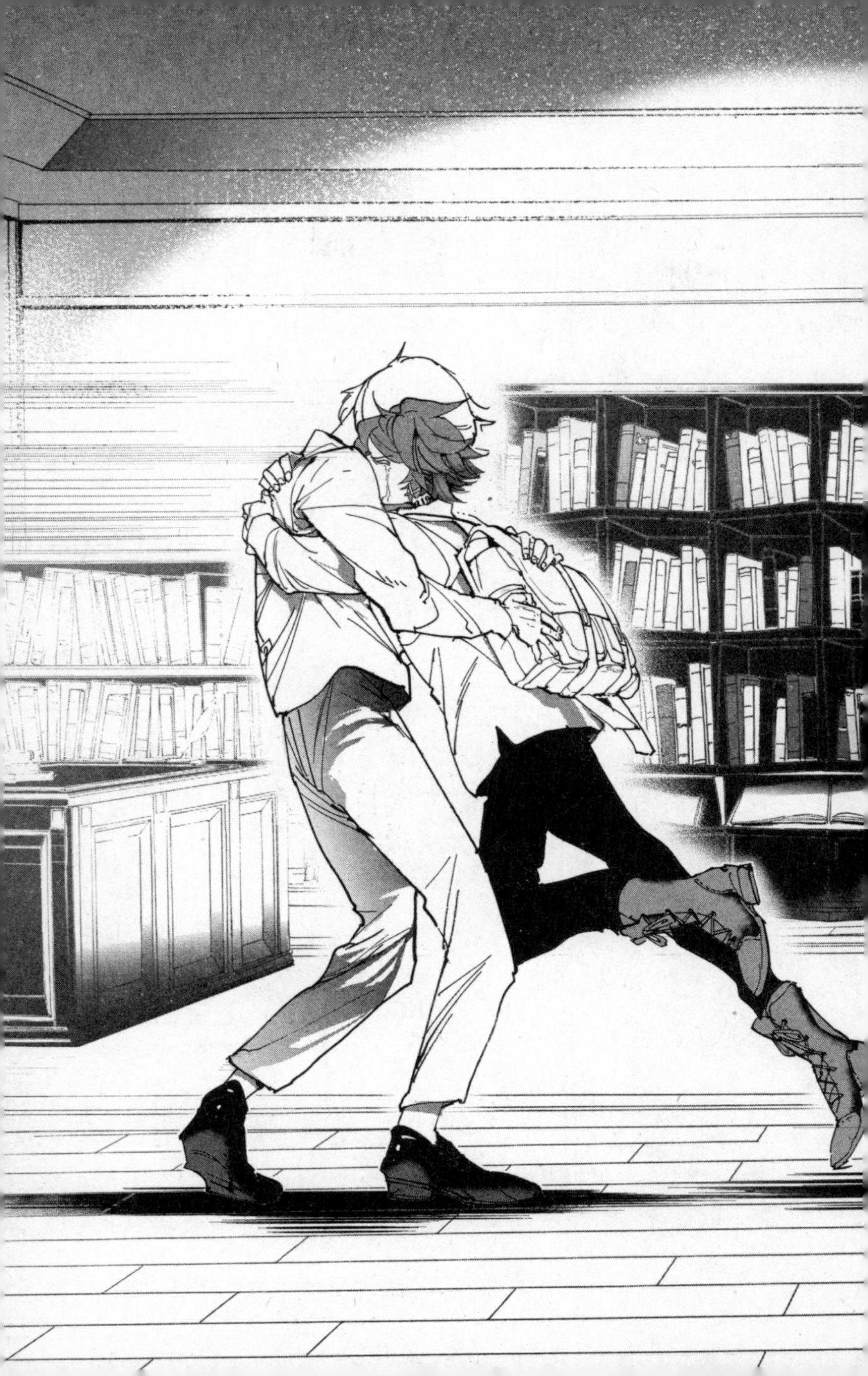

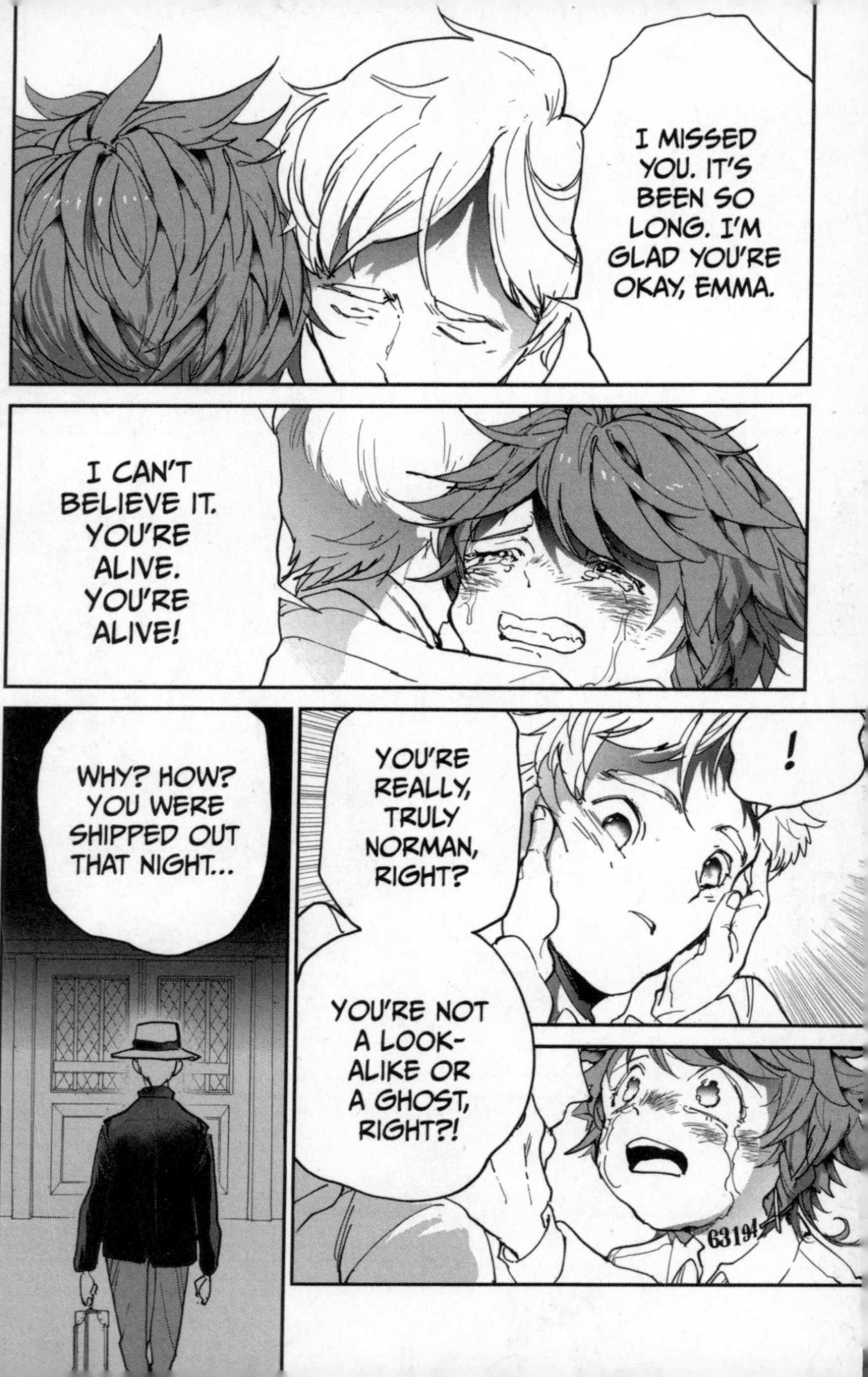
I MISSED YOU. IT'S BEEN SO LONG. I'M GLAD YOU'RE OKAY, EMMA.
I CAN'T BELIEVE IT. YOU'RE ALIVE. YOU'RE ALIVE!
!
YOU'RE REALLY, TRULY NORMAN, RIGHT?
YOU'RE NOT A LOOK-ALIKE OR A GHOST, RIGHT?!
63194
WHY? HOW? YOU WERE SHIPPED OUT THAT NIGHT...

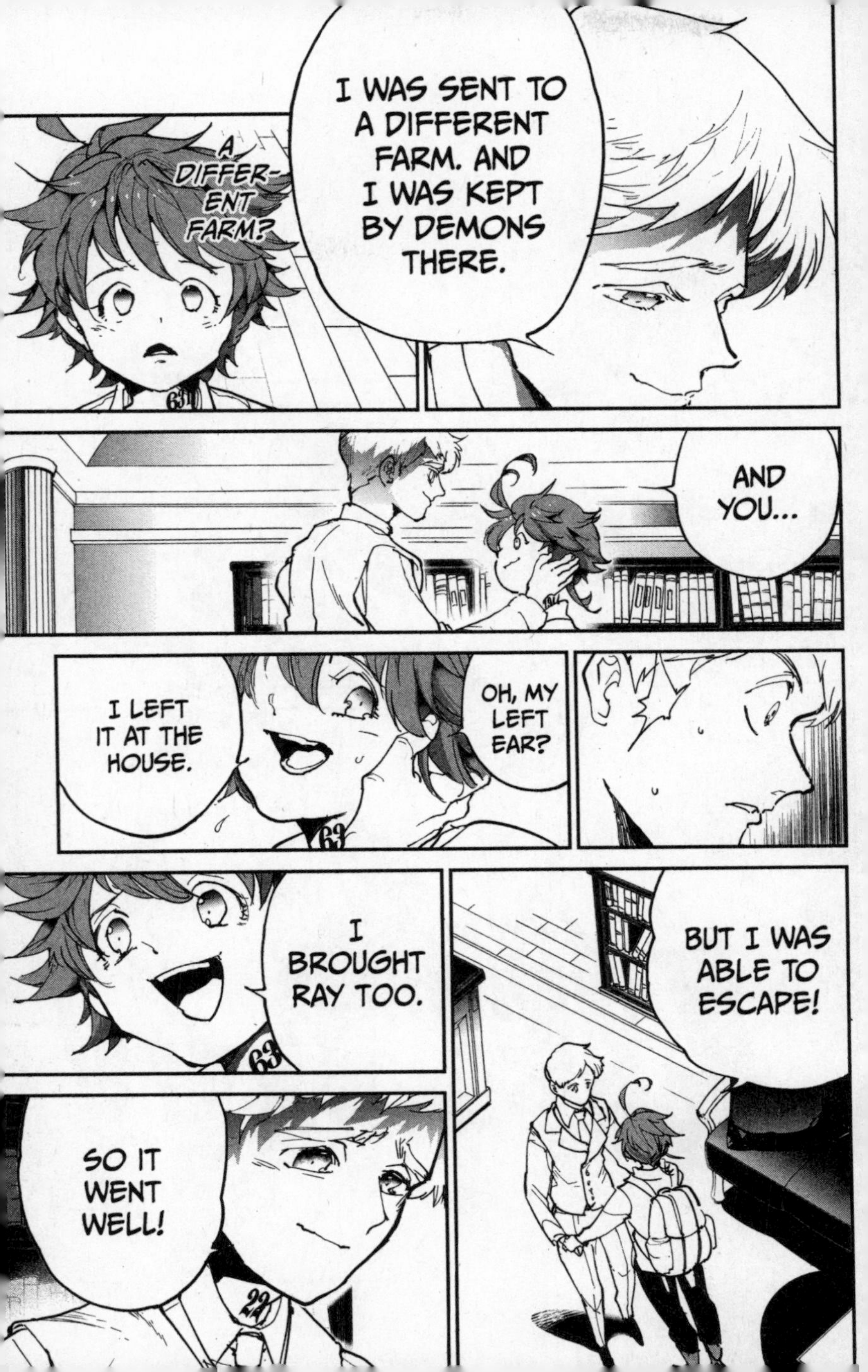
I WAS SENT TO A DIFFERENT FARM. AND I WAS KEPT BY DEMONS THERE.
A DIFFERENT FARM?
AND YOU...
OH, MY LEFT EAR?
I LEFT IT AT THE HOUSE.
BUT I WAS ABLE TO ESCAPE!
I BROUGHT RAY TOO.
SO IT WENT WELL!

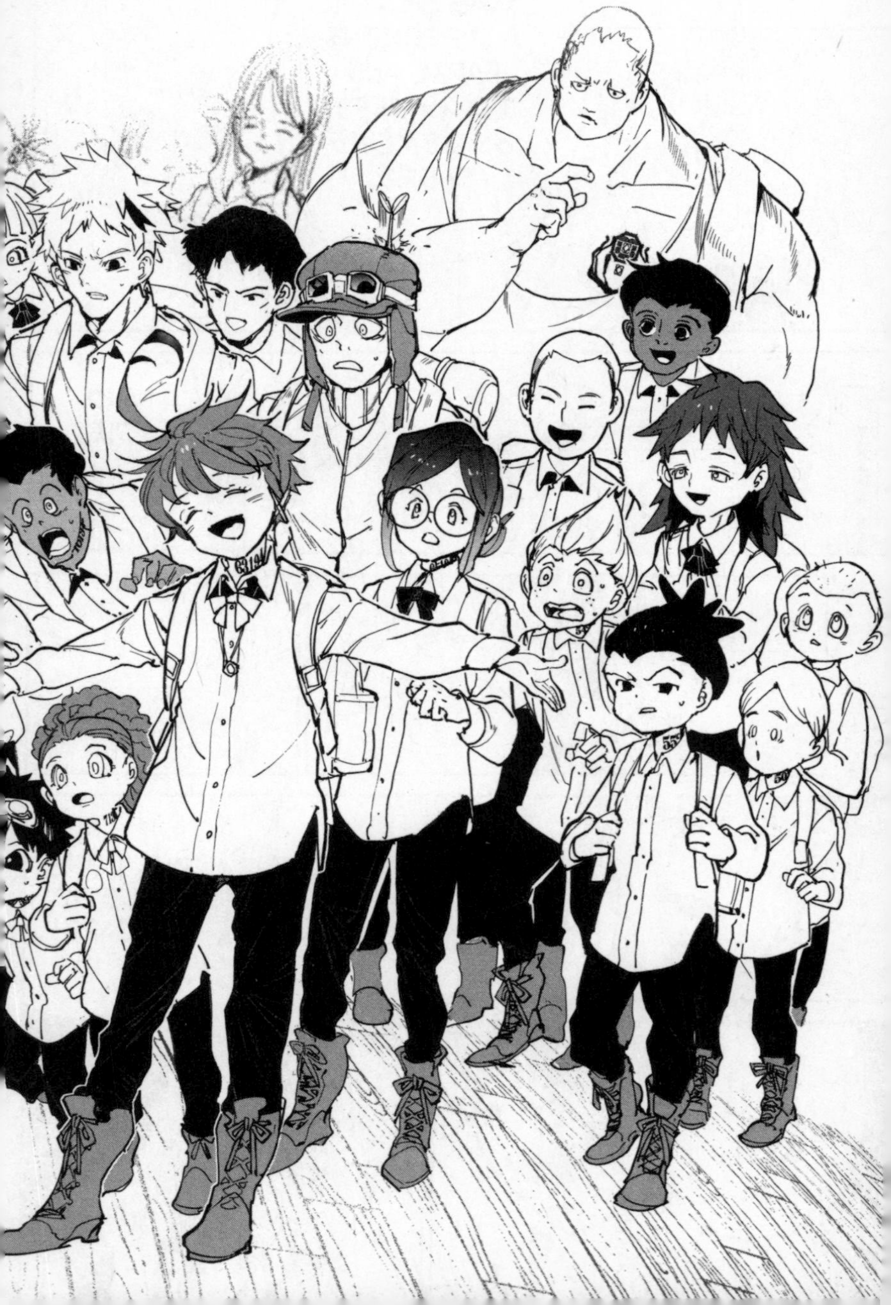

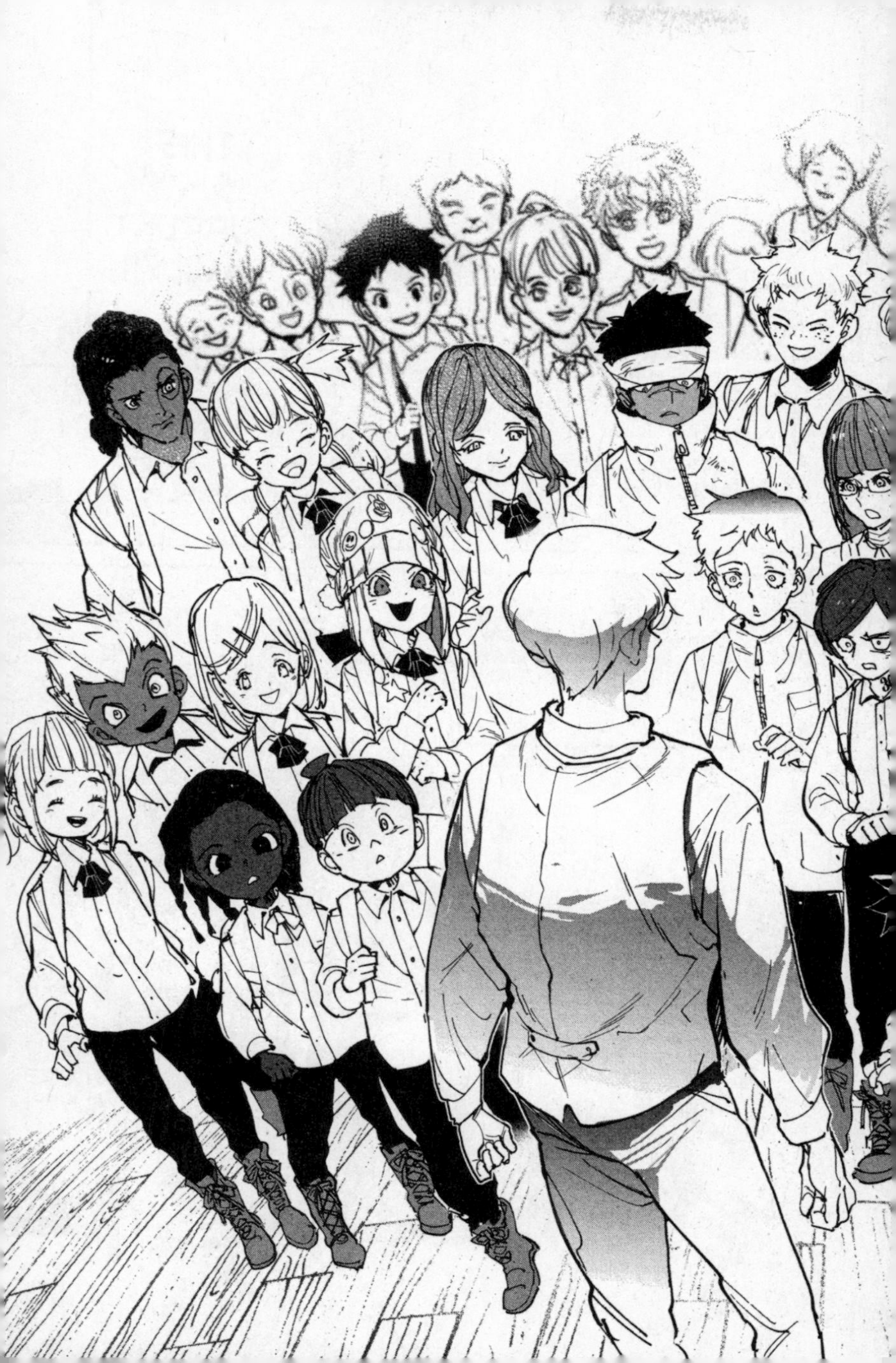

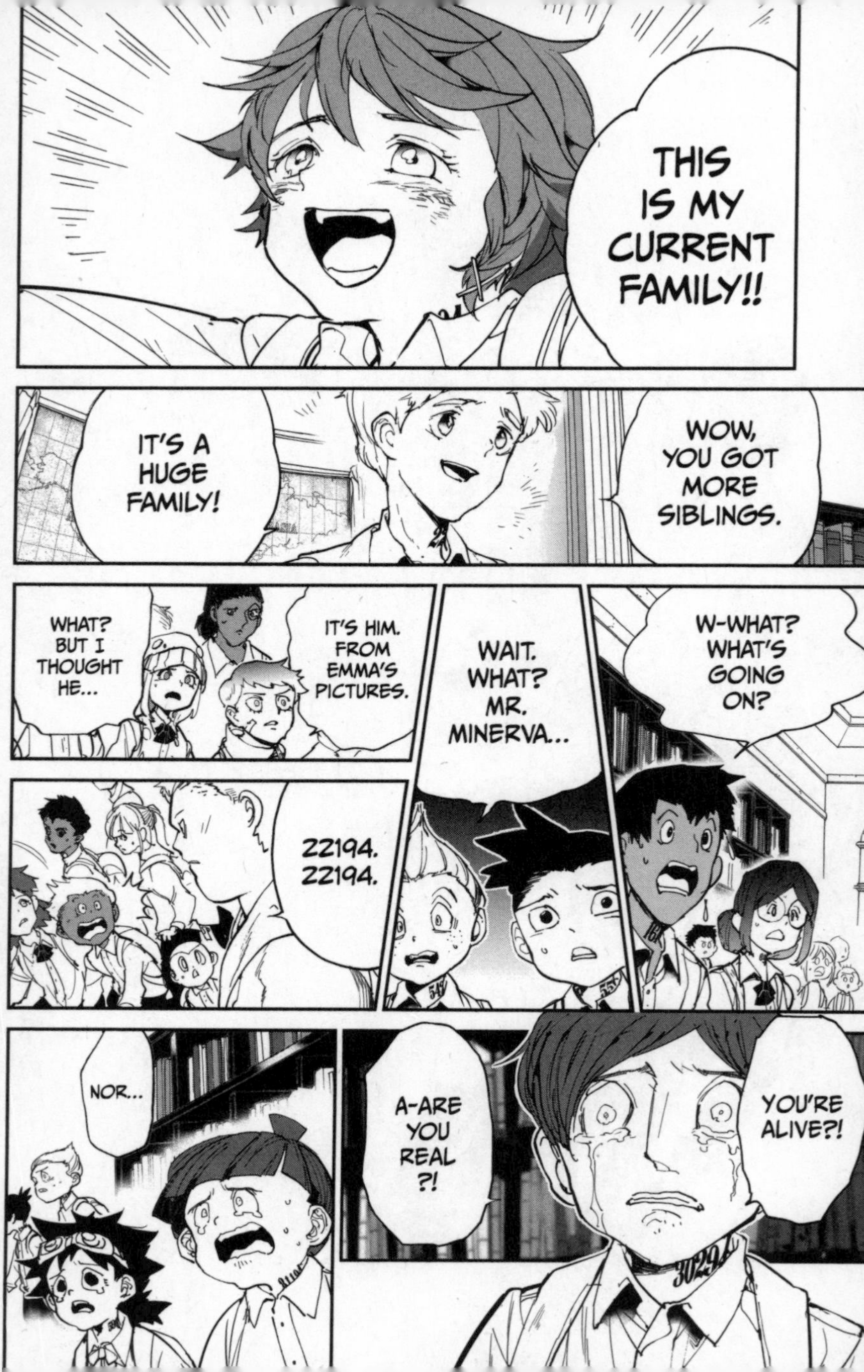
THIS IS MY CURRENT FAMILY!!
WOW, YOU GOT MORE SIBLINGS.
IT'S A HUGE FAMILY!
W-WHAT? WHAT'S GOING ON?
WAIT. WHAT? MR. MINERVA...
IT'S HIM. FROM EMMA'S PICTURES.
WHAT? BUT I THOUGHT HE...
22194. 22194.
YOU'RE ALIVE?!
A-ARE YOU REAL ?!
NOR...

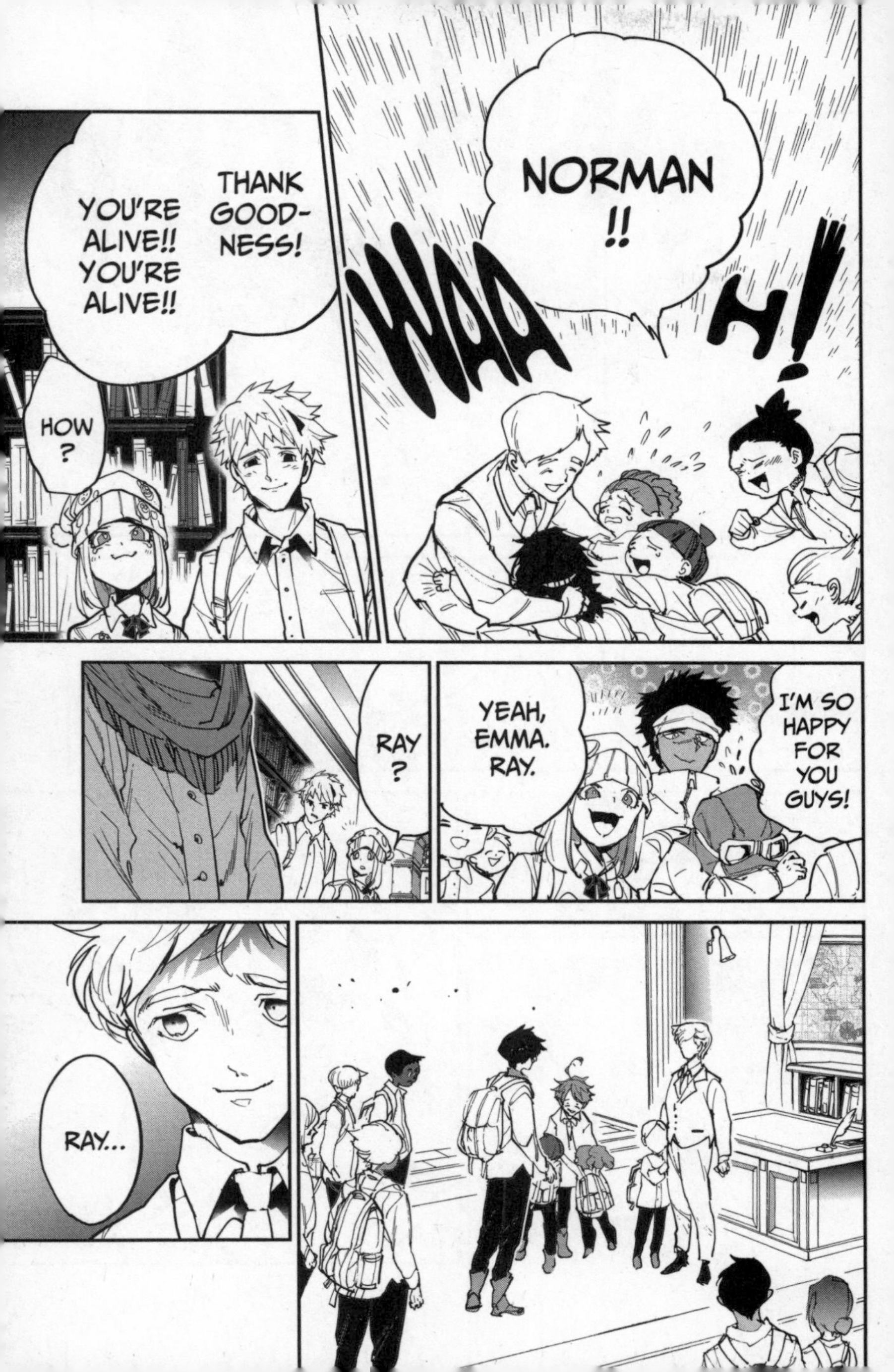
NORMAN!!
WAAH!
THANK GOODNESS!
YOU'RE ALIVE!! YOU'RE ALIVE!!
HOW?
I'M SO HAPPY FOR YOU GUYS!
YEAH, EMMA. RAY.
RAY?
RAY...

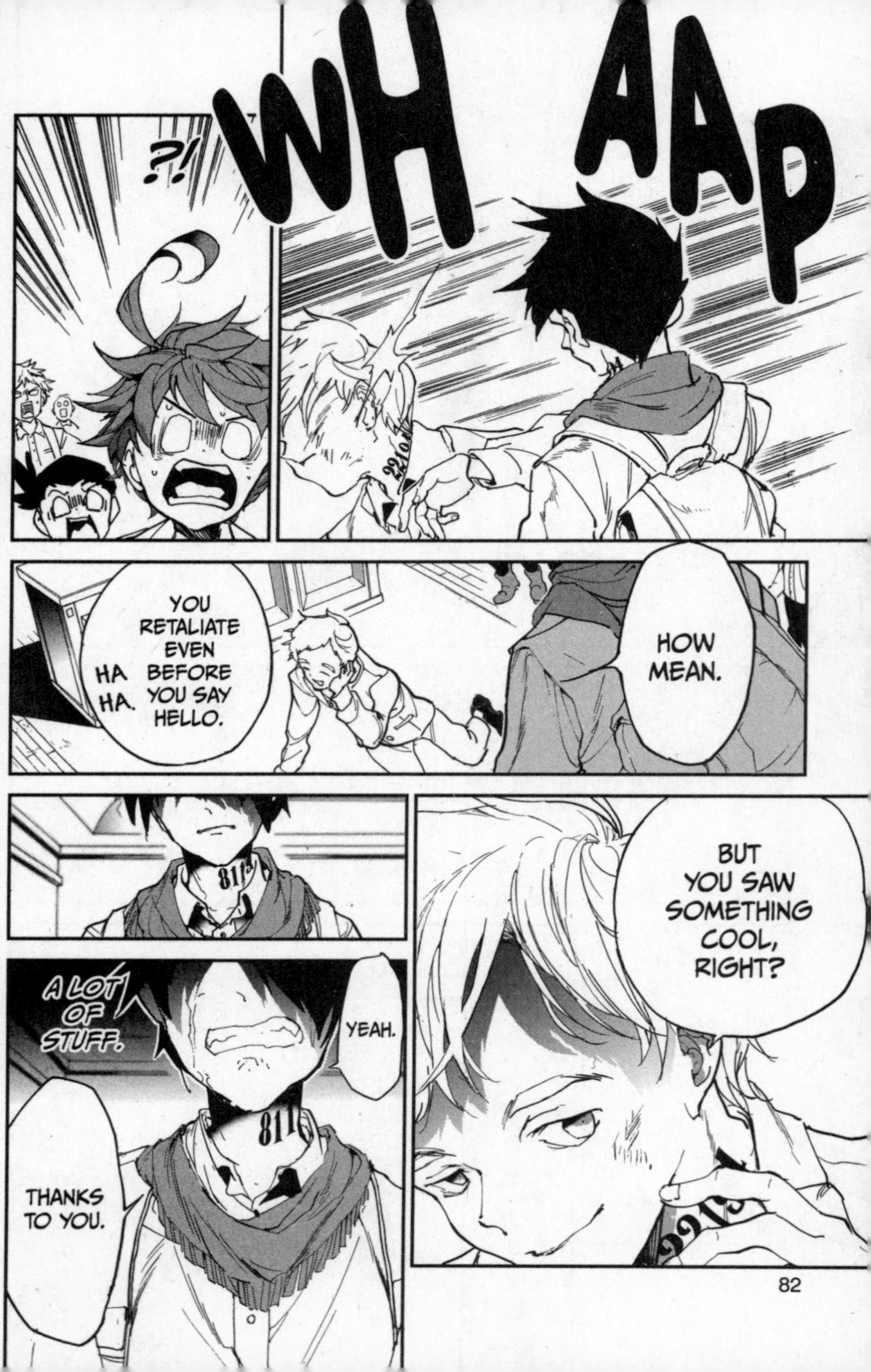
WHAAAP
?!
HOW MEAN.
YOU RETALIATE EVEN BEFORE YOU SAY HELLO.
HA HA.
BUT YOU SAW SOMETHING COOL, RIGHT?
YEAH.
A LOT OF STUFF.
THANKS TO YOU.

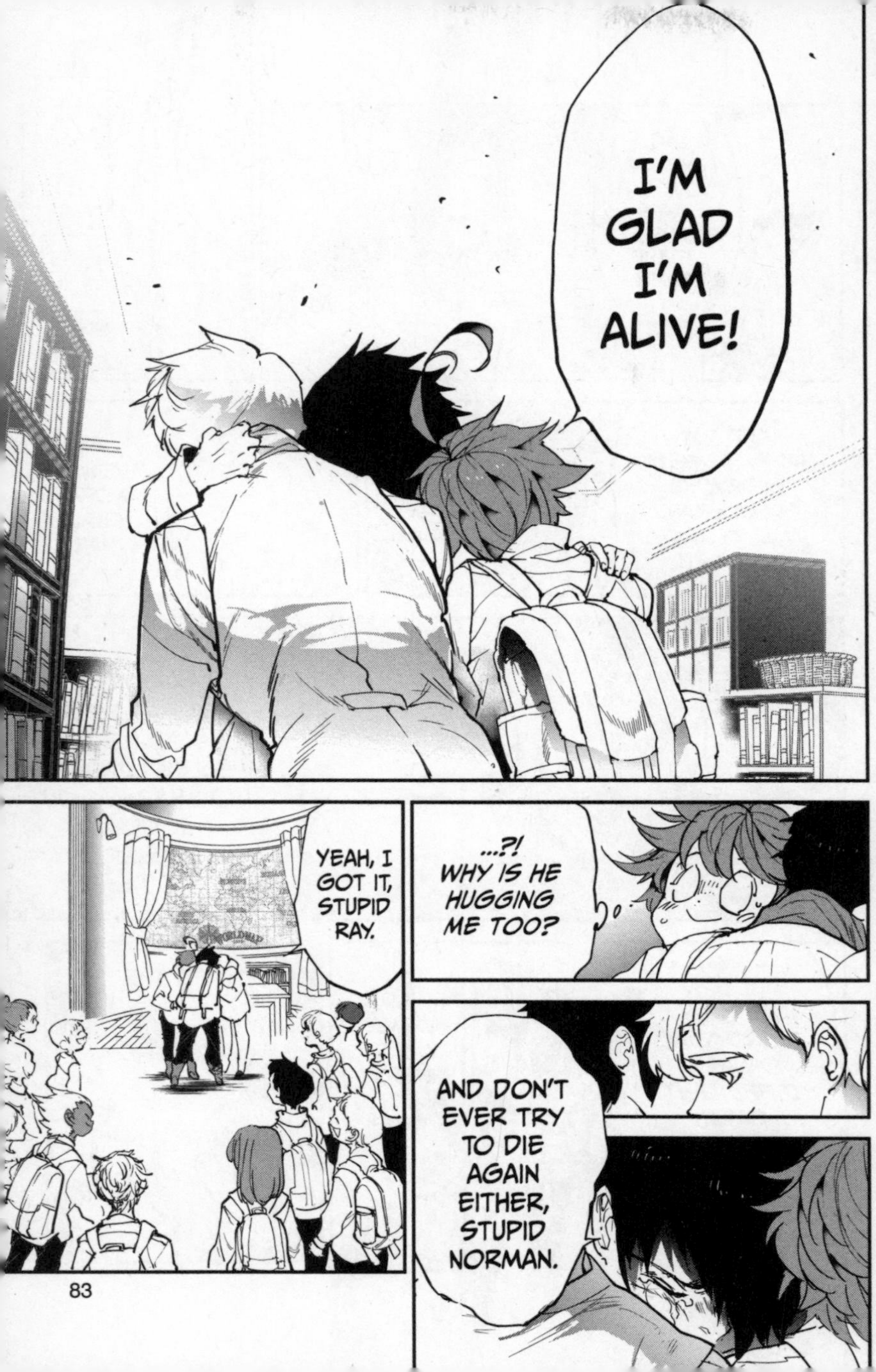
I'M GLAD I'M ALIVE!
...?! WHY IS HE HUGGING ME TOO?
AND DON'T EVER TRY TO DIE AGAIN EITHER, STUPID NORMAN.
YEAH, I GOT IT, STUPID RAY.

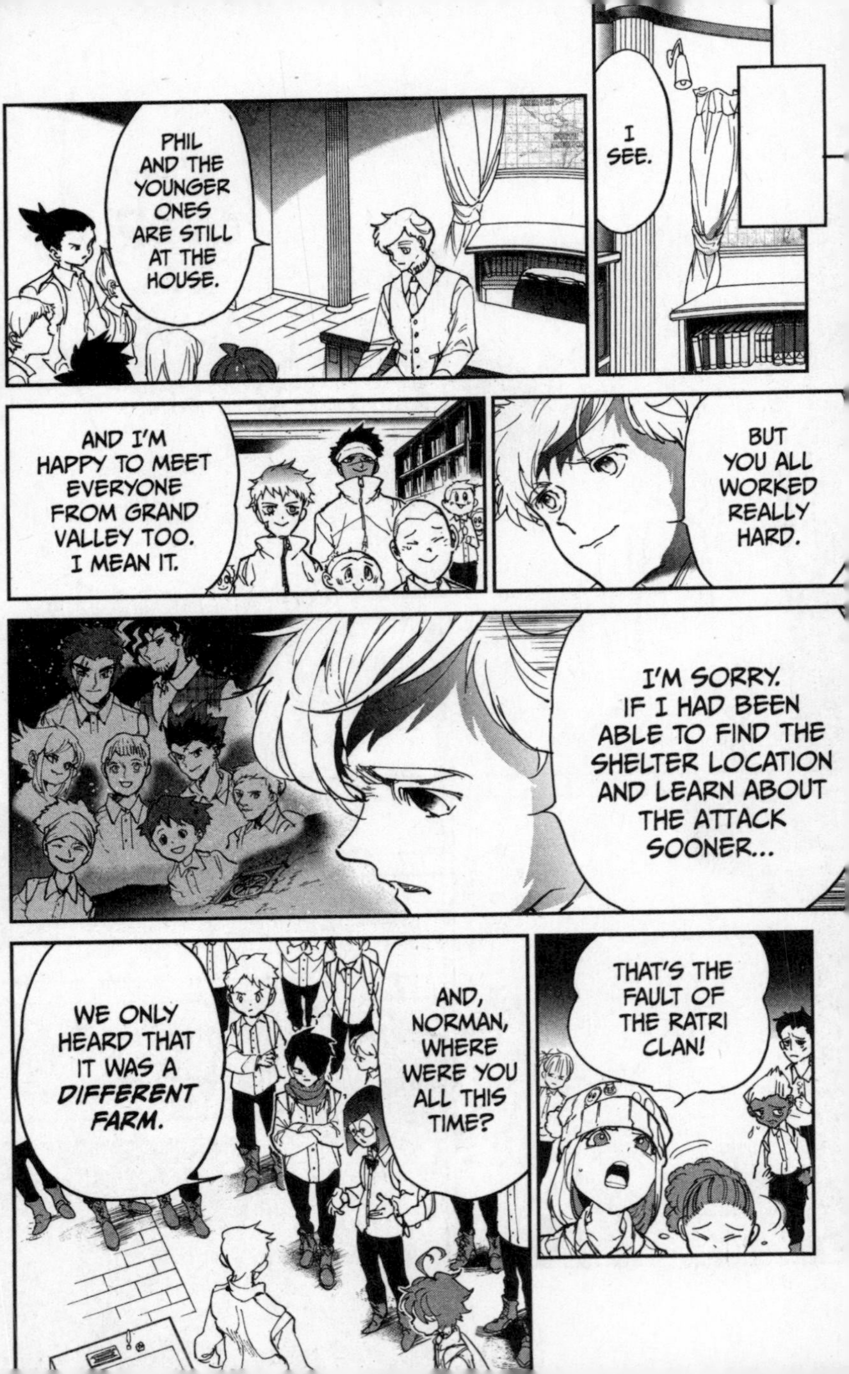
I SEE.
PHIL AND THE YOUNGER ONES ARE STILL AT THE HOUSE.
BUT YOU ALL WORKED REALLY HARD.
AND I'M HAPPY TO MEET EVERYONE FROM GRAND VALLEY TOO. I MEAN IT.
I'M SORRY. IF I HAD BEEN ABLE TO FIND THE SHELTER LOCATION AND LEARN ABOUT THE ATTACK SOONER...
THAT'S THE FAULT OF THE RATRI CLAN!
AND, NORMAN, WHERE WERE YOU ALL THIS TIME?
WE ONLY HEARD THAT IT WAS A *DIFFERENT* FARM.

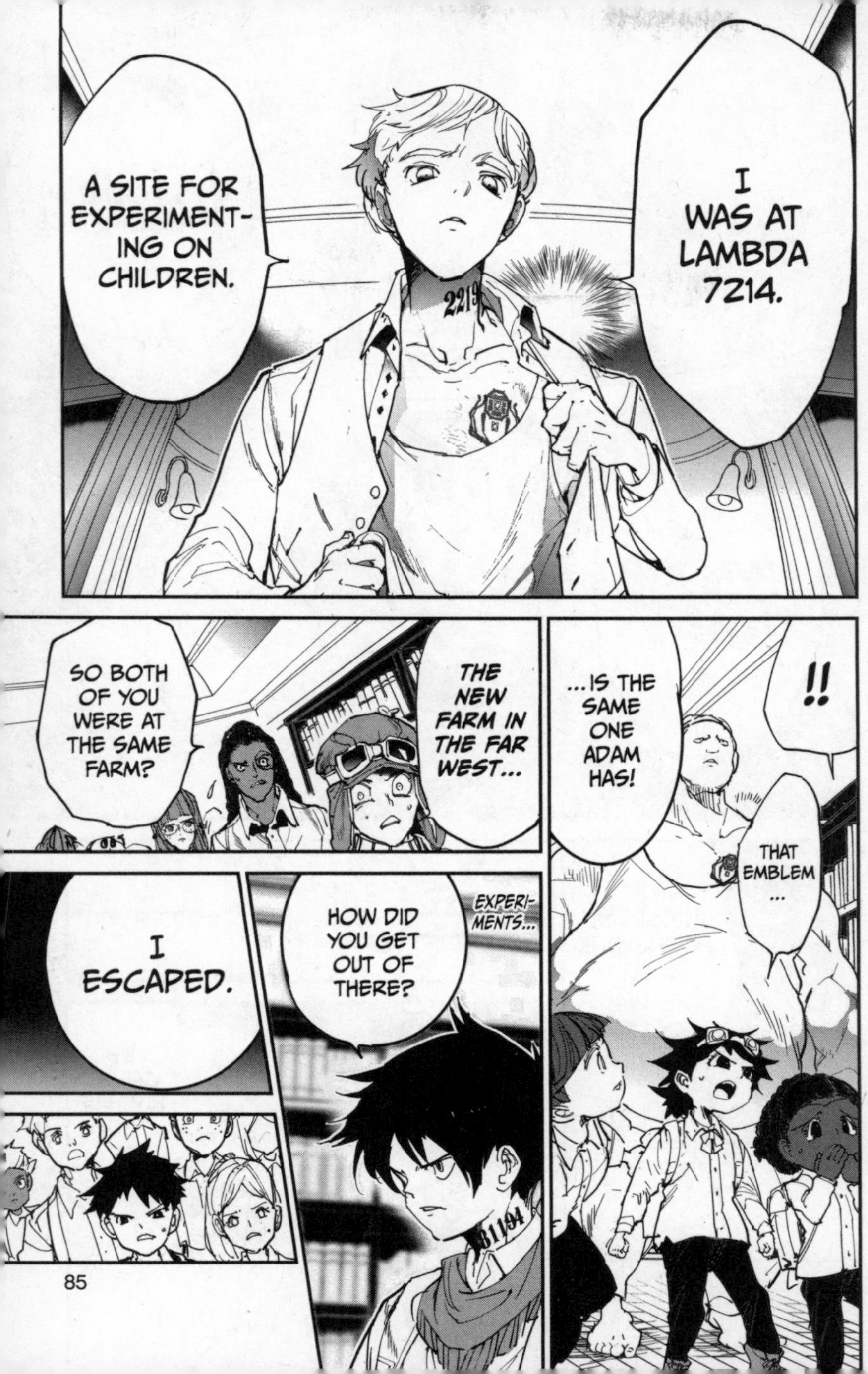
I WAS AT LAMBDA 7214.
A SITE FOR EXPERIMENT-ING ON CHILDREN.
!!
THAT EMBLEM ...
...IS THE SAME ONE ADAM HAS!
THE NEW FARM IN THE FAR WEST...
SO BOTH OF YOU WERE AT THE SAME FARM?
EXPERIMENTS...
HOW DID YOU GET OUT OF THERE?
I ESCAPED.

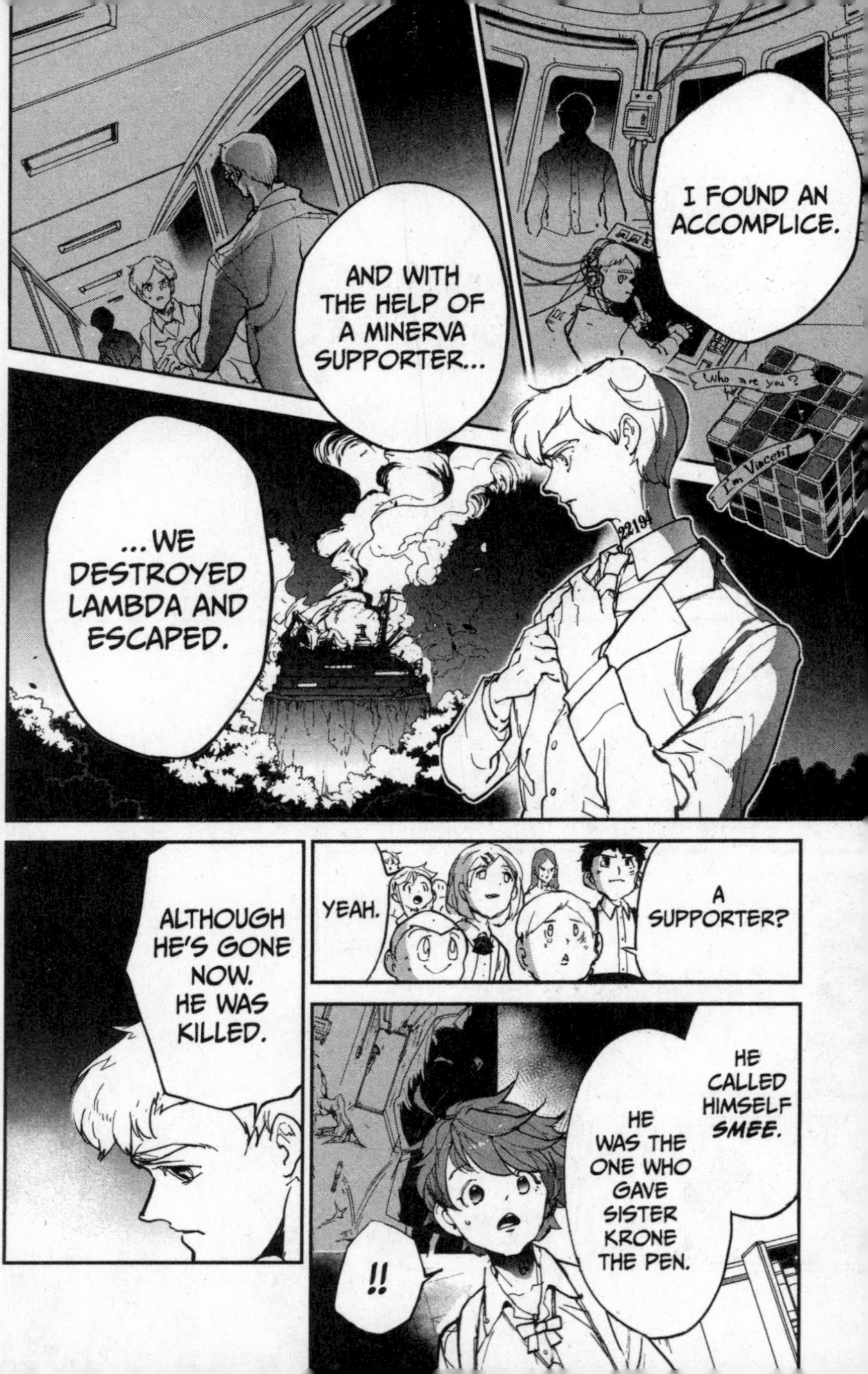
I FOUND AN ACCOMPLICE.
AND WITH THE HELP OF A MINERVA SUPPORTER...
Who are you?
I'm Vincent
22194
...WE DESTROYED LAMBDA AND ESCAPED.
A SUPPORTER?
YEAH.
HE CALLED HIMSELF *SMEE*.
HE WAS THE ONE WHO GAVE SISTER KRONE THE PEN.
!!
ALTHOUGH HE'S GONE NOW.
HE WAS KILLED.

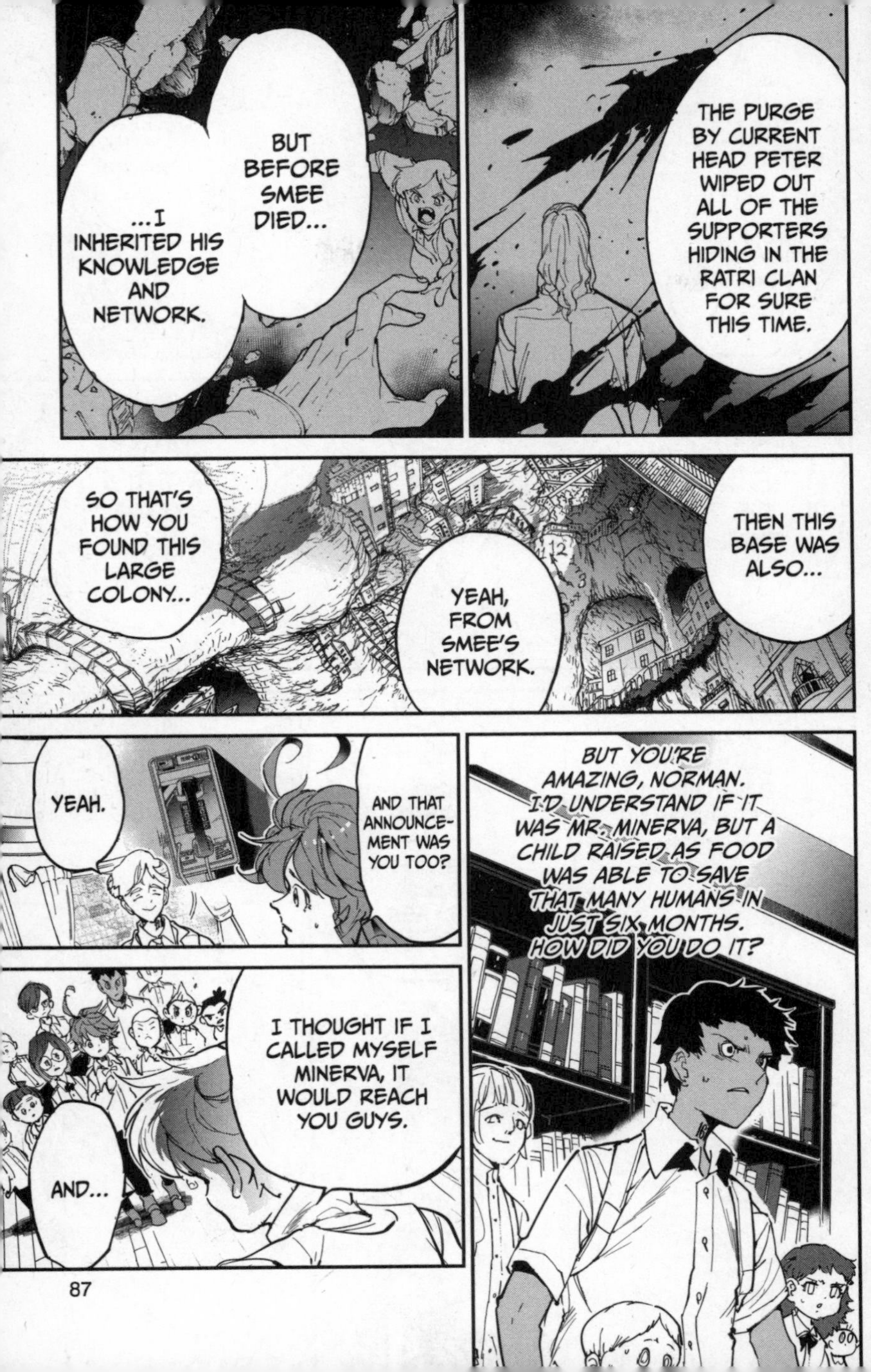
THE PURGE BY CURRENT HEAD PETER WIPED OUT ALL OF THE SUPPORTERS HIDING IN THE RATRI CLAN FOR SURE THIS TIME.
BUT BEFORE SMEE DIED...
...I INHERITED HIS KNOWLEDGE AND NETWORK.
THEN THIS BASE WAS ALSO...
YEAH, FROM SMEE'S NETWORK.
SO THAT'S HOW YOU FOUND THIS LARGE COLONY...
BUT YOU'RE AMAZING, NORMAN. I'D UNDERSTAND IF IT WAS MR. MINERVA, BUT A CHILD RAISED AS FOOD WAS ABLE TO SAVE THAT MANY HUMANS IN JUST SIX MONTHS. HOW DID YOU DO IT?
AND THAT ANNOUNCEMENT WAS YOU TOO?
YEAH.
I THOUGHT IF I CALLED MYSELF MINERVA, IT WOULD REACH YOU GUYS.
AND...

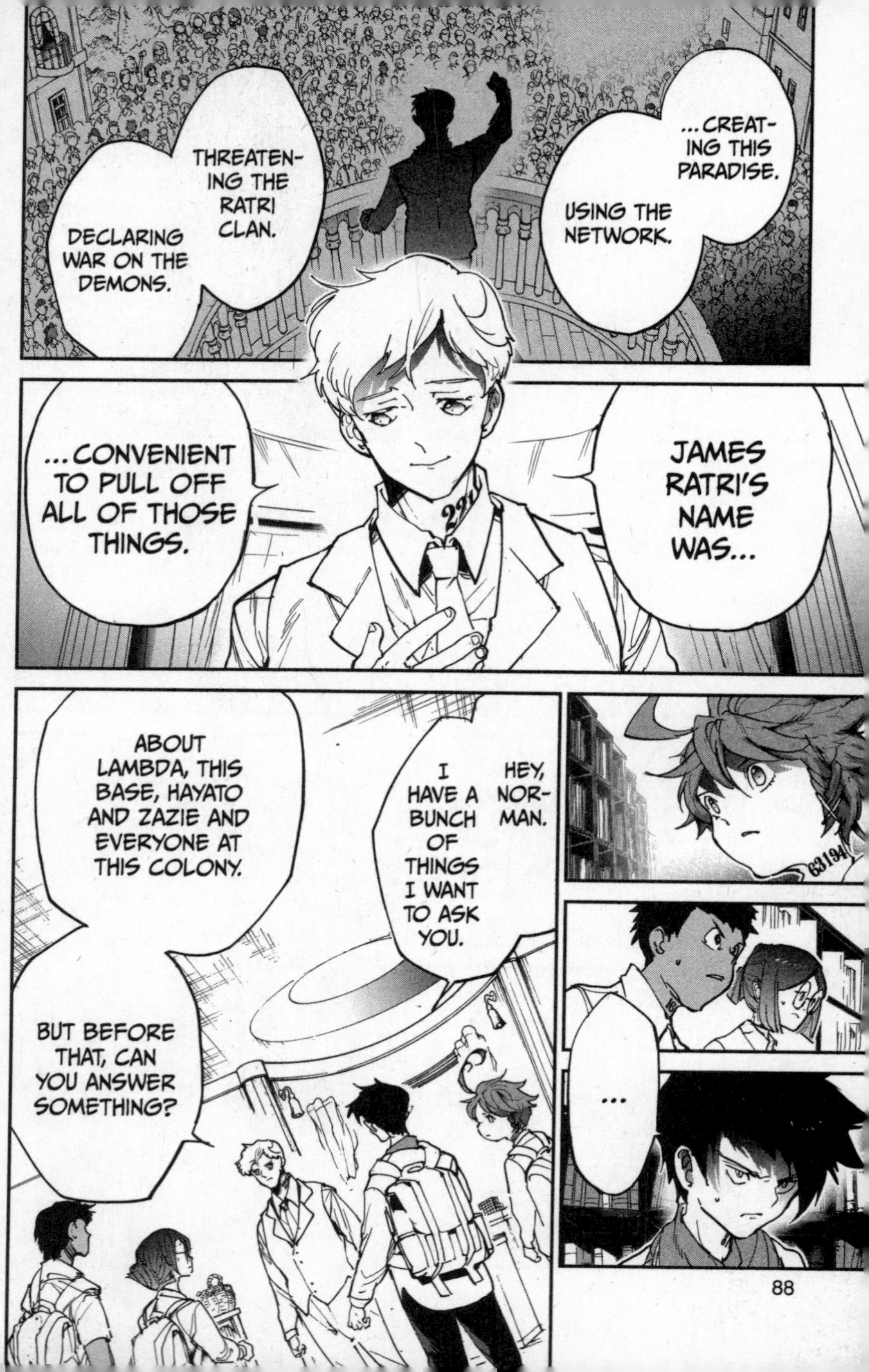
...CREAT-
ING THIS
PARADISE.
USING THE
NETWORK.
THREATEN-
ING THE
RATRI
CLAN.
DECLARING
WAR ON THE
DEMONS.
JAMES
RATRI'S
NAME
WAS...
...CONVENIENT
TO PULL OFF
ALL OF THOSE
THINGS.
...
HEY,
NOR-
MAN.
I
HAVE A
BUNCH
OF
THINGS
I WANT
TO ASK
YOU.
ABOUT
LAMBDA, THIS
BASE, HAYATO
AND ZAZIE AND
EVERYONE AT
THIS COLONY.
BUT BEFORE
THAT, CAN
YOU ANSWER
SOMETHING?

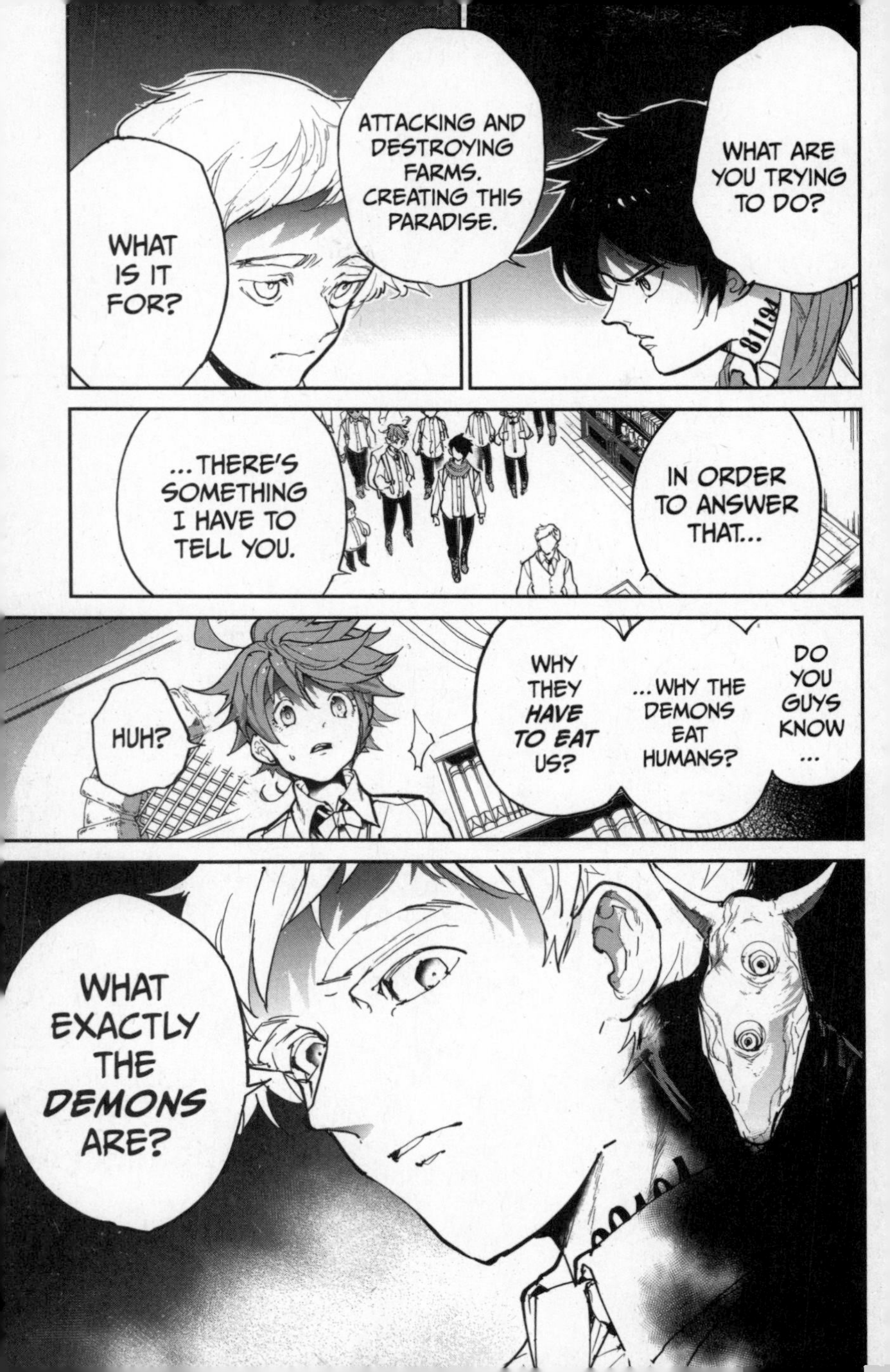
WHAT ARE YOU TRYING TO DO?
ATTACKING AND DESTROYING FARMS. CREATING THIS PARADISE.
WHAT IS IT FOR?
IN ORDER TO ANSWER THAT...
...THERE'S SOMETHING I HAVE TO TELL YOU.
DO YOU GUYS KNOW...
...WHY THE DEMONS EAT HUMANS?
WHY THEY *HAVE TO EAT* US?
HUH?
WHAT EXACTLY THE *DEMONS* ARE?

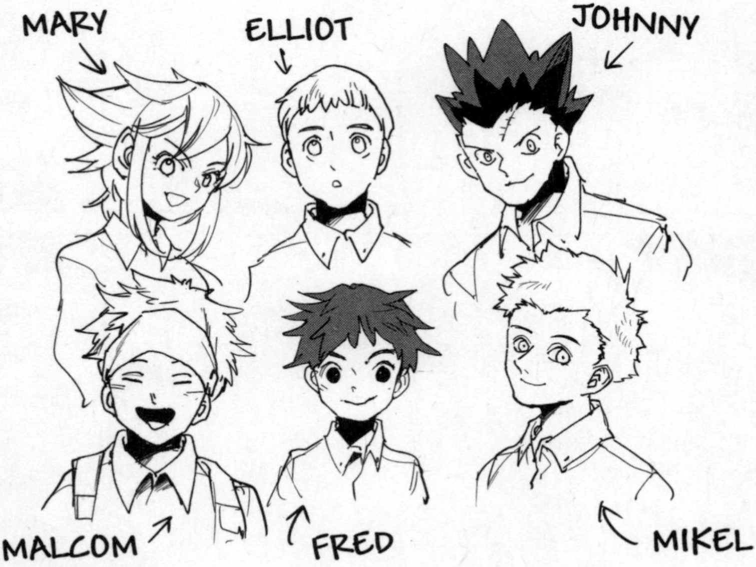
JOHNNY
ELLIOT
MARY
MIKEL
FRED
MALCOM

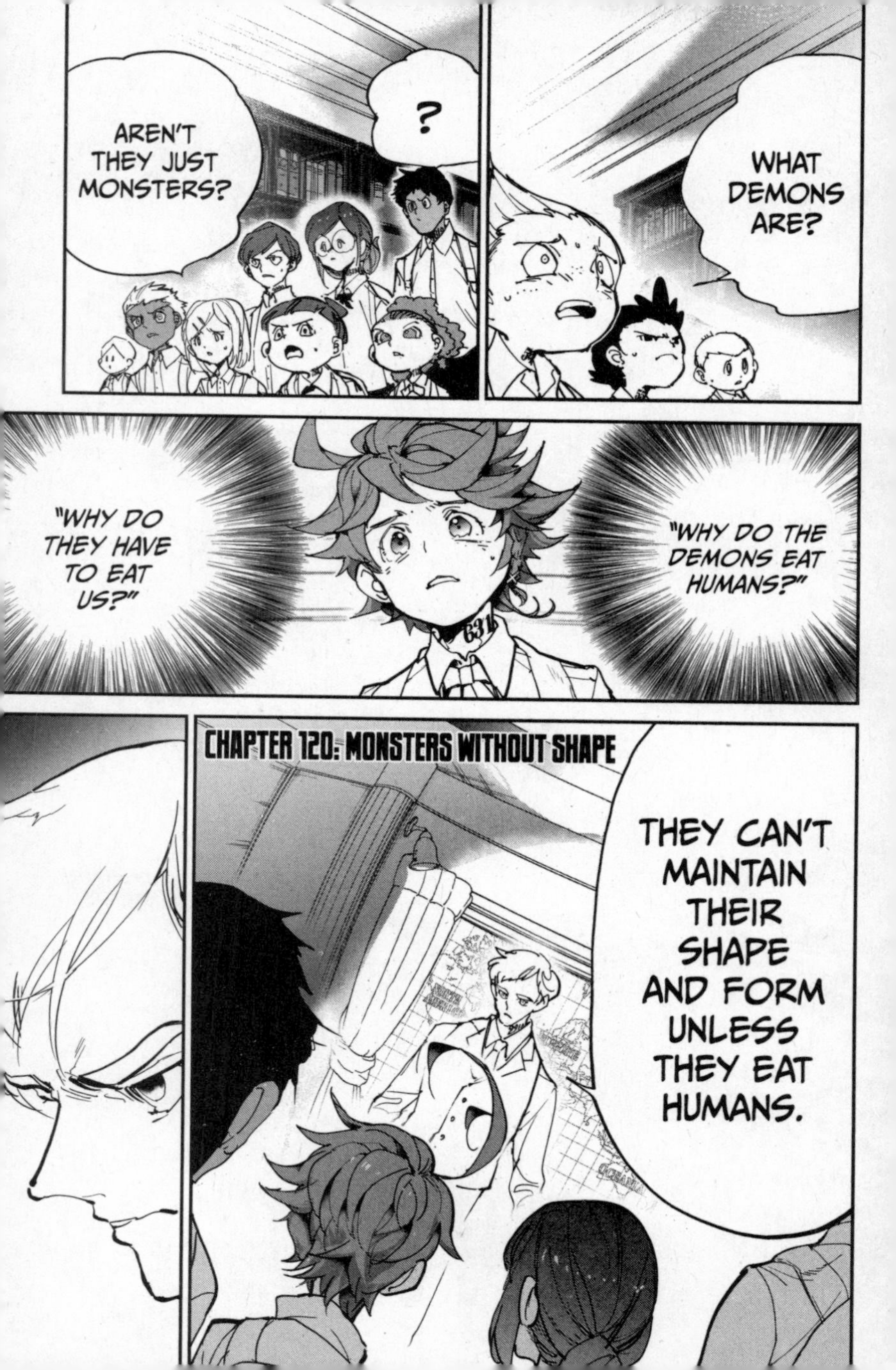
WHAT DEMONS ARE?
?
AREN'T THEY JUST MONSTERS?
"WHY DO THE DEMONS EAT HUMANS?"
"WHY DO THEY HAVE TO EAT US?"
CHAPTER 120: MONSTERS WITHOUT SHAPE
THEY CAN'T MAINTAIN THEIR SHAPE AND FORM UNLESS THEY EAT HUMANS.

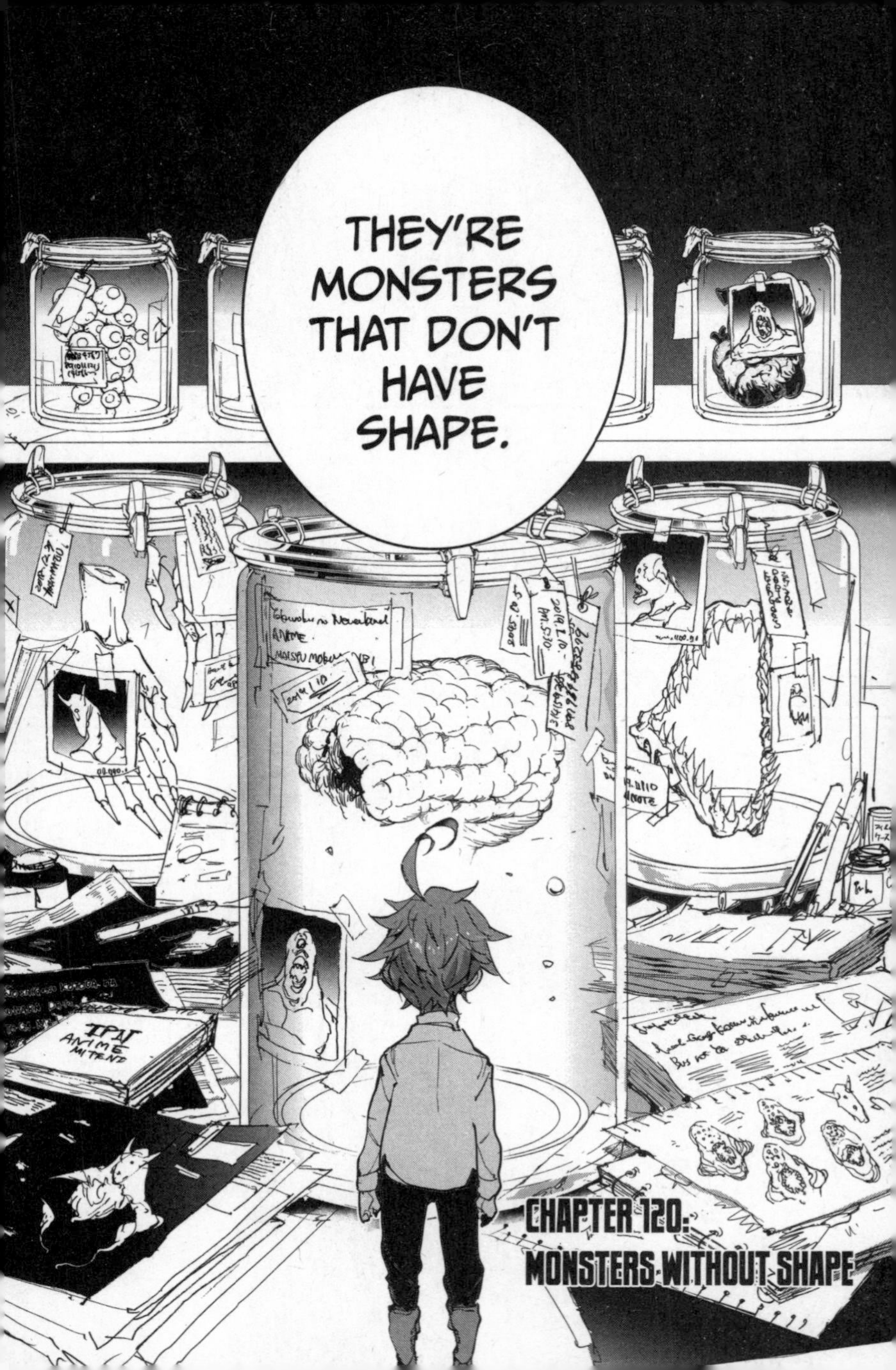
THEY'RE MONSTERS THAT DON'T HAVE SHAPE.
CHAPTER 120: MONSTERS WITHOUT SHAPE

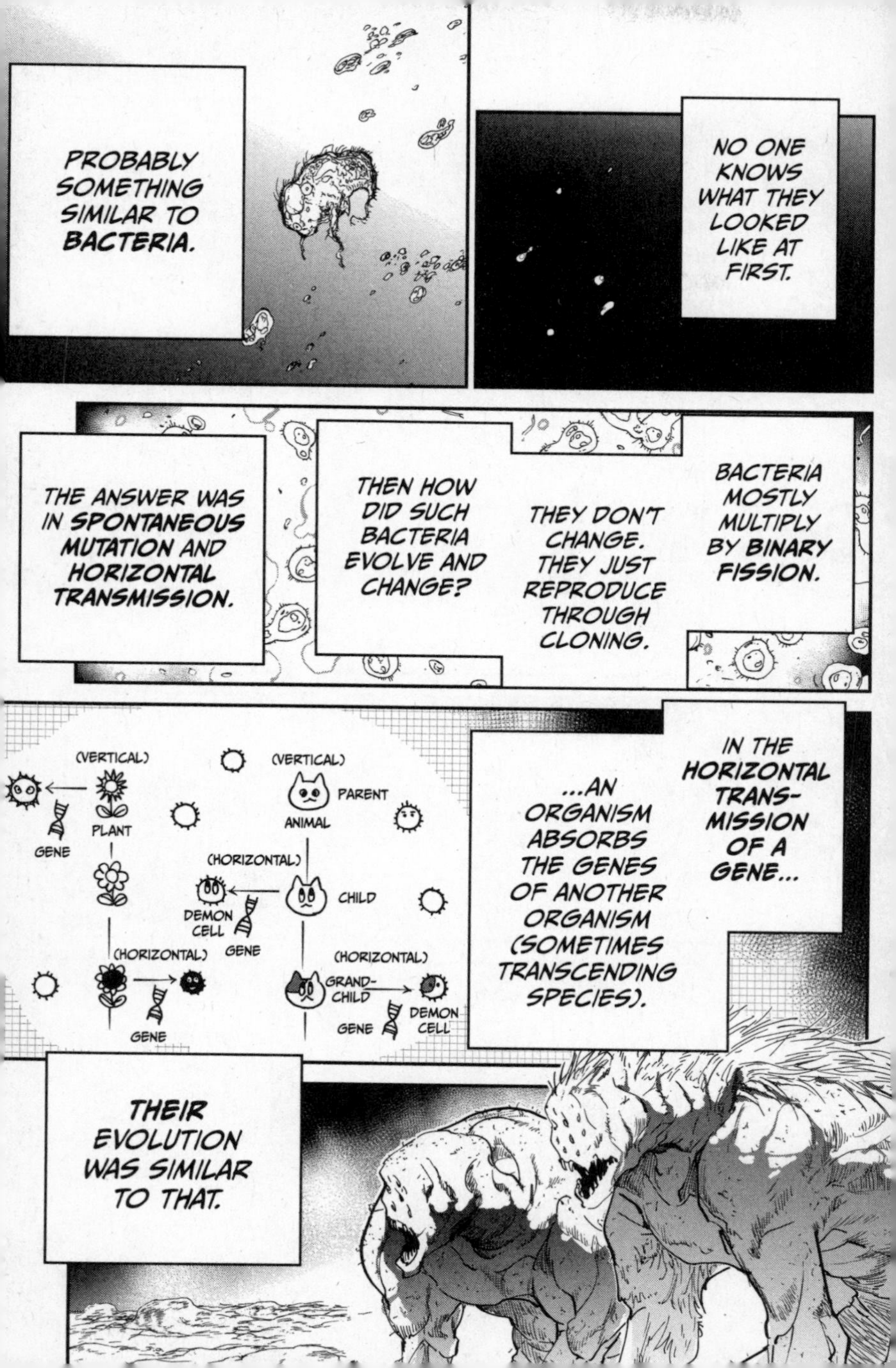
NO ONE KNOWS WHAT THEY LOOKED LIKE AT FIRST.
PROBABLY SOMETHING SIMILAR TO BACTERIA.
BACTERIA MOSTLY MULTIPLY BY BINARY FISSION.
THEY DON'T CHANGE. THEY JUST REPRODUCE THROUGH CLONING.
THEN HOW DID SUCH BACTERIA EVOLVE AND CHANGE?
THE ANSWER WAS IN SPONTANEOUS MUTATION AND HORIZONTAL TRANSMISSION.
IN THE HORIZONTAL TRANSMISSION OF A GENE...
...AN ORGANISM ABSORBS THE GENES OF ANOTHER ORGANISM (SOMETIMES TRANSCENDING SPECIES).
(VERTICAL)
PARENT
ANIMAL
(HORIZONTAL)
CHILD
DEMON CELL
GENE
(HORIZONTAL)
GRAND-CHILD
GENE
DEMON CELL
(VERTICAL)
PLANT
GENE
(HORIZONTAL)
GENE
THEIR EVOLUTION WAS SIMILAR TO THAT.

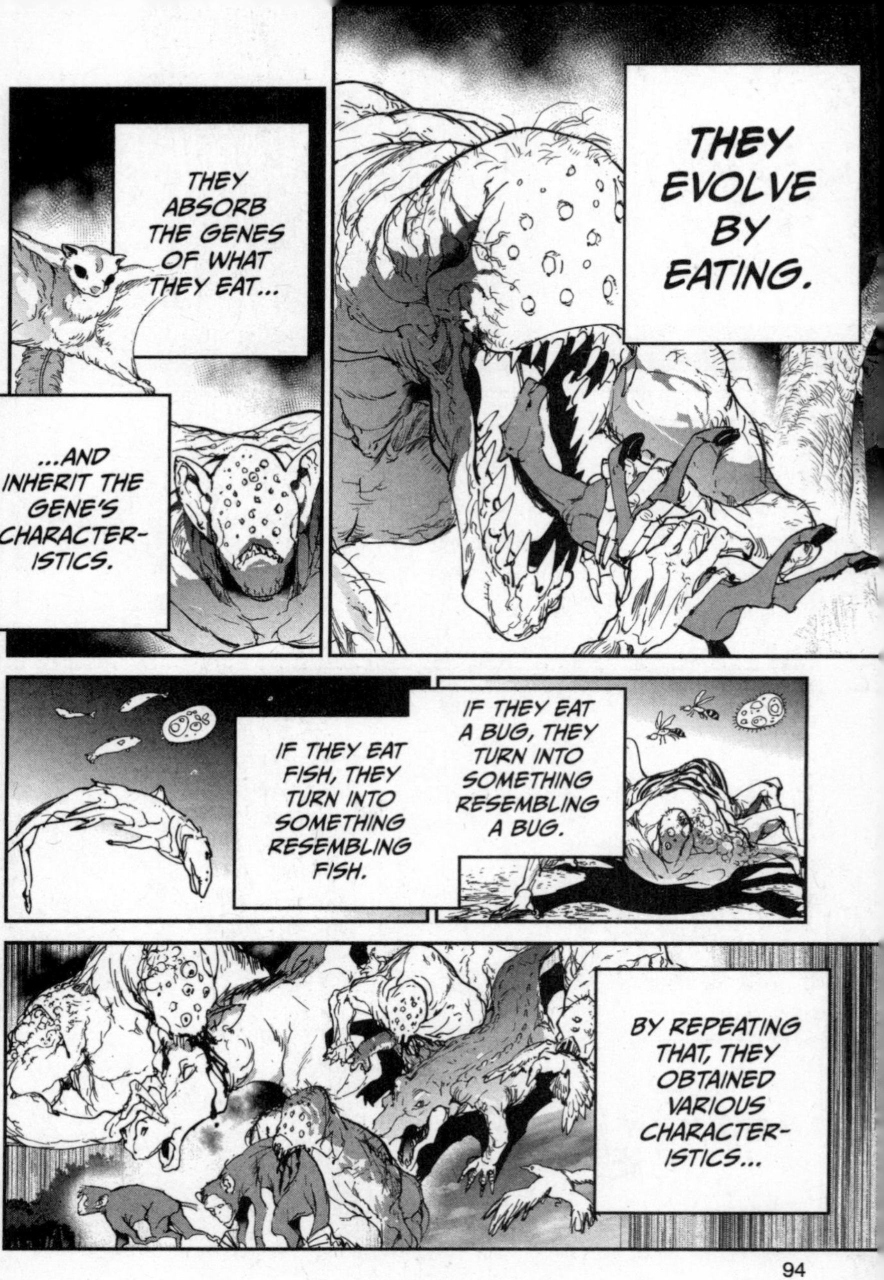
THEY EVOLVE BY EATING.
THEY ABSORB THE GENES OF WHAT THEY EAT...
...AND INHERIT THE GENE'S CHARACTER-ISTICS.
IF THEY EAT A BUG, THEY TURN INTO SOMETHING RESEMBLING A BUG.
IF THEY EAT FISH, THEY TURN INTO SOMETHING RESEMBLING FISH.
BY REPEATING THAT, THEY OBTAINED VARIOUS CHARACTER-ISTICS...

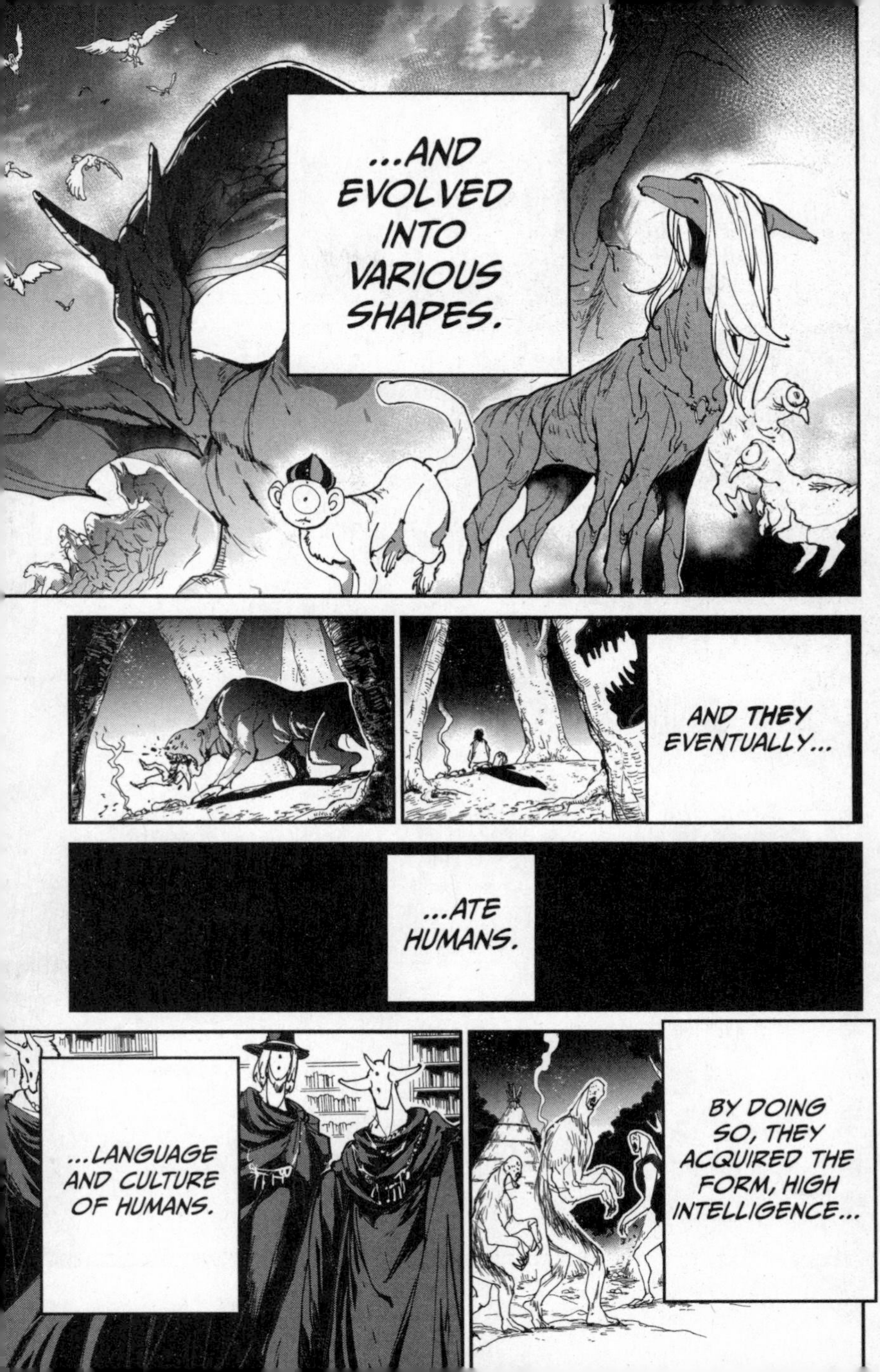
...AND EVOLVED INTO VARIOUS SHAPES.
AND THEY EVENTUALLY...
...ATE HUMANS.
BY DOING SO, THEY ACQUIRED THE FORM, HIGH INTELLIGENCE...
...LANGUAGE AND CULTURE OF HUMANS.

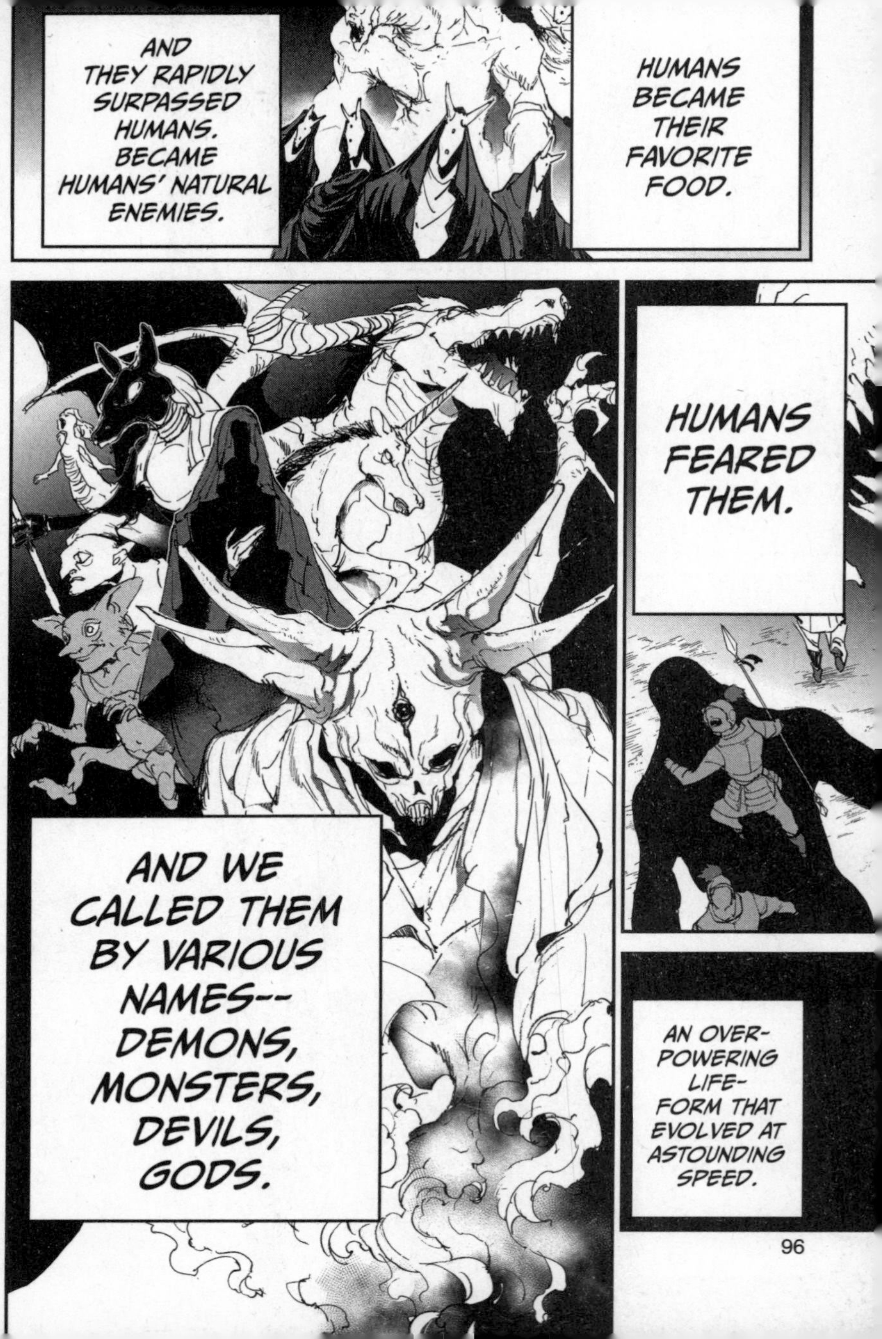
HUMANS BECAME THEIR FAVORITE FOOD.
AND THEY RAPIDLY SURPASSED HUMANS. BECAME HUMANS' NATURAL ENEMIES.
HUMANS FEARED THEM.
AN OVER-POWERING LIFE-FORM THAT EVOLVED AT ASTOUNDING SPEED.
AND WE CALLED THEM BY VARIOUS NAMES-- DEMONS, MONSTERS, DEVILS, GODS.

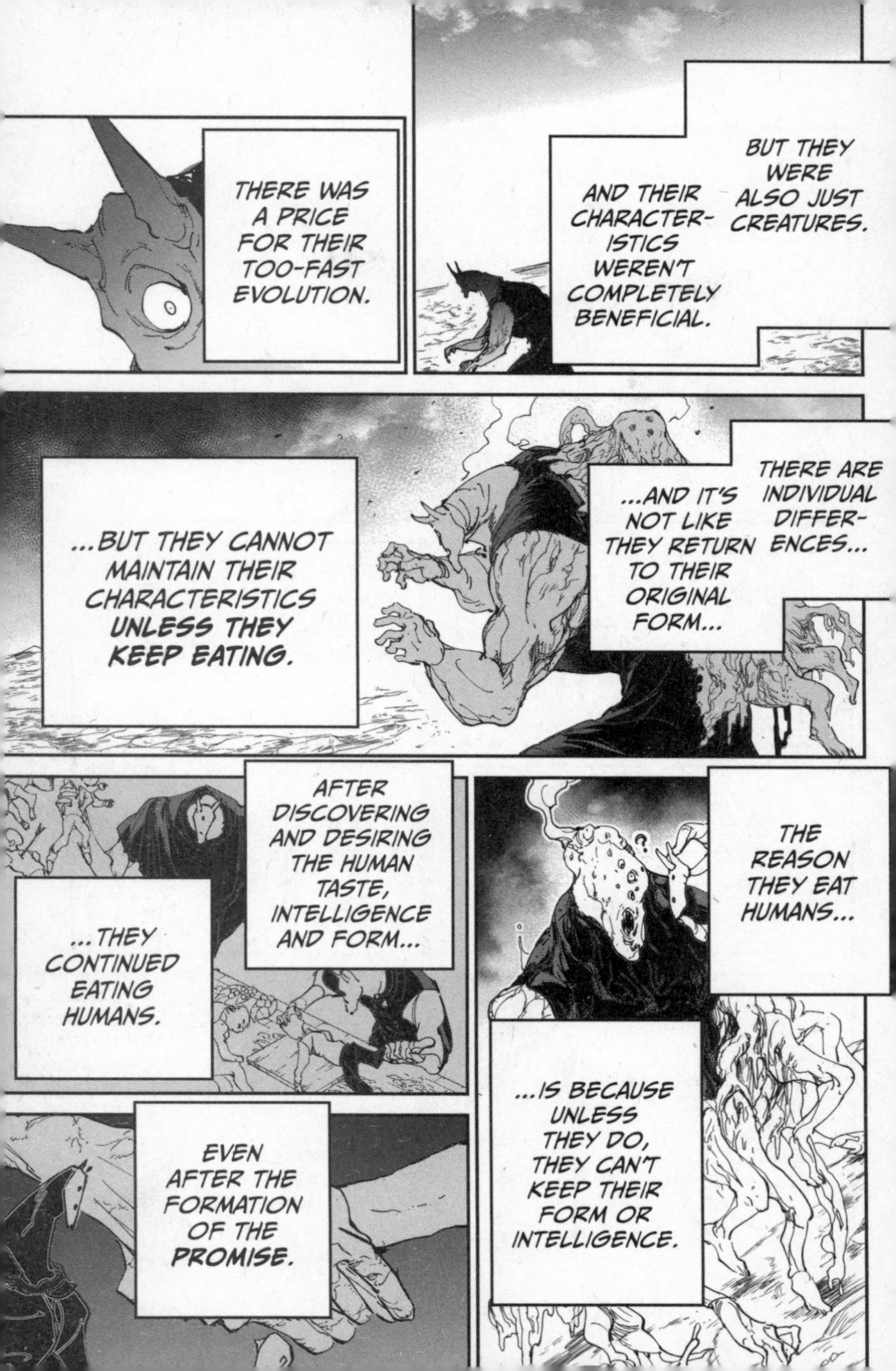
BUT THEY WERE ALSO JUST CREATURES.
AND THEIR CHARACTER-ISTICS WEREN'T COMPLETELY BENEFICIAL.
THERE WAS A PRICE FOR THEIR TOO-FAST EVOLUTION.
THERE ARE INDIVIDUAL DIFFER-ENCES...
...AND IT'S NOT LIKE THEY RETURN TO THEIR ORIGINAL FORM...
...BUT THEY CANNOT MAINTAIN THEIR CHARACTERISTICS UNLESS THEY KEEP EATING.
THE REASON THEY EAT HUMANS...
...IS BECAUSE UNLESS THEY DO, THEY CAN'T KEEP THEIR FORM OR INTELLIGENCE.
AFTER DISCOVERING AND DESIRING THE HUMAN TASTE, INTELLIGENCE AND FORM...
...THEY CONTINUED EATING HUMANS.
EVEN AFTER THE FORMATION OF THE PROMISE.

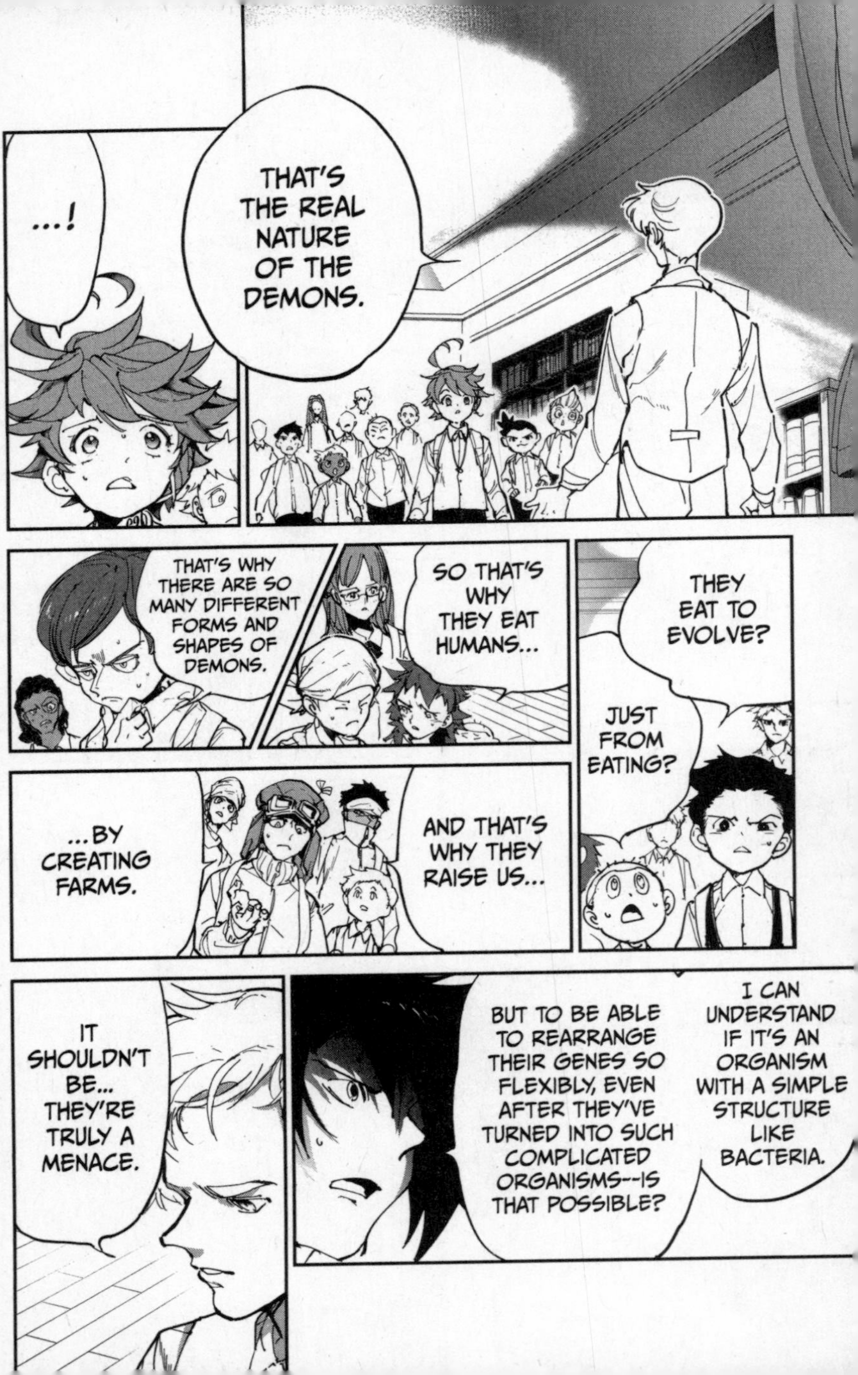

THAT'S THE REAL NATURE OF THE DEMONS.
...!
THEY EAT TO EVOLVE?
JUST FROM EATING?
SO THAT'S WHY THEY EAT HUMANS...
THAT'S WHY THERE ARE SO MANY DIFFERENT FORMS AND SHAPES OF DEMONS.
AND THAT'S WHY THEY RAISE US...
...BY CREATING FARMS.
I CAN UNDERSTAND IF IT'S AN ORGANISM WITH A SIMPLE STRUCTURE LIKE BACTERIA.
BUT TO BE ABLE TO REARRANGE THEIR GENES SO FLEXIBLY, EVEN AFTER THEY'VE TURNED INTO SUCH COMPLICATED ORGANISMS--IS THAT POSSIBLE?
IT SHOULDN'T BE... THEY'RE TRULY A MENACE.

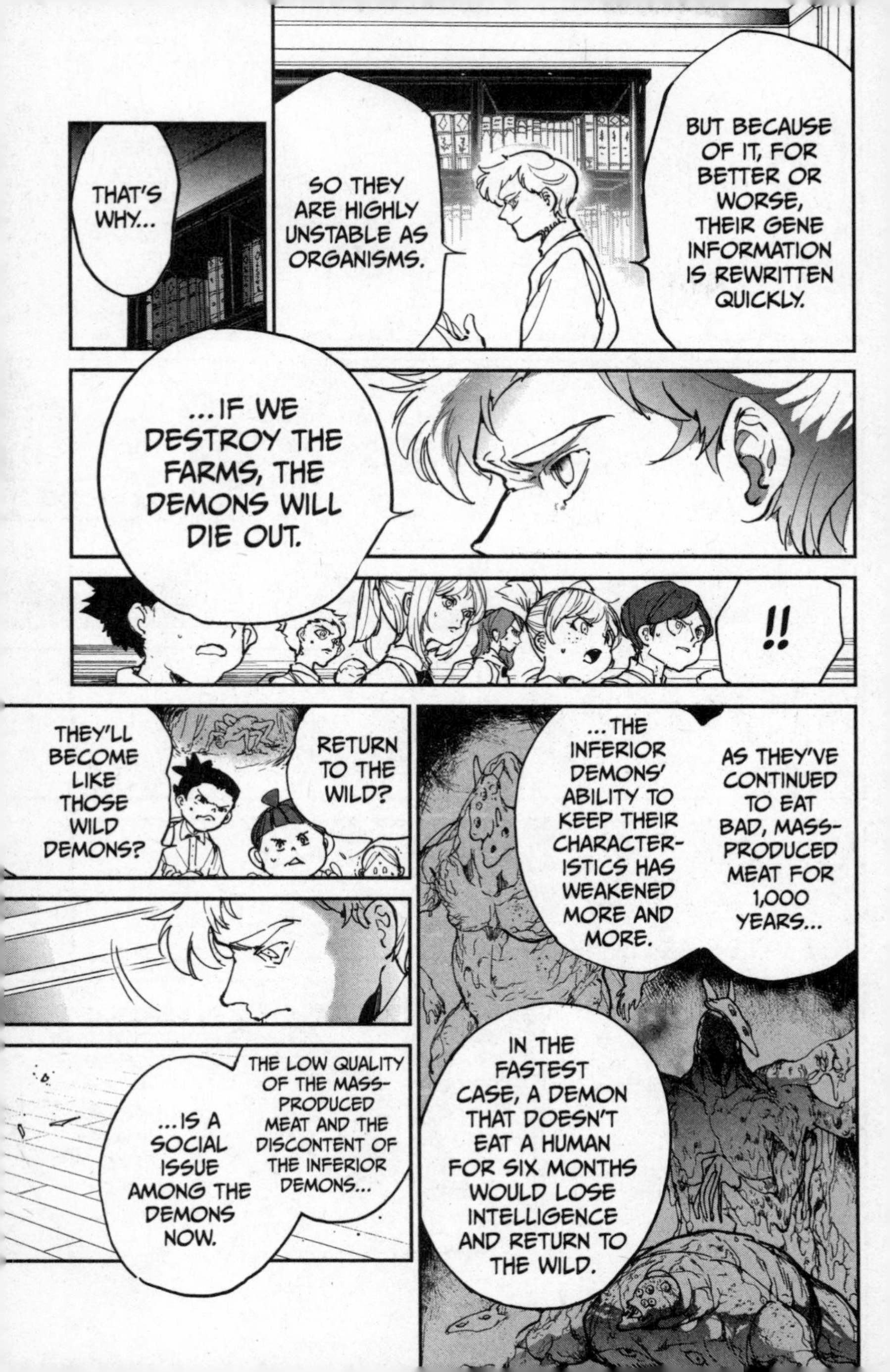
BUT BECAUSE OF IT, FOR BETTER OR WORSE, THEIR GENE INFORMATION IS REWRITTEN QUICKLY.
SO THEY ARE HIGHLY UNSTABLE AS ORGANISMS.
THAT'S WHY...
...IF WE DESTROY THE FARMS, THE DEMONS WILL DIE OUT.
!!
AS THEY'VE CONTINUED TO EAT BAD, MASS-PRODUCED MEAT FOR 1,000 YEARS...
...THE INFERIOR DEMONS' ABILITY TO KEEP THEIR CHARACTER-ISTICS HAS WEAKENED MORE AND MORE.
IN THE FASTEST CASE, A DEMON THAT DOESN'T EAT A HUMAN FOR SIX MONTHS WOULD LOSE INTELLIGENCE AND RETURN TO THE WILD.
RETURN TO THE WILD?
THEY'LL BECOME LIKE THOSE WILD DEMONS?
THE LOW QUALITY OF THE MASS-PRODUCED MEAT AND THE DISCONTENT OF THE INFERIOR DEMONS...
...IS A SOCIAL ISSUE AMONG THE DEMONS NOW.

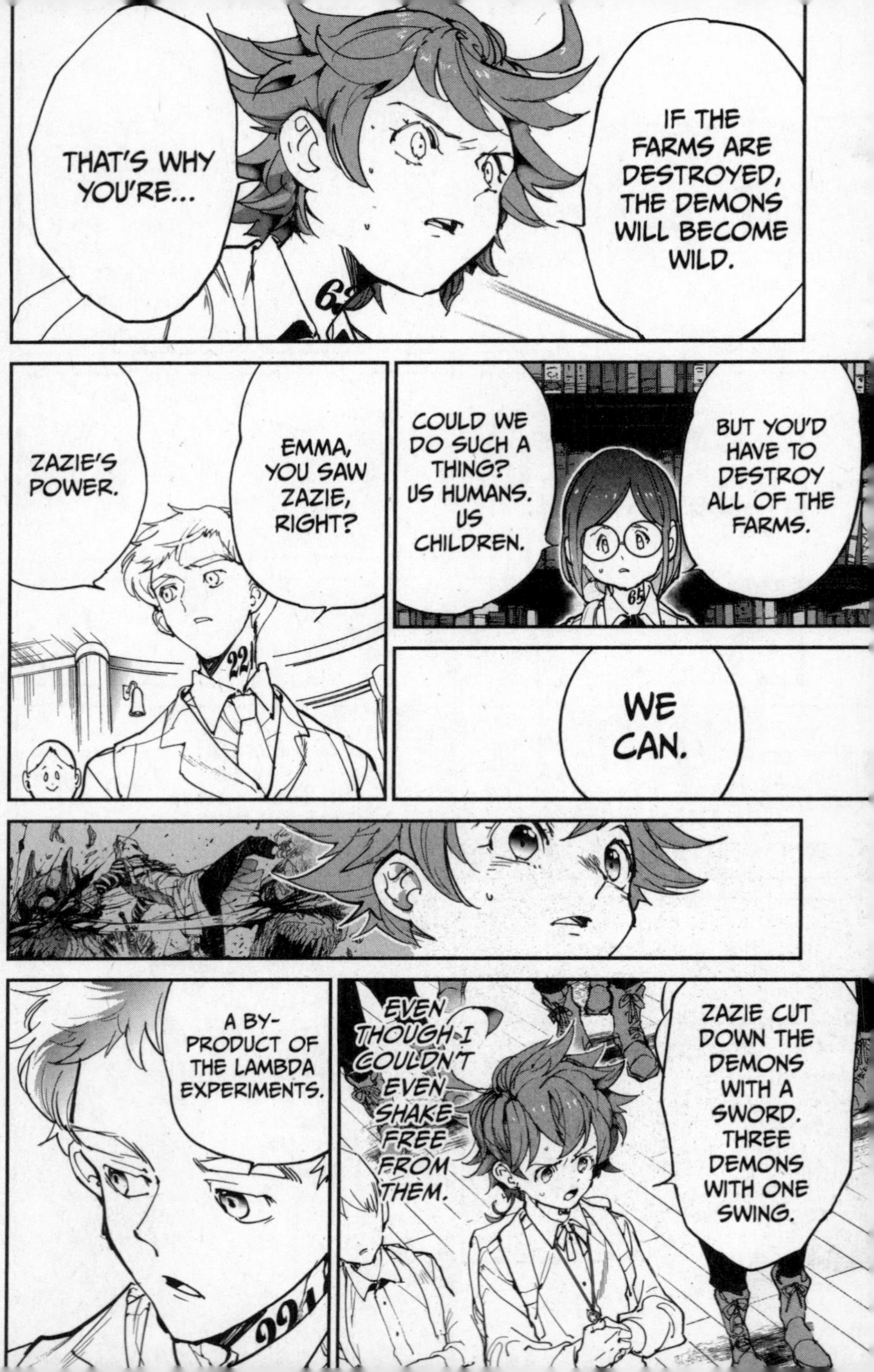
IF THE FARMS ARE DESTROYED, THE DEMONS WILL BECOME WILD.
THAT'S WHY YOU'RE...
BUT YOU'D HAVE TO DESTROY ALL OF THE FARMS.
COULD WE DO SUCH A THING? US HUMANS. US CHILDREN.
WE CAN.
EMMA, YOU SAW ZAZIE, RIGHT?
ZAZIE'S POWER.
ZAZIE CUT DOWN THE DEMONS WITH A SWORD. THREE DEMONS WITH ONE SWING.
EVEN THOUGH I COULDN'T EVEN SHAKE FREE FROM THEM.
A BY-PRODUCT OF THE LAMBDA EXPERIMENTS.

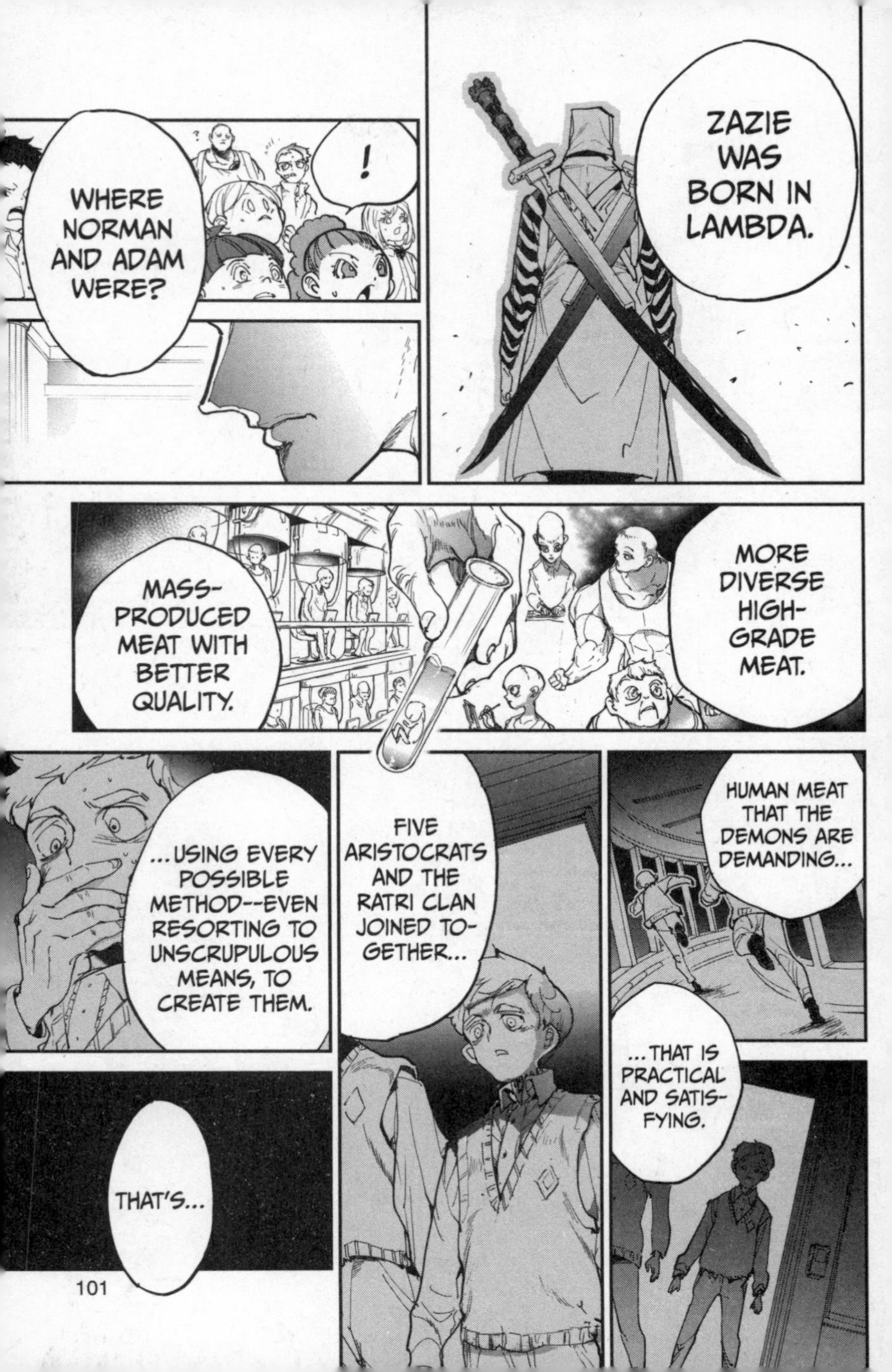

ZAZIE WAS BORN IN LAMBDA.
!
WHERE NORMAN AND ADAM WERE?
MORE DIVERSE HIGH-GRADE MEAT.
MASS-PRODUCED MEAT WITH BETTER QUALITY.
HUMAN MEAT THAT THE DEMONS ARE DEMANDING...
...THAT IS PRACTICAL AND SATIS-FYING.
FIVE ARISTOCRATS AND THE RATRI CLAN JOINED TO-GETHER...
...USING EVERY POSSIBLE METHOD--EVEN RESORTING TO UNSCRUPULOUS MEANS, TO CREATE THEM.
THAT'S...

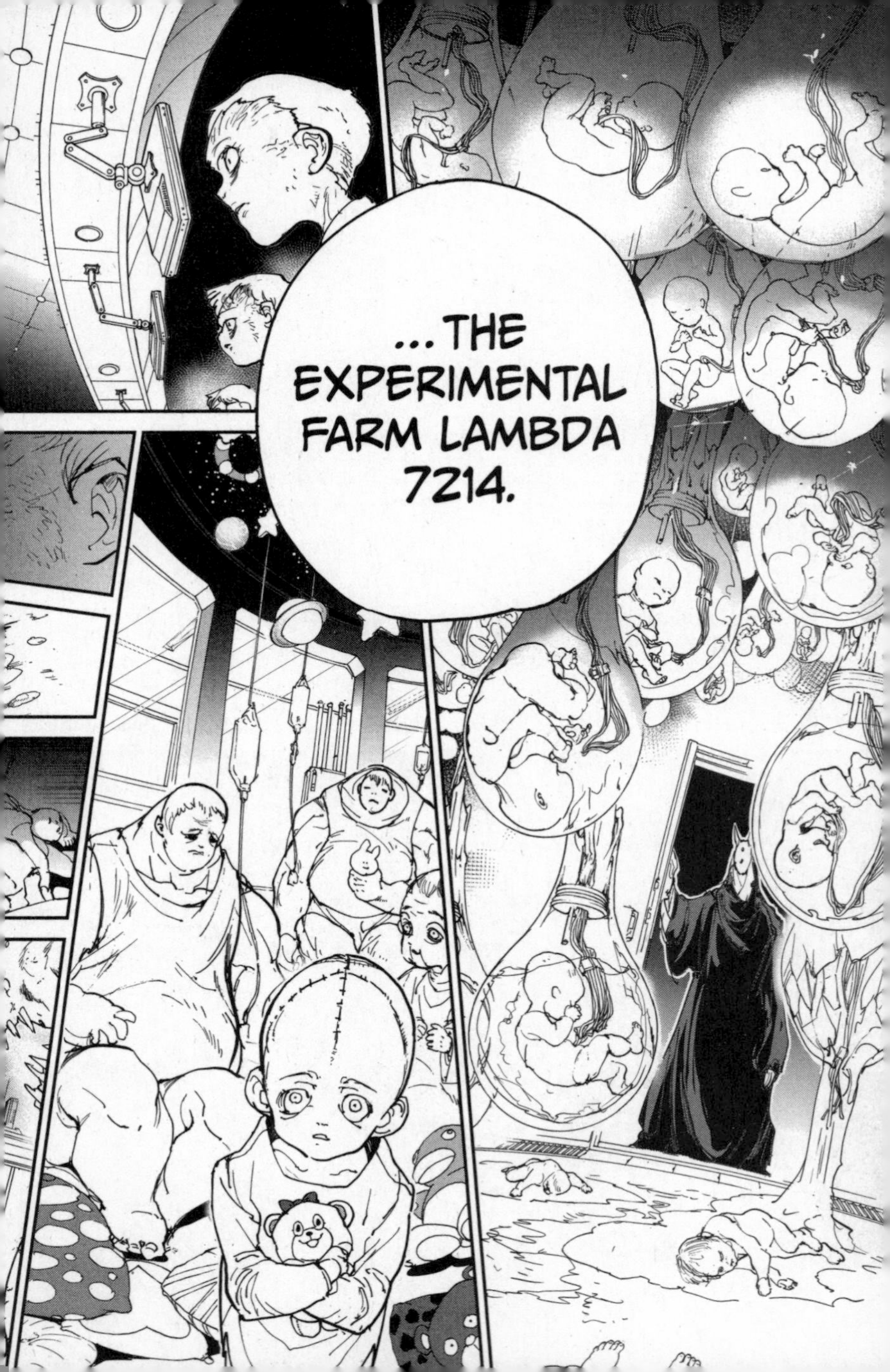
...THE EXPERIMENTAL FARM LAMBDA 7214.

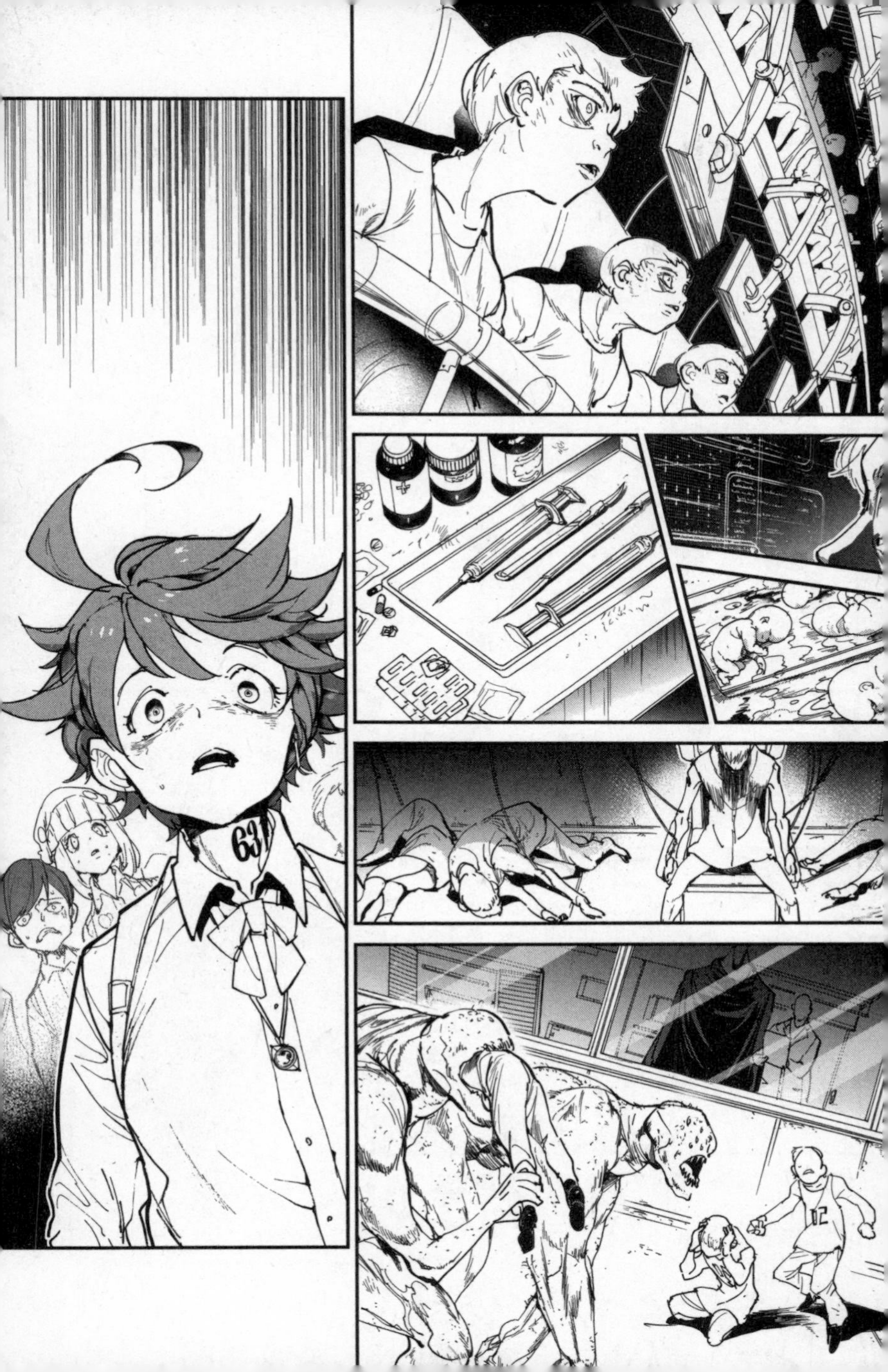

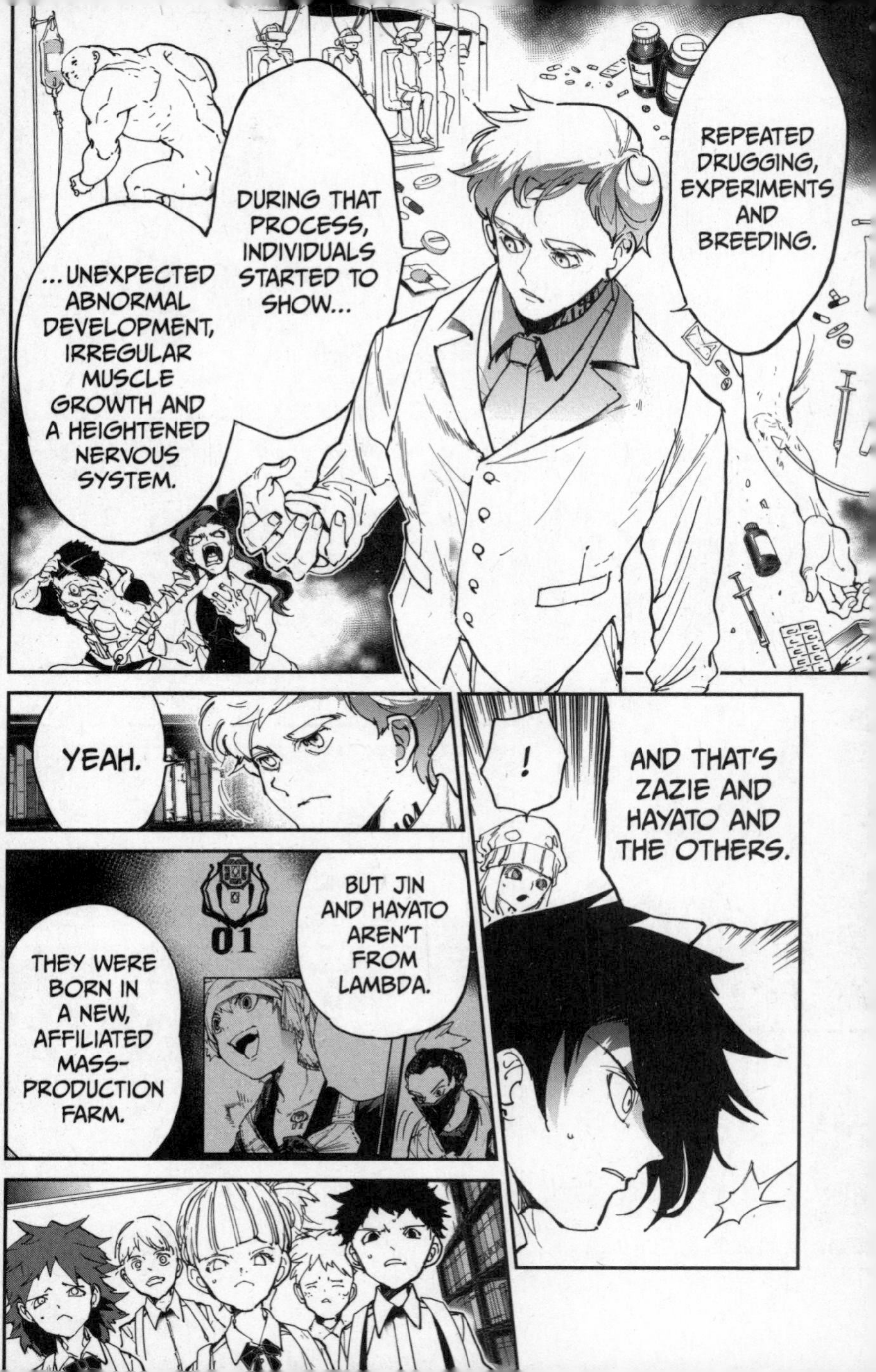
REPEATED DRUGGING, EXPERIMENTS AND BREEDING.
DURING THAT PROCESS, INDIVIDUALS STARTED TO SHOW...
...UNEXPECTED ABNORMAL DEVELOPMENT, IRREGULAR MUSCLE GROWTH AND A HEIGHTENED NERVOUS SYSTEM.
AND THAT'S ZAZIE AND HAYATO AND THE OTHERS.
!
YEAH.
01
BUT JIN AND HAYATO AREN'T FROM LAMBDA.
THEY WERE BORN IN A NEW, AFFILIATED MASS-PRODUCTION FARM.

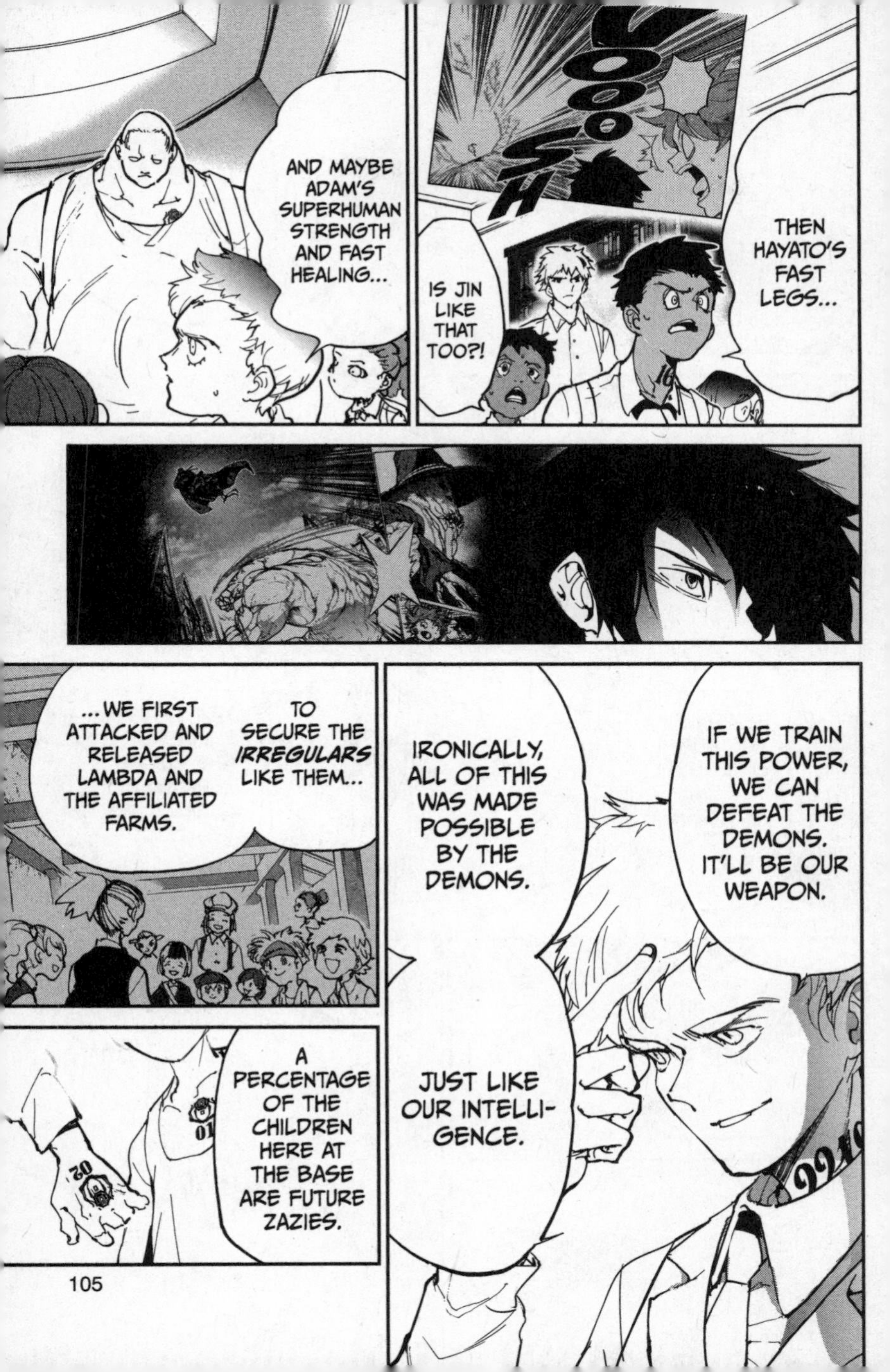
OOOOSH
THEN HAYATO'S FAST LEGS...
IS JIN LIKE THAT TOO?!
AND MAYBE ADAM'S SUPERHUMAN STRENGTH AND FAST HEALING...
IF WE TRAIN THIS POWER, WE CAN DEFEAT THE DEMONS. IT'LL BE OUR WEAPON.
IRONICALLY, ALL OF THIS WAS MADE POSSIBLE BY THE DEMONS.
JUST LIKE OUR INTELLI-GENCE.
TO SECURE THE *IRREGULARS* LIKE THEM...
...WE FIRST ATTACKED AND RELEASED LAMBDA AND THE AFFILIATED FARMS.
A PERCENTAGE OF THE CHILDREN HERE AT THE BASE ARE FUTURE ZAZIES.

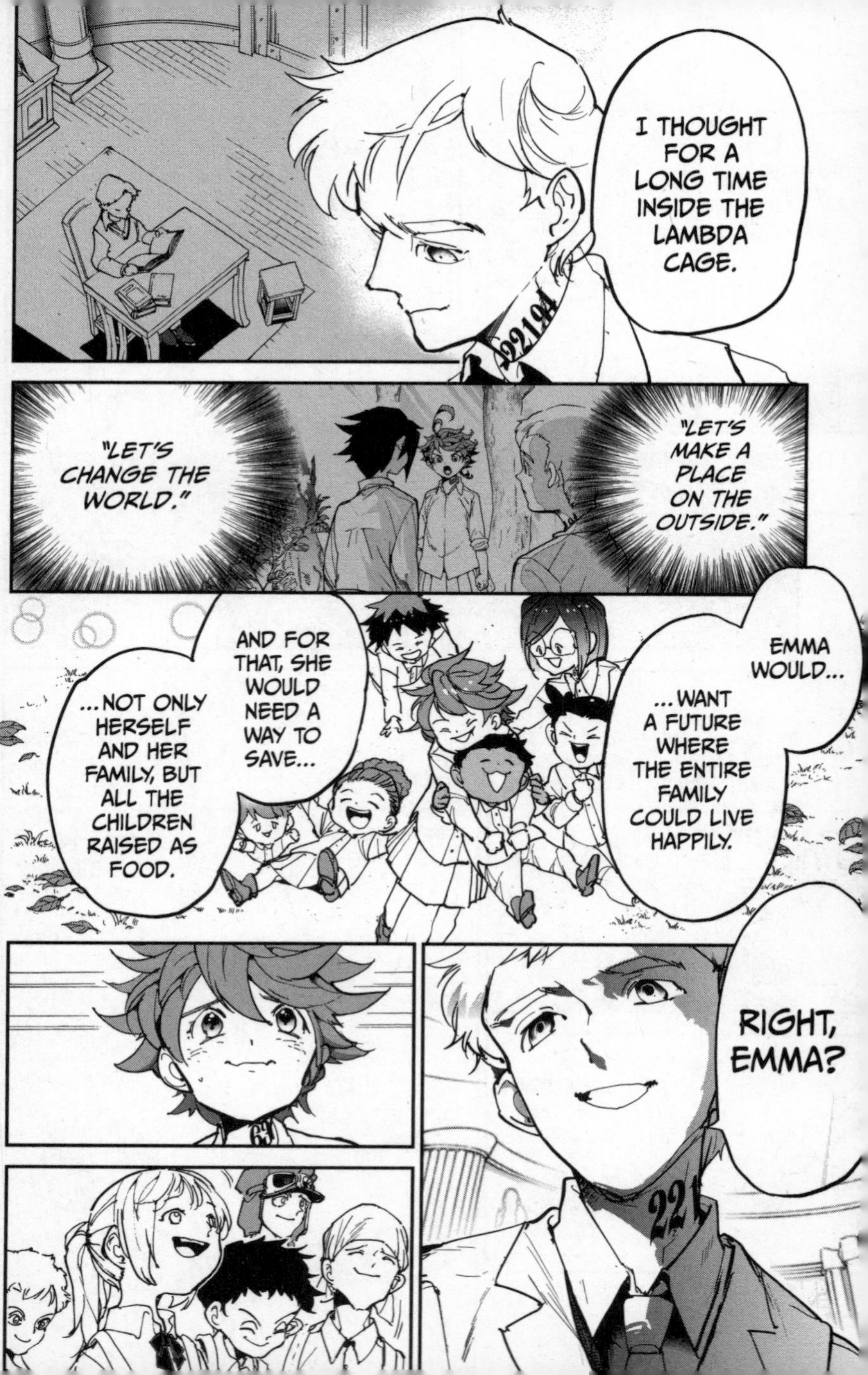
I THOUGHT FOR A LONG TIME INSIDE THE LAMBDA CAGE.
"LET'S MAKE A PLACE ON THE OUTSIDE."
"LET'S CHANGE THE WORLD."
EMMA WOULD...
...WANT A FUTURE WHERE THE ENTIRE FAMILY COULD LIVE HAPPILY.
AND FOR THAT, SHE WOULD NEED A WAY TO SAVE...
...NOT ONLY HERSELF AND HER FAMILY, BUT ALL THE CHILDREN RAISED AS FOOD.
RIGHT, EMMA?

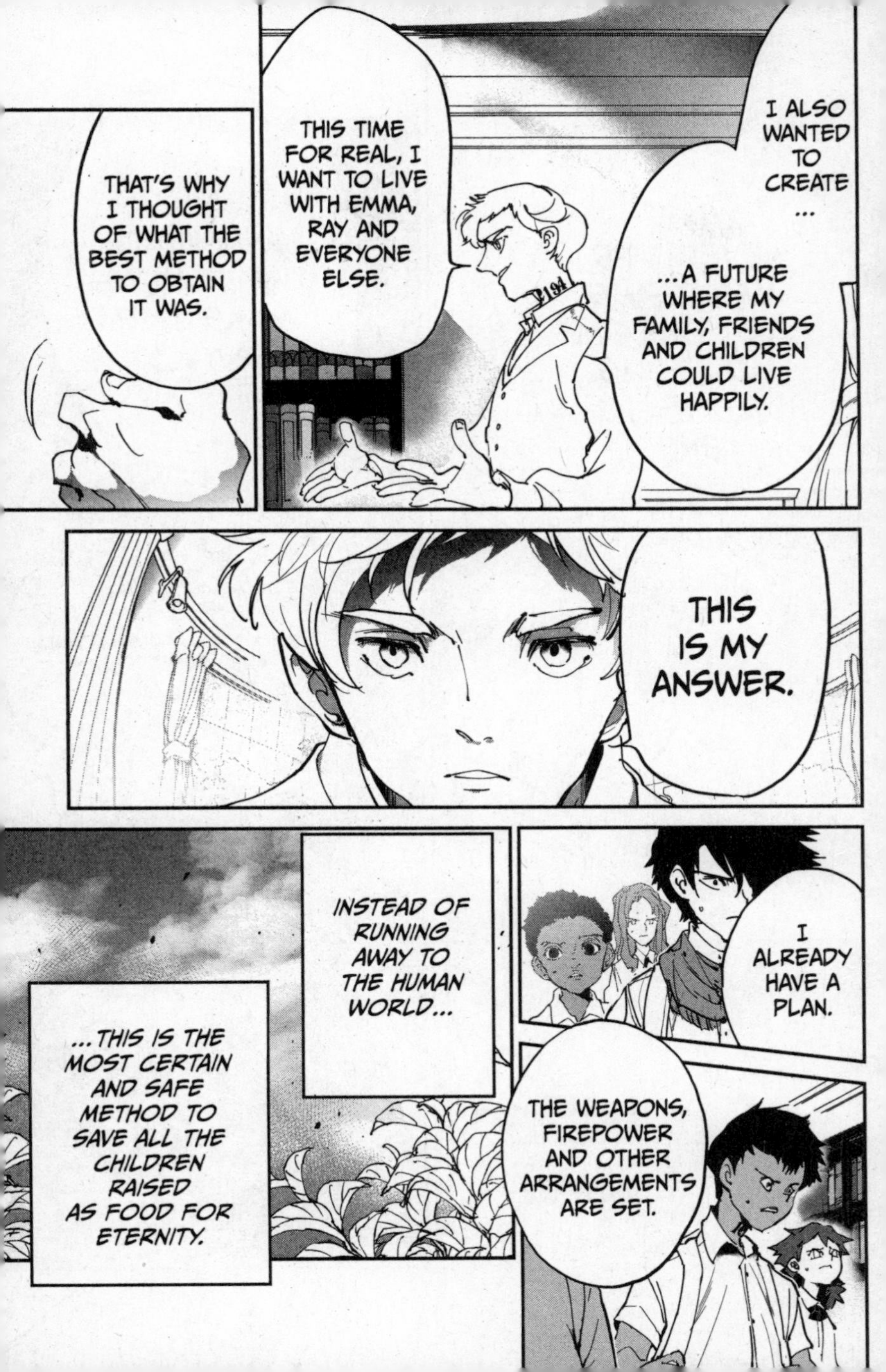
I ALSO WANTED TO CREATE ...
...A FUTURE WHERE MY FAMILY, FRIENDS AND CHILDREN COULD LIVE HAPPILY.
THIS TIME FOR REAL, I WANT TO LIVE WITH EMMA, RAY AND EVERYONE ELSE.
THAT'S WHY I THOUGHT OF WHAT THE BEST METHOD TO OBTAIN IT WAS.
THIS IS MY ANSWER.
I ALREADY HAVE A PLAN.
THE WEAPONS, FIREPOWER AND OTHER ARRANGEMENTS ARE SET.
INSTEAD OF RUNNING AWAY TO THE HUMAN WORLD...
...THIS IS THE MOST CERTAIN AND SAFE METHOD TO SAVE ALL THE CHILDREN RAISED AS FOOD FOR ETERNITY.

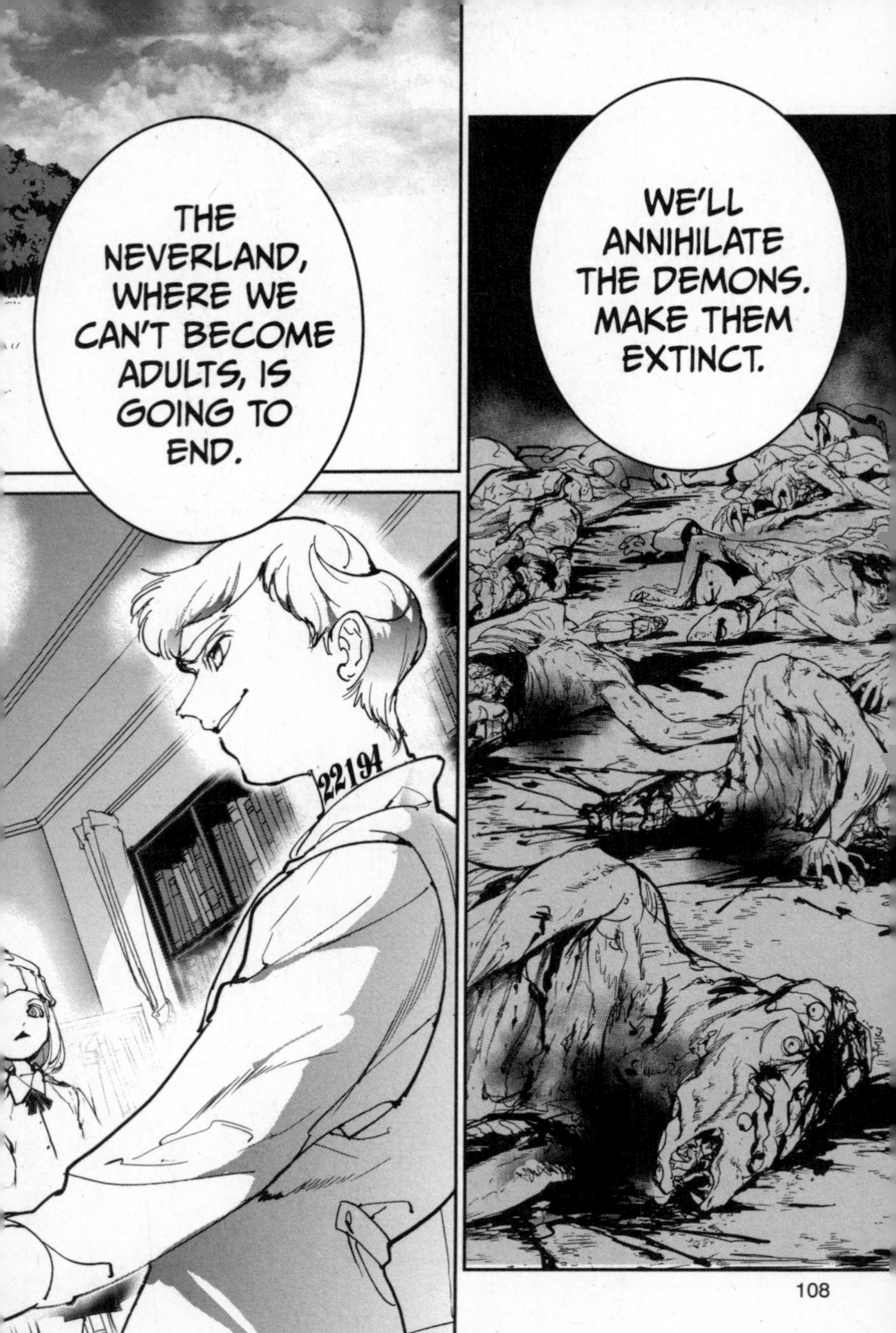
WE'LL ANNIHILATE THE DEMONS. MAKE THEM EXTINCT.
THE NEVERLAND, WHERE WE CAN'T BECOME ADULTS, IS GOING TO END.
22194

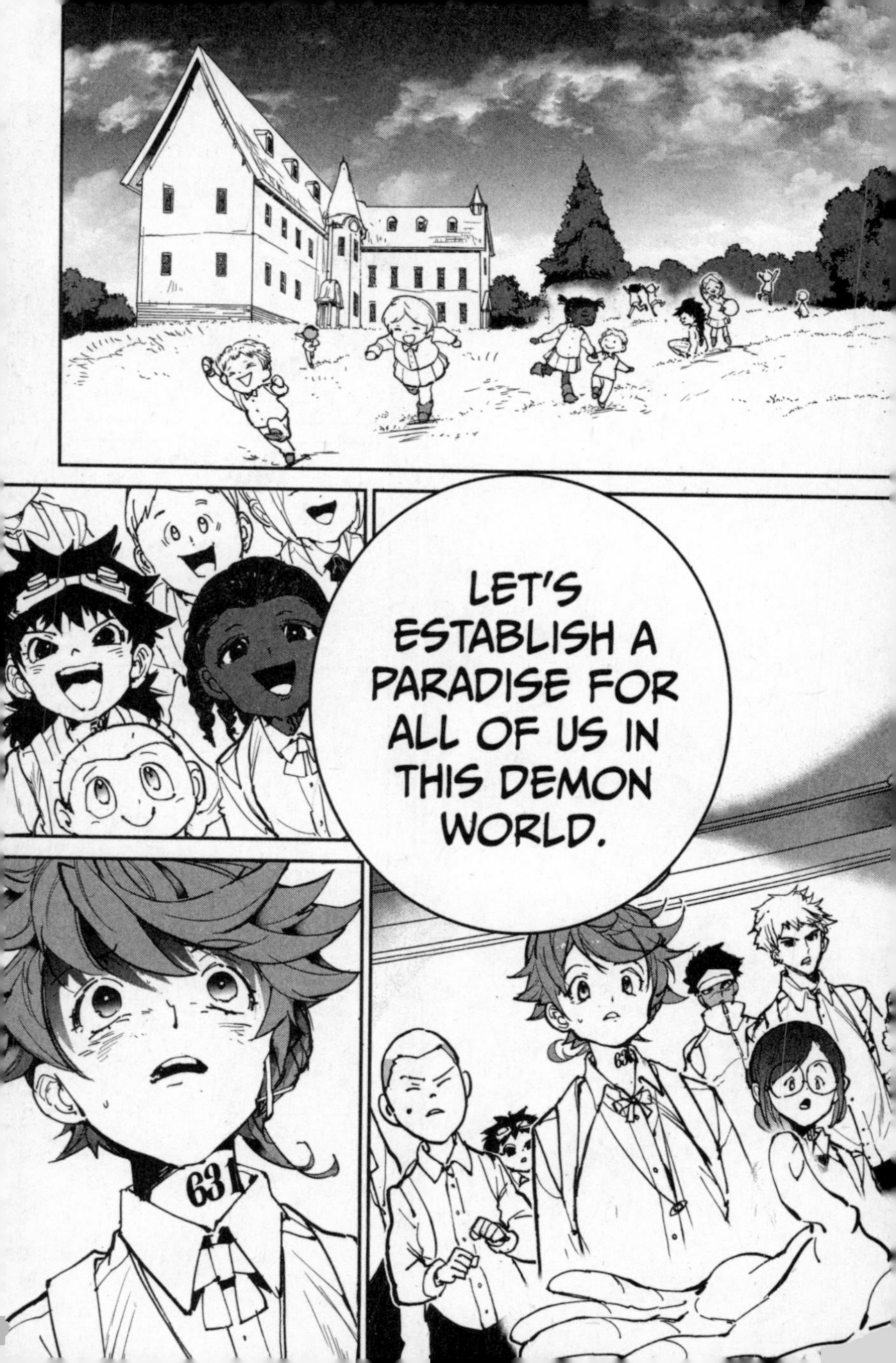
LET'S ESTABLISH A PARADISE FOR ALL OF US IN THIS DEMON WORLD.

HEIGHT

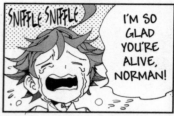

SNIFFLE SNIFFLE
I'M SO GLAD YOU'RE ALIVE, NORMAN!
TOUCHED
EMMA ...
SORTA FIST PUMP!

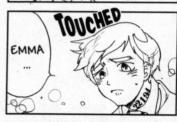

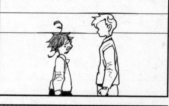

YOU REALLY GREW, NORMAN.
HEE HEE
I'M SO JEAL-OUS...
...THAT ALL OF YOU GOT TALLER.
YOU GOT TALLER TOO.

SIDE STORY 12...FIN

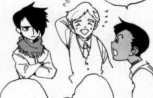

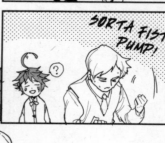

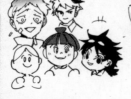

CHAPTER 121: ISN'T THIS GREAT

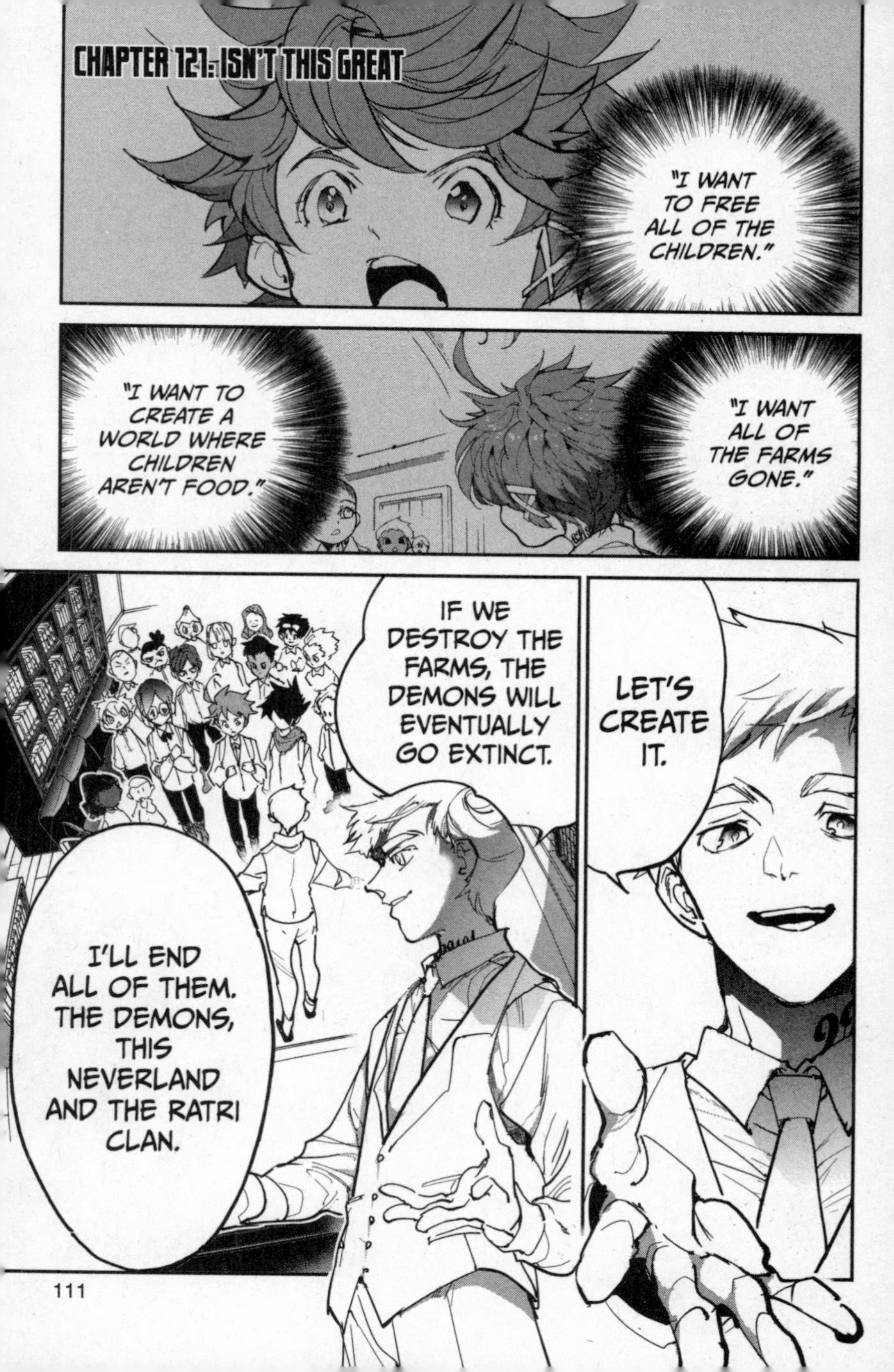
"I WANT TO FREE ALL OF THE CHILDREN."
"I WANT ALL OF THE FARMS GONE."
"I WANT TO CREATE A WORLD WHERE CHILDREN AREN'T FOOD."
LET'S CREATE IT.
IF WE DESTROY THE FARMS, THE DEMONS WILL EVENTUALLY GO EXTINCT.
I'LL END ALL OF THEM. THE DEMONS, THIS NEVERLAND AND THE RATRI CLAN.

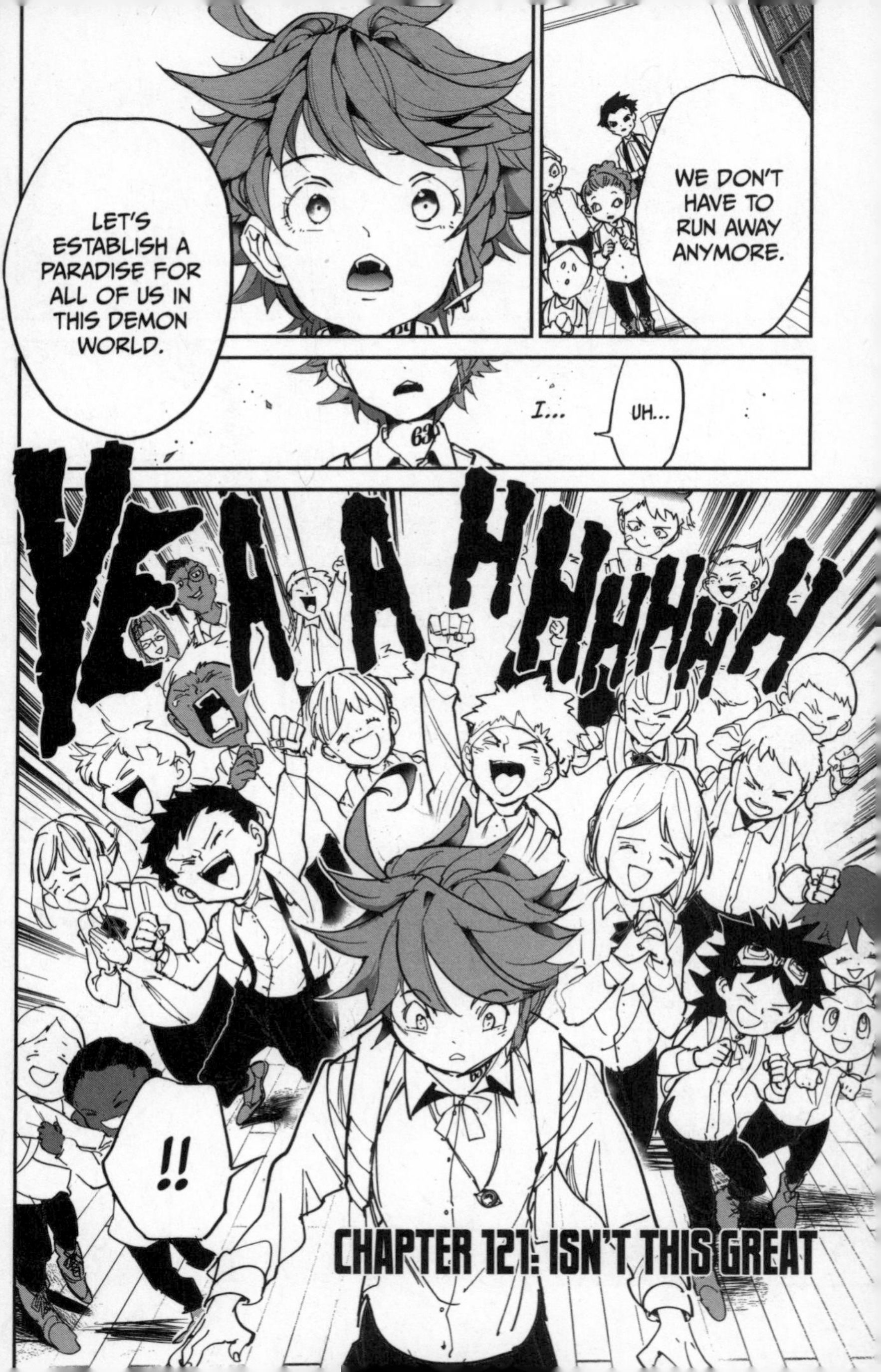
WE DON'T HAVE TO RUN AWAY ANYMORE.
LET'S ESTABLISH A PARADISE FOR ALL OF US IN THIS DEMON WORLD.
UH...
I...
YEAAAHHHHHH
!!
CHAPTER 121: ISN'T THIS GREAT

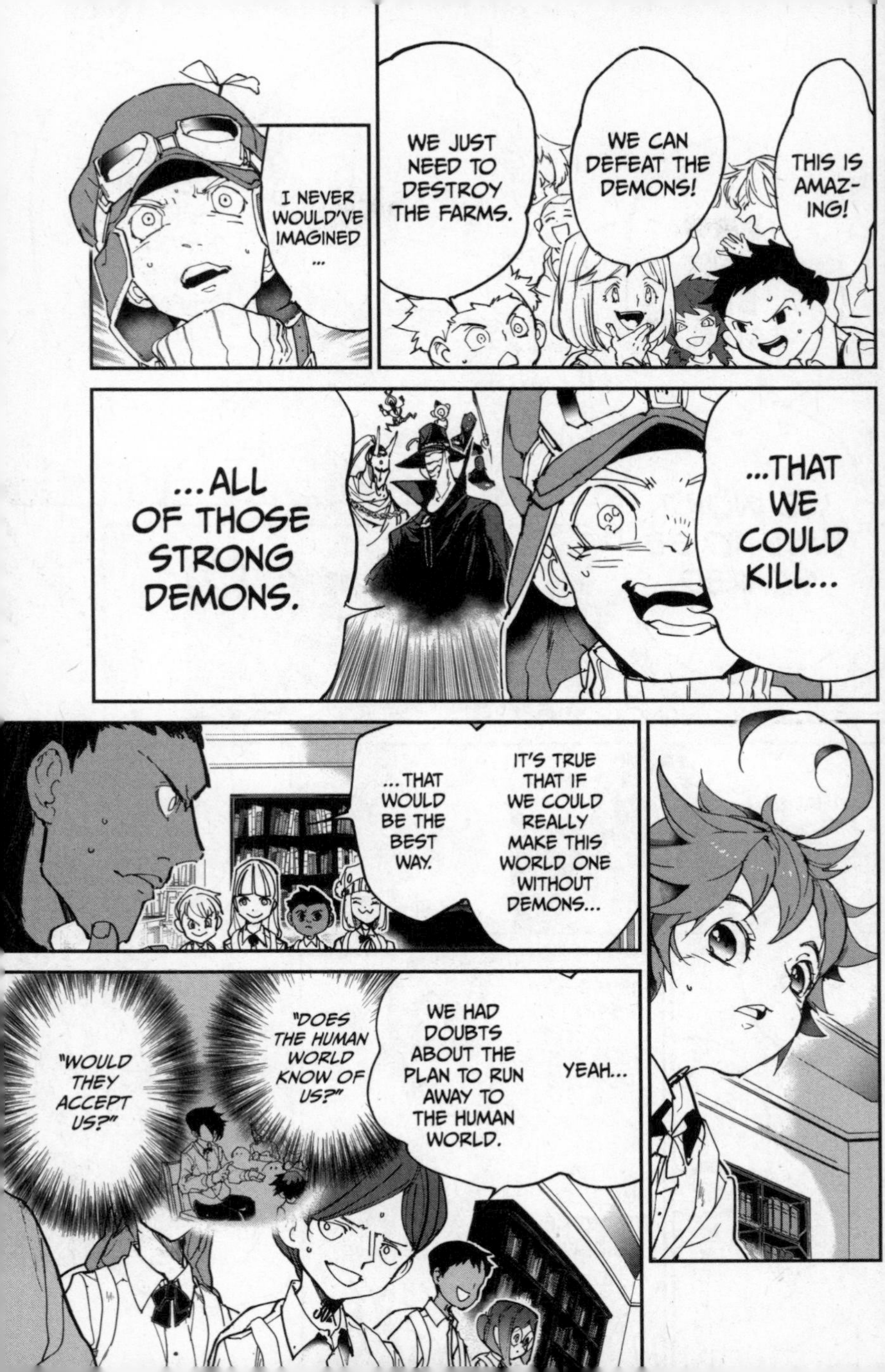
THIS IS AMAZ-ING!
WE CAN DEFEAT THE DEMONS!
WE JUST NEED TO DESTROY THE FARMS.
I NEVER WOULD'VE IMAGINED ...
...THAT WE COULD KILL...
...ALL OF THOSE STRONG DEMONS.
IT'S TRUE THAT IF WE COULD REALLY MAKE THIS WORLD ONE WITHOUT DEMONS...
...THAT WOULD BE THE BEST WAY.
YEAH...
WE HAD DOUBTS ABOUT THE PLAN TO RUN AWAY TO THE HUMAN WORLD.
"DOES THE HUMAN WORLD KNOW OF US?"
"WOULD THEY ACCEPT US?"

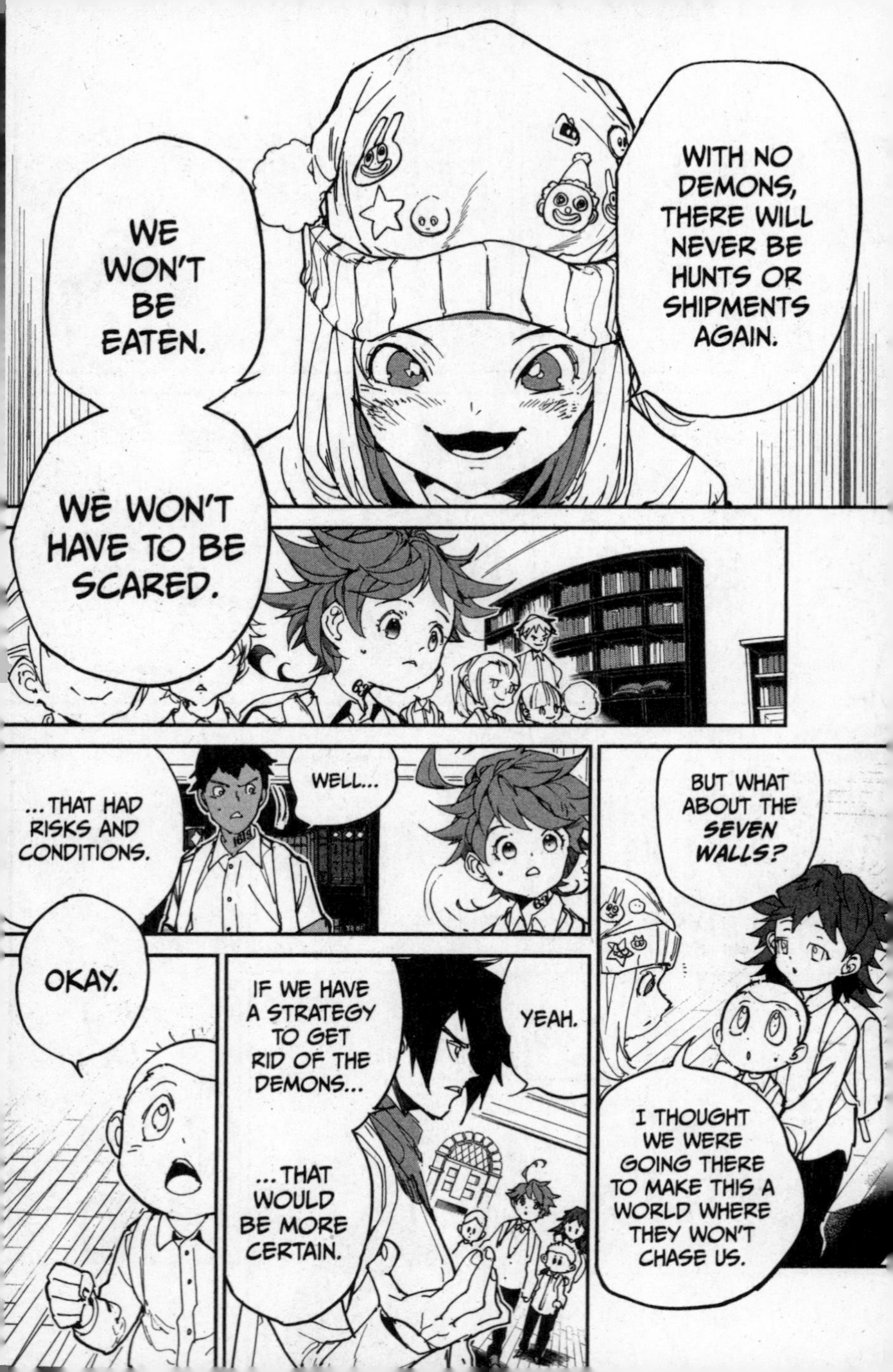
WITH NO DEMONS, THERE WILL NEVER BE HUNTS OR SHIPMENTS AGAIN.
WE WON'T BE EATEN.
WE WON'T HAVE TO BE SCARED.
BUT WHAT ABOUT THE *SEVEN WALLS?*
I THOUGHT WE WERE GOING THERE TO MAKE THIS A WORLD WHERE THEY WON'T CHASE US.
WELL...
...THAT HAD RISKS AND CONDITIONS.
YEAH.
IF WE HAVE A STRATEGY TO GET RID OF THE DEMONS...
...THAT WOULD BE MORE CERTAIN.
OKAY.

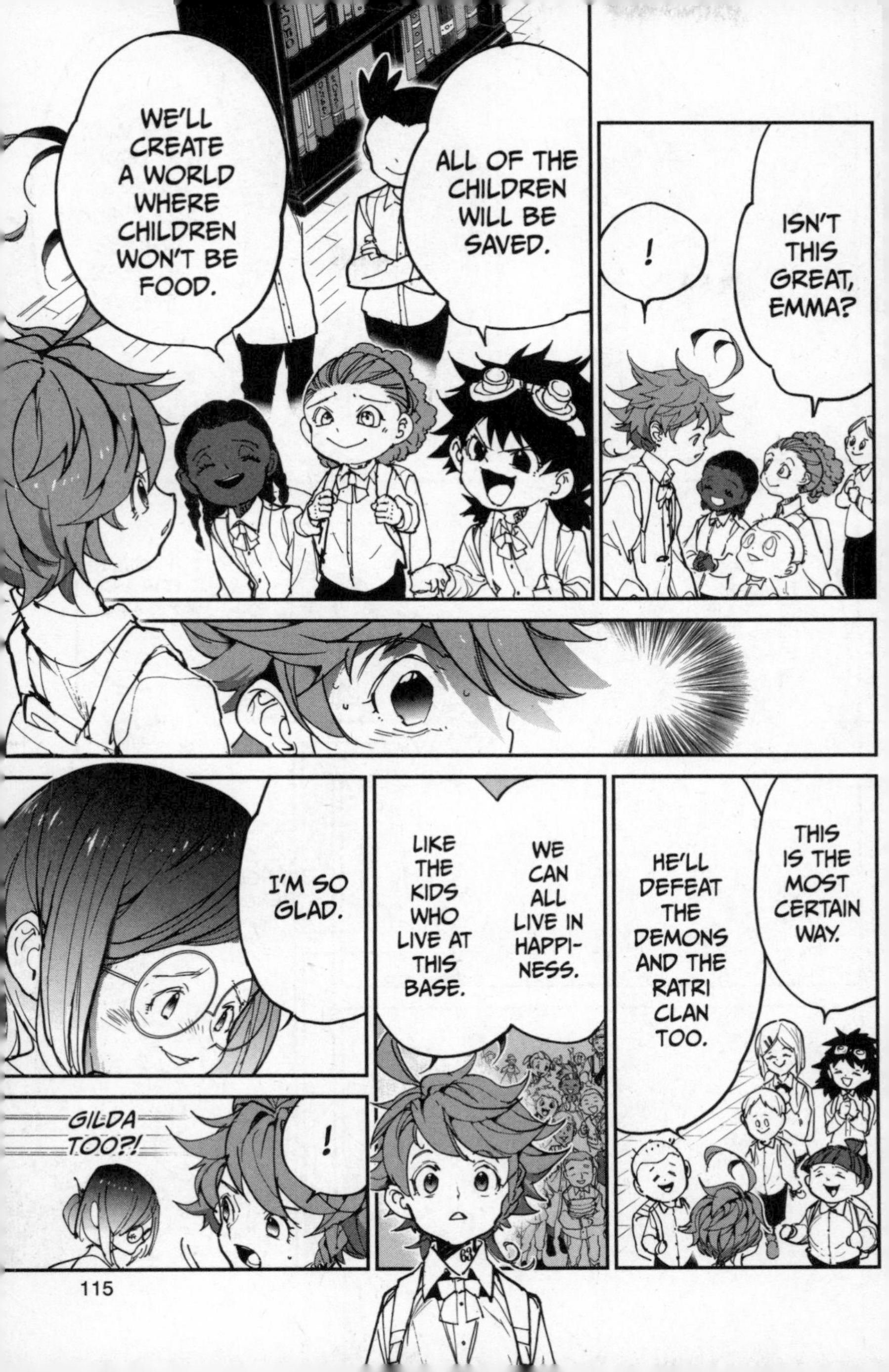
ISN'T THIS GREAT, EMMA?
!
ALL OF THE CHILDREN WILL BE SAVED.
WE'LL CREATE A WORLD WHERE CHILDREN WON'T BE FOOD.
THIS IS THE MOST CERTAIN WAY.
HE'LL DEFEAT THE DEMONS AND THE RATRI CLAN TOO.
WE CAN ALL LIVE IN HAPPINESS.
LIKE THE KIDS WHO LIVE AT THIS BASE.
I'M SO GLAD.
!
GILDA TOO?!

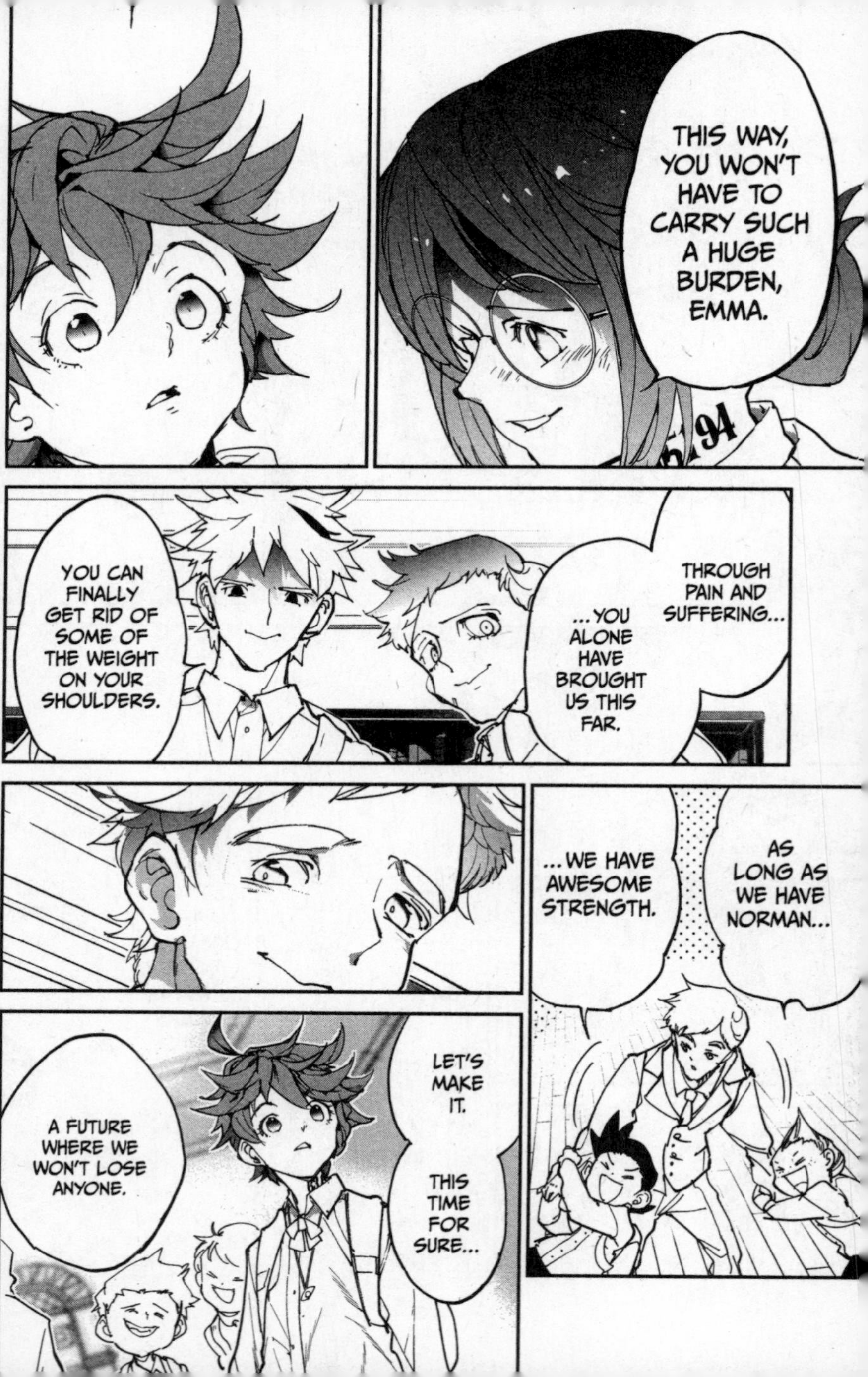
THIS WAY, YOU WON'T HAVE TO CARRY SUCH A HUGE BURDEN, EMMA.
THROUGH PAIN AND SUFFERING...
...YOU ALONE HAVE BROUGHT US THIS FAR.
YOU CAN FINALLY GET RID OF SOME OF THE WEIGHT ON YOUR SHOULDERS.
AS LONG AS WE HAVE NORMAN...
...WE HAVE AWESOME STRENGTH.
LET'S MAKE IT.
THIS TIME FOR SURE...
A FUTURE WHERE WE WON'T LOSE ANYONE.

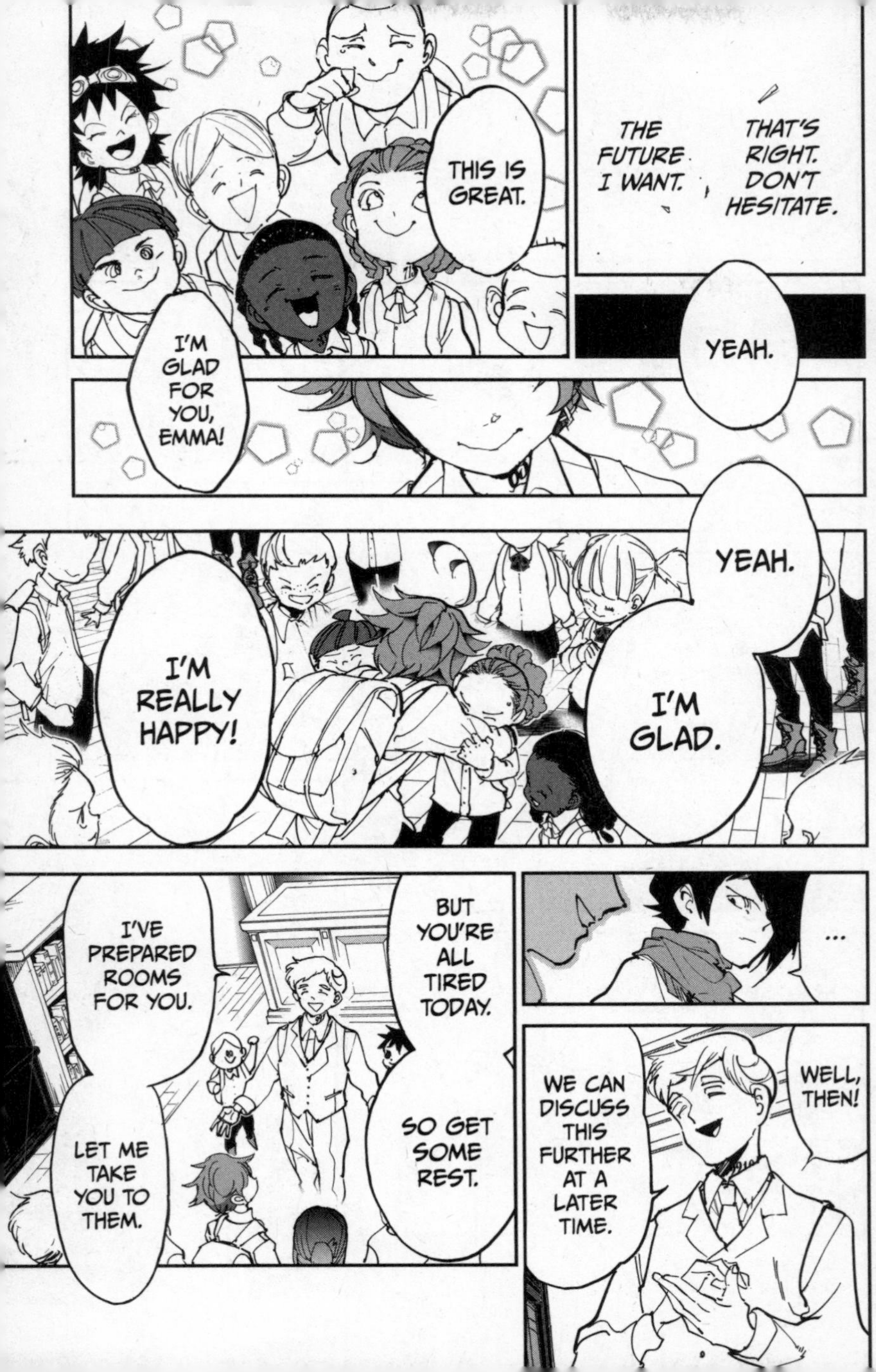
THAT'S RIGHT. DON'T HESITATE.
THE FUTURE I WANT.
THIS IS GREAT.
I'M GLAD FOR YOU, EMMA!
YEAH.
YEAH.
I'M GLAD.
I'M REALLY HAPPY!
...
WELL, THEN!
WE CAN DISCUSS THIS FURTHER AT A LATER TIME.
BUT YOU'RE ALL TIRED TODAY.
SO GET SOME REST.
I'VE PREPARED ROOMS FOR YOU.
LET ME TAKE YOU TO THEM.

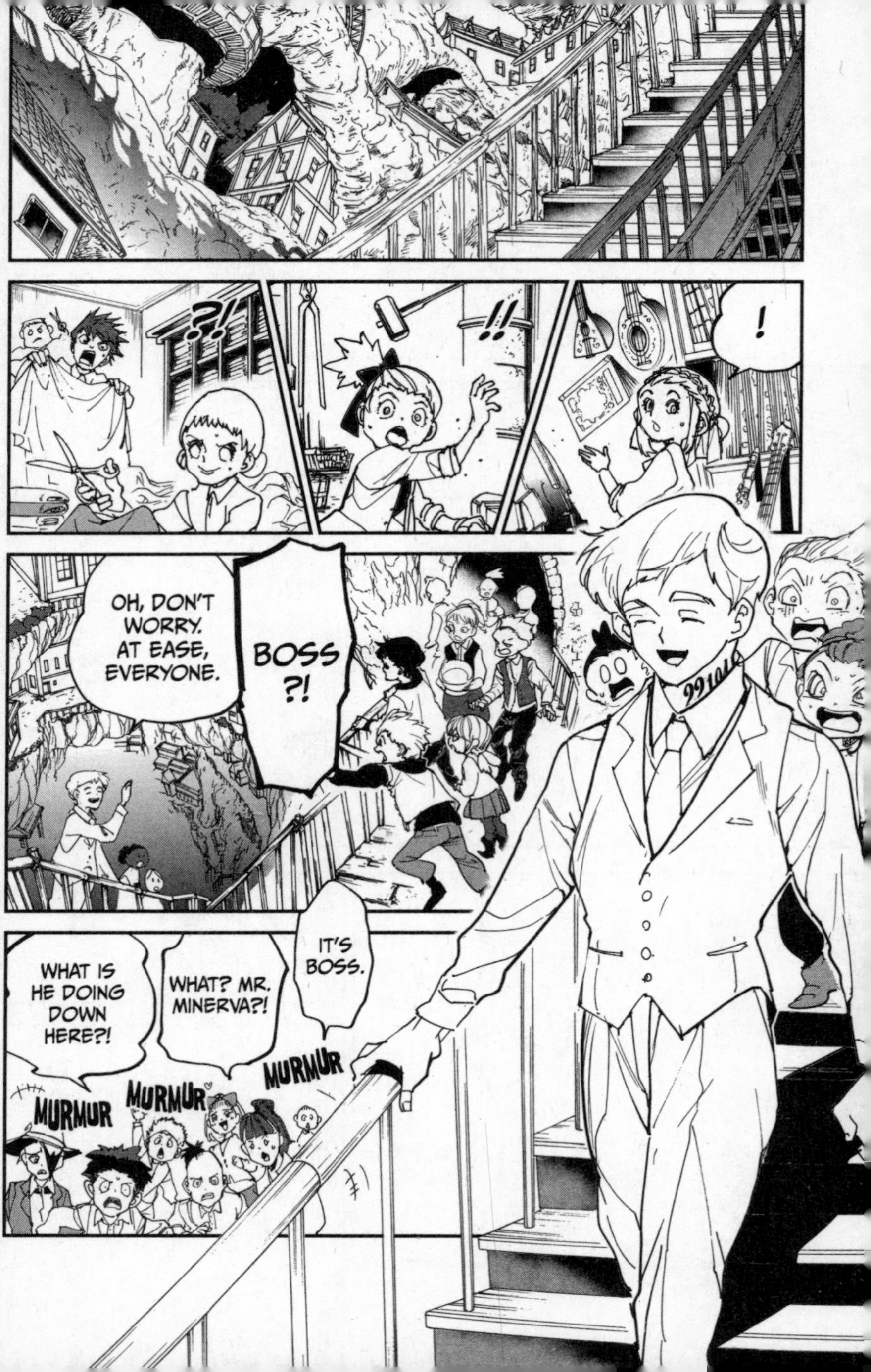
!
!!
?!
BOSS ?!
OH, DON'T WORRY. AT EASE, EVERYONE.
IT'S BOSS.
WHAT? MR. MINERVA?!
WHAT IS HE DOING DOWN HERE?!
MURMUR
MURMUR
MURMUR

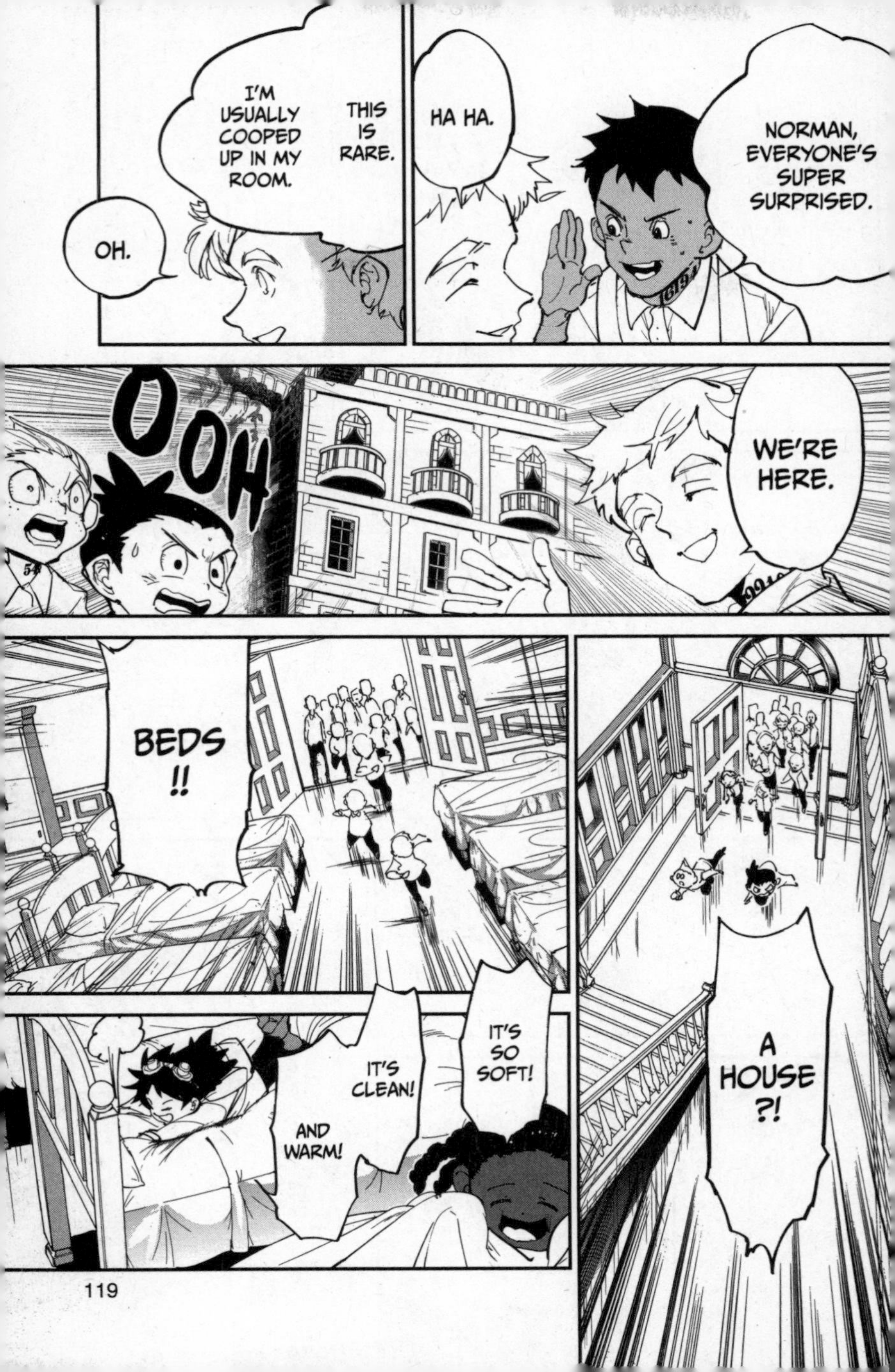
NORMAN, EVERYONE'S SUPER SURPRISED.
HA HA.
THIS IS RARE.
I'M USUALLY COOPED UP IN MY ROOM.
OH.
WE'RE HERE.
OOH
A HOUSE ?!
BEDS !!
IT'S SO SOFT!
IT'S CLEAN!
AND WARM!

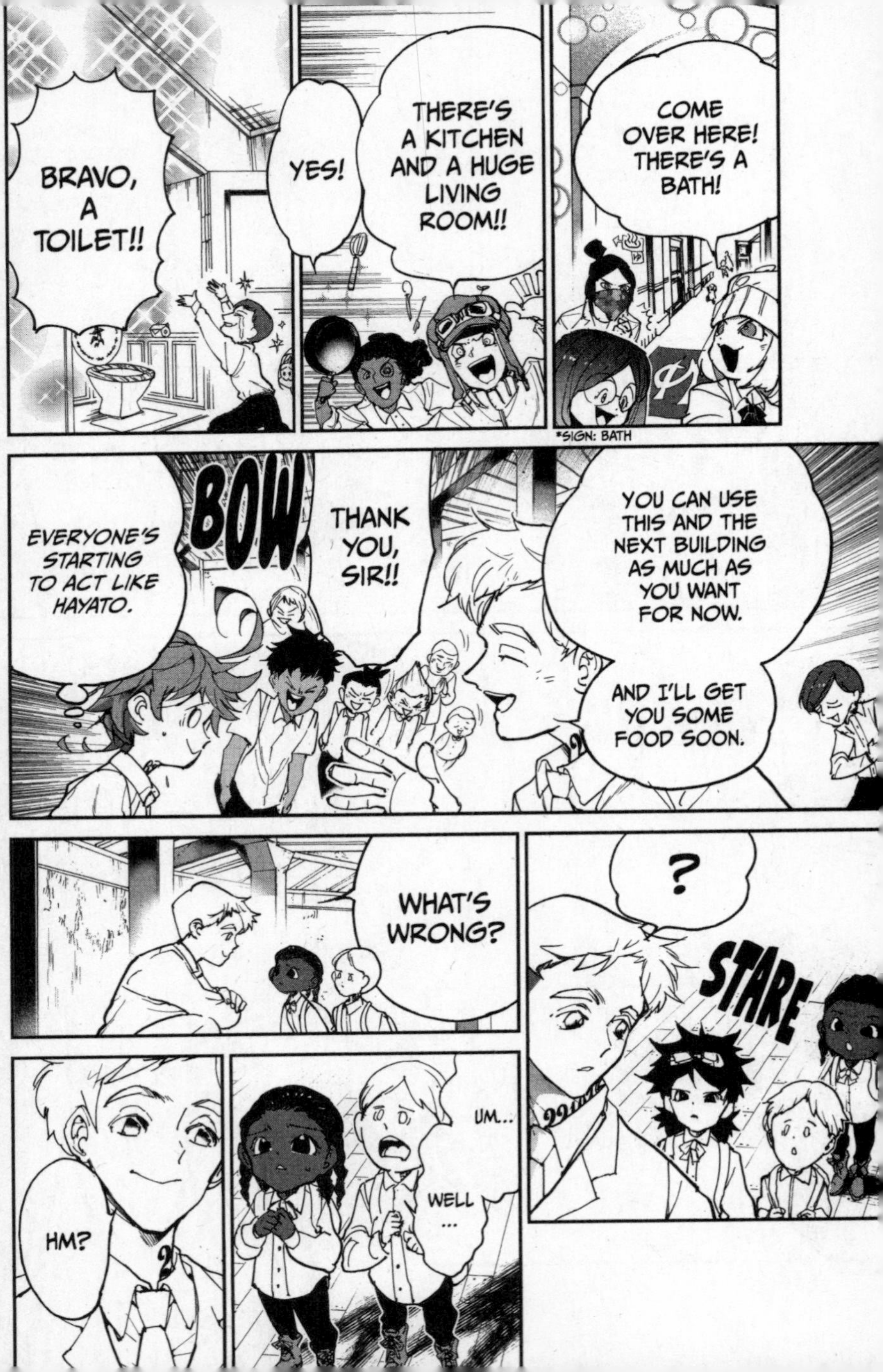
COME OVER HERE! THERE'S A BATH!
*SIGN: BATH
THERE'S A KITCHEN AND A HUGE LIVING ROOM!!
YES!
BRAVO, A TOILET!!
YOU CAN USE THIS AND THE NEXT BUILDING AS MUCH AS YOU WANT FOR NOW.
AND I'LL GET YOU SOME FOOD SOON.
THANK YOU, SIR!!
BOW
EVERYONE'S STARTING TO ACT LIKE HAYATO.
?
STARE
WHAT'S WRONG?
UM...
WELL ...
HM?

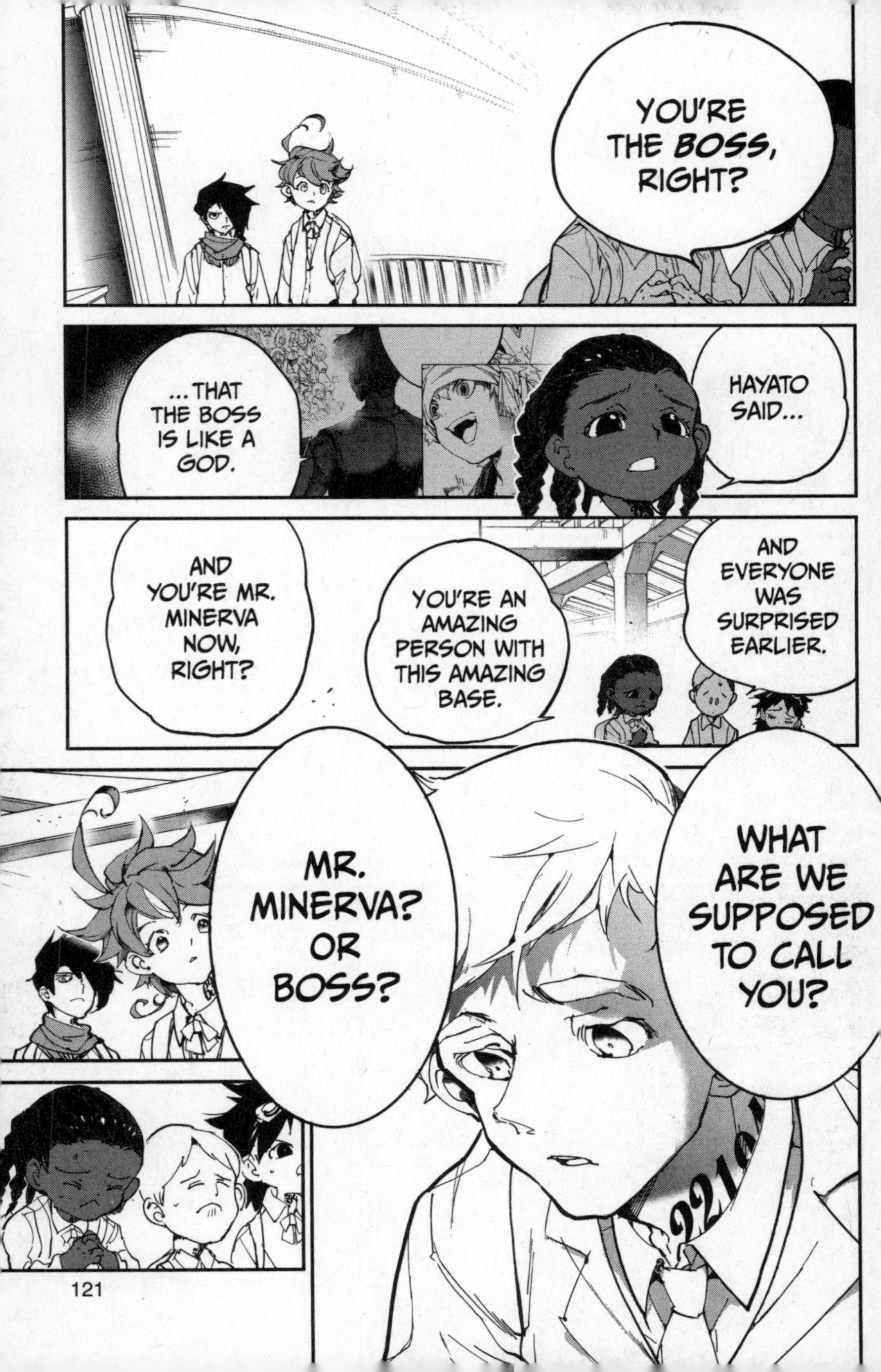
YOU'RE THE BOSS, RIGHT?
HAYATO SAID...
...THAT THE BOSS IS LIKE A GOD.
AND EVERYONE WAS SURPRISED EARLIER.
YOU'RE AN AMAZING PERSON WITH THIS AMAZING BASE.
AND YOU'RE MR. MINERVA NOW, RIGHT?
WHAT ARE WE SUPPOSED TO CALL YOU?
MR. MINERVA? OR BOSS?
22194

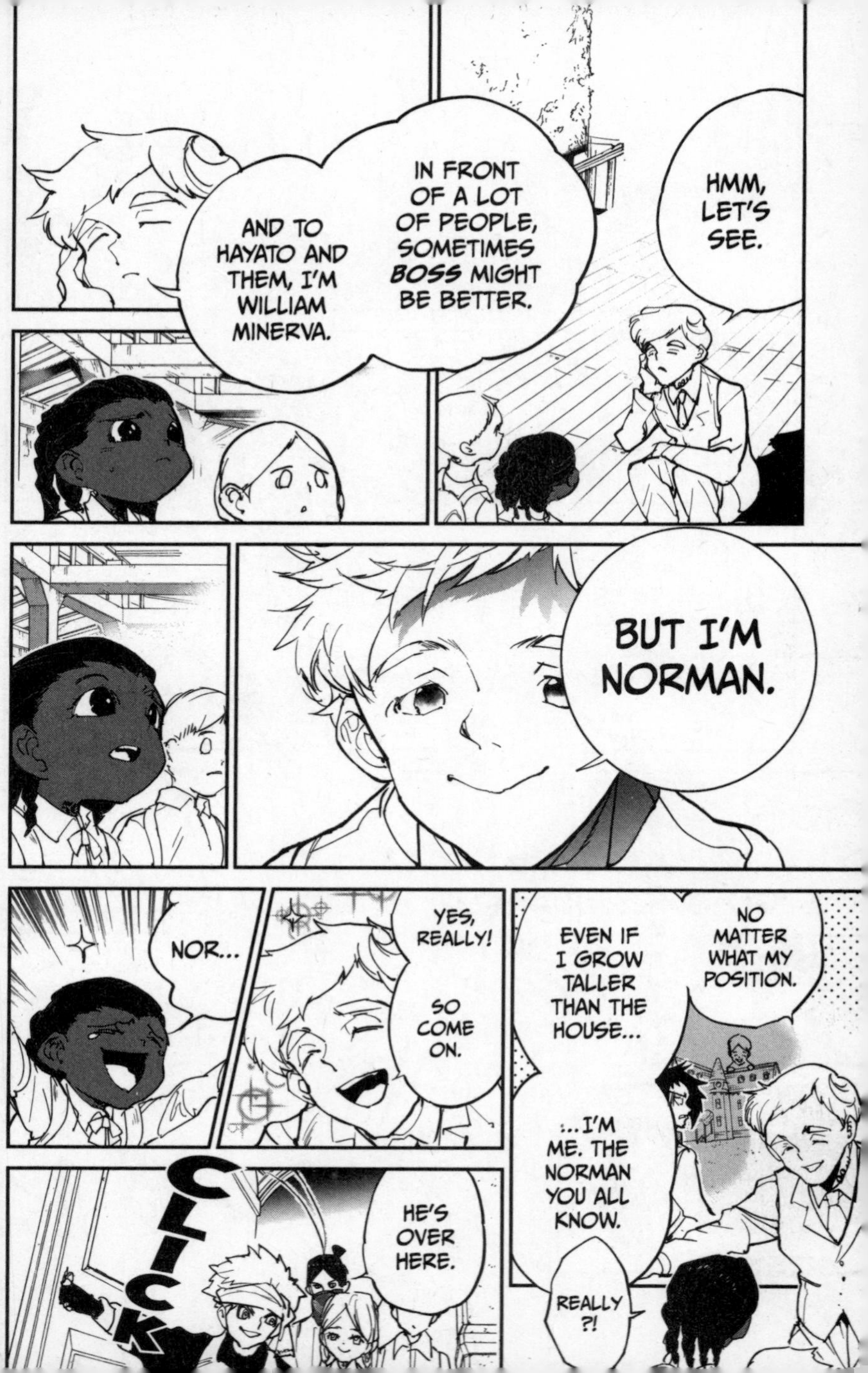
HMM, LET'S SEE.
IN FRONT OF A LOT OF PEOPLE, SOMETIMES *BOSS* MIGHT BE BETTER.
AND TO HAYATO AND THEM, I'M WILLIAM MINERVA.
BUT I'M NORMAN.
NO MATTER WHAT MY POSITION.
EVEN IF I GROW TALLER THAN THE HOUSE...
...I'M ME. THE NORMAN YOU ALL KNOW.
REALLY?!
YES, REALLY!
SO COME ON.
NOR...
HE'S OVER HERE.
CLICK

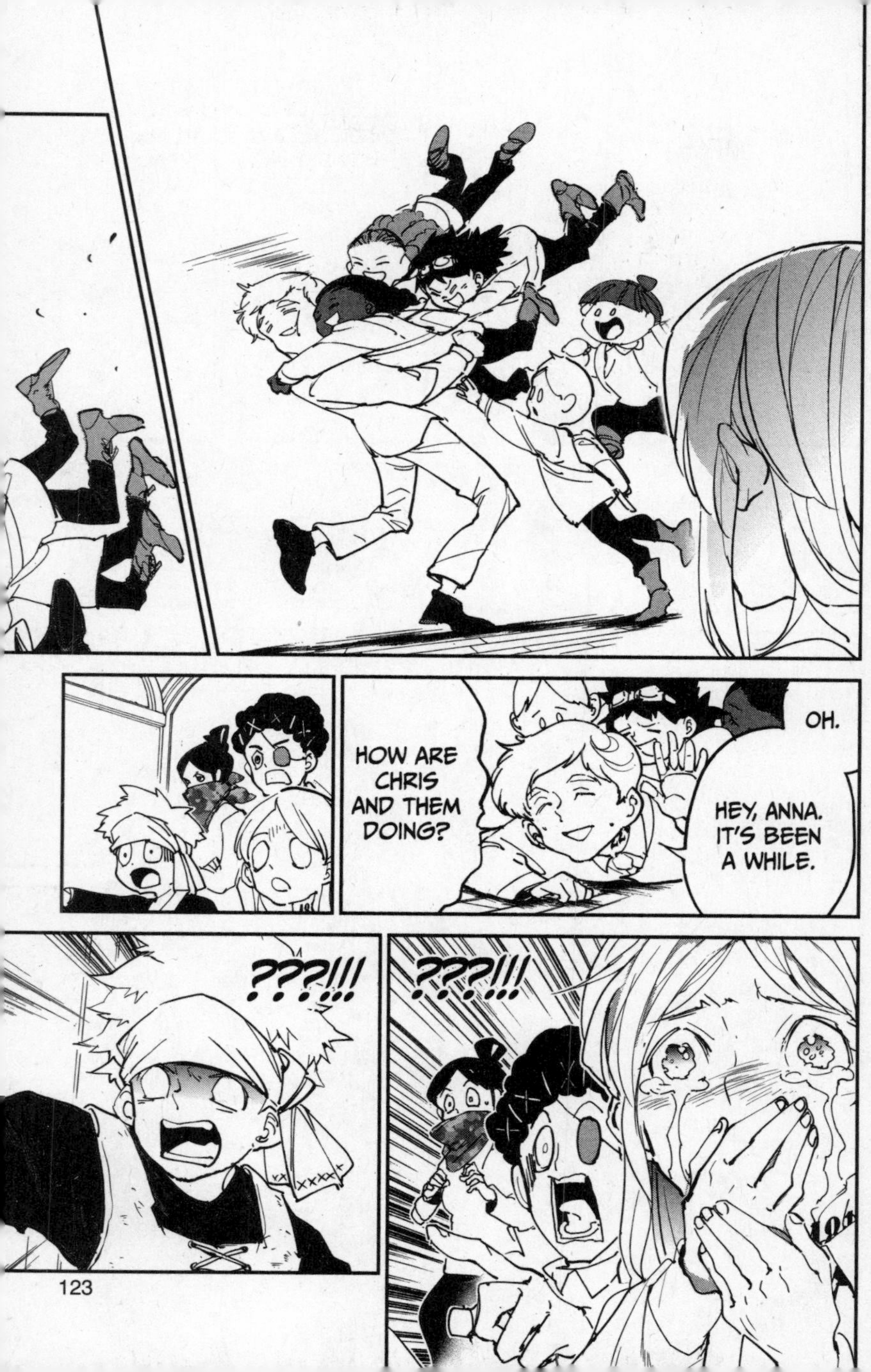
OH.
HEY, ANNA. IT'S BEEN A WHILE.
HOW ARE CHRIS AND THEM DOING?
???!!!
???!!!

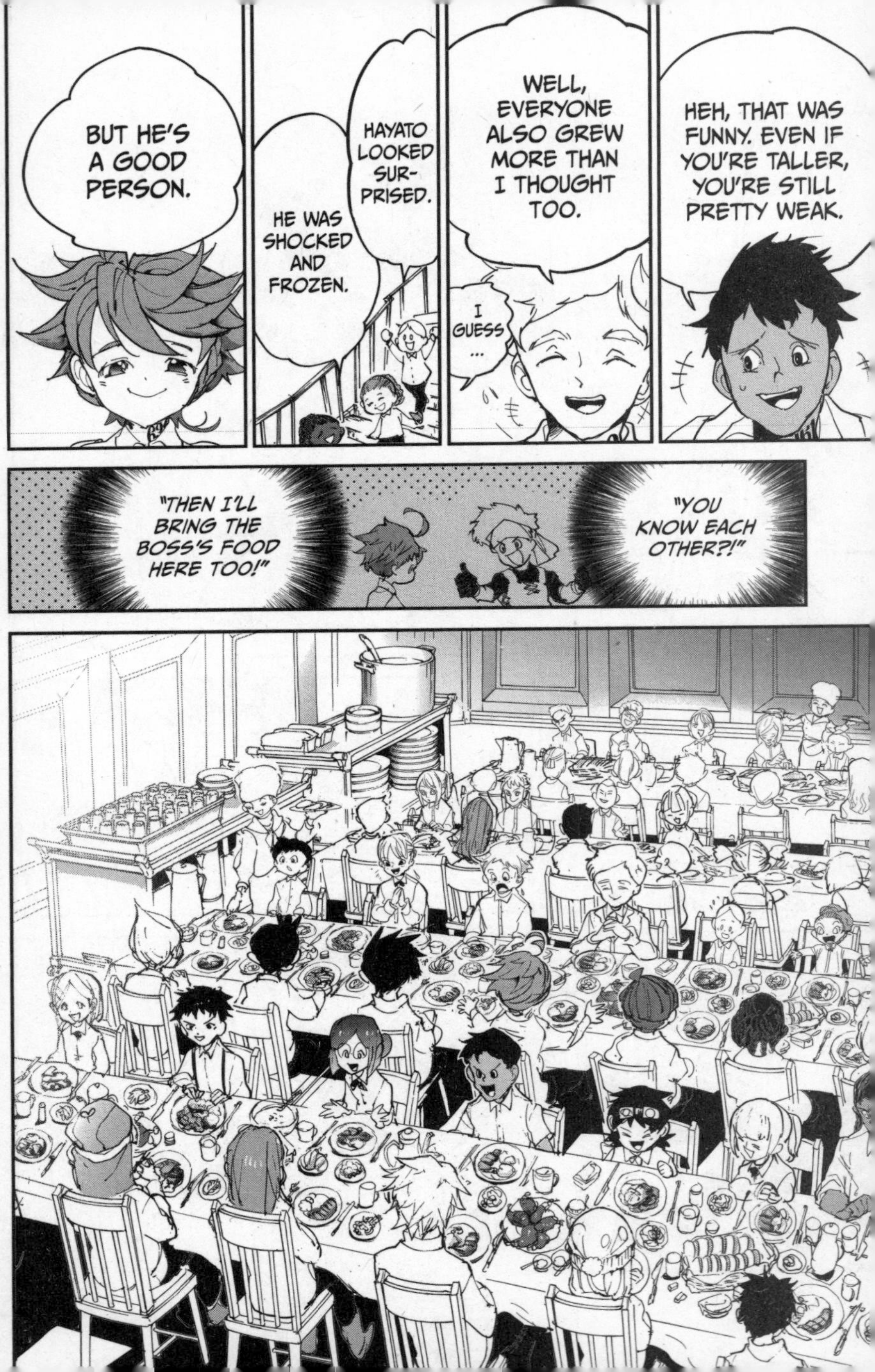
HEH, THAT WAS FUNNY. EVEN IF YOU'RE TALLER, YOU'RE STILL PRETTY WEAK.
WELL, EVERYONE ALSO GREW MORE THAN I THOUGHT TOO.
I GUESS...
HAYATO LOOKED SUR-PRISED.
HE WAS SHOCKED AND FROZEN.
BUT HE'S A GOOD PERSON.
"YOU KNOW EACH OTHER?!"
"THEN I'LL BRING THE BOSS'S FOOD HERE TOO!"

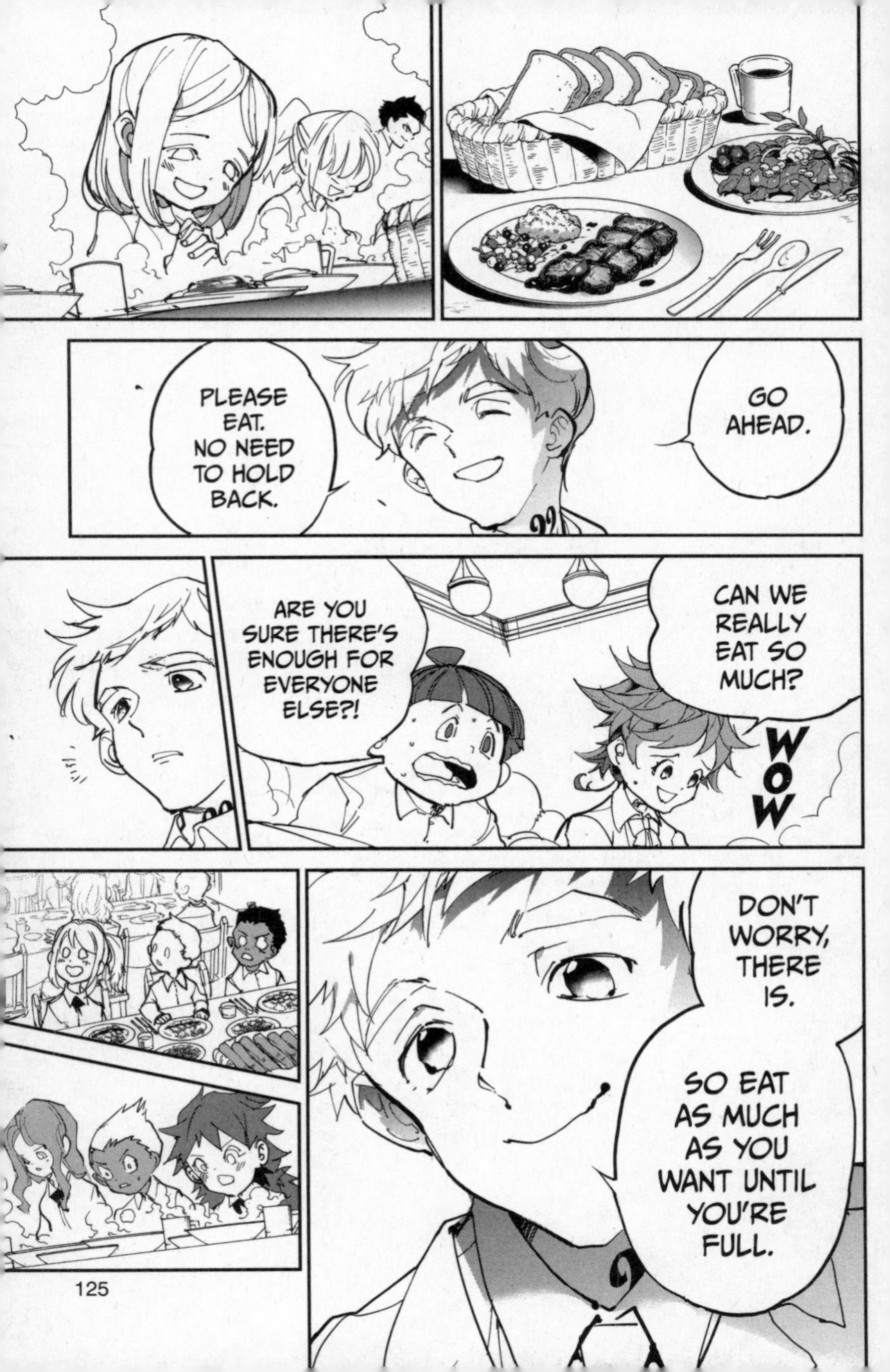
GO AHEAD.
PLEASE EAT. NO NEED TO HOLD BACK.
CAN WE REALLY EAT SO MUCH?
WOW
ARE YOU SURE THERE'S ENOUGH FOR EVERYONE ELSE?!
DON'T WORRY, THERE IS.
SO EAT AS MUCH AS YOU WANT UNTIL YOU'RE FULL.

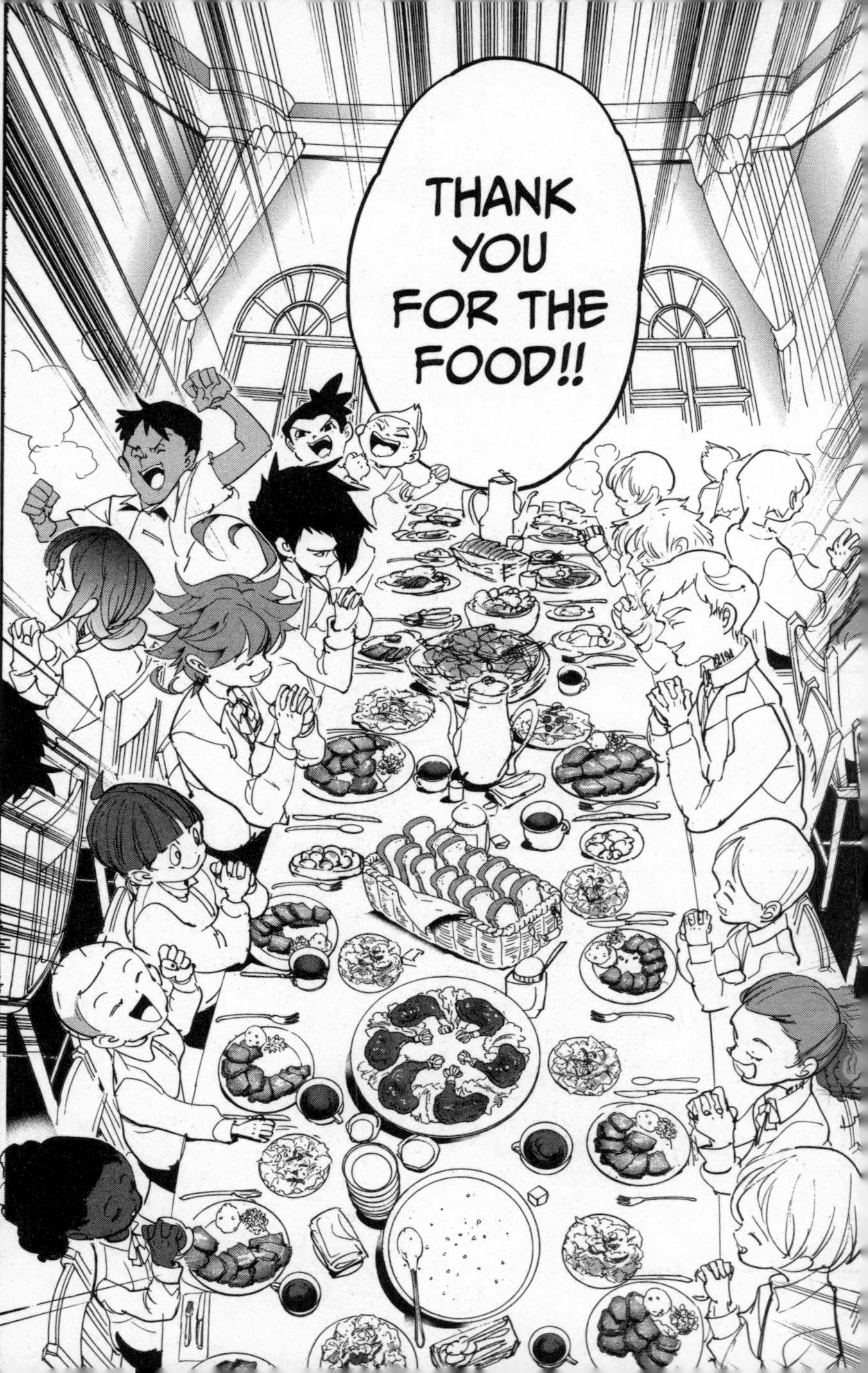
THANK YOU FOR THE FOOD!!

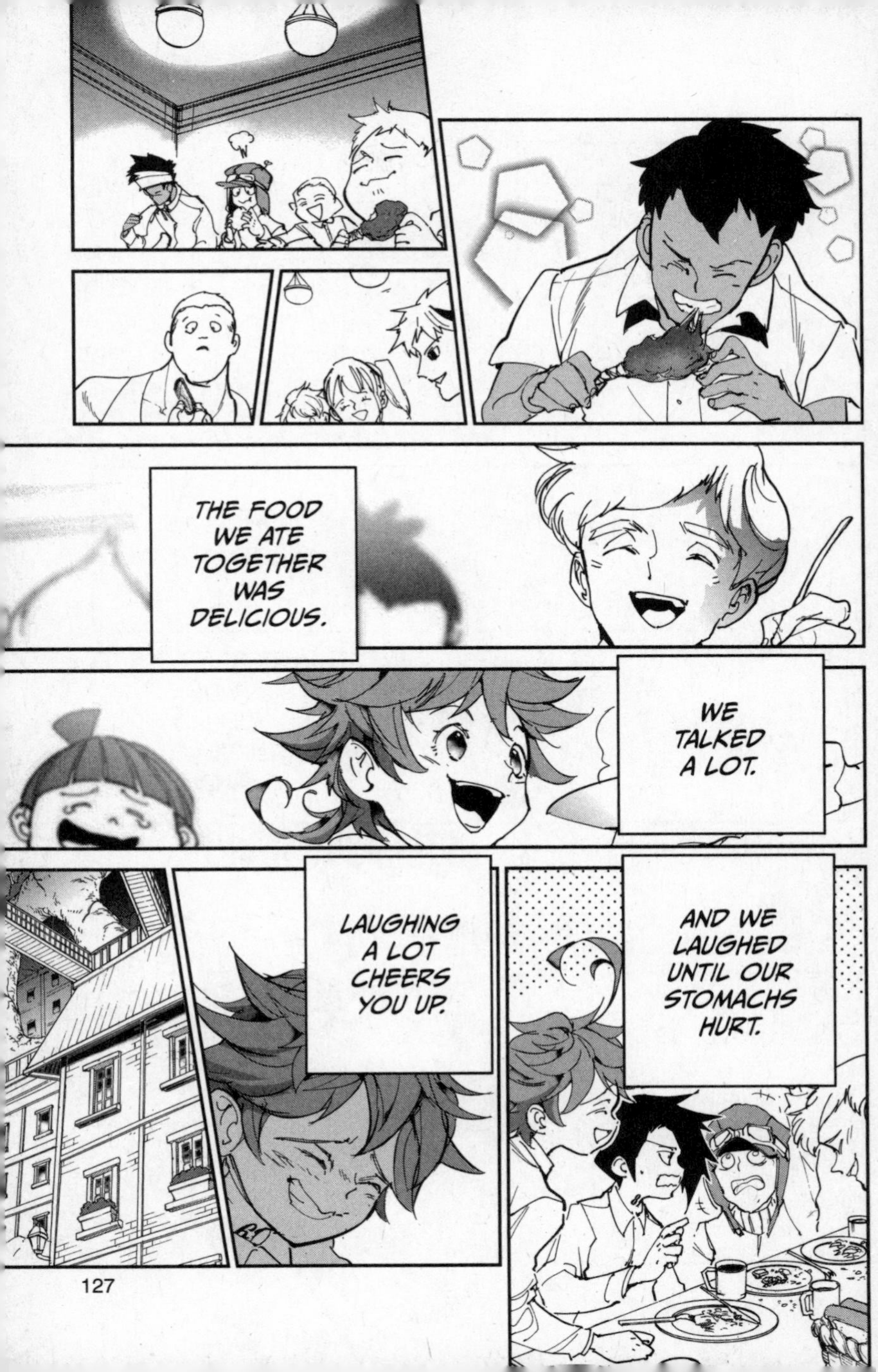
THE FOOD WE ATE TOGETHER WAS DELICIOUS.
WE TALKED A LOT.
AND WE LAUGHED UNTIL OUR STOMACHS HURT.
LAUGHING A LOT CHEERS YOU UP.

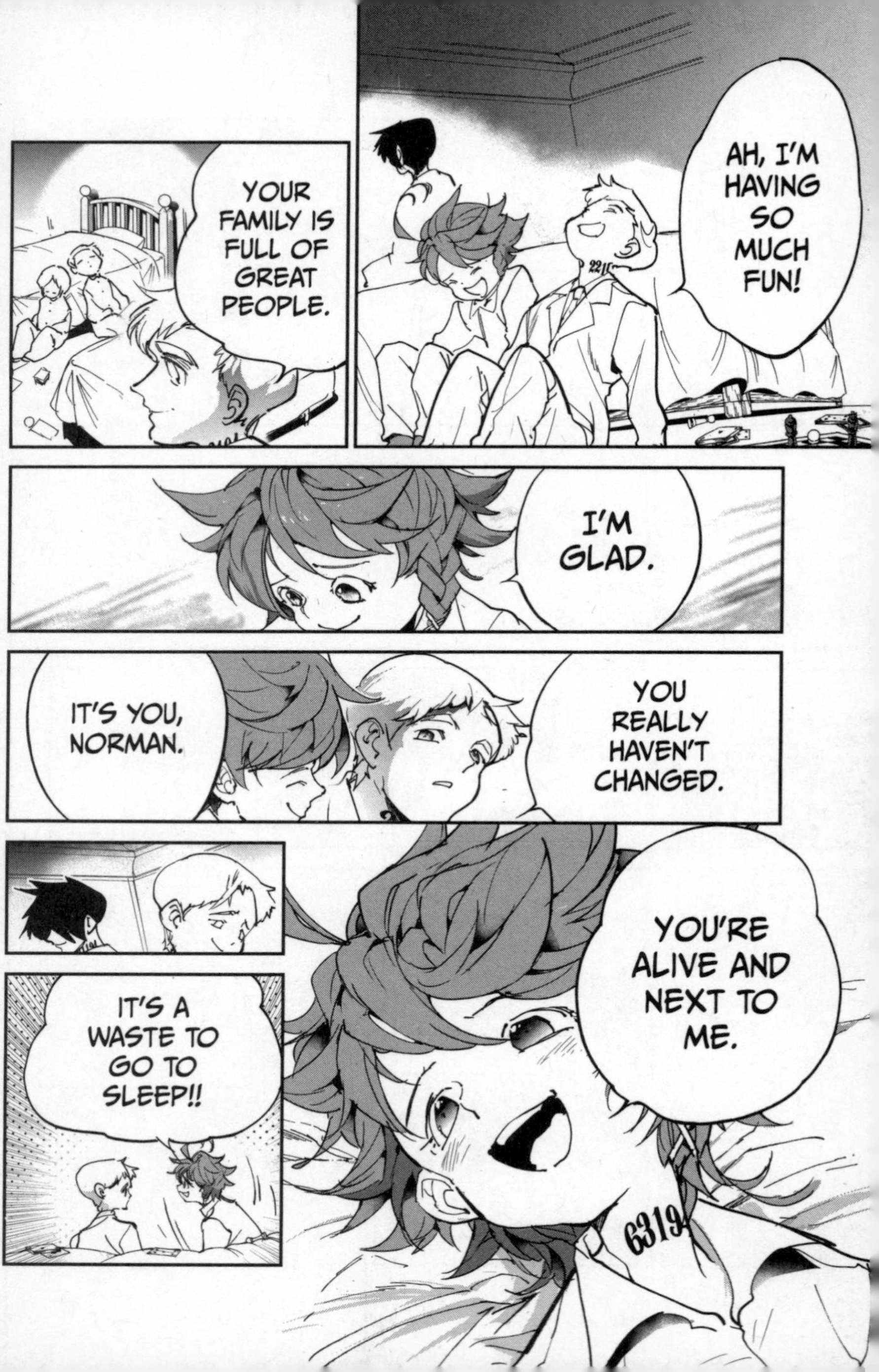
AH, I'M HAVING SO MUCH FUN!
YOUR FAMILY IS FULL OF GREAT PEOPLE.
I'M GLAD.
YOU REALLY HAVEN'T CHANGED.
IT'S YOU, NORMAN.
YOU'RE ALIVE AND NEXT TO ME.
6319
IT'S A WASTE TO GO TO SLEEP!!

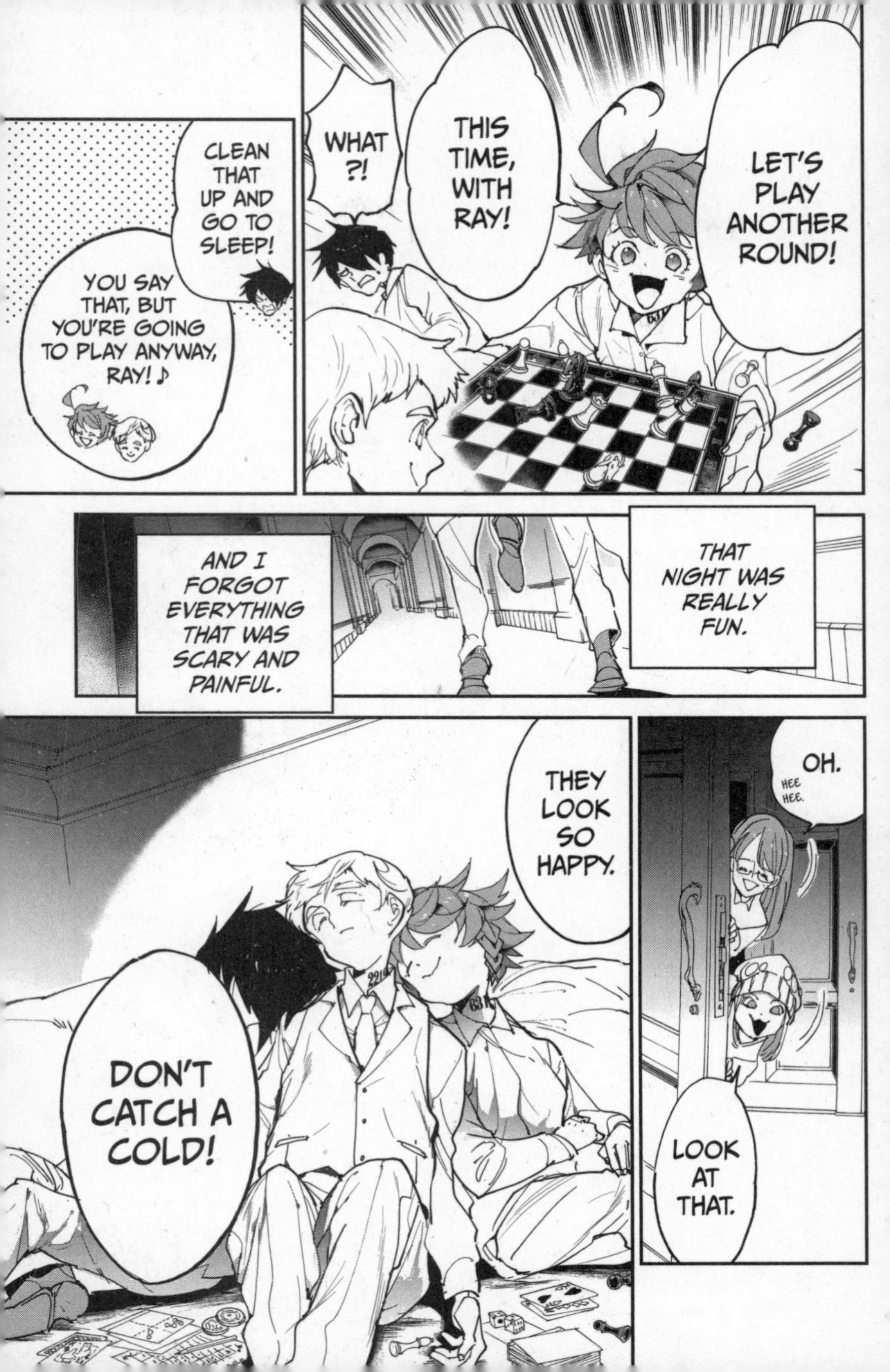
LET'S PLAY ANOTHER ROUND!
THIS TIME, WITH RAY!
WHAT?!
CLEAN THAT UP AND GO TO SLEEP!
YOU SAY THAT, BUT YOU'RE GOING TO PLAY ANYWAY, RAY! ♪
THAT NIGHT WAS REALLY FUN.
AND I FORGOT EVERYTHING THAT WAS SCARY AND PAINFUL.
OH.
HEE HEE.
LOOK AT THAT.
THEY LOOK SO HAPPY.
DON'T CATCH A COLD!

POWER

YAY
WHOA
TADAA
!!
TA DAAAA
HOW DO THEY DO IT ?!

WHAT'S THE MATTER, BOSS?
NOTHING.
?
I'M GONNA START LIFTING WEIGHTS.

SIDE STORY 13...FIN

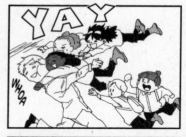

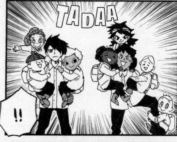

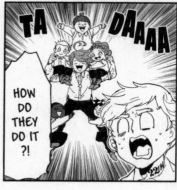

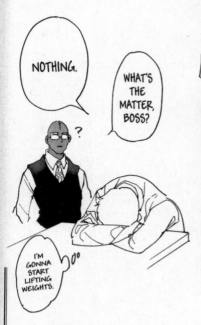

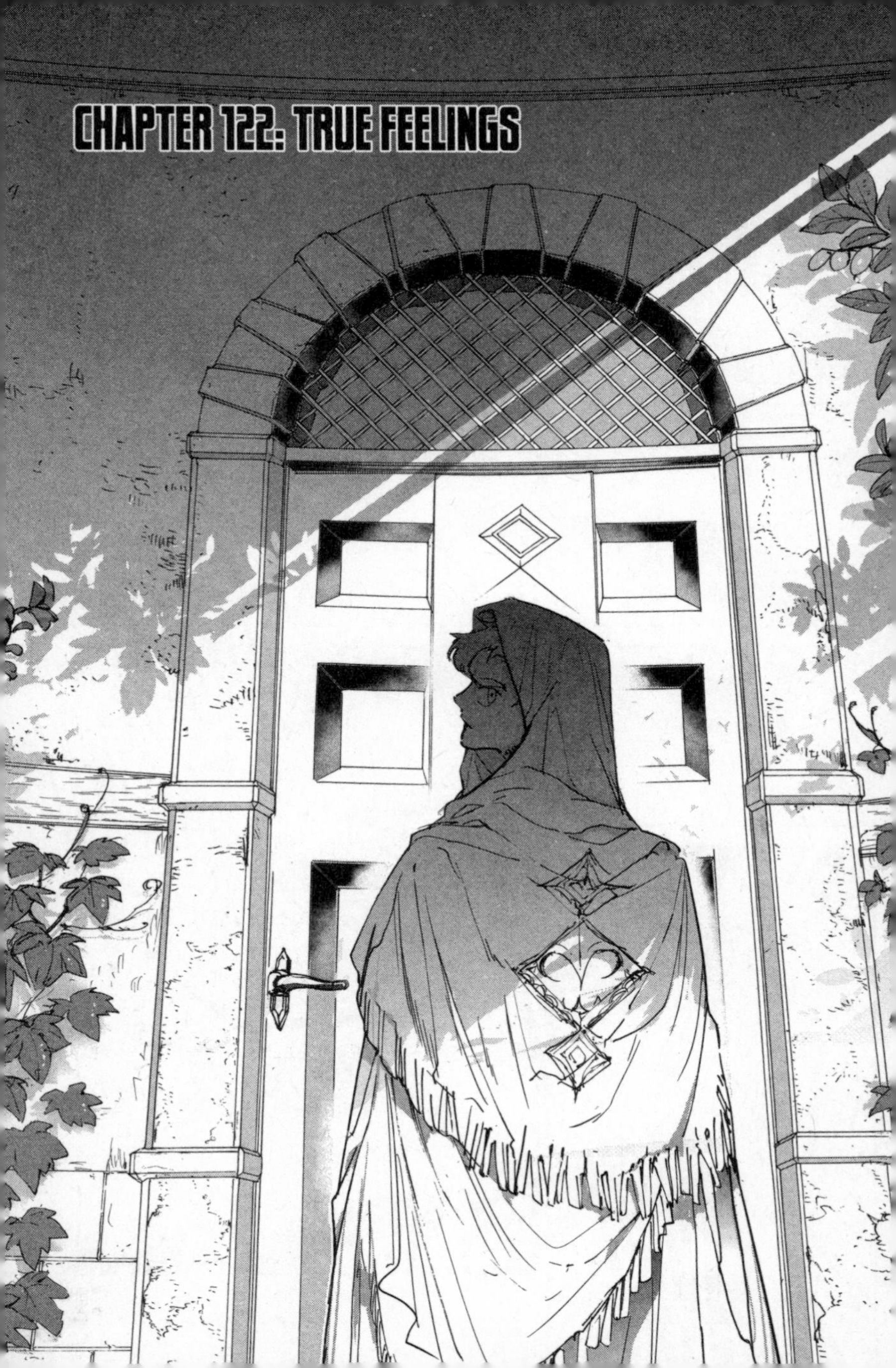
CHAPTER 122: TRUE FEELINGS

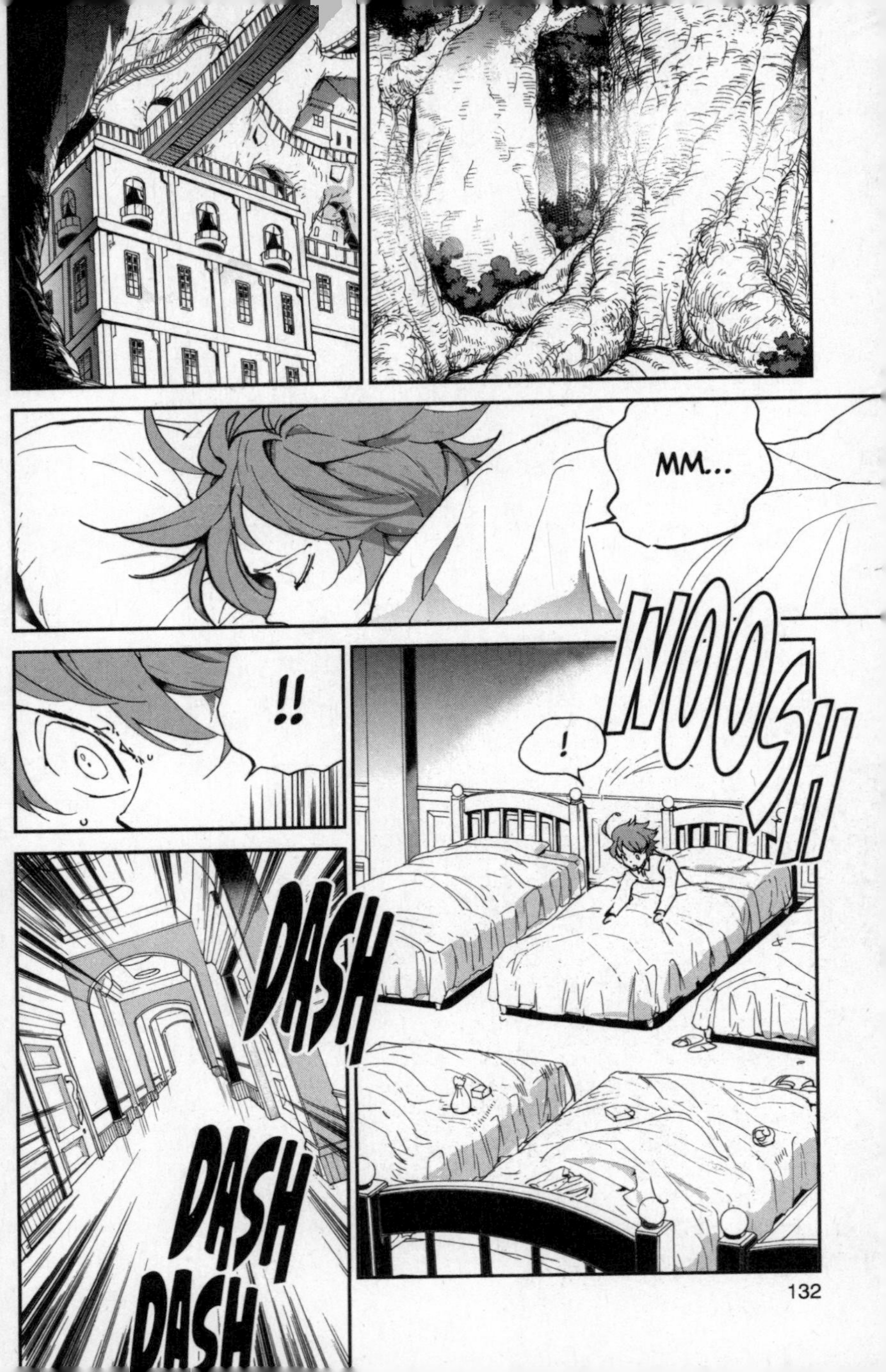
MM...
!
WOOSH
!!
DASH
DASH
DASH

OH, MORNING, EMMA.

GOOD MORN- ING!

VOOSH

I'M SORRY! I OVER- SLEPT!!

*FIRST TIME OVER- SLEEPING, EVER

WE DID TOO.

HEE HEE.

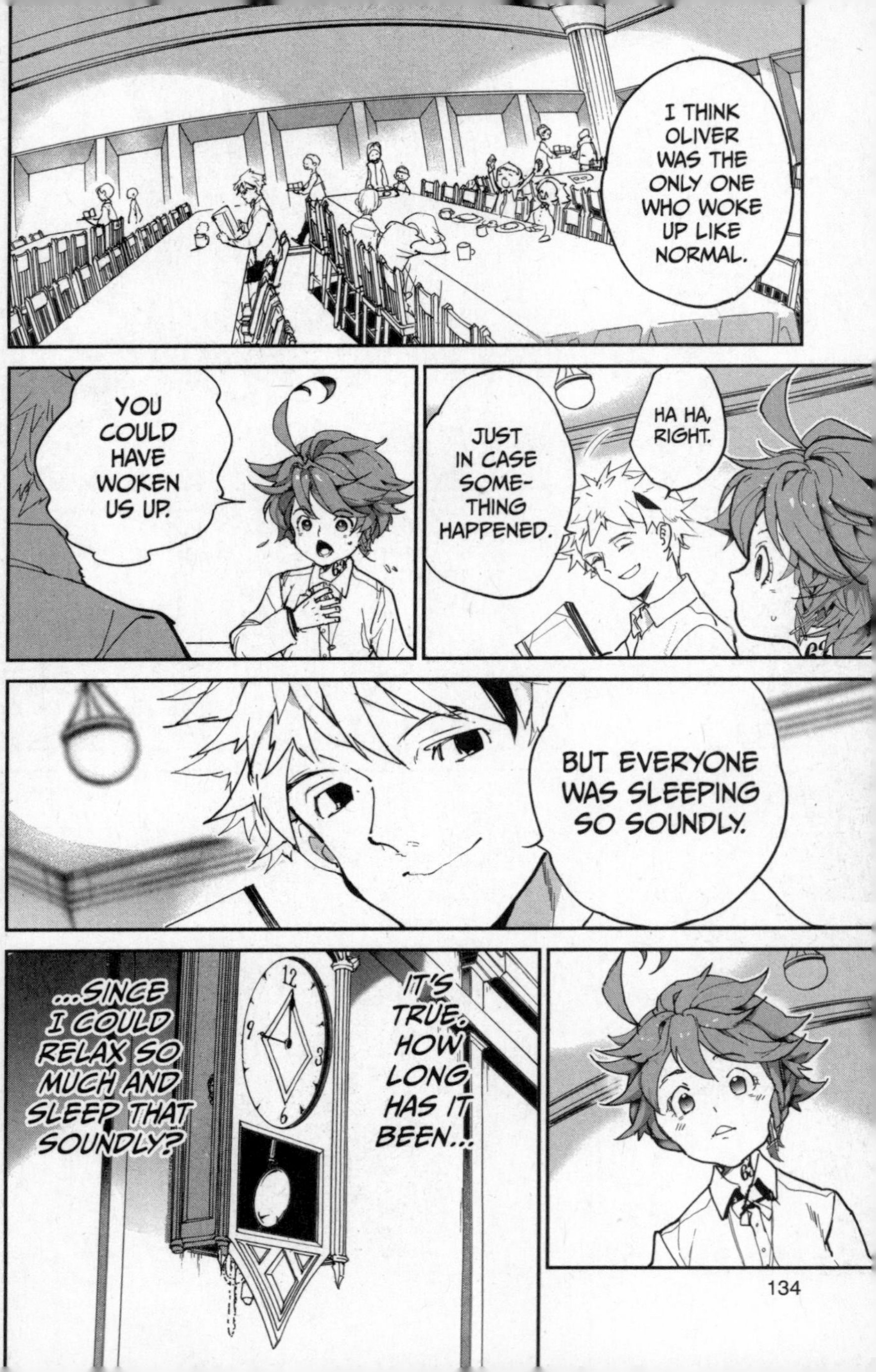

I THINK OLIVER WAS THE ONLY ONE WHO WOKE UP LIKE NORMAL.
HA HA, RIGHT.
JUST IN CASE SOME- THING HAPPENED.
YOU COULD HAVE WOKEN US UP.
BUT EVERYONE WAS SLEEPING SO SOUNDLY.
IT'S TRUE. HOW LONG HAS IT BEEN...
...SINCE I COULD RELAX SO MUCH AND SLEEP THAT SOUNDLY?

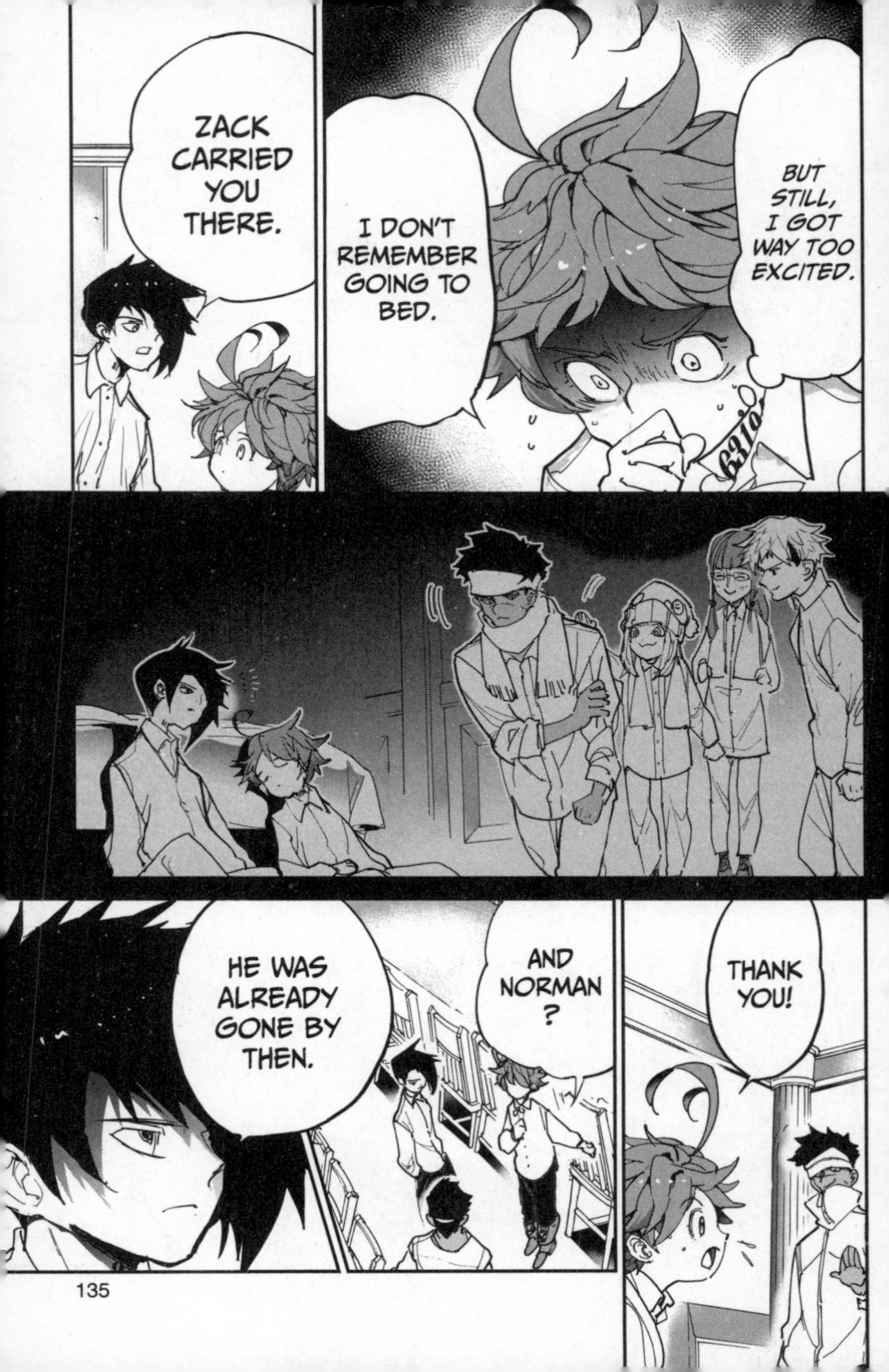
BUT STILL, I GOT WAY TOO EXCITED.
I DON'T REMEMBER GOING TO BED.
ZACK CARRIED YOU THERE.
THANK YOU!
AND NORMAN?
HE WAS ALREADY GONE BY THEN.

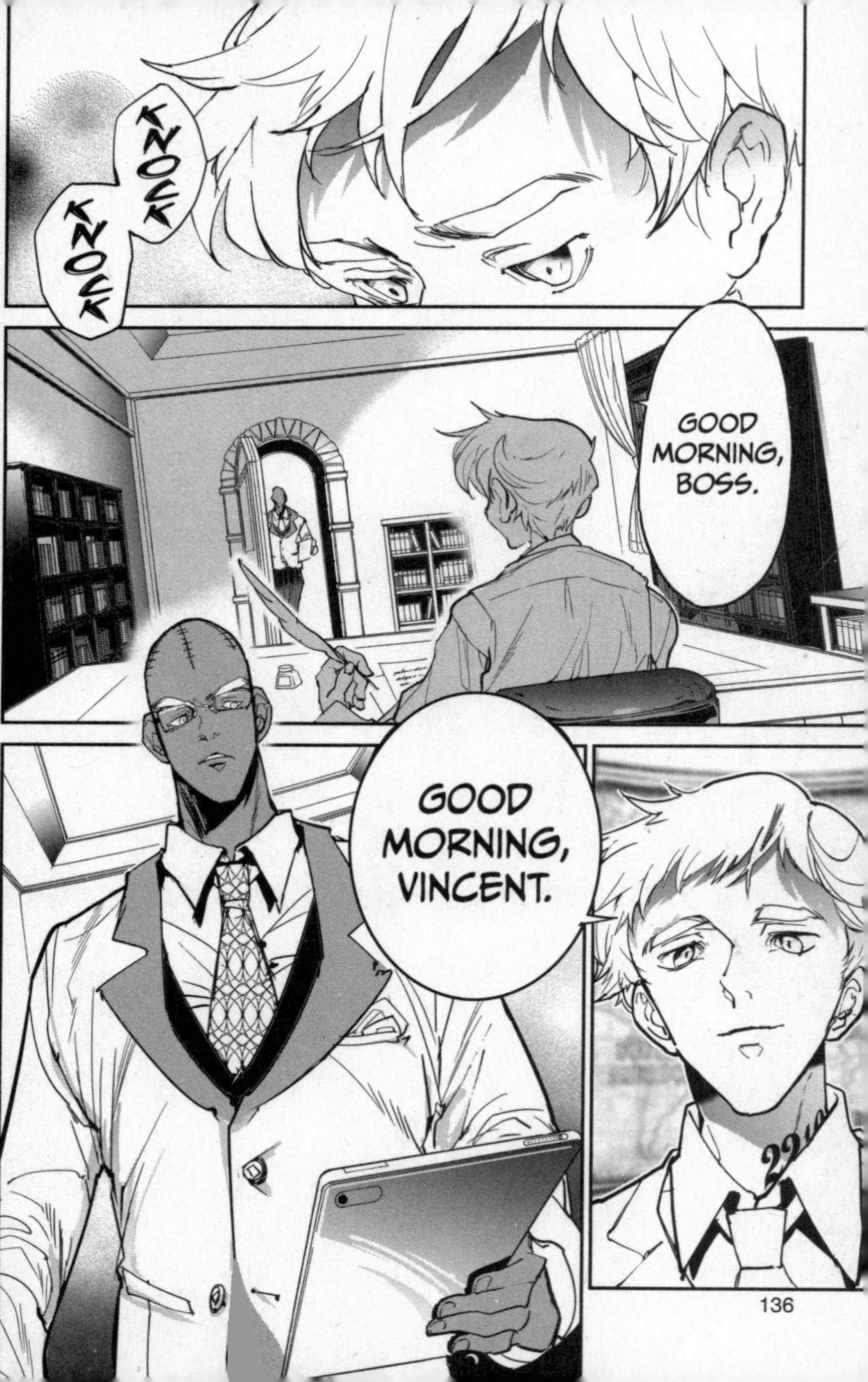
KNOCK KNOCK
GOOD MORNING, BOSS.
GOOD MORNING, VINCENT.

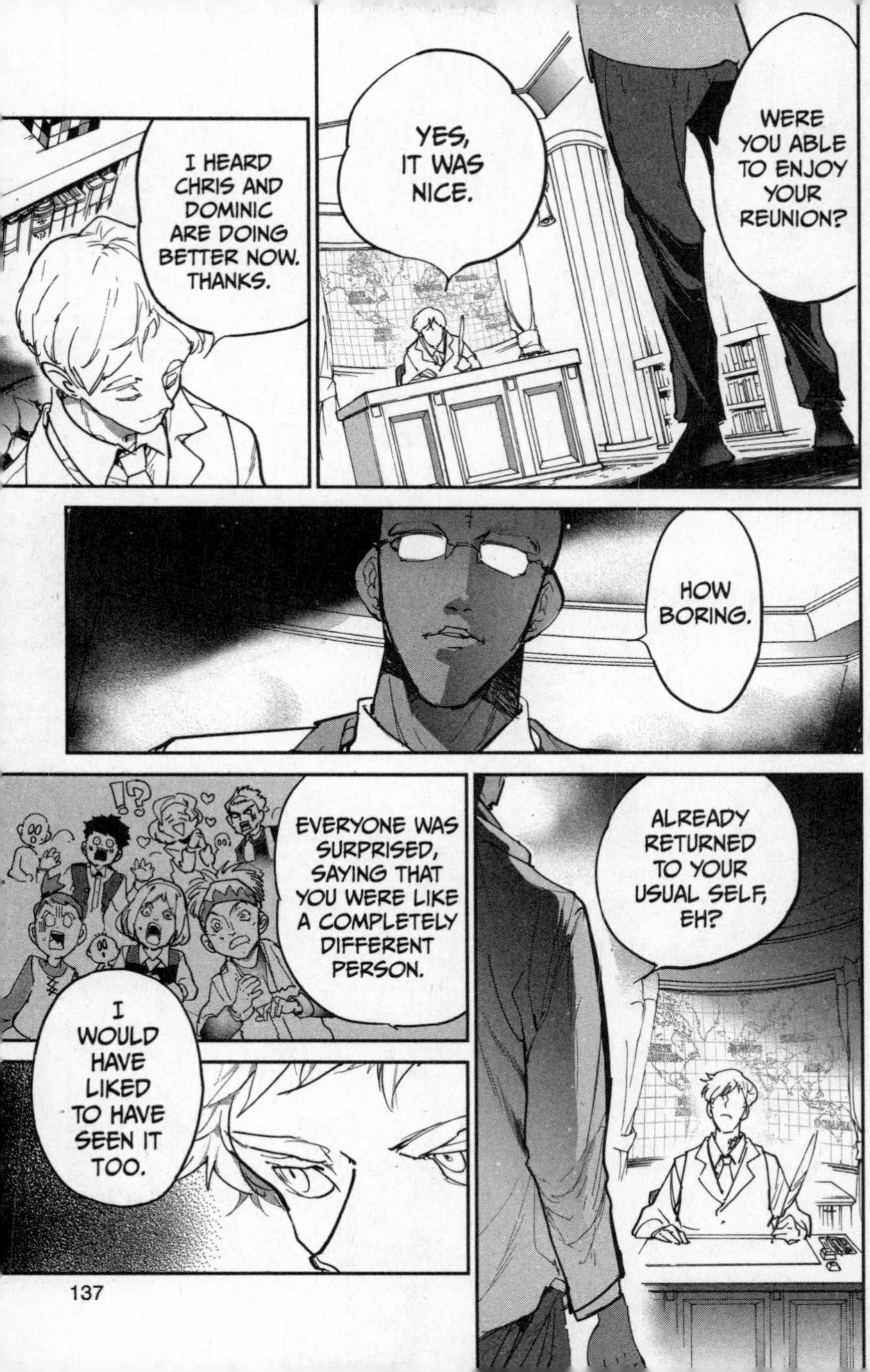
WERE YOU ABLE TO ENJOY YOUR REUNION?
YES, IT WAS NICE.
I HEARD CHRIS AND DOMINIC ARE DOING BETTER NOW. THANKS.
HOW BORING.
ALREADY RETURNED TO YOUR USUAL SELF, EH?
EVERYONE WAS SURPRISED, SAYING THAT YOU WERE LIKE A COMPLETELY DIFFERENT PERSON.
!?
I WOULD HAVE LIKED TO HAVE SEEN IT TOO.

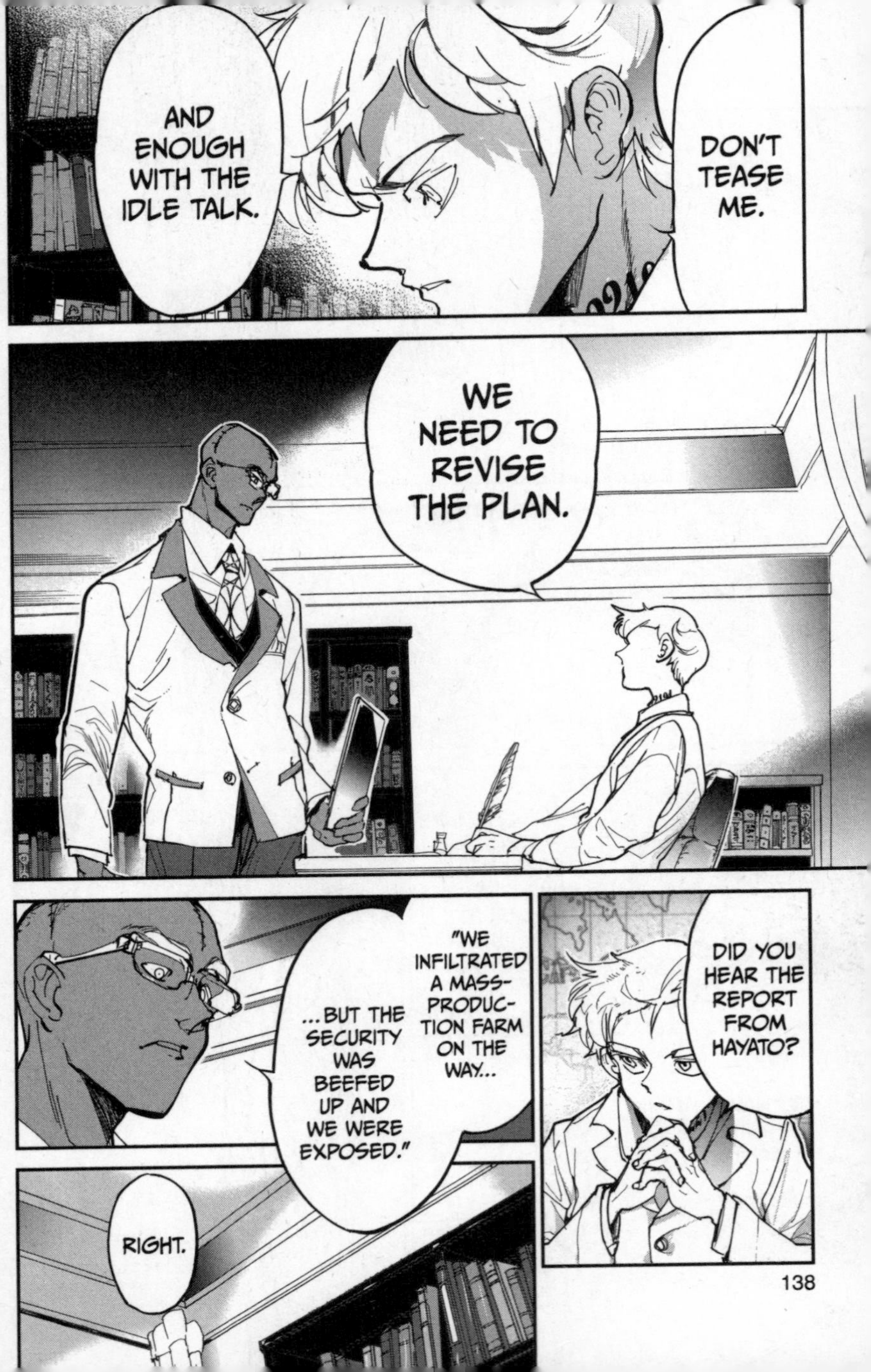
DON'T TEASE ME.
AND ENOUGH WITH THE IDLE TALK.
WE NEED TO REVISE THE PLAN.
DID YOU HEAR THE REPORT FROM HAYATO?
"WE INFILTRATED A MASS-PRODUCTION FARM ON THE WAY...
...BUT THE SECURITY WAS BEEFED UP AND WE WERE EXPOSED."
RIGHT.

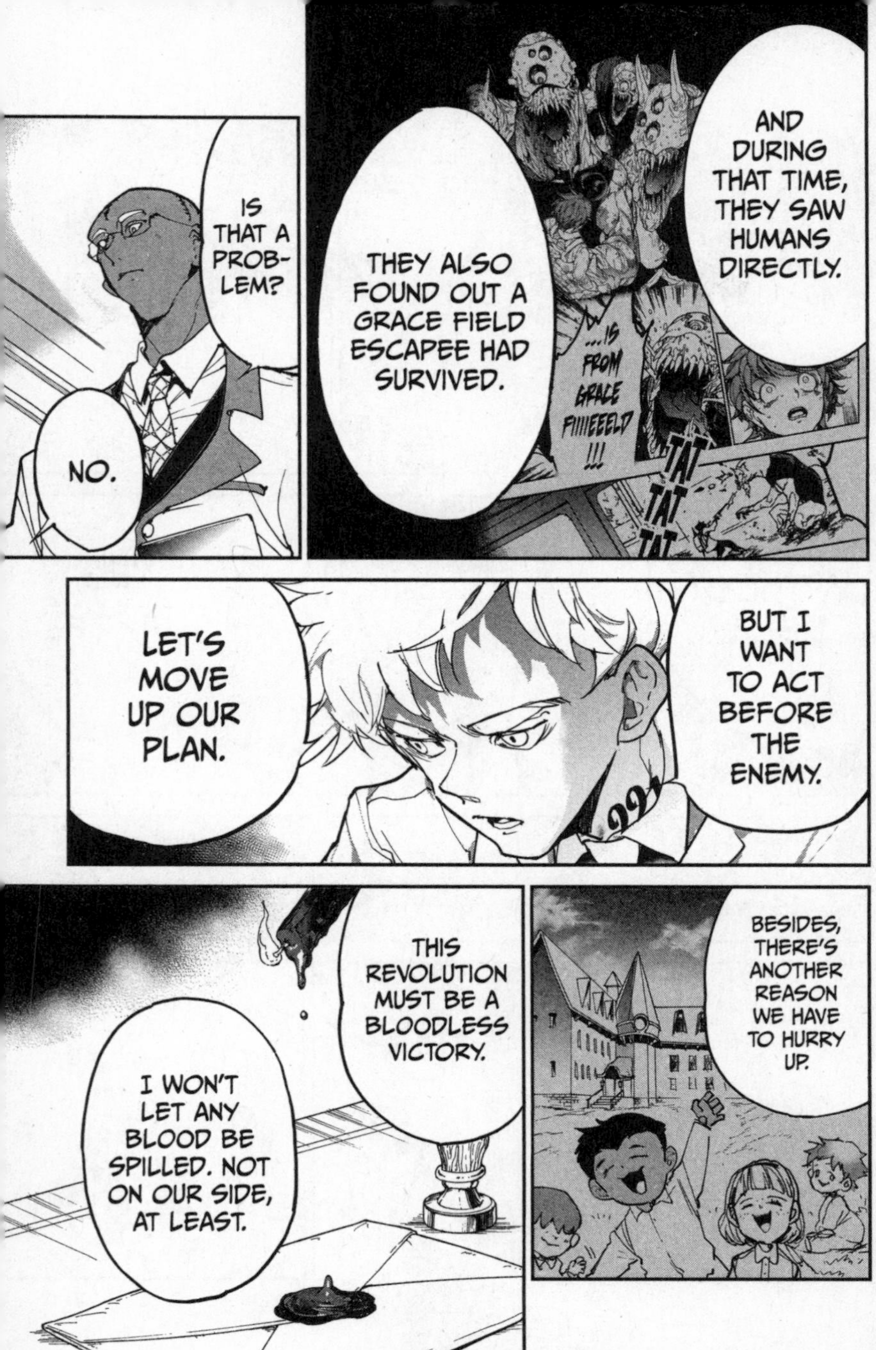
AND DURING THAT TIME, THEY SAW HUMANS DIRECTLY.
THEY ALSO FOUND OUT A GRACE FIELD ESCAPEE HAD SURVIVED.
...IS FROM GRACE FIIIIEEELD!!!
TAT TAT TAT
IS THAT A PROB-LEM?
NO.
BUT I WANT TO ACT BEFORE THE ENEMY.
LET'S MOVE UP OUR PLAN.
BESIDES, THERE'S ANOTHER REASON WE HAVE TO HURRY UP.
THIS REVOLUTION MUST BE A BLOODLESS VICTORY.
I WON'T LET ANY BLOOD BE SPILLED. NOT ON OUR SIDE, AT LEAST.

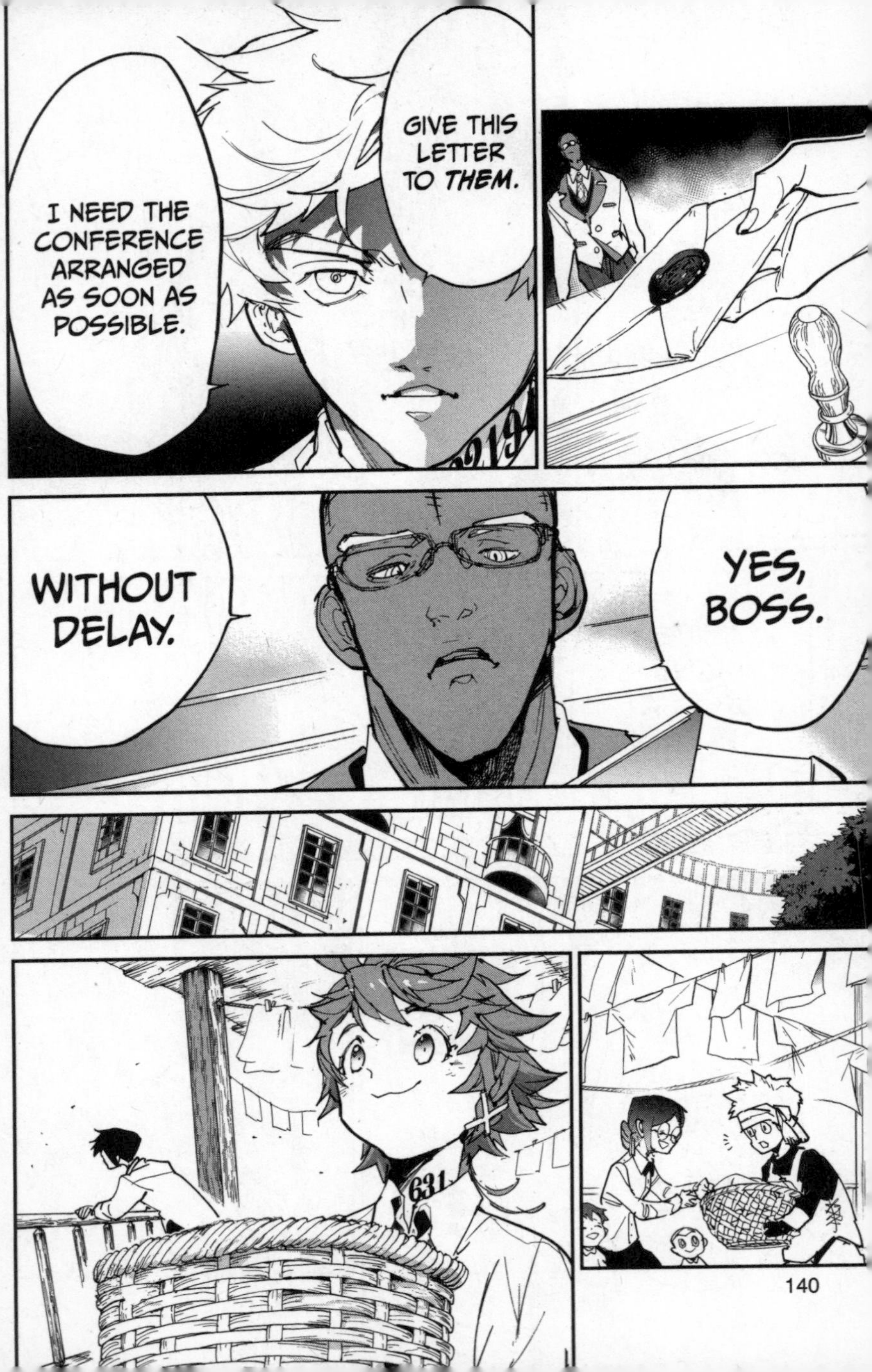
GIVE THIS LETTER TO *THEM*.
I NEED THE CONFERENCE ARRANGED AS SOON AS POSSIBLE.
YES, BOSS.
WITHOUT DELAY.

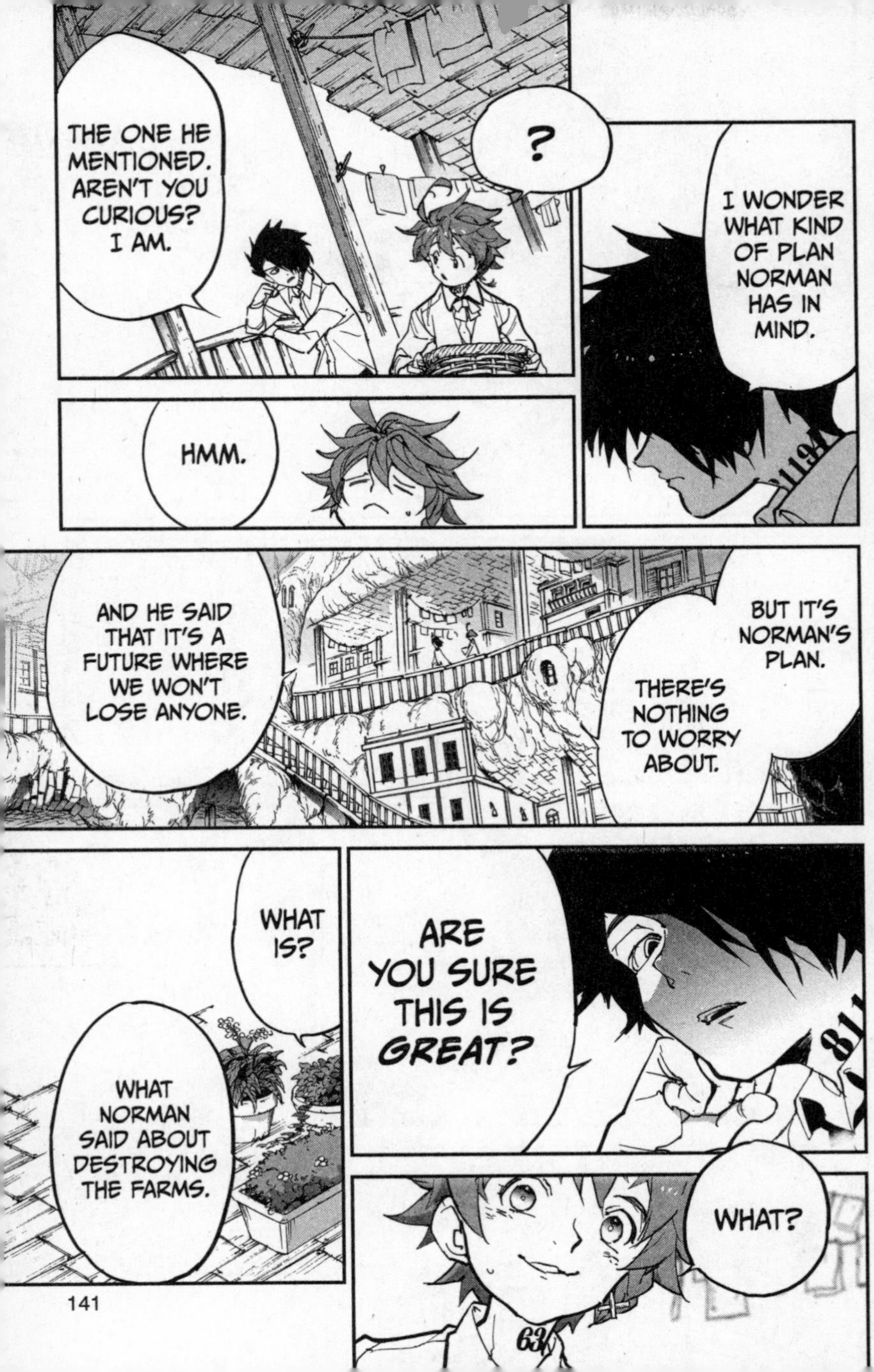
I WONDER WHAT KIND OF PLAN NORMAN HAS IN MIND.
?
THE ONE HE MENTIONED. AREN'T YOU CURIOUS? I AM.
HMM.
BUT IT'S NORMAN'S PLAN.
THERE'S NOTHING TO WORRY ABOUT.
AND HE SAID THAT IT'S A FUTURE WHERE WE WON'T LOSE ANYONE.
ARE YOU SURE THIS IS *GREAT?*
WHAT?
WHAT IS?
WHAT NORMAN SAID ABOUT DESTROYING THE FARMS.

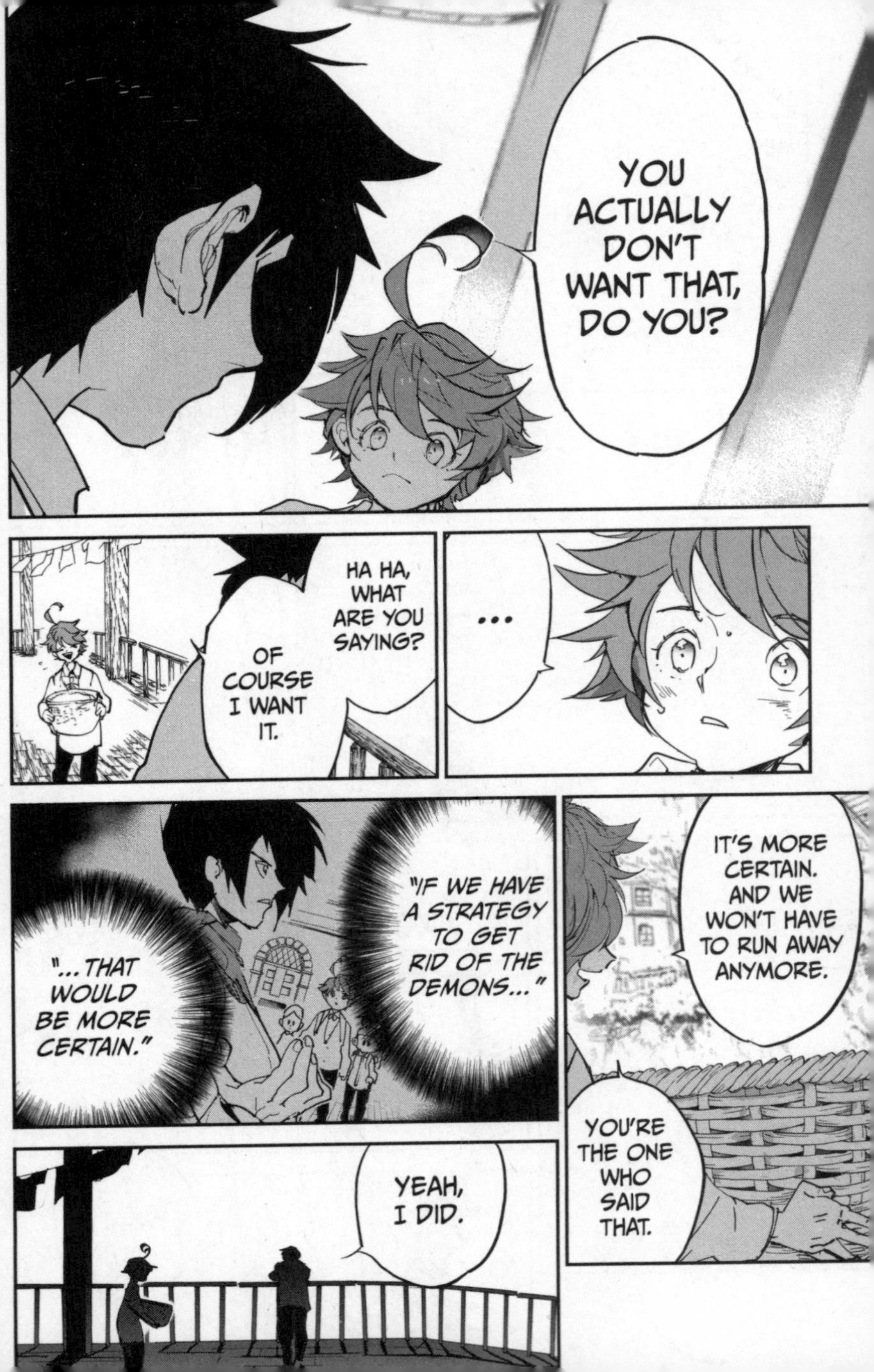
YOU ACTUALLY DON'T WANT THAT, DO YOU?
...
HA HA, WHAT ARE YOU SAYING?
OF COURSE I WANT IT.
IT'S MORE CERTAIN. AND WE WON'T HAVE TO RUN AWAY ANYMORE.
YOU'RE THE ONE WHO SAID THAT.
"IF WE HAVE A STRATEGY TO GET RID OF THE DEMONS..."
"...THAT WOULD BE MORE CERTAIN."
YEAH, I DID.

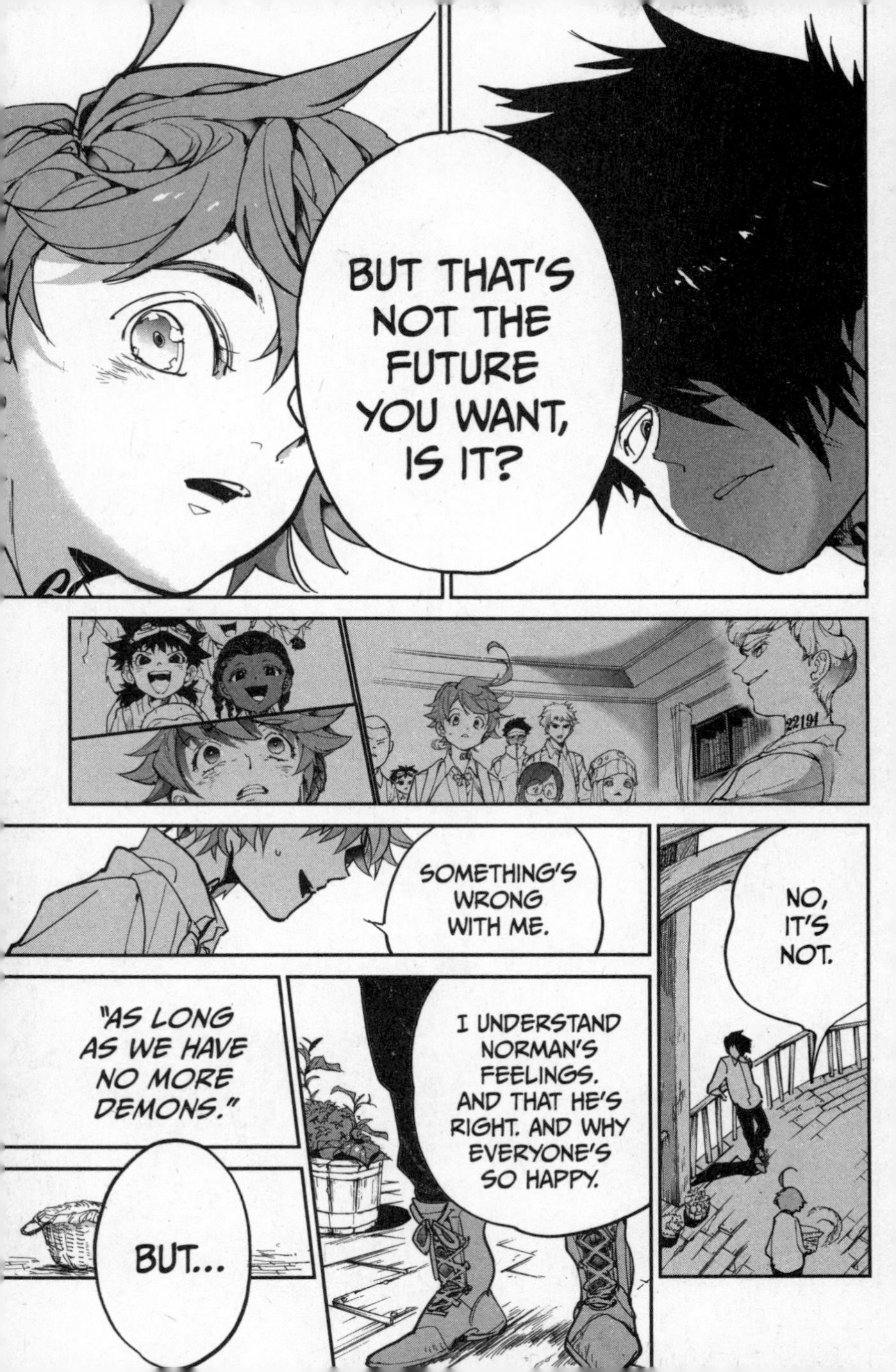
BUT THAT'S NOT THE FUTURE YOU WANT, IS IT?
22194
NO, IT'S NOT.
SOMETHING'S WRONG WITH ME.
I UNDERSTAND NORMAN'S FEELINGS. AND THAT HE'S RIGHT. AND WHY EVERYONE'S SO HAPPY.
"AS LONG AS WE HAVE NO MORE DEMONS."
BUT...

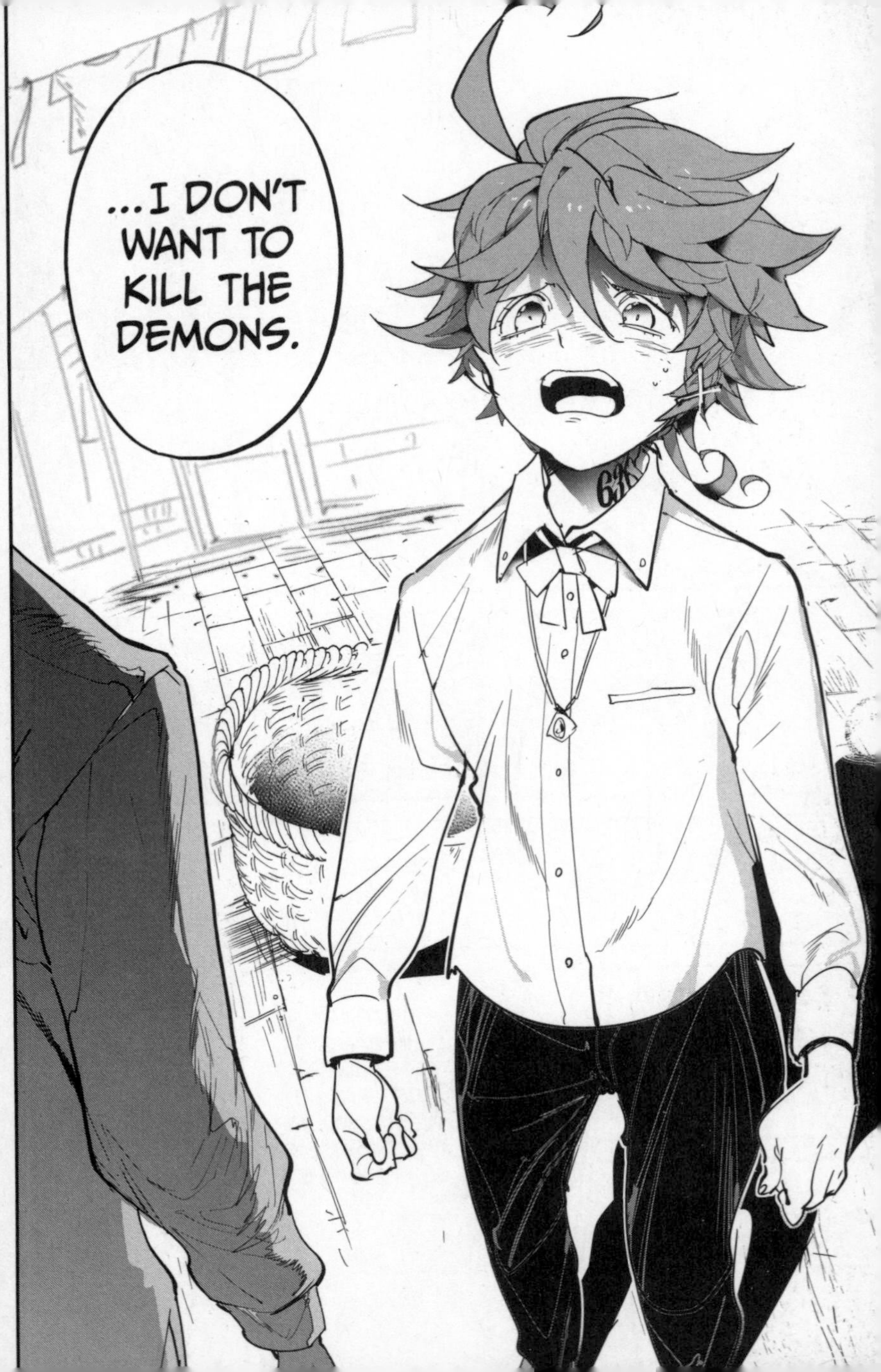
...I DON'T WANT TO KILL THE DEMONS.

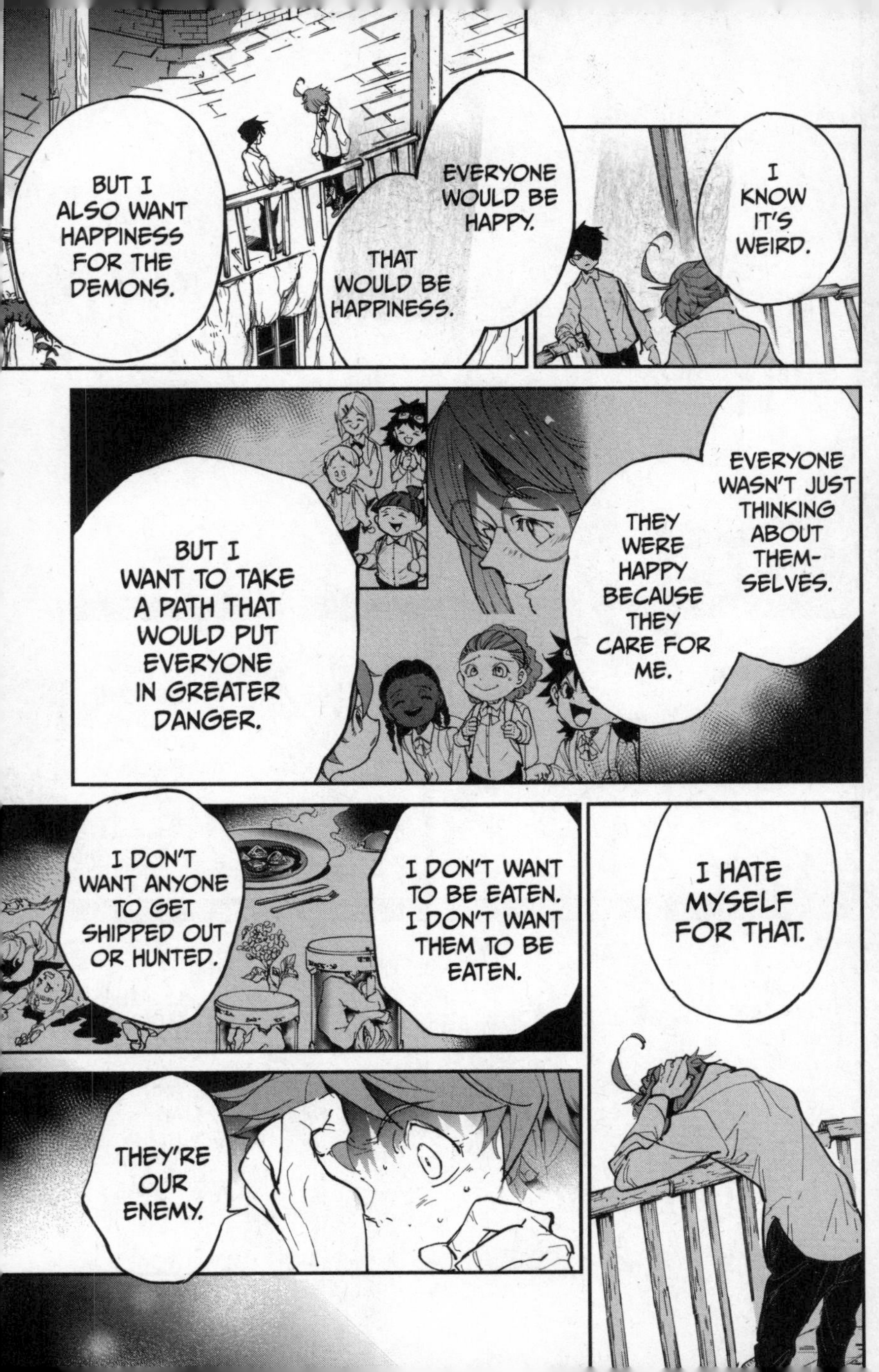
I KNOW IT'S WEIRD.
EVERYONE WOULD BE HAPPY.
THAT WOULD BE HAPPINESS.
BUT I ALSO WANT HAPPINESS FOR THE DEMONS.
EVERYONE WASN'T JUST THINKING ABOUT THEM-SELVES.
THEY WERE HAPPY BECAUSE THEY CARE FOR ME.
BUT I WANT TO TAKE A PATH THAT WOULD PUT EVERYONE IN GREATER DANGER.
I DON'T WANT TO BE EATEN. I DON'T WANT THEM TO BE EATEN.
I DON'T WANT ANYONE TO GET SHIPPED OUT OR HUNTED.
THEY'RE OUR ENEMY.
I HATE MYSELF FOR THAT.

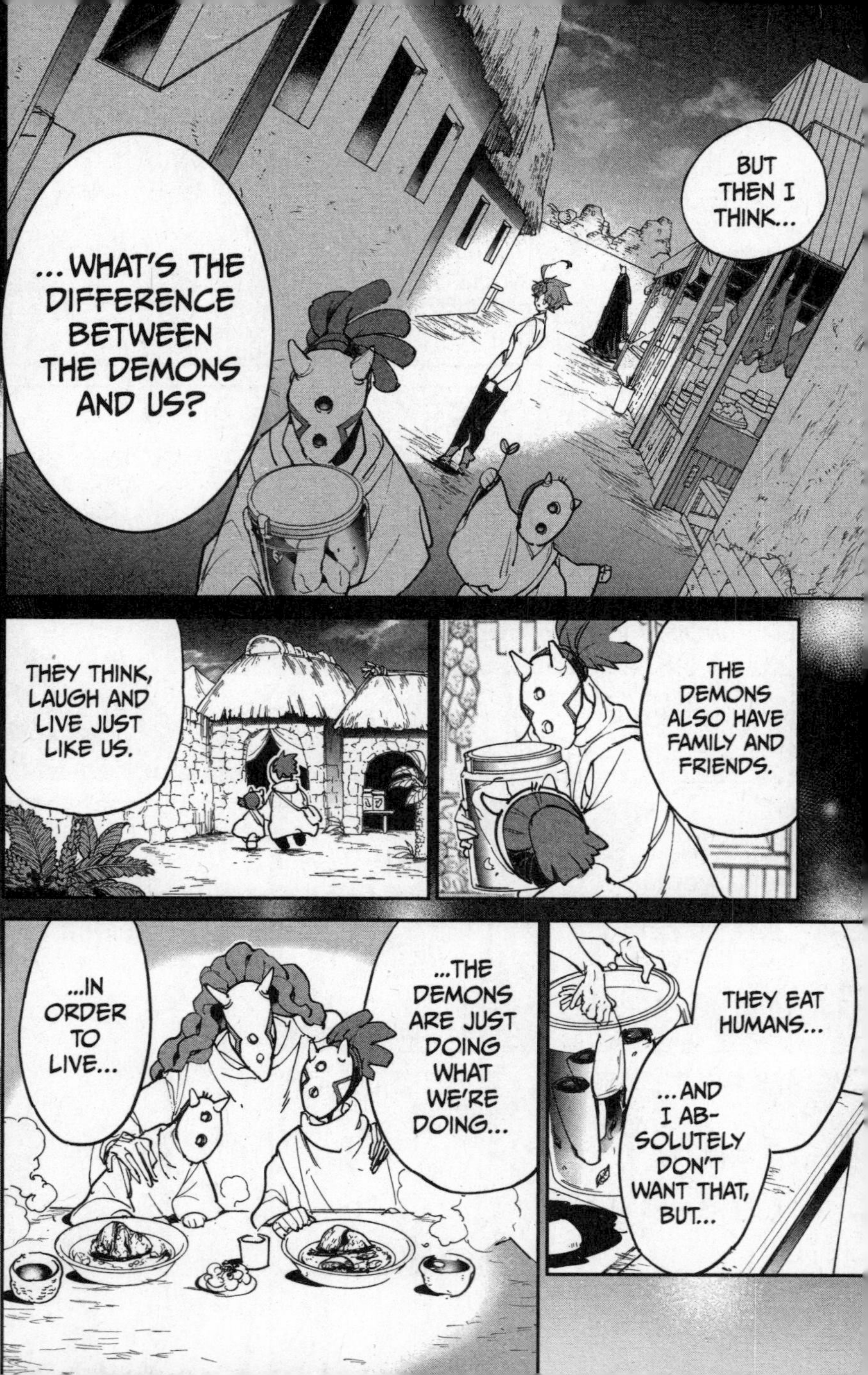
BUT THEN I THINK...
...WHAT'S THE DIFFERENCE BETWEEN THE DEMONS AND US?
THE DEMONS ALSO HAVE FAMILY AND FRIENDS.
THEY THINK, LAUGH AND LIVE JUST LIKE US.
THEY EAT HUMANS...
...AND I AB-SOLUTELY DON'T WANT THAT, BUT...
...THE DEMONS ARE JUST DOING WHAT WE'RE DOING...
...IN ORDER TO LIVE...

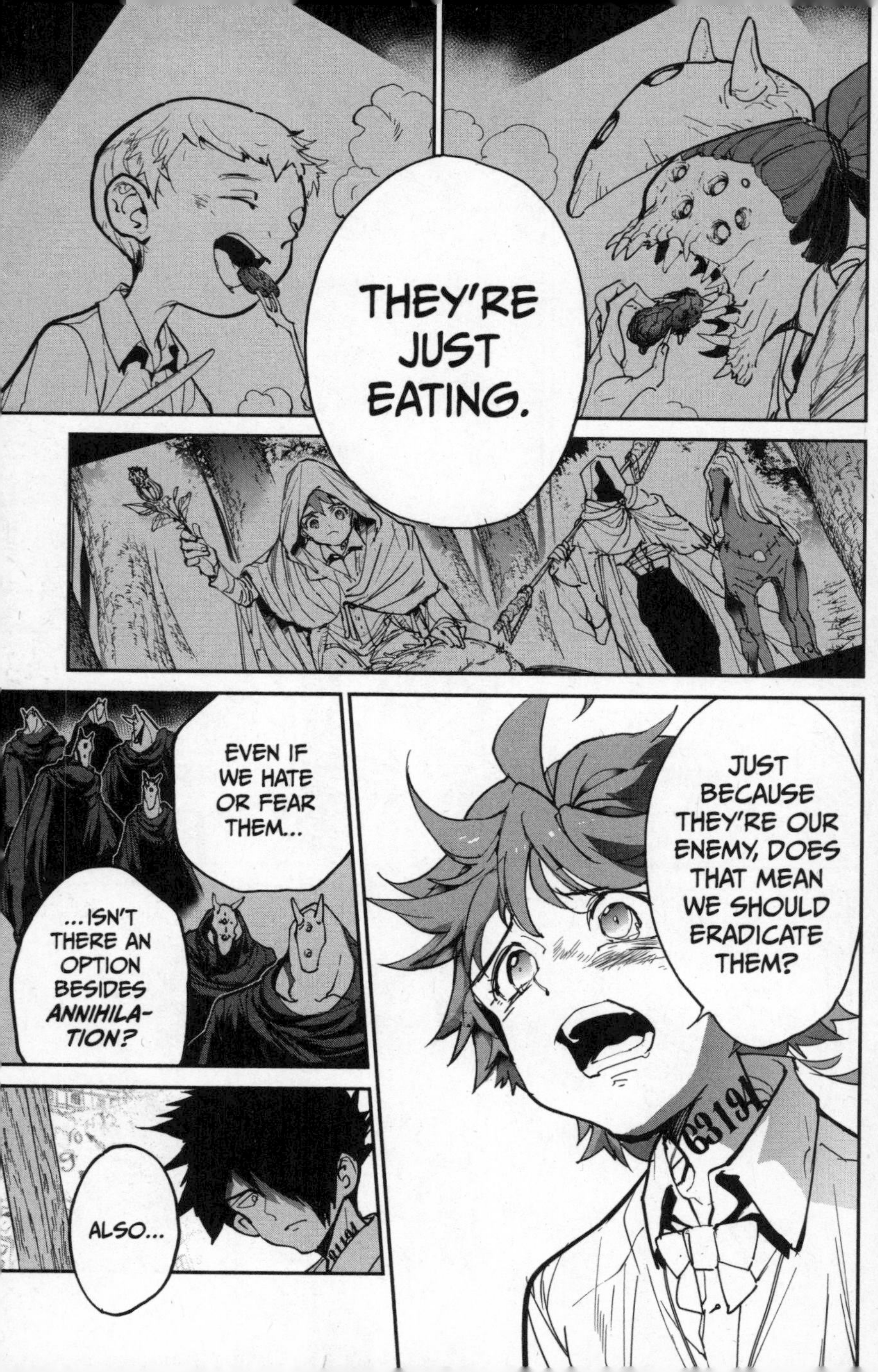
THEY'RE JUST EATING.
JUST BECAUSE THEY'RE OUR ENEMY, DOES THAT MEAN WE SHOULD ERADICATE THEM?
EVEN IF WE HATE OR FEAR THEM...
...ISN'T THERE AN OPTION BESIDES *ANNIHILATION?*
ALSO...

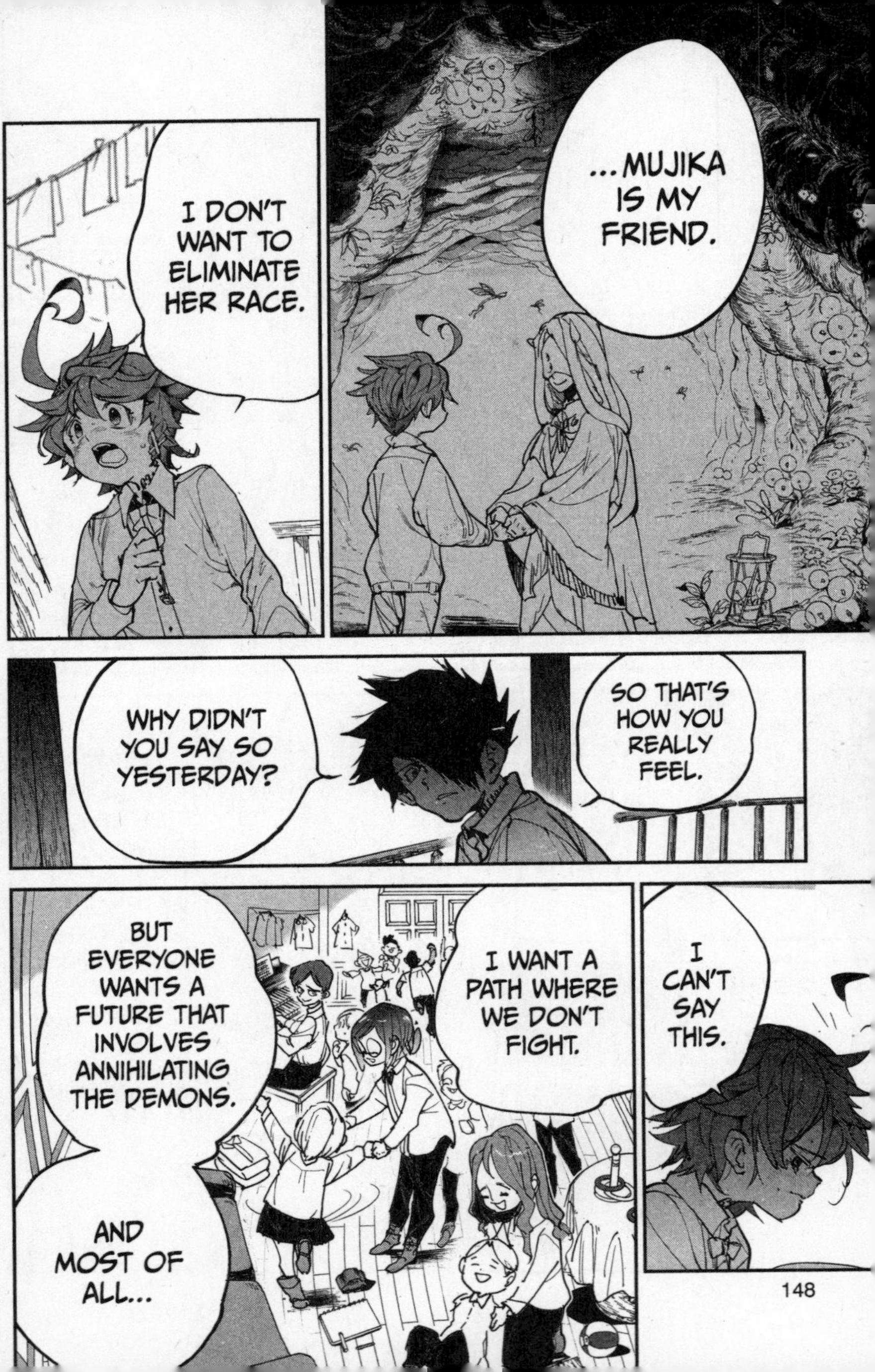

...MUJIKA IS MY FRIEND.
I DON'T WANT TO ELIMINATE HER RACE.
SO THAT'S HOW YOU REALLY FEEL.
WHY DIDN'T YOU SAY SO YESTERDAY?
I CAN'T SAY THIS.
I WANT A PATH WHERE WE DON'T FIGHT.
BUT EVERYONE WANTS A FUTURE THAT INVOLVES ANNIHILATING THE DEMONS.
AND MOST OF ALL...

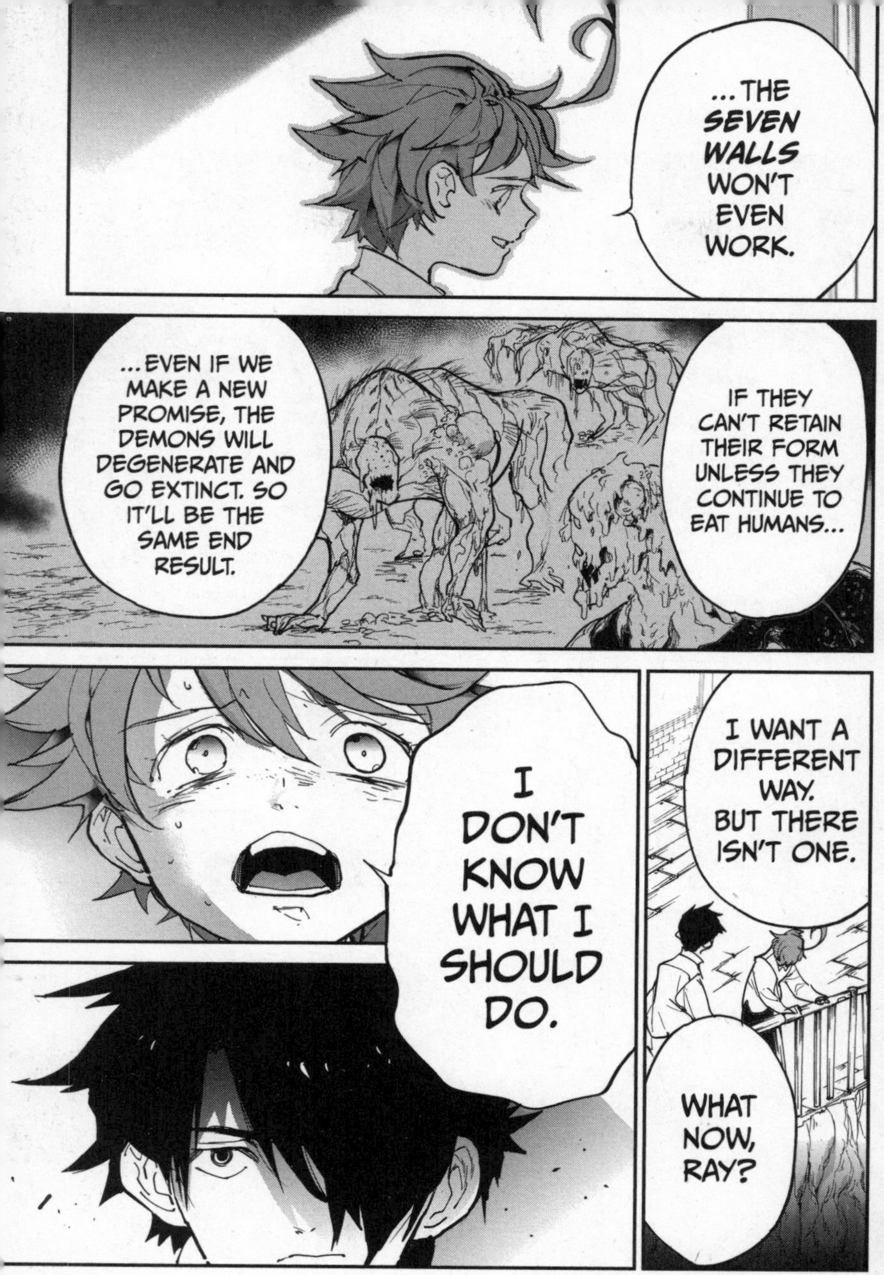
...THE SEVEN WALLS WON'T EVEN WORK.
IF THEY CAN'T RETAIN THEIR FORM UNLESS THEY CONTINUE TO EAT HUMANS...
...EVEN IF WE MAKE A NEW PROMISE, THE DEMONS WILL DEGENERATE AND GO EXTINCT. SO IT'LL BE THE SAME END RESULT.
I WANT A DIFFERENT WAY. BUT THERE ISN'T ONE.
WHAT NOW, RAY?
I DON'T KNOW WHAT I SHOULD DO.

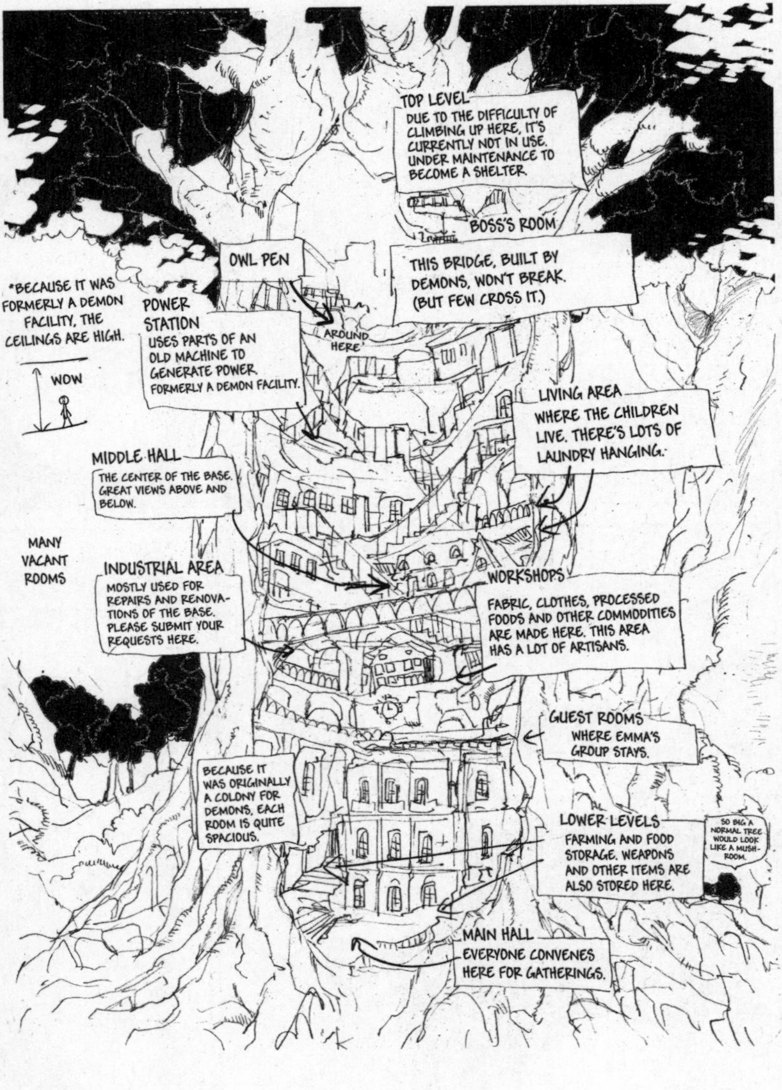

TOP LEVEL
DUE TO THE DIFFICULTY OF CLIMBING UP HERE, IT'S CURRENTLY NOT IN USE. UNDER MAINTENANCE TO BECOME A SHELTER.
BOSS'S ROOM
THIS BRIDGE, BUILT BY DEMONS, WON'T BREAK. (BUT FEW CROSS IT.)
OWL PEN
AROUND HERE
*BECAUSE IT WAS FORMERLY A DEMON FACILITY, THE CEILINGS ARE HIGH.
WOW
POWER STATION
USES PARTS OF AN OLD MACHINE TO GENERATE POWER. FORMERLY A DEMON FACILITY.
LIVING AREA
WHERE THE CHILDREN LIVE. THERE'S LOTS OF LAUNDRY HANGING.
MIDDLE HALL
THE CENTER OF THE BASE. GREAT VIEWS ABOVE AND BELOW.
MANY VACANT ROOMS
WORKSHOPS
FABRIC, CLOTHES, PROCESSED FOODS AND OTHER COMMODITIES ARE MADE HERE. THIS AREA HAS A LOT OF ARTISANS.
INDUSTRIAL AREA
MOSTLY USED FOR REPAIRS AND RENOVATIONS OF THE BASE. PLEASE SUBMIT YOUR REQUESTS HERE.
GUEST ROOMS
WHERE EMMA'S GROUP STAYS.
BECAUSE IT WAS ORIGINALLY A COLONY FOR DEMONS, EACH ROOM IS QUITE SPACIOUS.
SO BIG A NORMAL TREE WOULD LOOK LIKE A MUSHROOM.
LOWER LEVELS
FARMING AND FOOD STORAGE. WEAPONS AND OTHER ITEMS ARE ALSO STORED HERE.
MAIN HALL
EVERYONE CONVENES HERE FOR GATHERINGS.

CHAPTER 123: AN IMPORTANT CHOICE

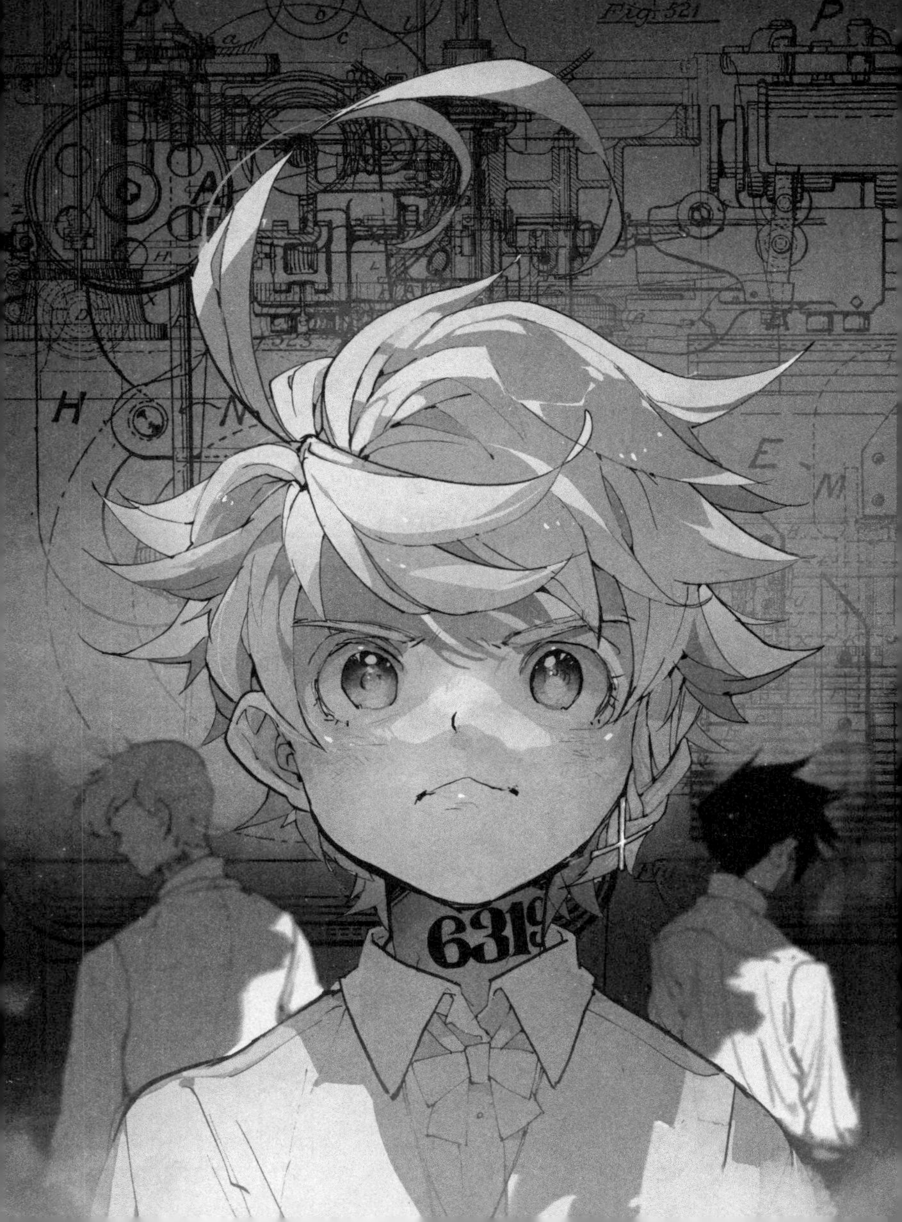

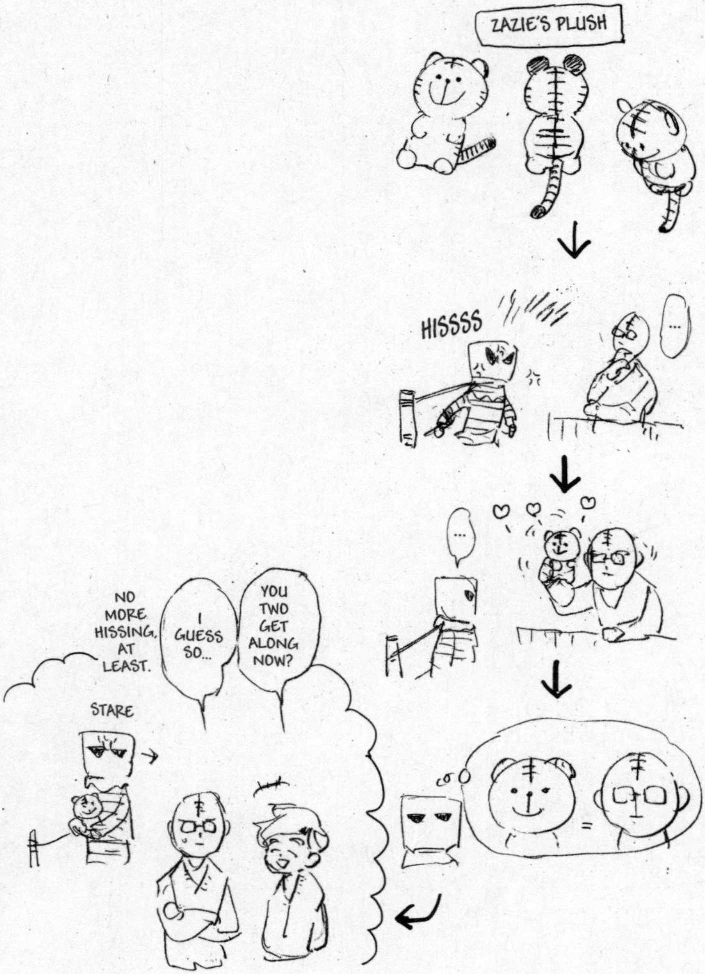
ZAZIE'S PLUSH
...
HISSSS
...
YOU TWO GET ALONG NOW?
I GUESS SO...
NO MORE HISSING, AT LEAST.
STARE

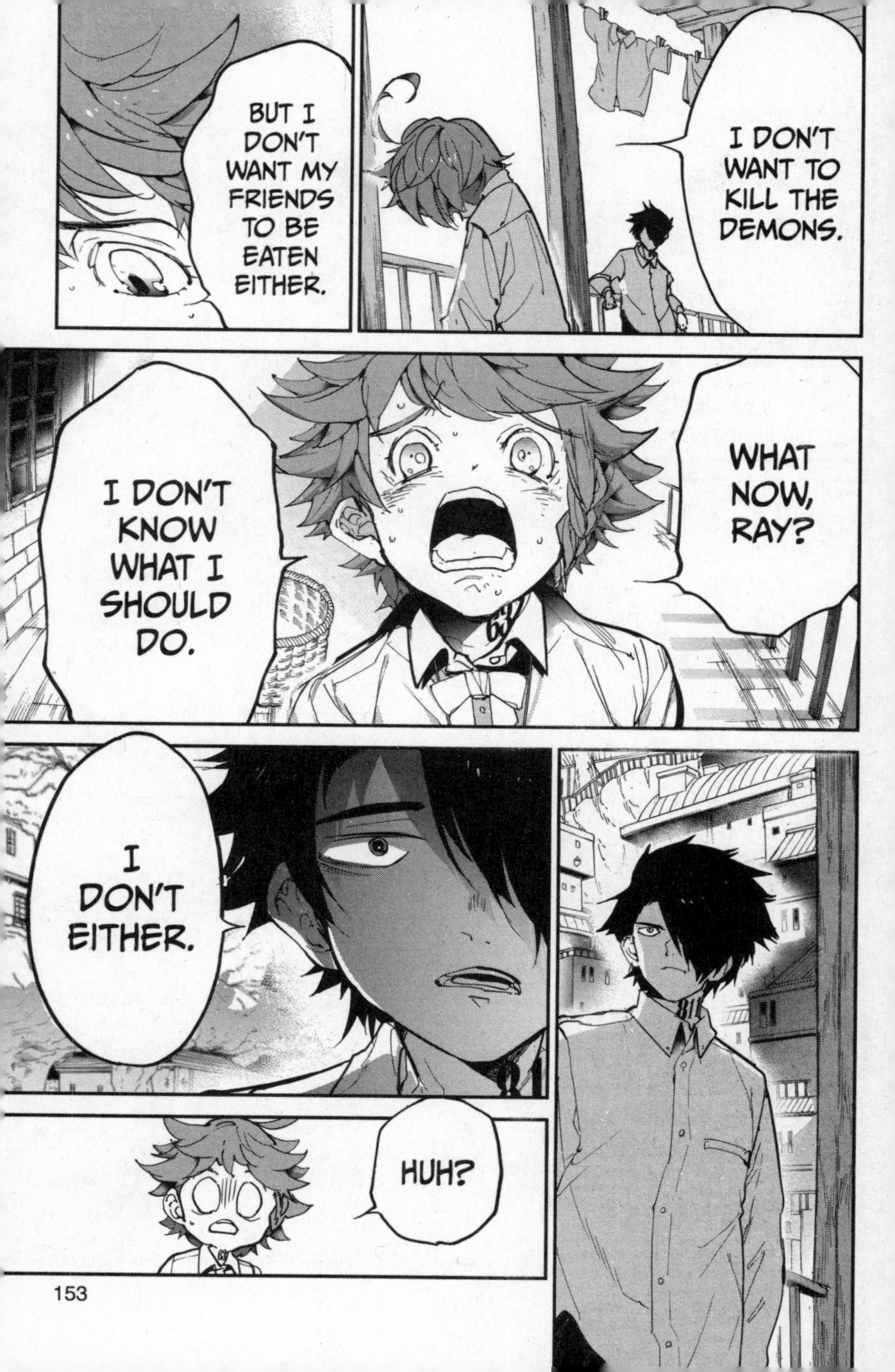
I DON'T WANT TO KILL THE DEMONS.
BUT I DON'T WANT MY FRIENDS TO BE EATEN EITHER.
WHAT NOW, RAY?
I DON'T KNOW WHAT I SHOULD DO.
I DON'T EITHER.
HUH?

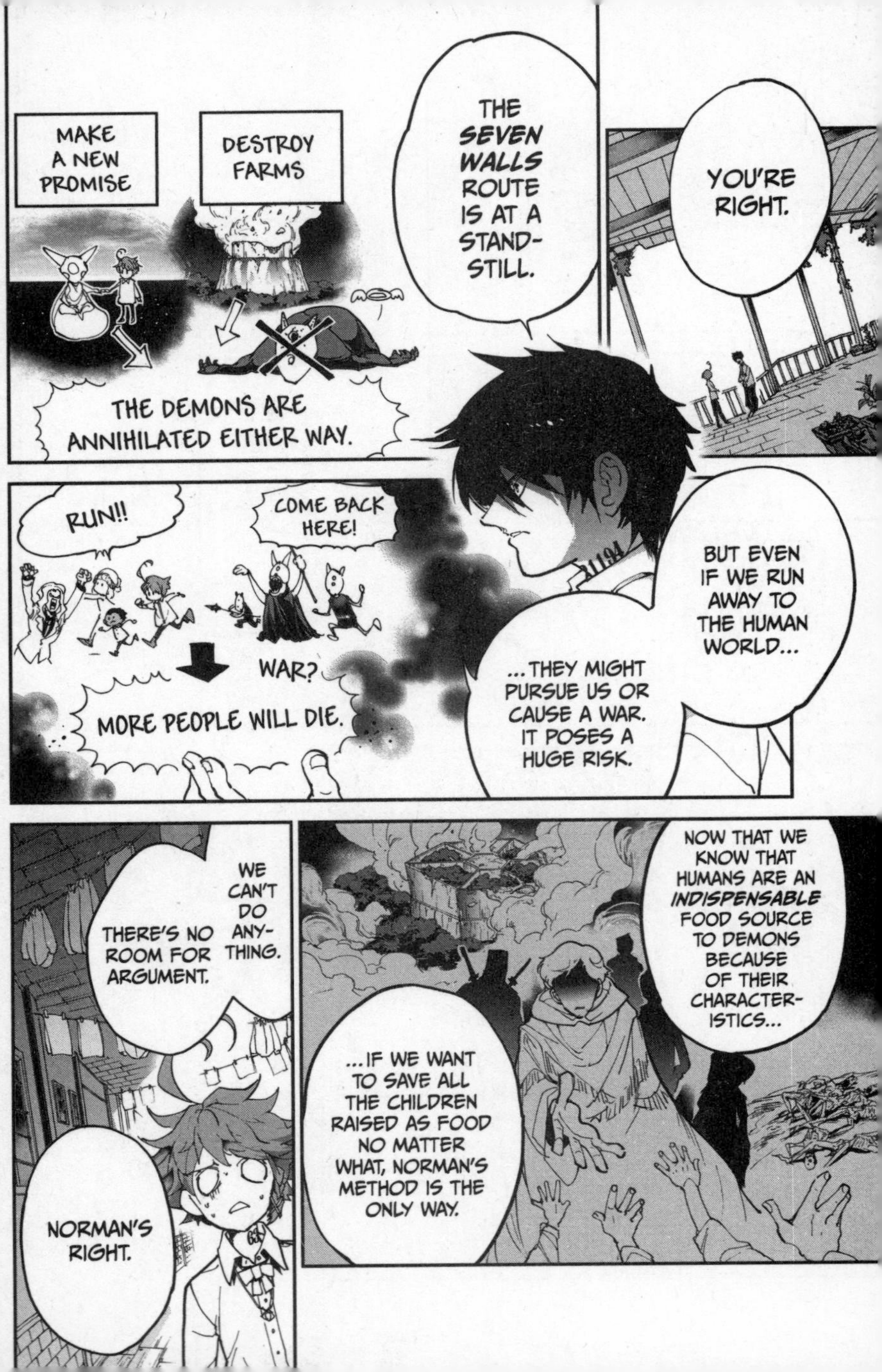
YOU'RE RIGHT.
THE *SEVEN WALLS* ROUTE IS AT A STANDSTILL.
DESTROY FARMS
MAKE A NEW PROMISE
THE DEMONS ARE ANNIHILATED EITHER WAY.
BUT EVEN IF WE RUN AWAY TO THE HUMAN WORLD...
...THEY MIGHT PURSUE US OR CAUSE A WAR. IT POSES A HUGE RISK.
COME BACK HERE!
RUN!!
WAR?
MORE PEOPLE WILL DIE.
NOW THAT WE KNOW THAT HUMANS ARE AN *INDISPENSABLE* FOOD SOURCE TO DEMONS BECAUSE OF THEIR CHARACTERISTICS...
...IF WE WANT TO SAVE ALL THE CHILDREN RAISED AS FOOD NO MATTER WHAT, NORMAN'S METHOD IS THE ONLY WAY.
WE CAN'T DO ANYTHING.
THERE'S NO ROOM FOR ARGUMENT.
NORMAN'S RIGHT.

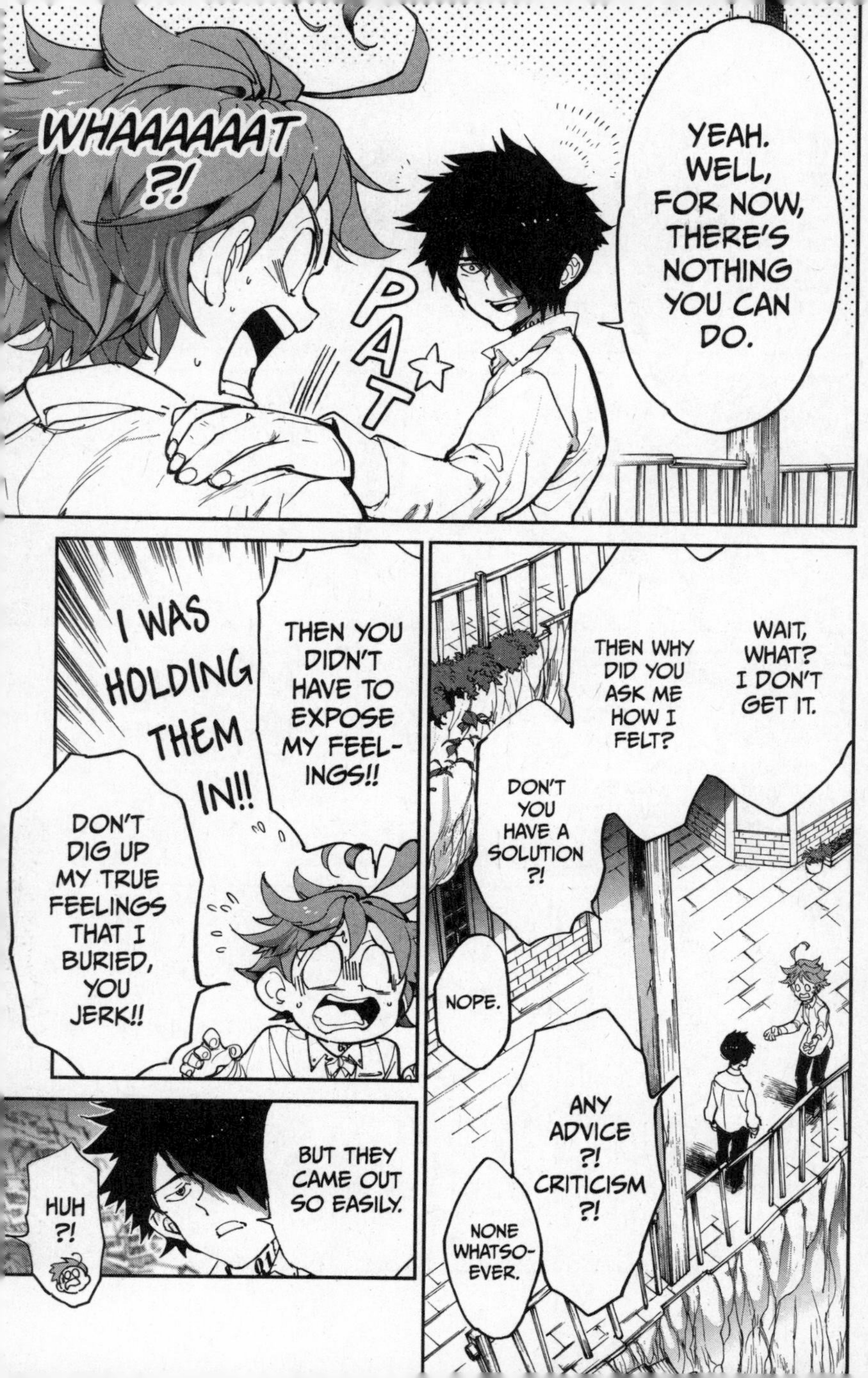
YEAH. WELL, FOR NOW, THERE'S NOTHING YOU CAN DO.
PAT
WHAAAAAAT ?!
WAIT, WHAT? I DON'T GET IT.
THEN WHY DID YOU ASK ME HOW I FELT?
DON'T YOU HAVE A SOLUTION ?!
NOPE.
ANY ADVICE ?! CRITICISM ?!
NONE WHATSO-EVER.
THEN YOU DIDN'T HAVE TO EXPOSE MY FEEL-INGS!!
I WAS HOLDING THEM IN!!
DON'T DIG UP MY TRUE FEELINGS THAT I BURIED, YOU JERK!!
BUT THEY CAME OUT SO EASILY.
HUH ?!

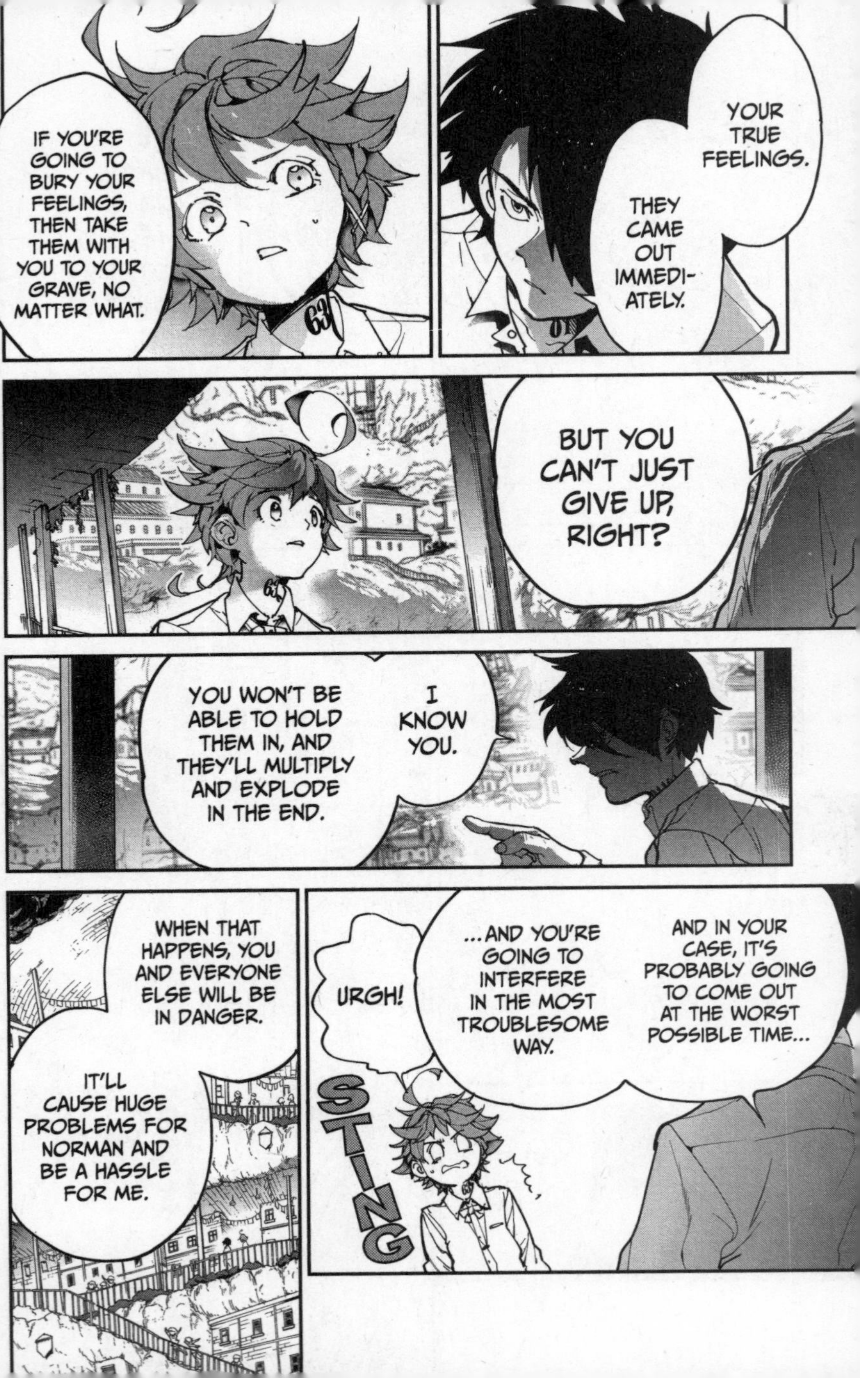
YOUR TRUE FEELINGS.
THEY CAME OUT IMMEDI-ATELY.
IF YOU'RE GOING TO BURY YOUR FEELINGS, THEN TAKE THEM WITH YOU TO YOUR GRAVE, NO MATTER WHAT.
BUT YOU CAN'T JUST GIVE UP, RIGHT?
I KNOW YOU.
YOU WON'T BE ABLE TO HOLD THEM IN, AND THEY'LL MULTIPLY AND EXPLODE IN THE END.
AND IN YOUR CASE, IT'S PROBABLY GOING TO COME OUT AT THE WORST POSSIBLE TIME...
...AND YOU'RE GOING TO INTERFERE IN THE MOST TROUBLESOME WAY.
URGH!
STING
WHEN THAT HAPPENS, YOU AND EVERYONE ELSE WILL BE IN DANGER.
IT'LL CAUSE HUGE PROBLEMS FOR NORMAN AND BE A HASSLE FOR ME.

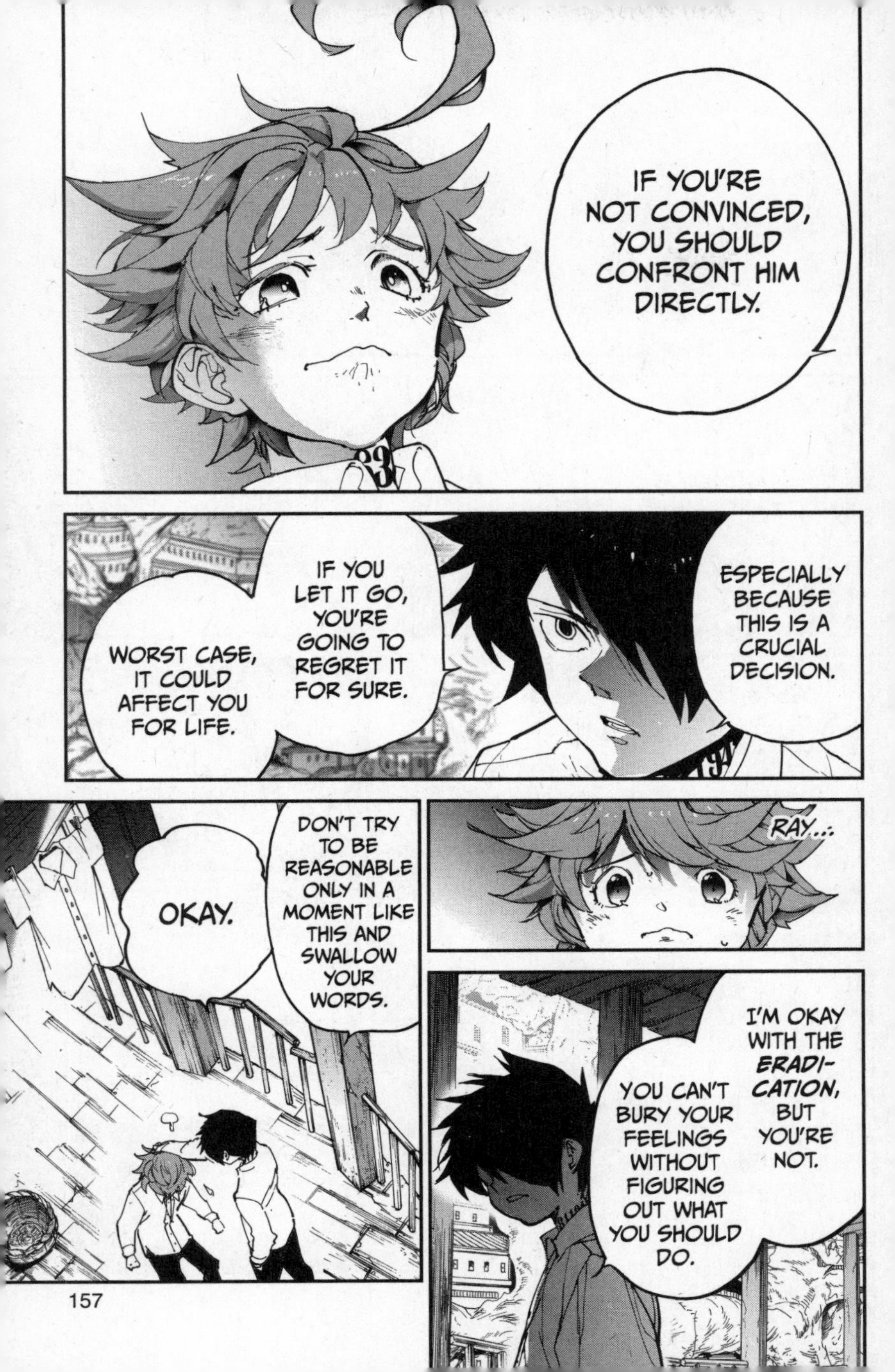
IF YOU'RE NOT CONVINCED, YOU SHOULD CONFRONT HIM DIRECTLY.
ESPECIALLY BECAUSE THIS IS A CRUCIAL DECISION.
IF YOU LET IT GO, YOU'RE GOING TO REGRET IT FOR SURE.
WORST CASE, IT COULD AFFECT YOU FOR LIFE.
RAY...
I'M OKAY WITH THE *ERADICATION*, BUT YOU'RE NOT.
YOU CAN'T BURY YOUR FEELINGS WITHOUT FIGURING OUT WHAT YOU SHOULD DO.
DON'T TRY TO BE REASONABLE ONLY IN A MOMENT LIKE THIS AND SWALLOW YOUR WORDS.
OKAY.

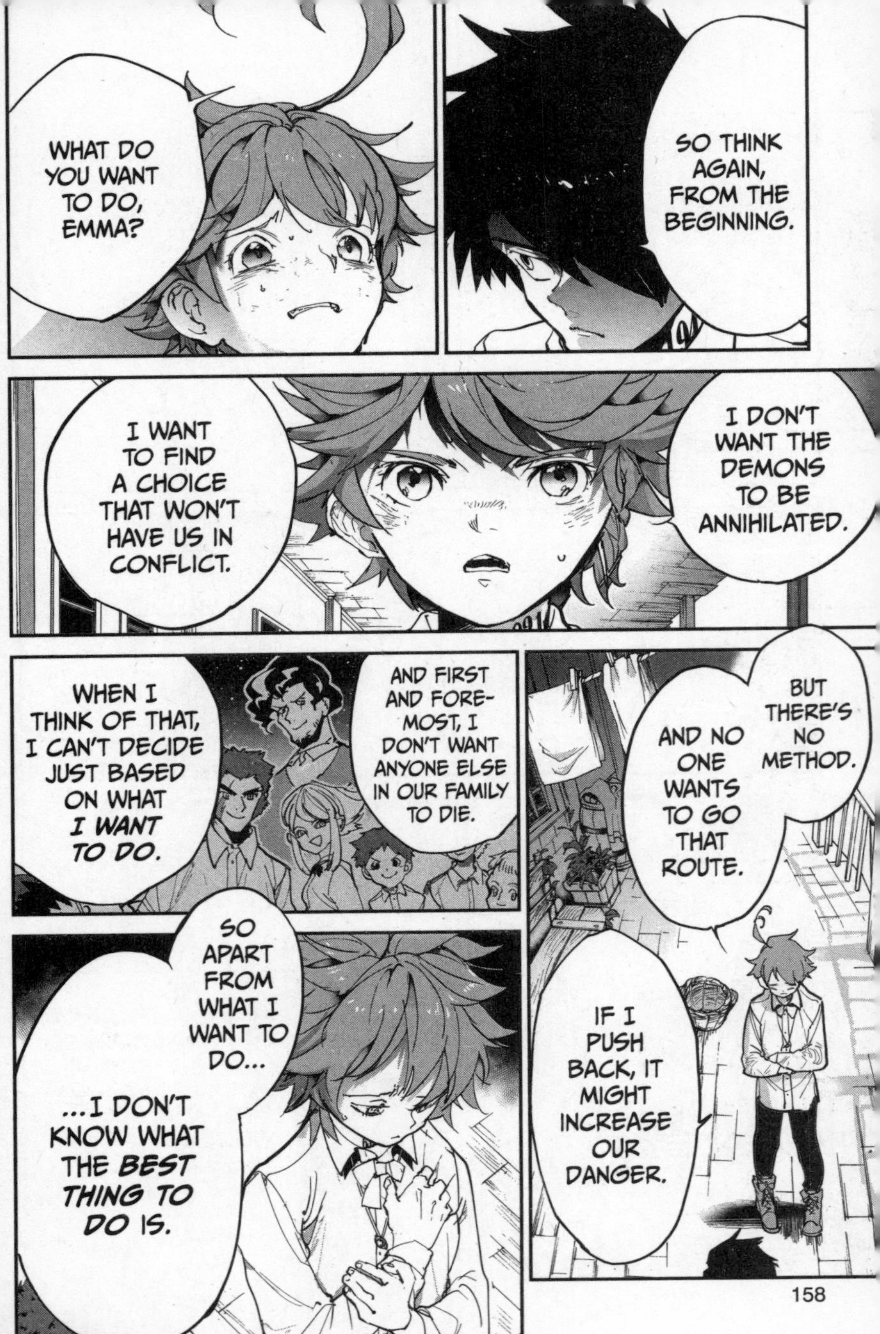
SO THINK AGAIN, FROM THE BEGINNING.
WHAT DO YOU WANT TO DO, EMMA?
I DON'T WANT THE DEMONS TO BE ANNIHILATED.
I WANT TO FIND A CHOICE THAT WON'T HAVE US IN CONFLICT.
BUT THERE'S NO METHOD.
AND NO ONE WANTS TO GO THAT ROUTE.
IF I PUSH BACK, IT MIGHT INCREASE OUR DANGER.
AND FIRST AND FORE-MOST, I DON'T WANT ANYONE ELSE IN OUR FAMILY TO DIE.
WHEN I THINK OF THAT, I CAN'T DECIDE JUST BASED ON WHAT *I WANT TO DO.*
SO APART FROM WHAT I WANT TO DO...
...I DON'T KNOW WHAT THE *BEST THING TO DO* IS.

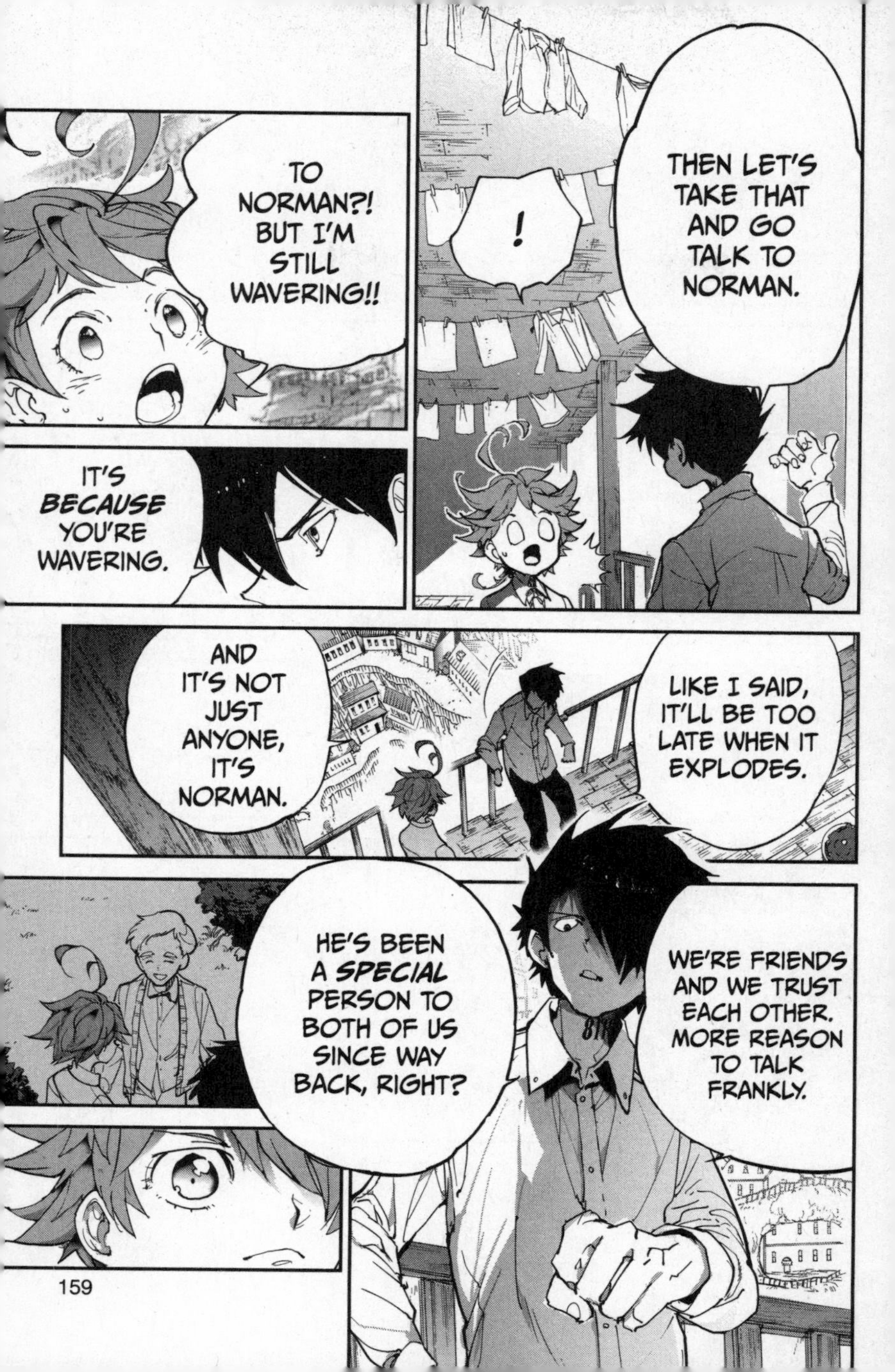
THEN LET'S TAKE THAT AND GO TALK TO NORMAN.
!
TO NORMAN?! BUT I'M STILL WAVERING!!
IT'S *BECAUSE* YOU'RE WAVERING.
LIKE I SAID, IT'LL BE TOO LATE WHEN IT EXPLODES.
AND IT'S NOT JUST ANYONE, IT'S NORMAN.
WE'RE FRIENDS AND WE TRUST EACH OTHER. MORE REASON TO TALK FRANKLY.
HE'S BEEN A *SPECIAL* PERSON TO BOTH OF US SINCE WAY BACK, RIGHT?

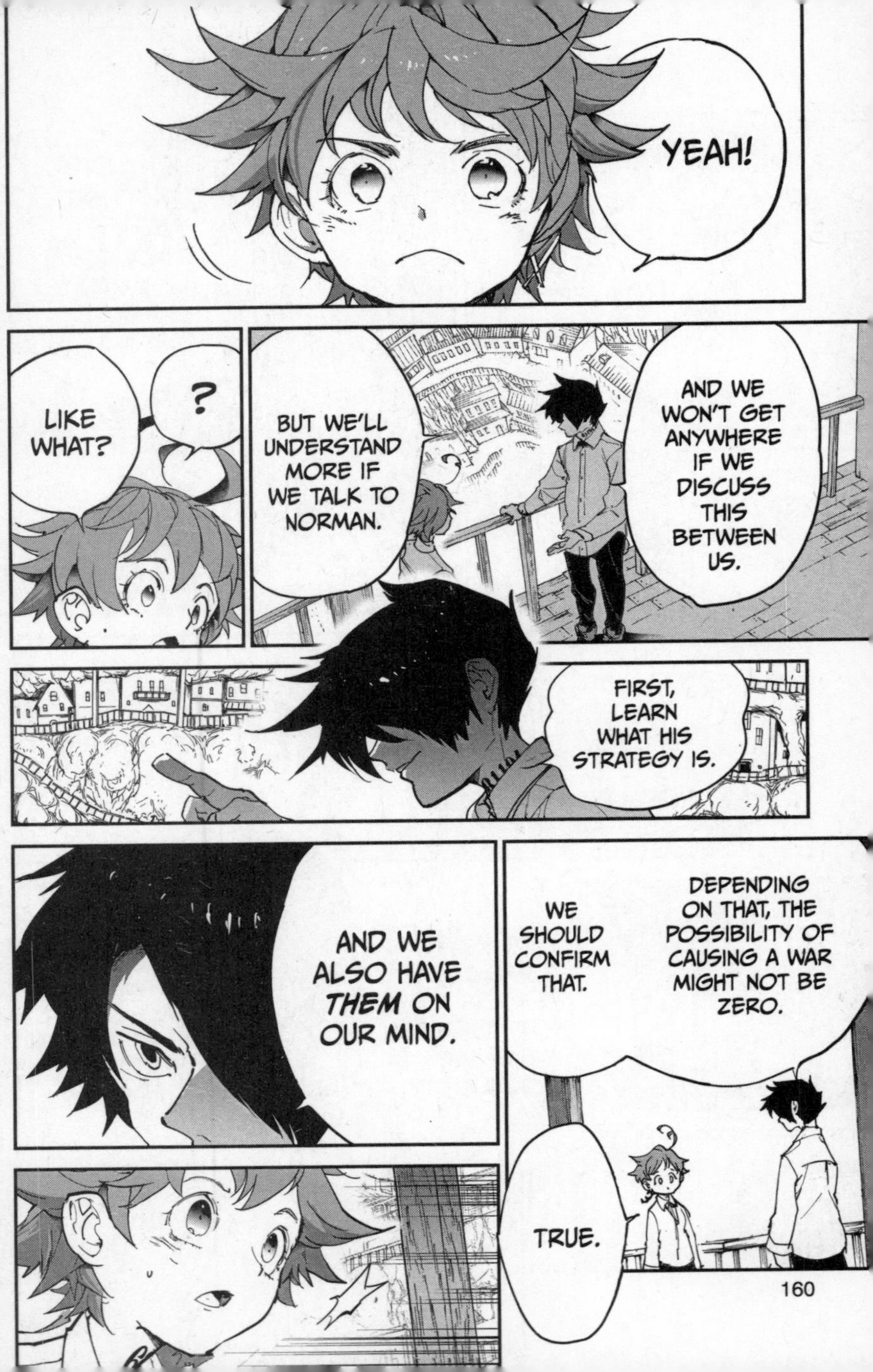
YEAH!
AND WE WON'T GET ANYWHERE IF WE DISCUSS THIS BETWEEN US.
BUT WE'LL UNDERSTAND MORE IF WE TALK TO NORMAN.
?
LIKE WHAT?
FIRST, LEARN WHAT HIS STRATEGY IS.
DEPENDING ON THAT, THE POSSIBILITY OF CAUSING A WAR MIGHT NOT BE ZERO.
WE SHOULD CONFIRM THAT.
TRUE.
AND WE ALSO HAVE *THEM* ON OUR MIND.

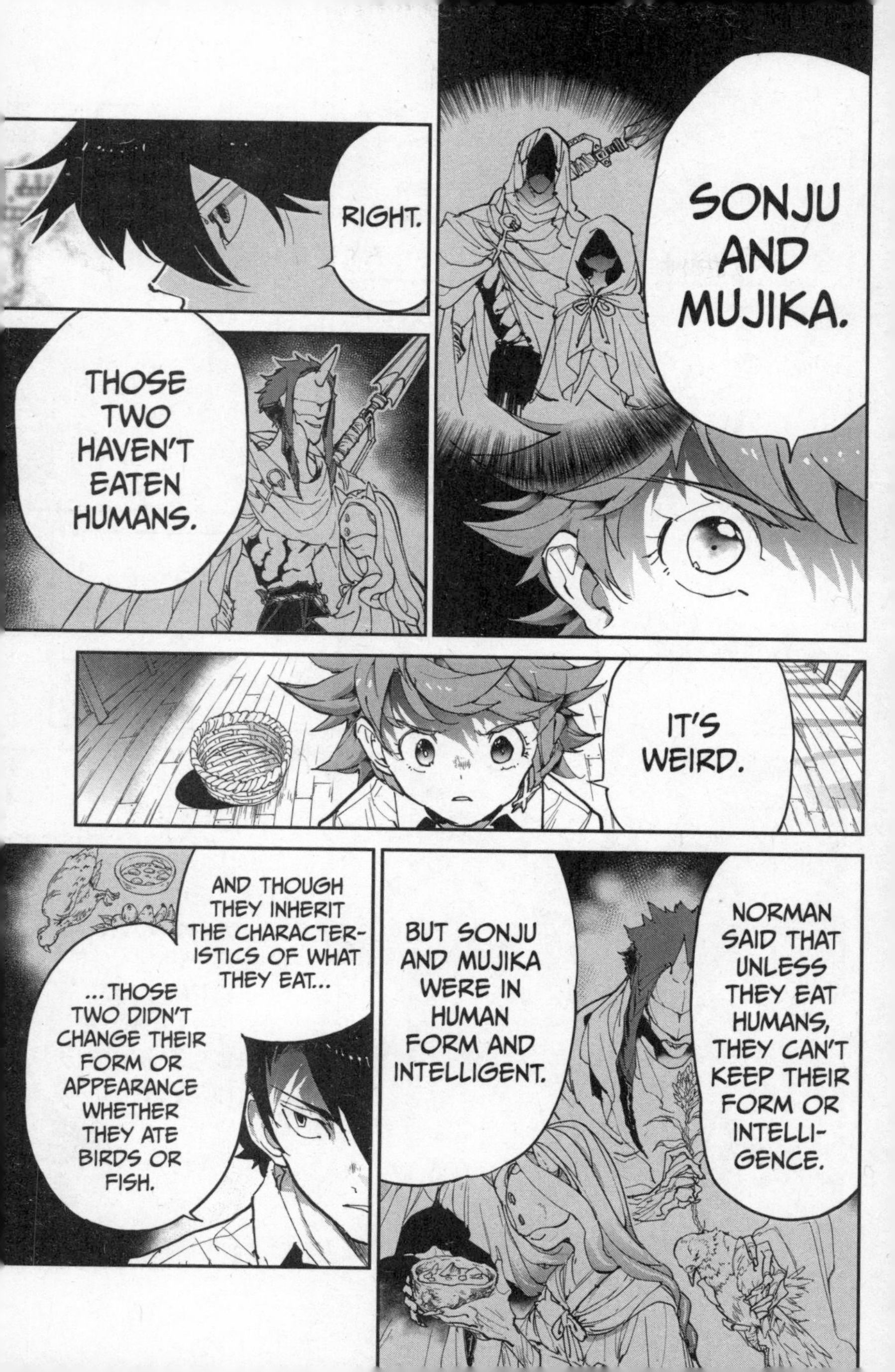
SONJU AND MUJIKA.
RIGHT.
THOSE TWO HAVEN'T EATEN HUMANS.
IT'S WEIRD.
NORMAN SAID THAT UNLESS THEY EAT HUMANS, THEY CAN'T KEEP THEIR FORM OR INTELLI-GENCE.
BUT SONJU AND MUJIKA WERE IN HUMAN FORM AND INTELLIGENT.
AND THOUGH THEY INHERIT THE CHARACTER-ISTICS OF WHAT THEY EAT...
...THOSE TWO DIDN'T CHANGE THEIR FORM OR APPEARANCE WHETHER THEY ATE BIRDS OR FISH.

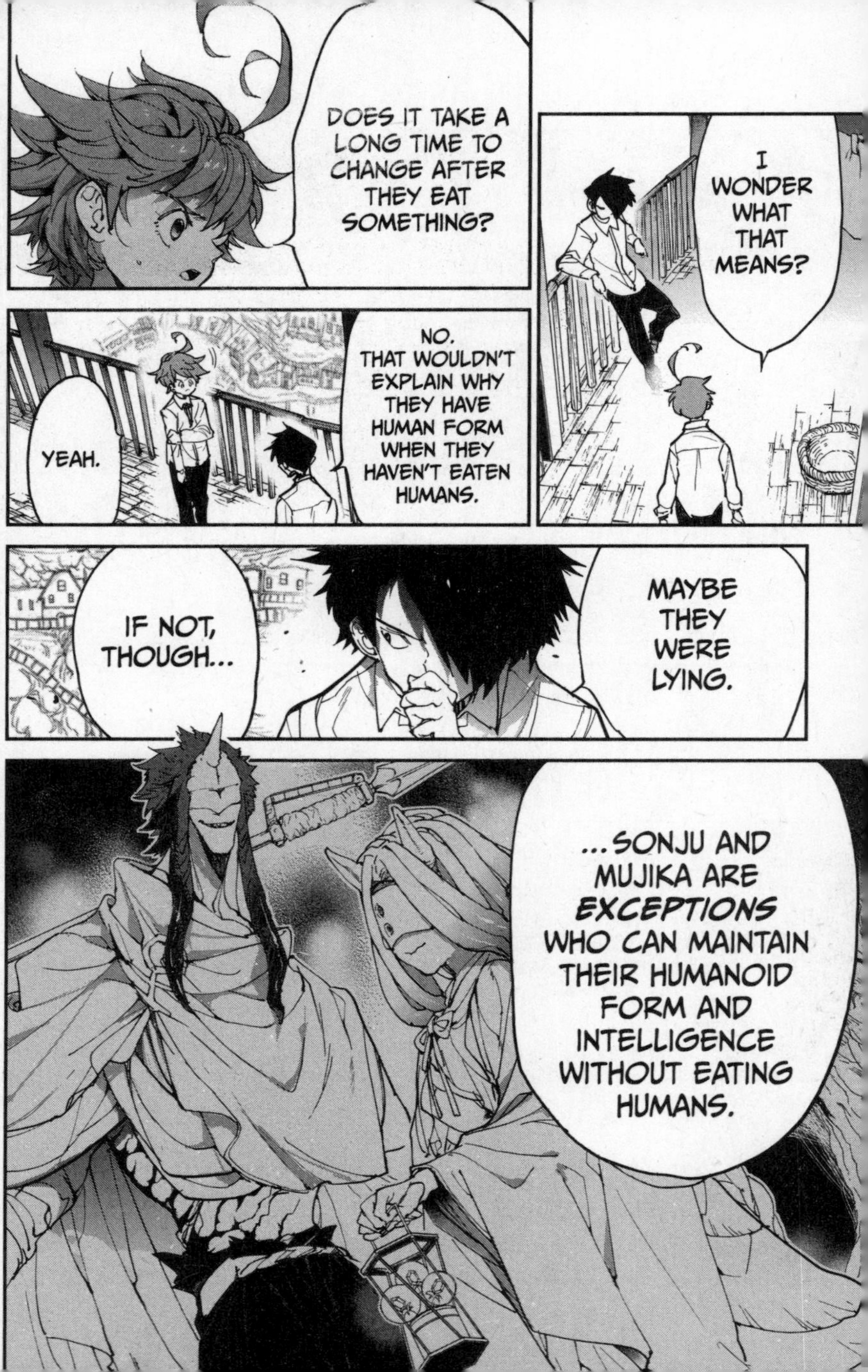
I WONDER WHAT THAT MEANS?
DOES IT TAKE A LONG TIME TO CHANGE AFTER THEY EAT SOMETHING?
NO. THAT WOULDN'T EXPLAIN WHY THEY HAVE HUMAN FORM WHEN THEY HAVEN'T EATEN HUMANS.
YEAH.
MAYBE THEY WERE LYING.
IF NOT, THOUGH...
...SONJU AND MUJIKA ARE *EXCEPTIONS* WHO CAN MAINTAIN THEIR HUMANOID FORM AND INTELLIGENCE WITHOUT EATING HUMANS.

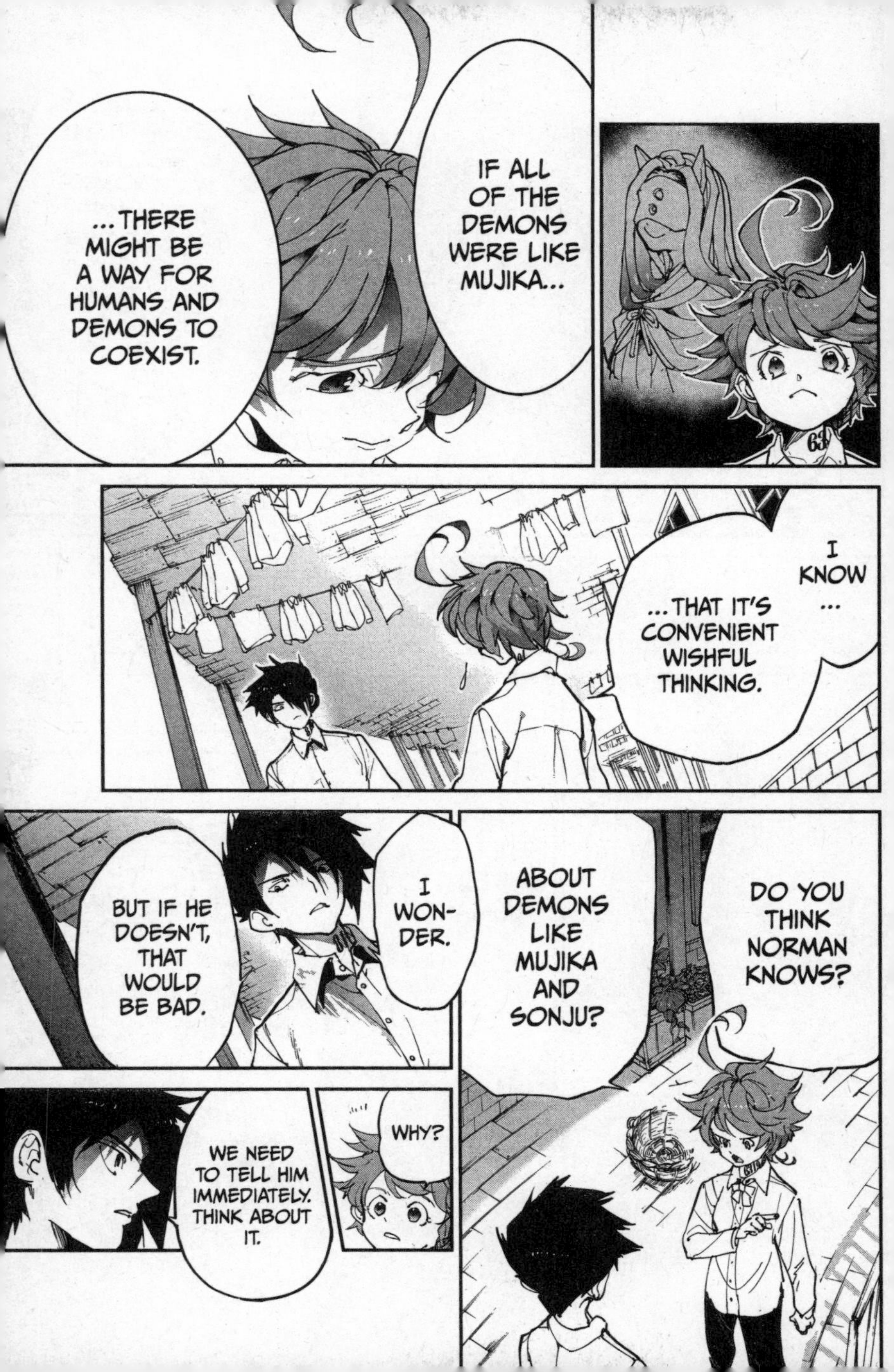

IF ALL OF THE DEMONS WERE LIKE MUJIKA...
...THERE MIGHT BE A WAY FOR HUMANS AND DEMONS TO COEXIST.
I KNOW...
...THAT IT'S CONVENIENT WISHFUL THINKING.
DO YOU THINK NORMAN KNOWS?
ABOUT DEMONS LIKE MUJIKA AND SONJU?
I WONDER.
BUT IF HE DOESN'T, THAT WOULD BE BAD.
WHY?
WE NEED TO TELL HIM IMMEDIATELY. THINK ABOUT IT.

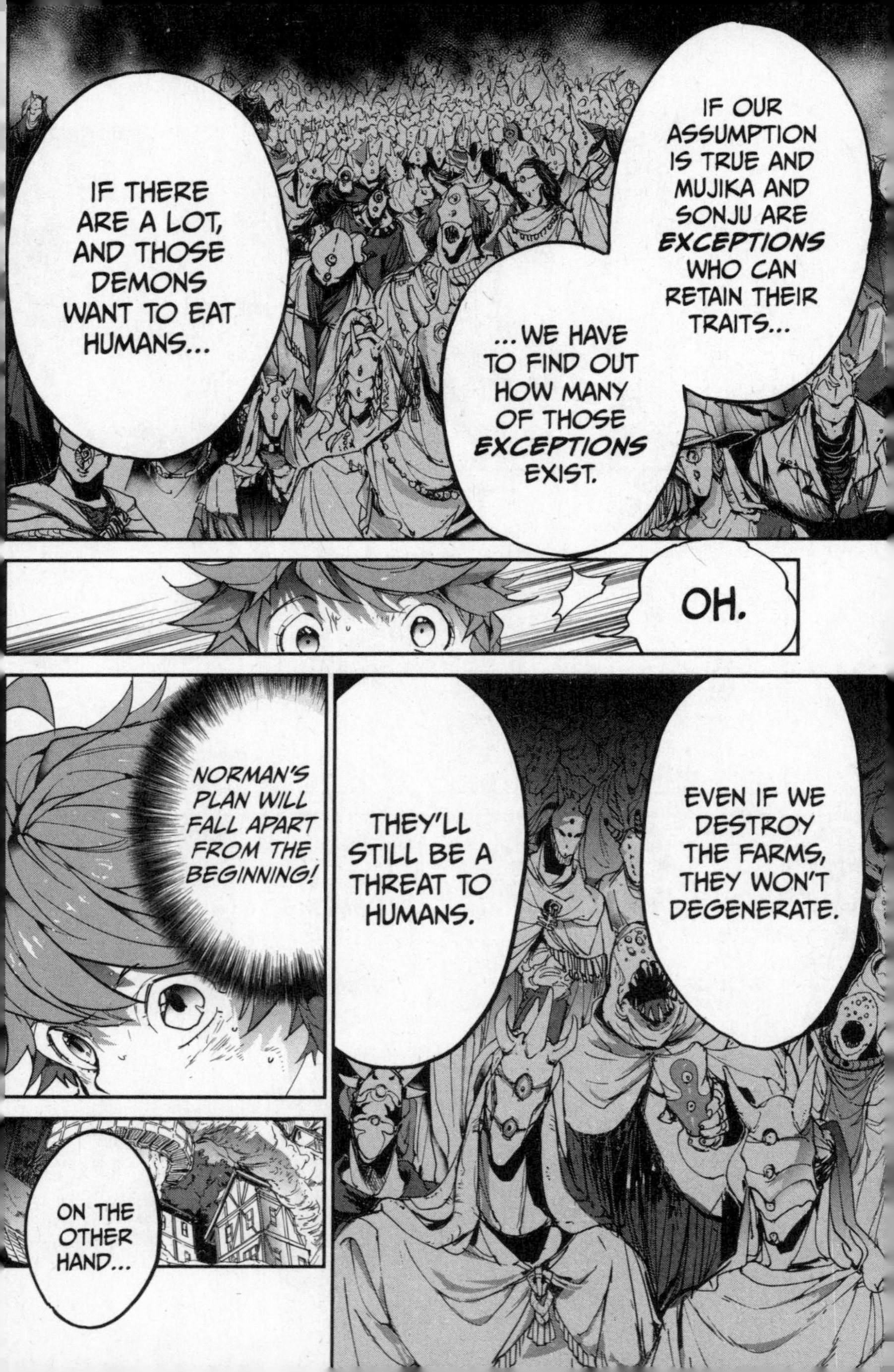
IF OUR ASSUMPTION IS TRUE AND MUJIKA AND SONJU ARE *EXCEPTIONS* WHO CAN RETAIN THEIR TRAITS...
...WE HAVE TO FIND OUT HOW MANY OF THOSE *EXCEPTIONS* EXIST.
IF THERE ARE A LOT, AND THOSE DEMONS WANT TO EAT HUMANS...
OH.
EVEN IF WE DESTROY THE FARMS, THEY WON'T DEGENERATE.
THEY'LL STILL BE A THREAT TO HUMANS.
NORMAN'S PLAN WILL FALL APART FROM THE BEGINNING!
ON THE OTHER HAND...

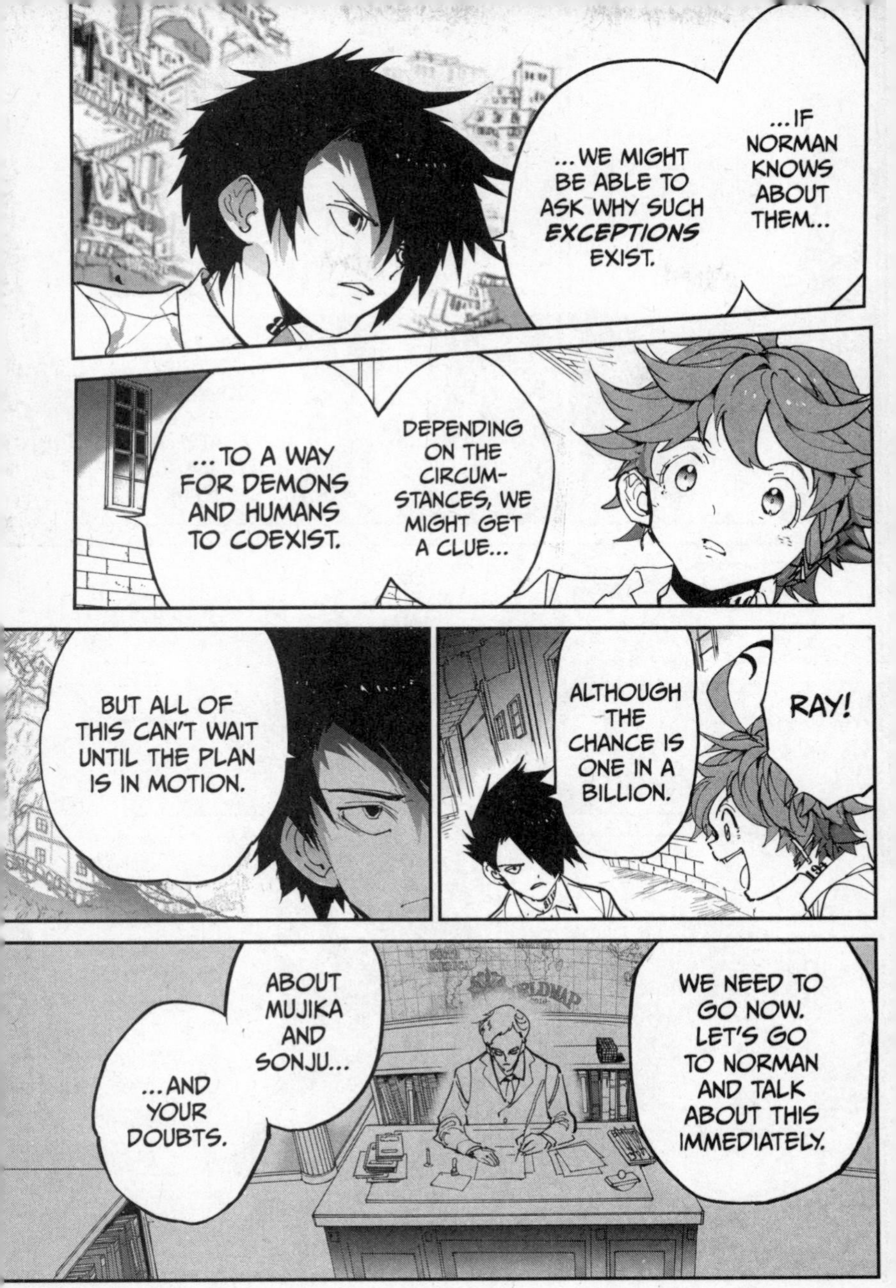
...IF NORMAN KNOWS ABOUT THEM...
...WE MIGHT BE ABLE TO ASK WHY SUCH *EXCEPTIONS* EXIST.
DEPENDING ON THE CIRCUM-STANCES, WE MIGHT GET A CLUE...
...TO A WAY FOR DEMONS AND HUMANS TO COEXIST.
RAY!
ALTHOUGH THE CHANCE IS ONE IN A BILLION.
BUT ALL OF THIS CAN'T WAIT UNTIL THE PLAN IS IN MOTION.
WE NEED TO GO NOW. LET'S GO TO NORMAN AND TALK ABOUT THIS IMMEDIATELY.
ABOUT MUJIKA AND SONJU...
...AND YOUR DOUBTS.

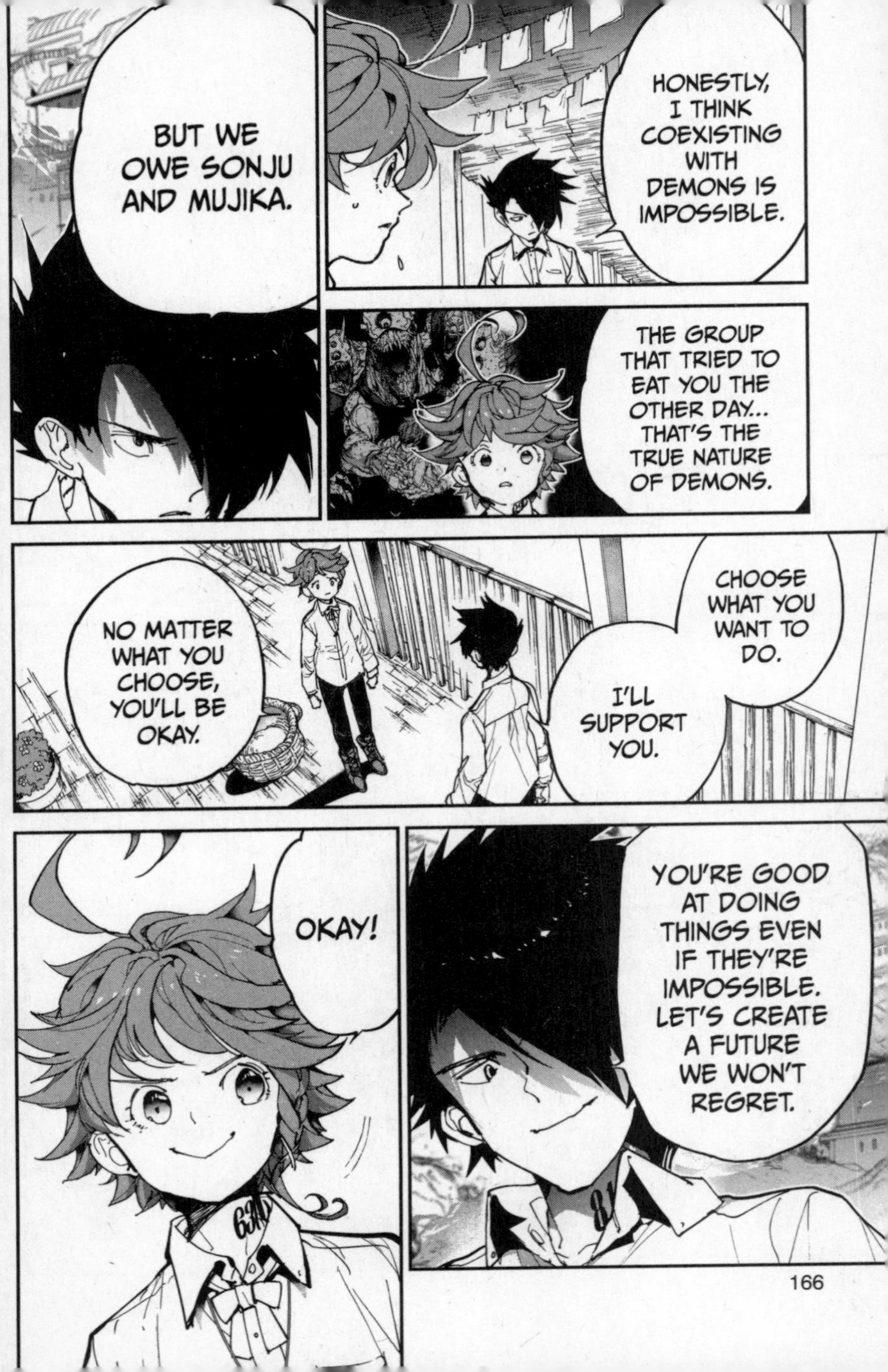
HONESTLY, I THINK COEXISTING WITH DEMONS IS IMPOSSIBLE.
THE GROUP THAT TRIED TO EAT YOU THE OTHER DAY... THAT'S THE TRUE NATURE OF DEMONS.
BUT WE OWE SONJU AND MUJIKA.
CHOOSE WHAT YOU WANT TO DO.
I'LL SUPPORT YOU.
NO MATTER WHAT YOU CHOOSE, YOU'LL BE OKAY.
YOU'RE GOOD AT DOING THINGS EVEN IF THEY'RE IMPOSSIBLE. LET'S CREATE A FUTURE WE WON'T REGRET.
OKAY!

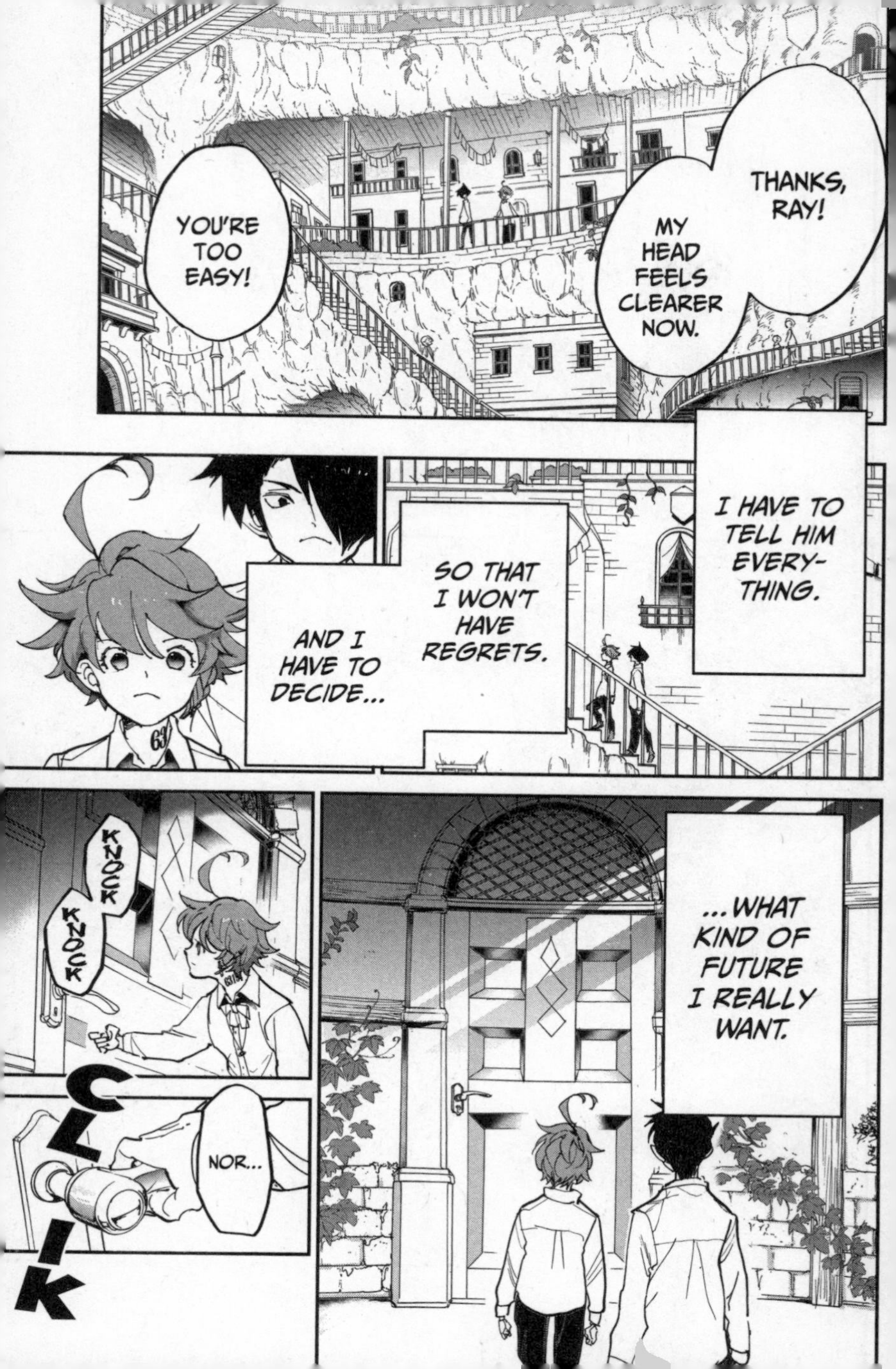
THANKS, RAY!
MY HEAD FEELS CLEARER NOW.
YOU'RE TOO EASY!
I HAVE TO TELL HIM EVERY-THING.
SO THAT I WON'T HAVE REGRETS.
AND I HAVE TO DECIDE...
...WHAT KIND OF FUTURE I REALLY WANT.
KNOCK KNOCK
CLIK
NOR...

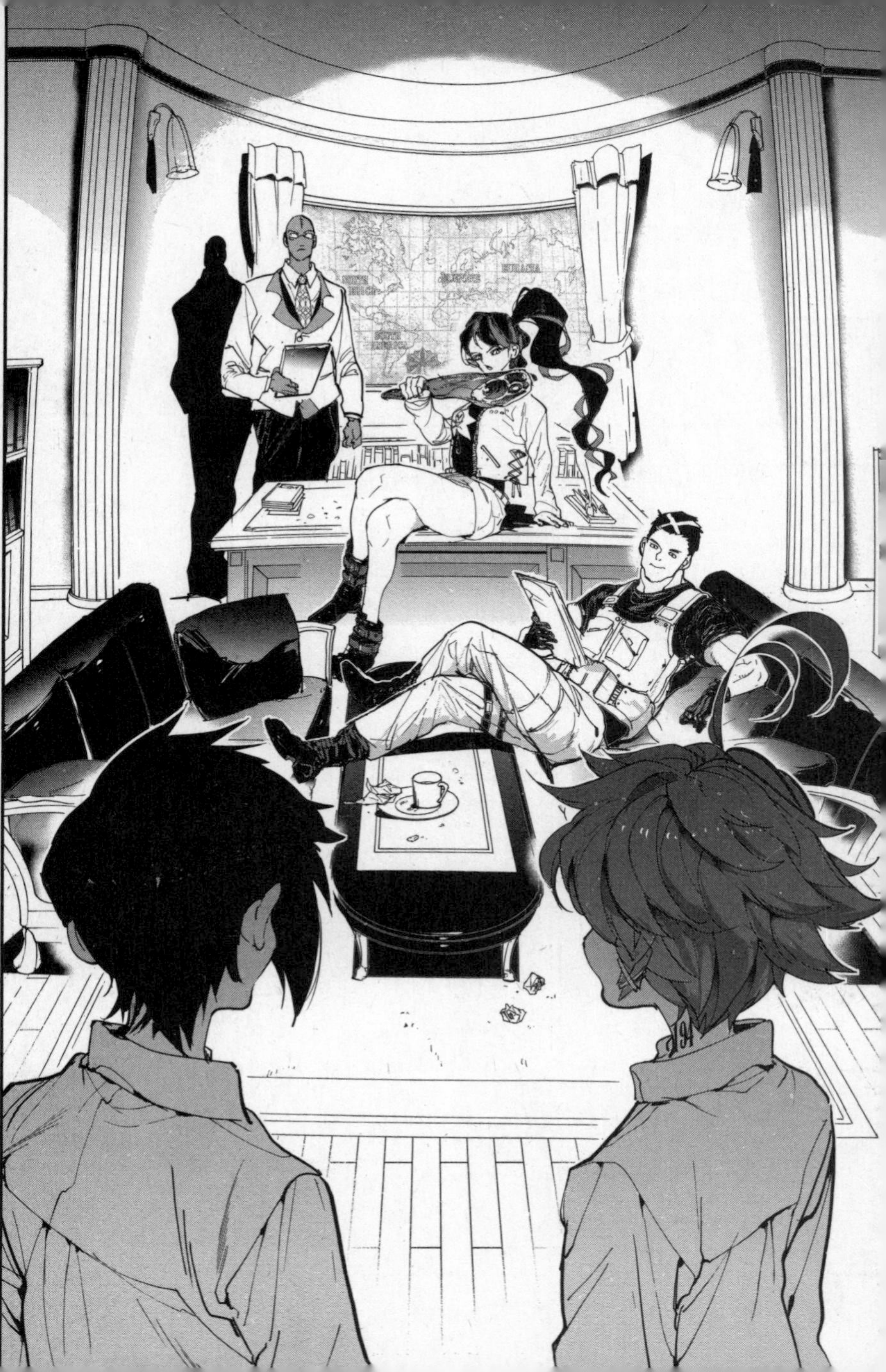
EURASIA

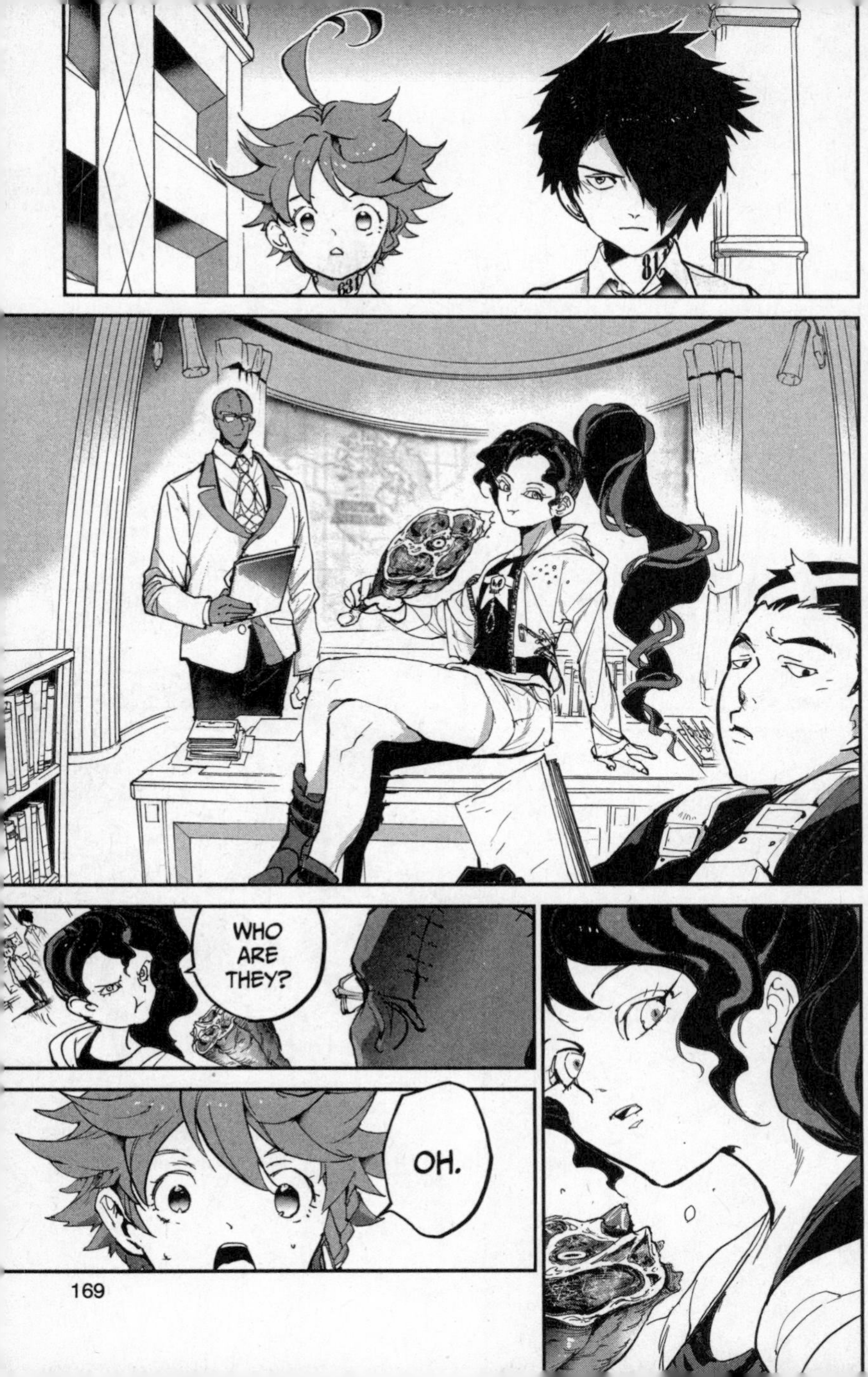
WHO ARE THEY?
OH.

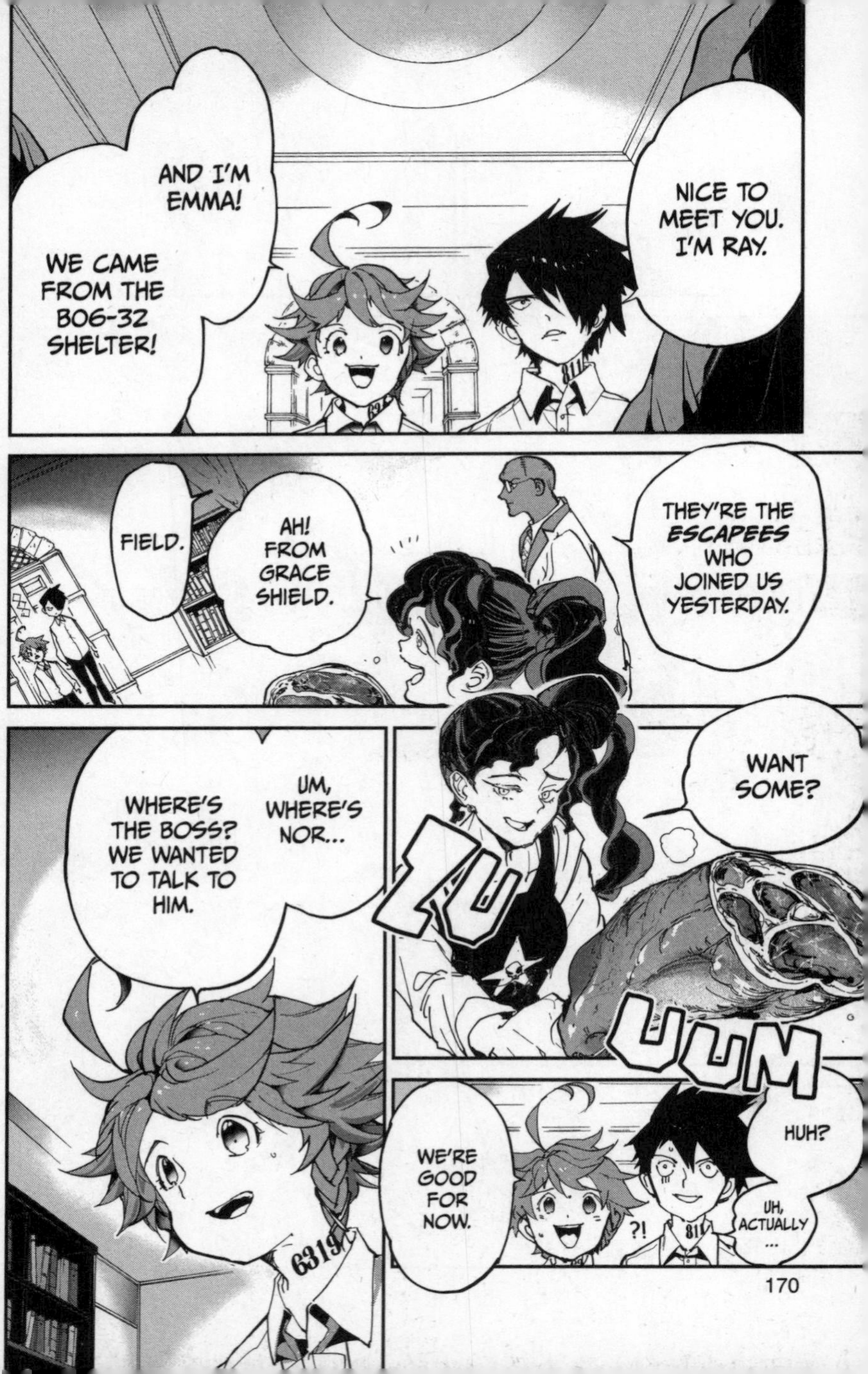
NICE TO MEET YOU. I'M RAY.
AND I'M EMMA!
WE CAME FROM THE B06-32 SHELTER!
THEY'RE THE *ESCAPEES* WHO JOINED US YESTERDAY.
AH! FROM GRACE SHIELD.
FIELD.
WANT SOME?
ZU
UUM
HUH?
UH, ACTUALLY ...
?!
WE'RE GOOD FOR NOW.
UM, WHERE'S NOR...
WHERE'S THE BOSS? WE WANTED TO TALK TO HIM.

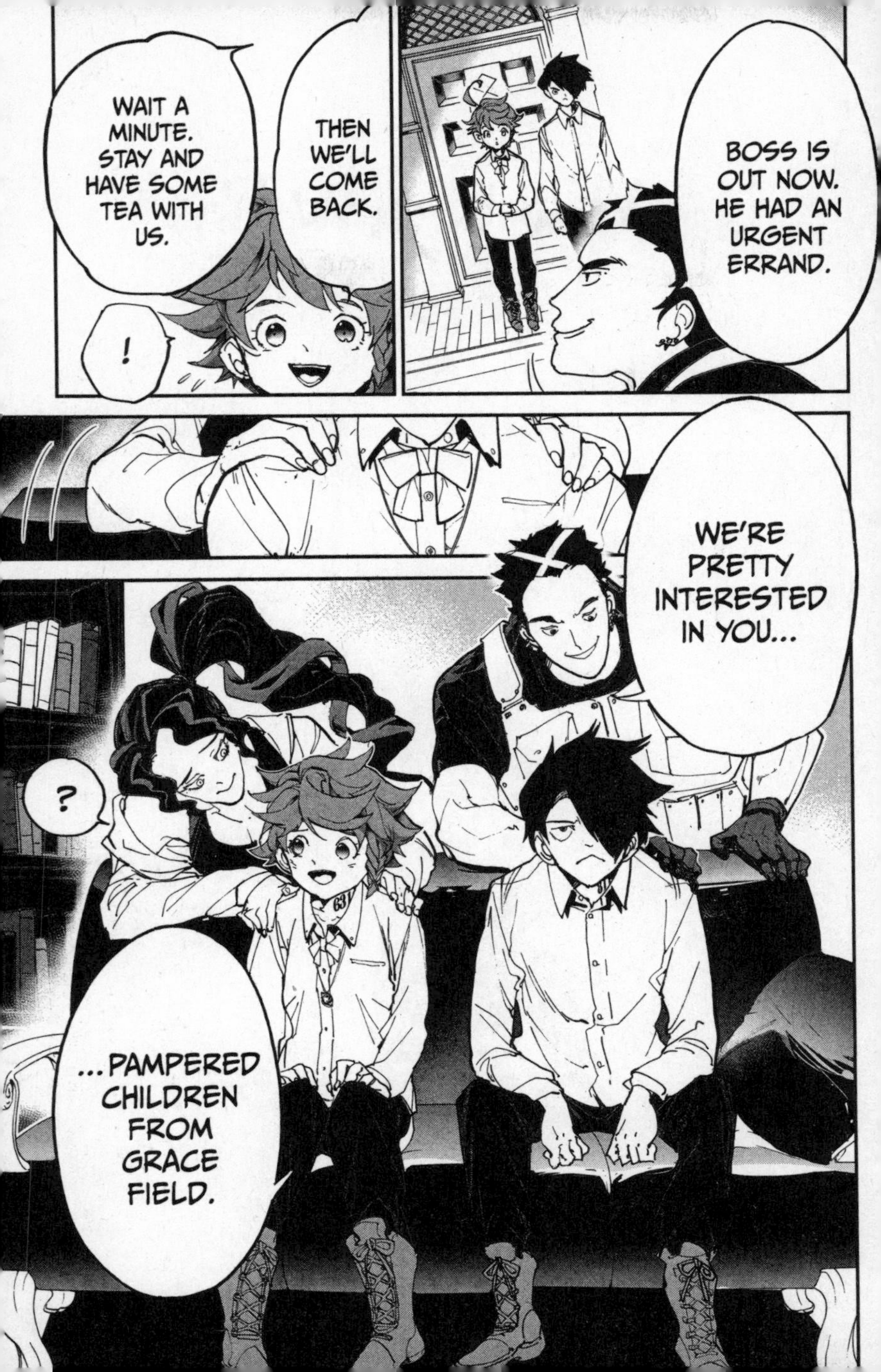
BOSS IS OUT NOW. HE HAD AN URGENT ERRAND.
THEN WE'LL COME BACK.
WAIT A MINUTE. STAY AND HAVE SOME TEA WITH US.
!
WE'RE PRETTY INTERESTED IN YOU...
?
...PAMPERED CHILDREN FROM GRACE FIELD.

How to draw Ray

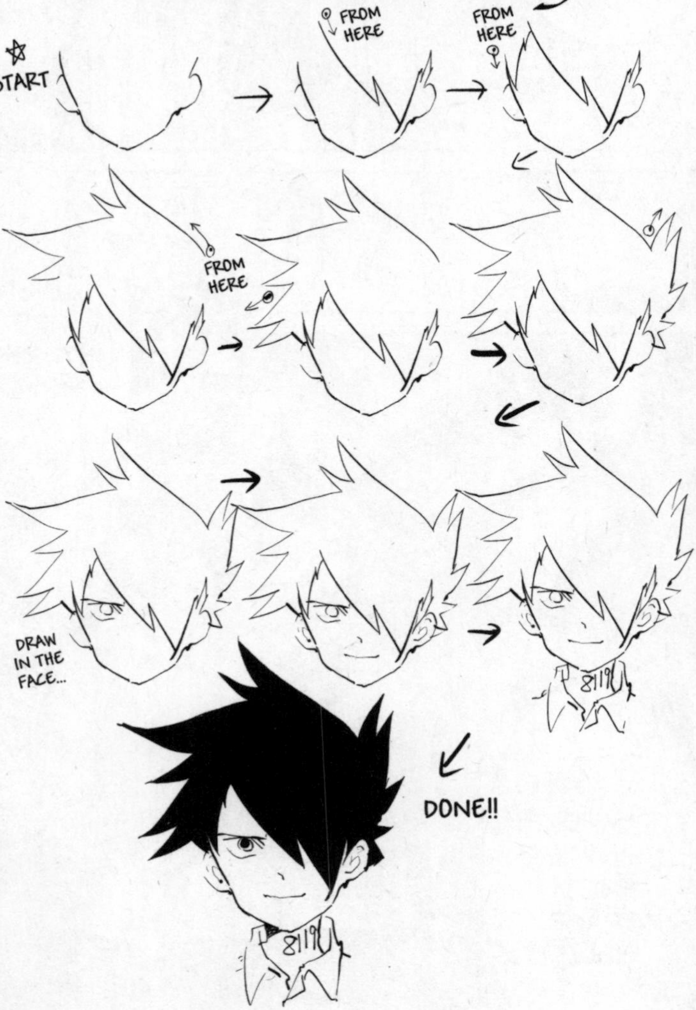
START
FROM HERE
FROM HERE
FROM HERE
DRAW IN THE FACE...
8119
DONE!!
8119

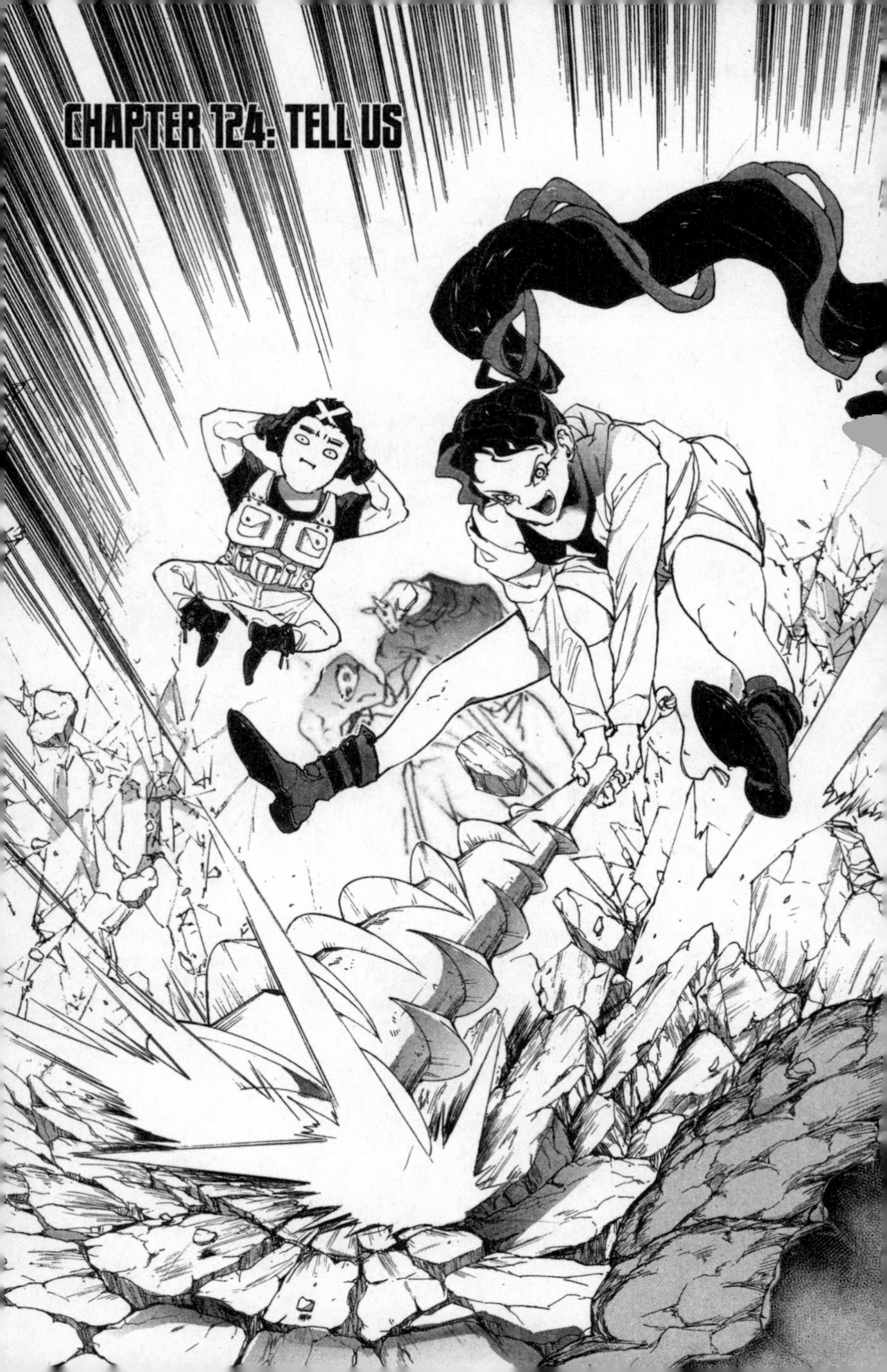
CHAPTER 124: TELL US

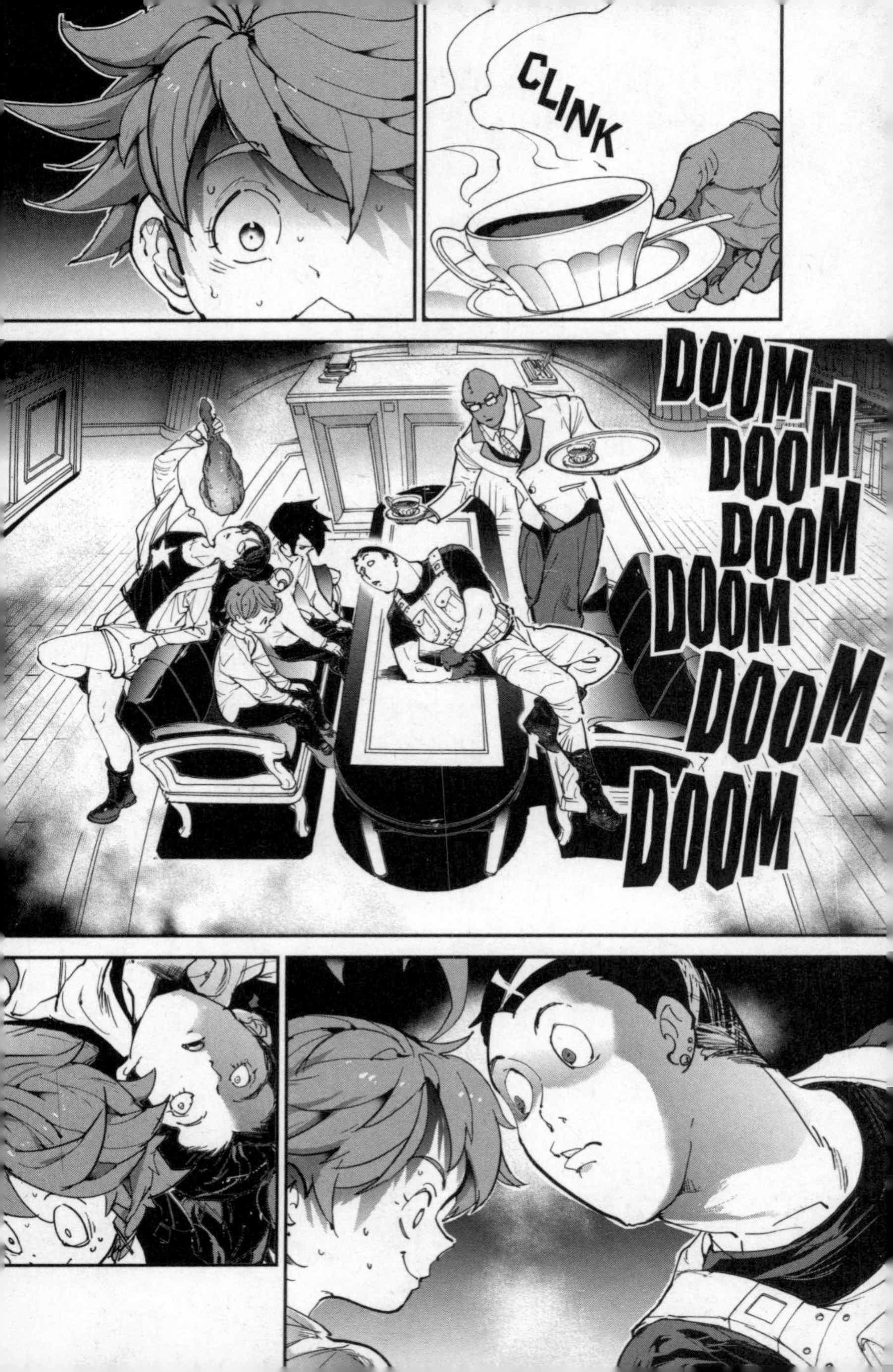
CLINK
DOOM
DOOM
DOOM
DOOM
DOOM
DOOM

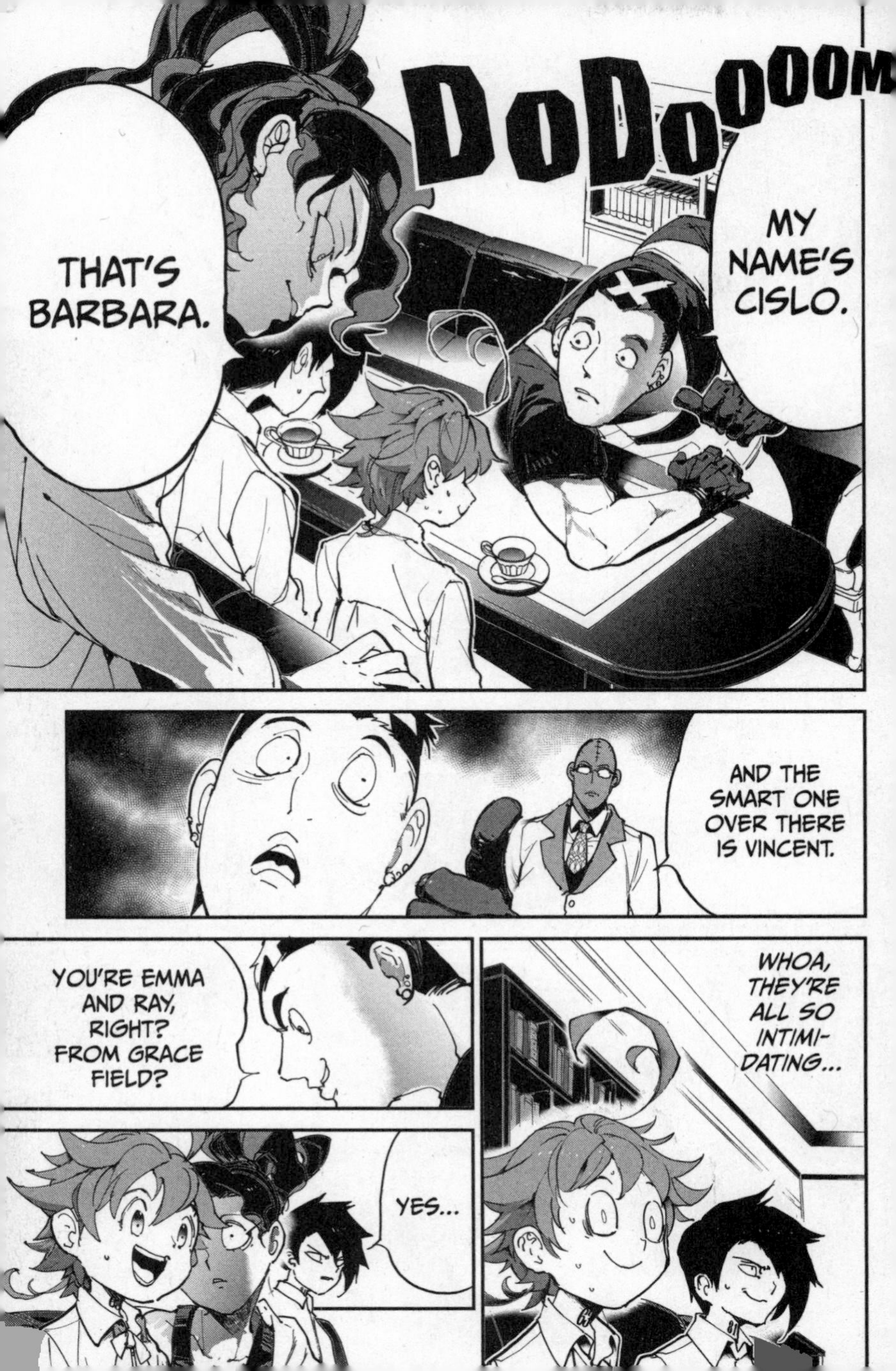
DoDoOOOOM
MY NAME'S CISLO.
THAT'S BARBARA.
AND THE SMART ONE OVER THERE IS VINCENT.
WHOA, THEY'RE ALL SO INTIMI-DATING...
YOU'RE EMMA AND RAY, RIGHT? FROM GRACE FIELD?
YES...

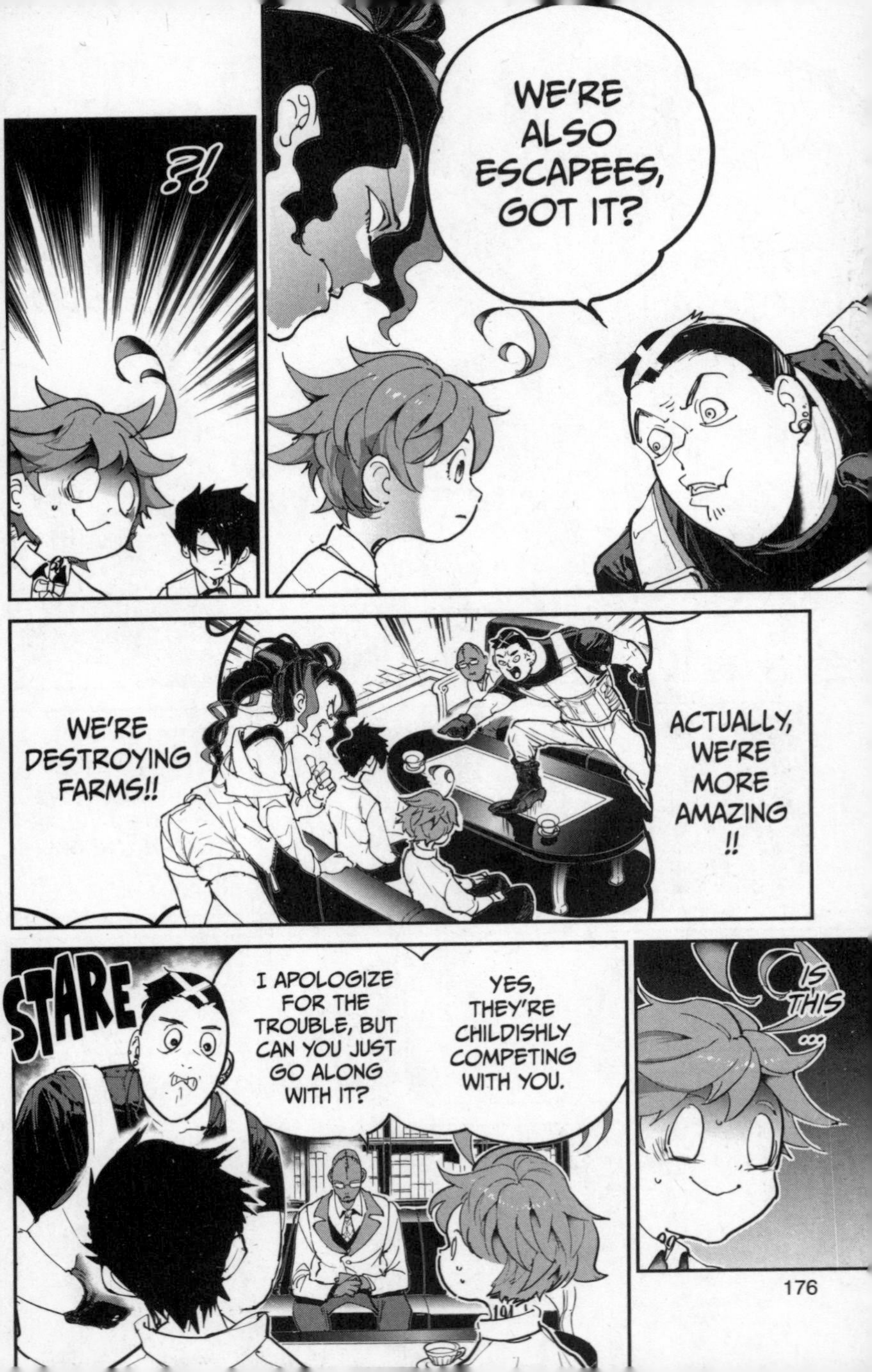
WE'RE ALSO ESCAPEES, GOT IT?
?!
ACTUALLY, WE'RE MORE AMAZING!!
WE'RE DESTROYING FARMS!!
IS THIS...
YES, THEY'RE CHILDISHLY COMPETING WITH YOU.
I APOLOGIZE FOR THE TROUBLE, BUT CAN YOU JUST GO ALONG WITH IT?
STARE

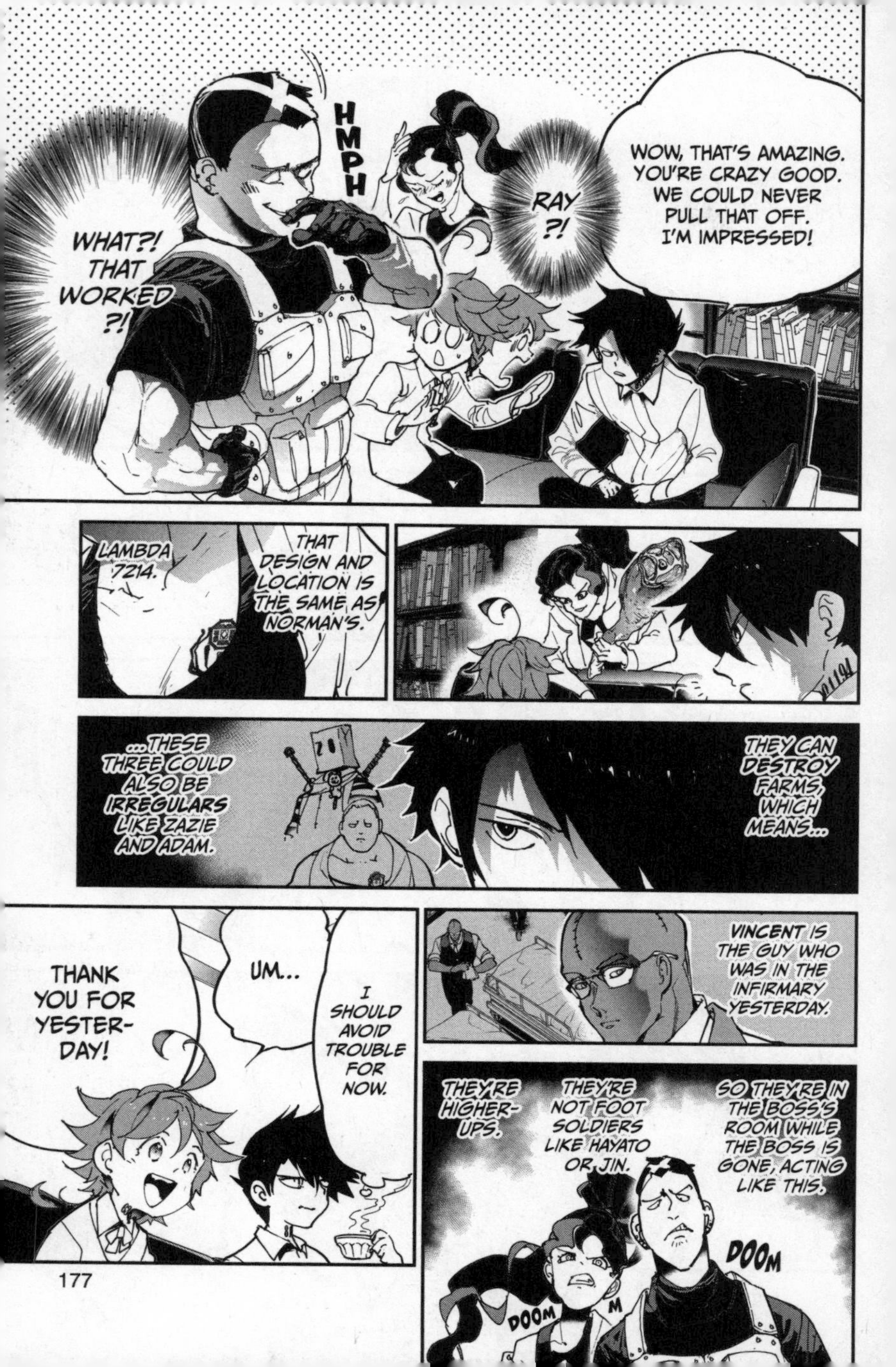
WOW, THAT'S AMAZING. YOU'RE CRAZY GOOD. WE COULD NEVER PULL THAT OFF. I'M IMPRESSED!
RAY ?!
HMPH
WHAT?! THAT WORKED ?!
THAT DESIGN AND LOCATION IS THE SAME AS NORMAN'S.
LAMBDA 7214.
THEY CAN DESTROY FARMS, WHICH MEANS...
...THESE THREE COULD ALSO BE IRREGULARS LIKE ZAZIE AND ADAM.
VINCENT IS THE GUY WHO WAS IN THE INFIRMARY YESTERDAY.
SO THEY'RE IN THE BOSS'S ROOM WHILE THE BOSS IS GONE, ACTING LIKE THIS.
THEY'RE NOT FOOT SOLDIERS LIKE HAYATO OR JIN.
THEY'RE HIGHER-UPS.
DOOM
M
DOOM
I SHOULD AVOID TROUBLE FOR NOW.
UM...
THANK YOU FOR YESTER-DAY!

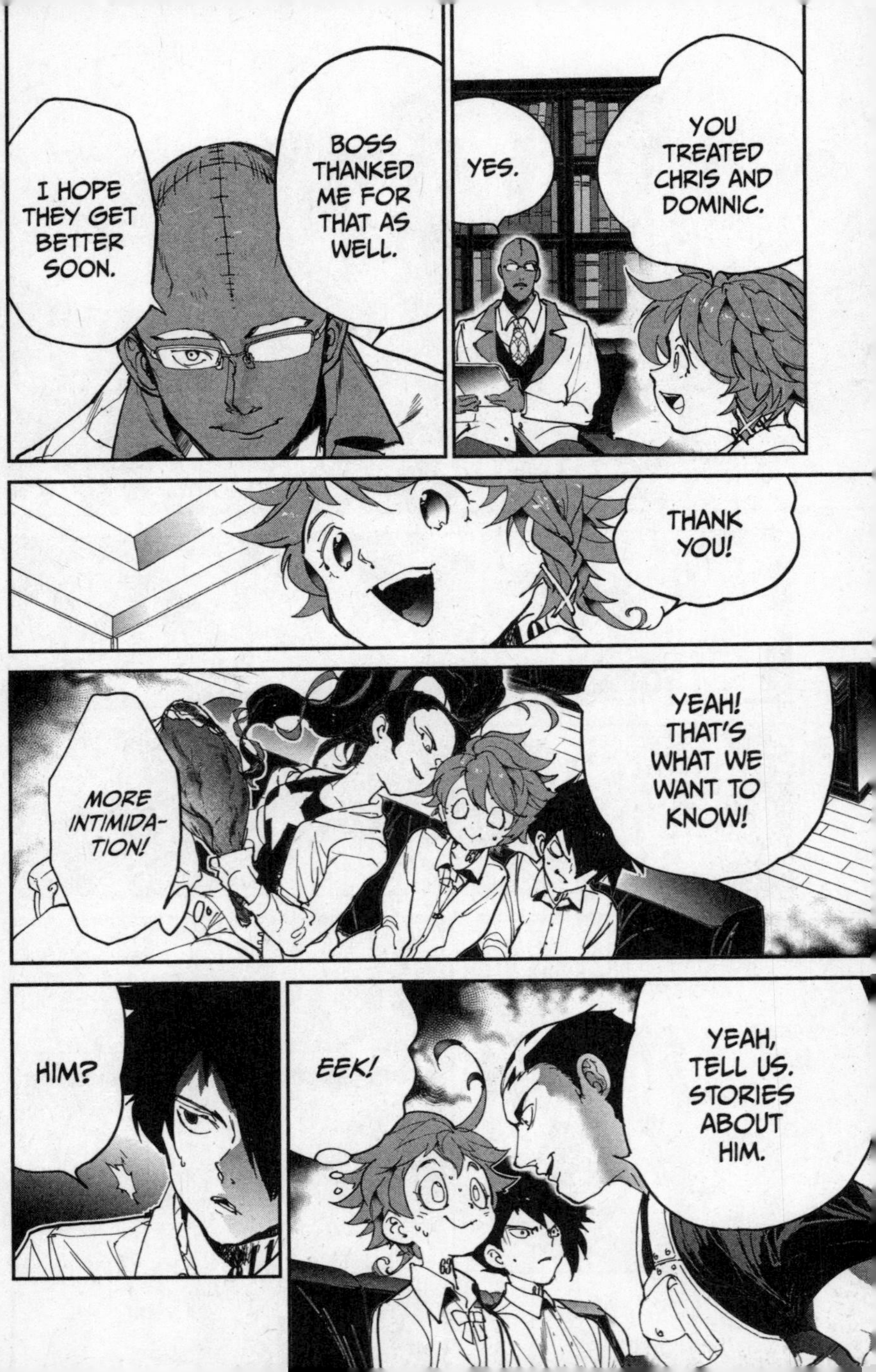
YOU TREATED CHRIS AND DOMINIC.
YES.
BOSS THANKED ME FOR THAT AS WELL.
I HOPE THEY GET BETTER SOON.
THANK YOU!
YEAH! THAT'S WHAT WE WANT TO KNOW!
MORE INTIMIDA-TION!
YEAH, TELL US. STORIES ABOUT HIM.
EEK!
HIM?

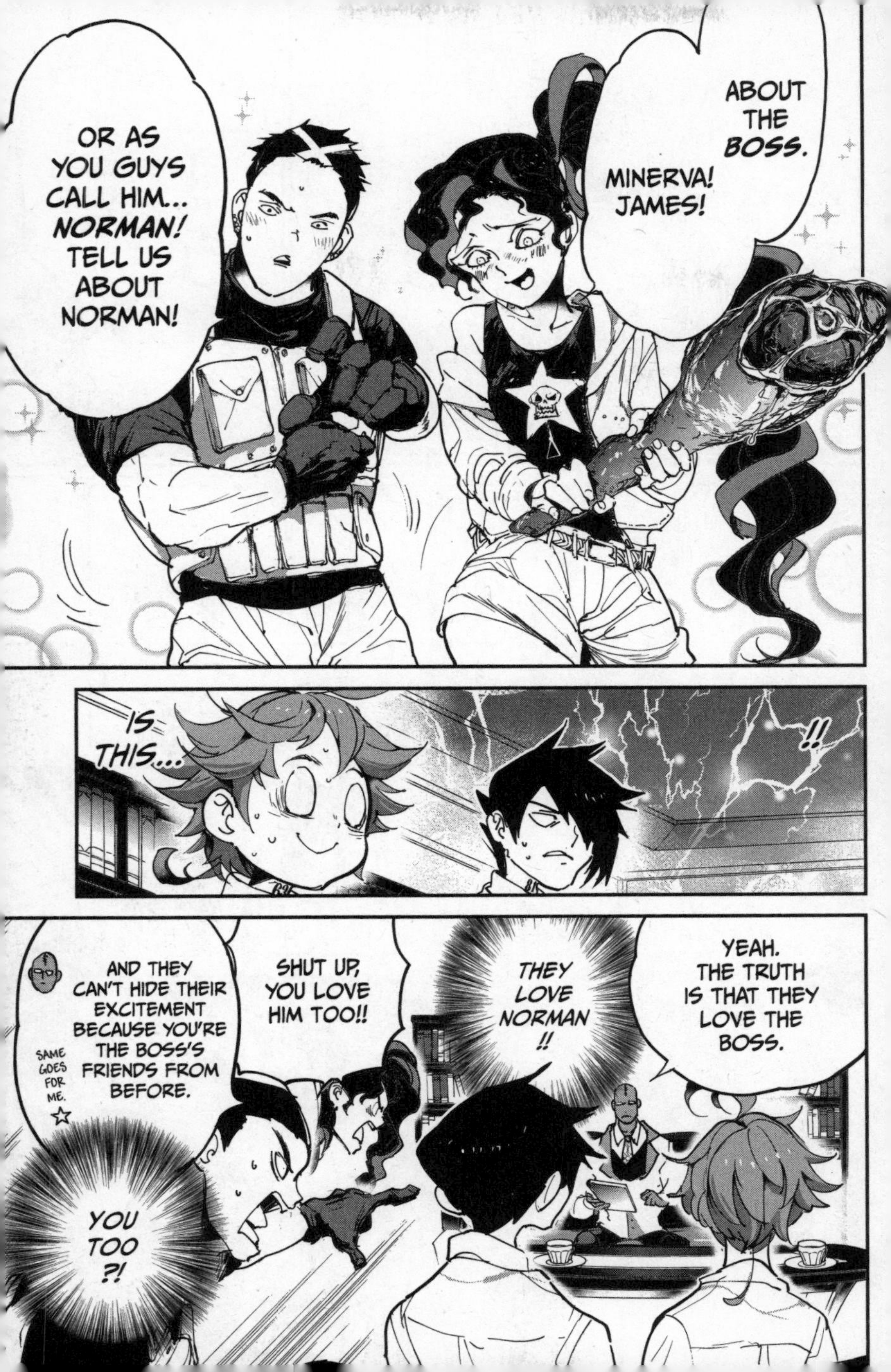
ABOUT THE BOSS.
MINERVA! JAMES!
OR AS YOU GUYS CALL HIM... NORMAN! TELL US ABOUT NORMAN!
!!
IS THIS...
YEAH. THE TRUTH IS THAT THEY LOVE THE BOSS.
THEY LOVE NORMAN !!
SHUT UP, YOU LOVE HIM TOO!!
AND THEY CAN'T HIDE THEIR EXCITEMENT BECAUSE YOU'RE THE BOSS'S FRIENDS FROM BEFORE.
SAME GOES FOR ME. ☆
YOU TOO ?!

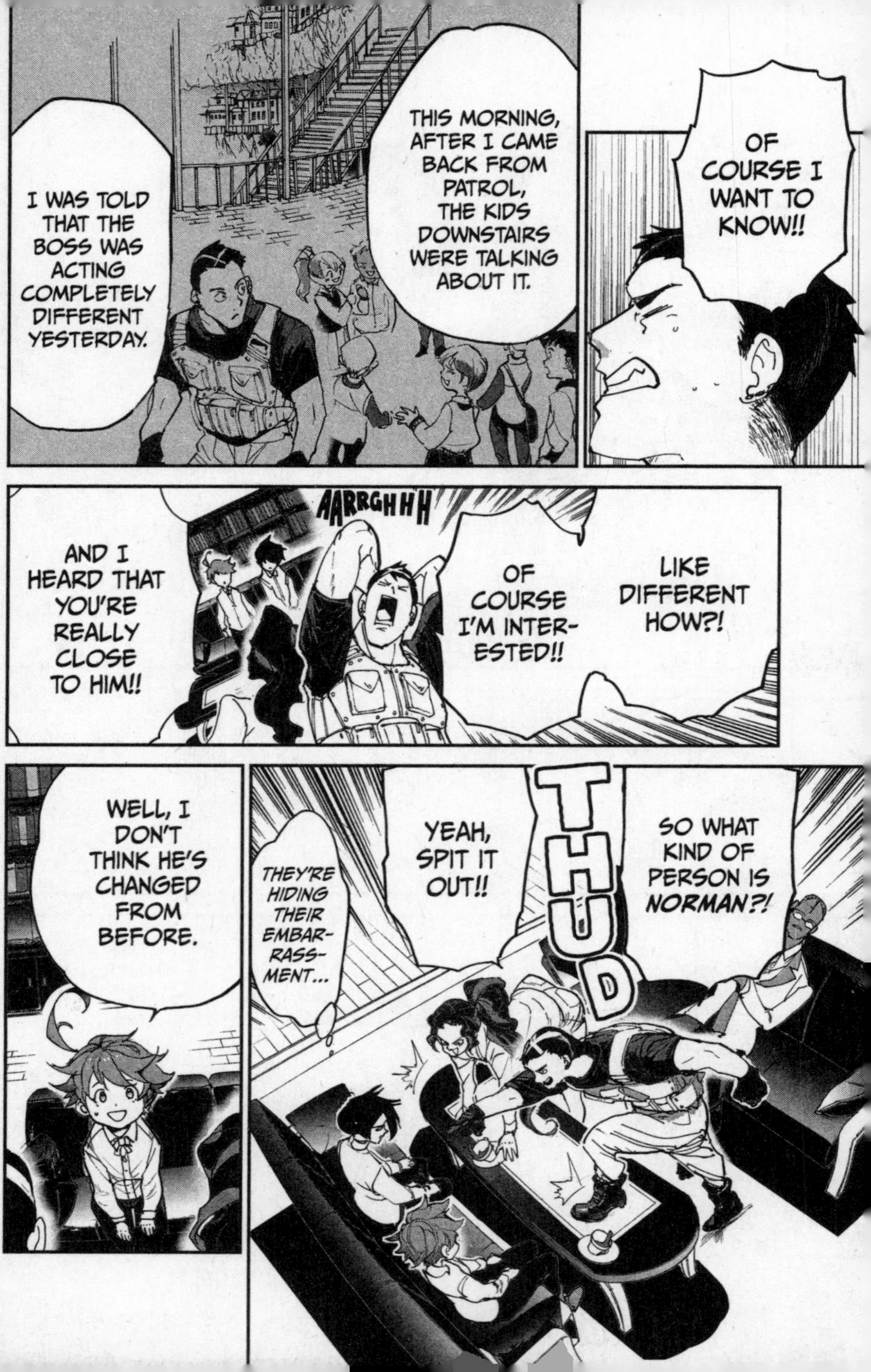

OF COURSE I WANT TO KNOW!!
THIS MORNING, AFTER I CAME BACK FROM PATROL, THE KIDS DOWNSTAIRS WERE TALKING ABOUT IT.
I WAS TOLD THAT THE BOSS WAS ACTING COMPLETELY DIFFERENT YESTERDAY.
LIKE DIFFERENT HOW?!
OF COURSE I'M INTER-ESTED!!
AARRGHHH
AND I HEARD THAT YOU'RE REALLY CLOSE TO HIM!!
SO WHAT KIND OF PERSON IS *NORMAN?!*
THUD
YEAH, SPIT IT OUT!!
THEY'RE HIDING THEIR EMBAR-RASS-MENT...
WELL, I DON'T THINK HE'S CHANGED FROM BEFORE.

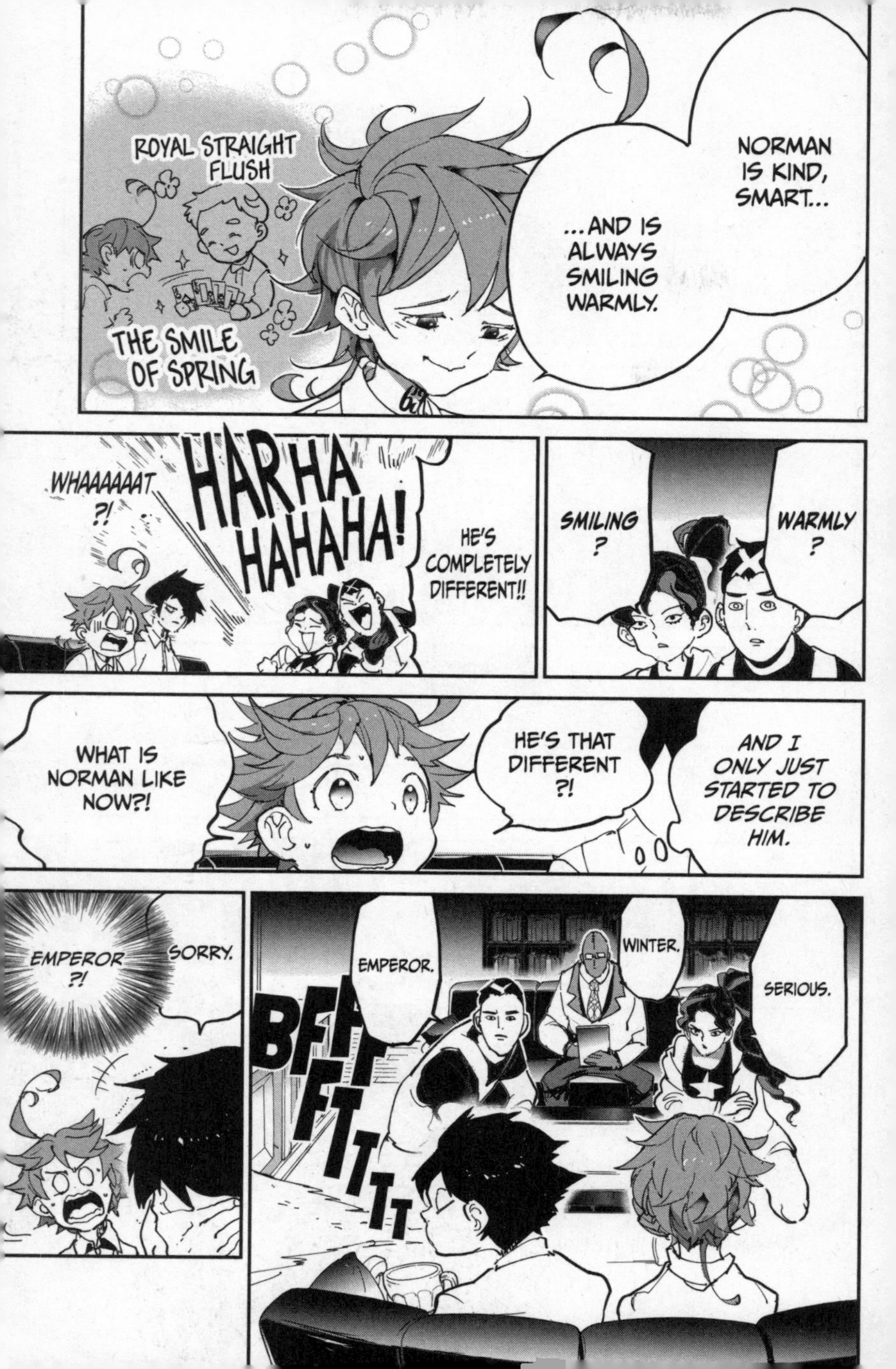
NORMAN IS KIND, SMART...
...AND IS ALWAYS SMILING WARMLY.
ROYAL STRAIGHT FLUSH
THE SMILE OF SPRING
WARMLY?
SMILING?
HE'S COMPLETELY DIFFERENT!!
HARHA HAHAHA!
WHAAAAAAT?!
AND I ONLY JUST STARTED TO DESCRIBE HIM.
HE'S THAT DIFFERENT?!
WHAT IS NORMAN LIKE NOW?!
SERIOUS.
WINTER.
EMPEROR.
BFFFTTTT
SORRY.
EMPEROR?!

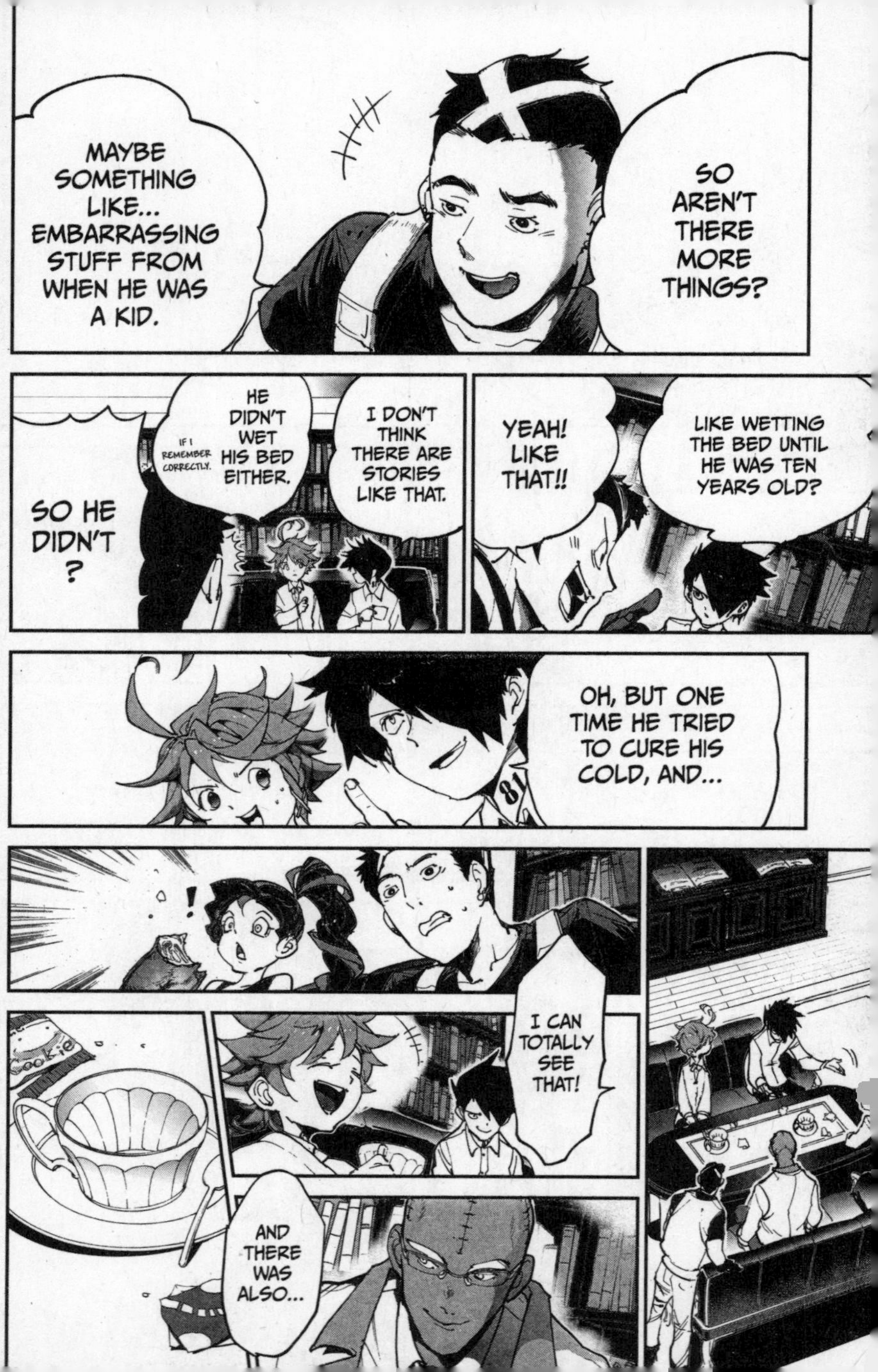
SO AREN'T THERE MORE THINGS?
MAYBE SOMETHING LIKE... EMBARRASSING STUFF FROM WHEN HE WAS A KID.
LIKE WETTING THE BED UNTIL HE WAS TEN YEARS OLD?
YEAH! LIKE THAT!!
I DON'T THINK THERE ARE STORIES LIKE THAT.
HE DIDN'T WET HIS BED EITHER.
IF I REMEMBER CORRECTLY.
SO HE DIDN'T ?
OH, BUT ONE TIME HE TRIED TO CURE HIS COLD, AND...
!
I CAN TOTALLY SEE THAT!
AND THERE WAS ALSO...

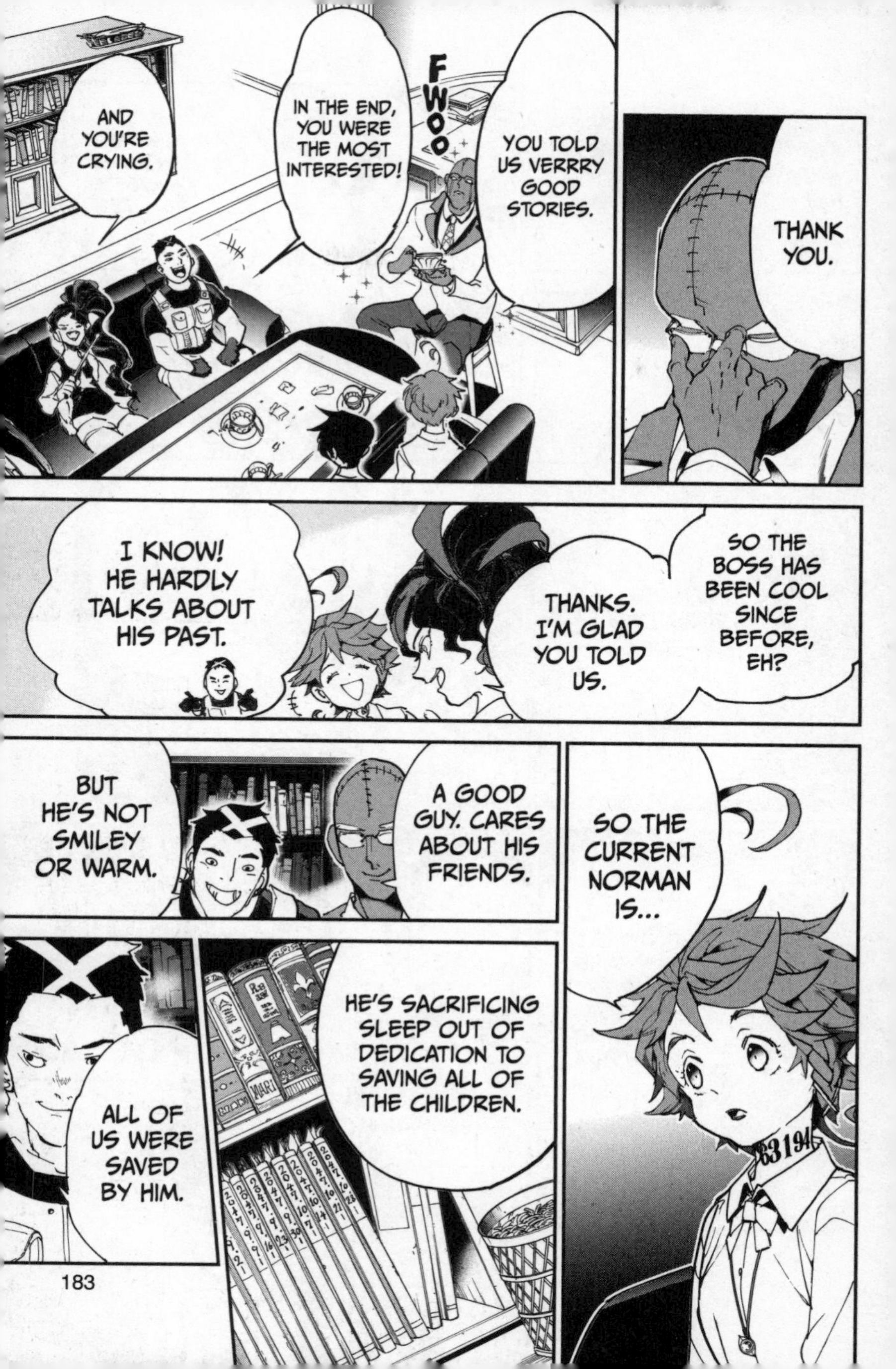
THANK YOU.
YOU TOLD US VERRRY GOOD STORIES.
FWOO
IN THE END, YOU WERE THE MOST INTERESTED!
AND YOU'RE CRYING.
SO THE BOSS HAS BEEN COOL SINCE BEFORE, EH?
THANKS. I'M GLAD YOU TOLD US.
I KNOW! HE HARDLY TALKS ABOUT HIS PAST.
SO THE CURRENT NORMAN IS...
63194
A GOOD GUY. CARES ABOUT HIS FRIENDS.
BUT HE'S NOT SMILEY OR WARM.
HE'S SACRIFICING SLEEP OUT OF DEDICATION TO SAVING ALL OF THE CHILDREN.
ALL OF US WERE SAVED BY HIM.

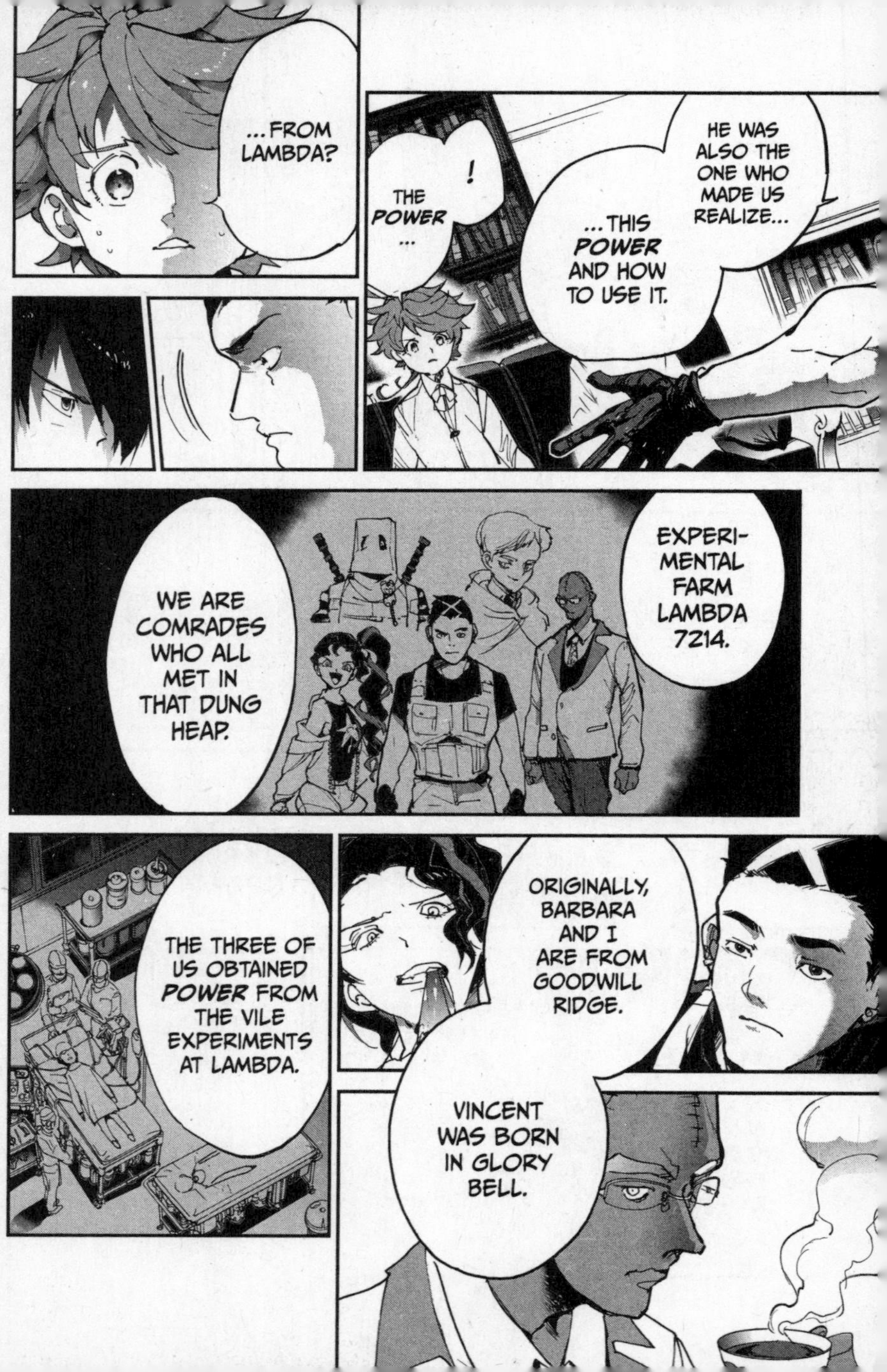

...FROM LAMBDA?
HE WAS ALSO THE ONE WHO MADE US REALIZE...
...THIS *POWER* AND HOW TO USE IT.
!
THE *POWER* ...
EXPERI-MENTAL FARM LAMBDA 7214.
WE ARE COMRADES WHO ALL MET IN THAT DUNG HEAP.
ORIGINALLY, BARBARA AND I ARE FROM GOODWILL RIDGE.
VINCENT WAS BORN IN GLORY BELL.
THE THREE OF US OBTAINED *POWER* FROM THE VILE EXPERIMENTS AT LAMBDA.

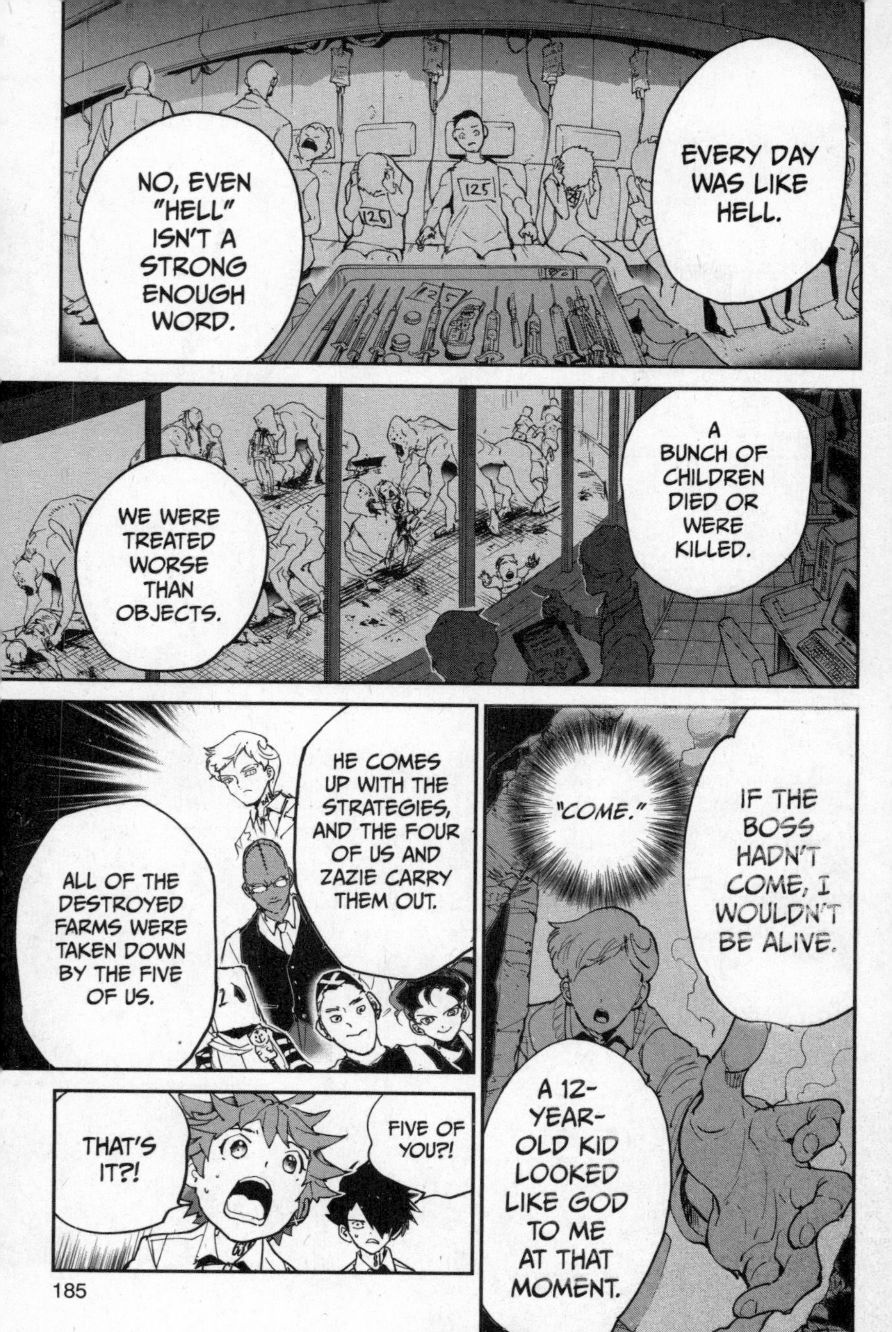
EVERY DAY WAS LIKE HELL.
NO, EVEN "HELL" ISN'T A STRONG ENOUGH WORD.
A BUNCH OF CHILDREN DIED OR WERE KILLED.
WE WERE TREATED WORSE THAN OBJECTS.
IF THE BOSS HADN'T COME, I WOULDN'T BE ALIVE.
"COME."
A 12-YEAR-OLD KID LOOKED LIKE GOD TO ME AT THAT MOMENT.
HE COMES UP WITH THE STRATEGIES, AND THE FOUR OF US AND ZAZIE CARRY THEM OUT.
ALL OF THE DESTROYED FARMS WERE TAKEN DOWN BY THE FIVE OF US.
FIVE OF YOU?!
THAT'S IT?!

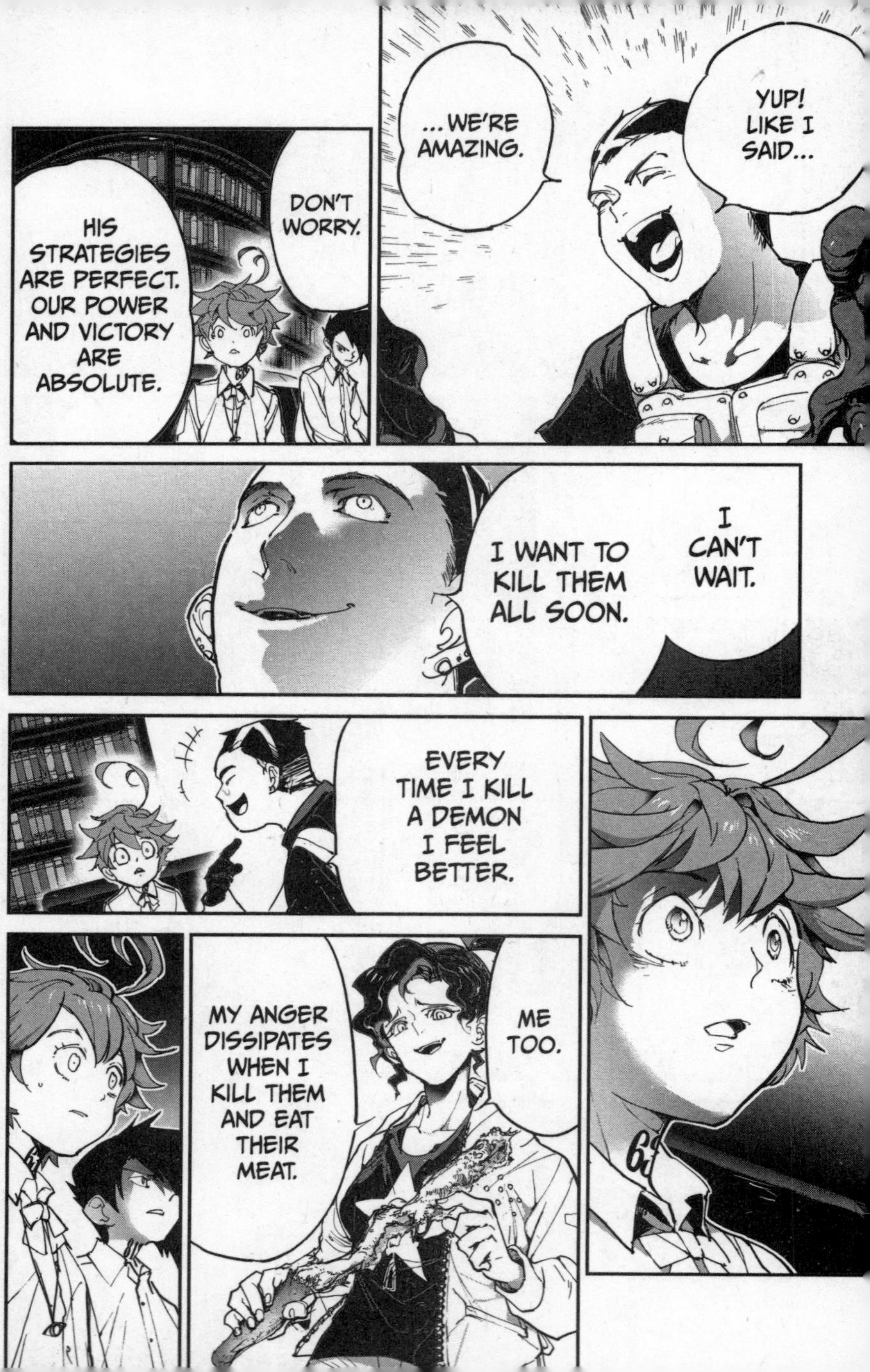
YUP! LIKE I SAID...
...WE'RE AMAZING.
DON'T WORRY.
HIS STRATEGIES ARE PERFECT. OUR POWER AND VICTORY ARE ABSOLUTE.
I CAN'T WAIT.
I WANT TO KILL THEM ALL SOON.
EVERY TIME I KILL A DEMON I FEEL BETTER.
ME TOO.
MY ANGER DISSIPATES WHEN I KILL THEM AND EAT THEIR MEAT.

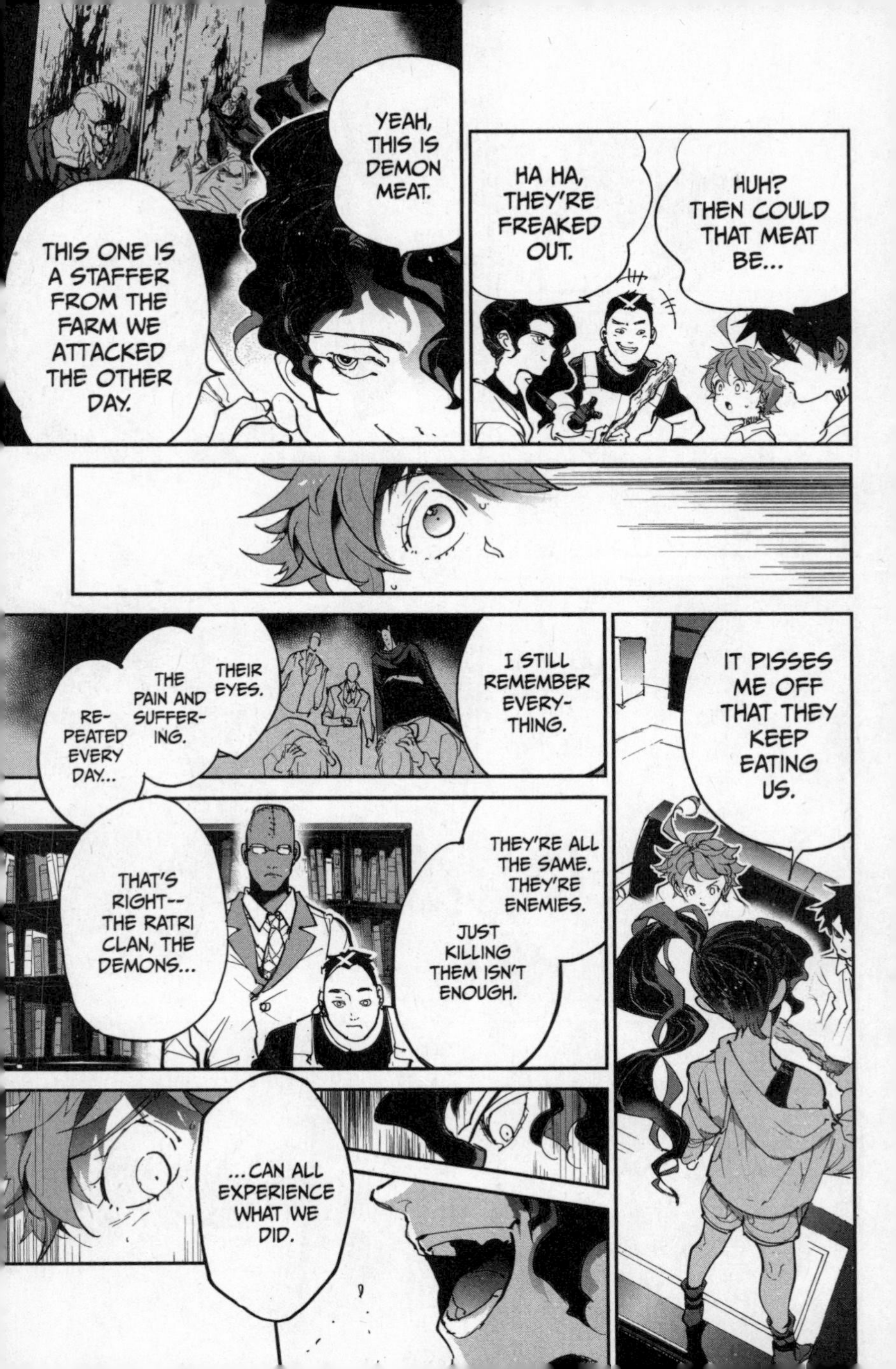
HUH? THEN COULD THAT MEAT BE...
HA HA, THEY'RE FREAKED OUT.
YEAH, THIS IS DEMON MEAT.
THIS ONE IS A STAFFER FROM THE FARM WE ATTACKED THE OTHER DAY.
IT PISSES ME OFF THAT THEY KEEP EATING US.
I STILL REMEMBER EVERY-THING.
THEIR EYES.
THE PAIN AND SUFFER-ING.
RE-PEATED EVERY DAY...
THEY'RE ALL THE SAME. THEY'RE ENEMIES.
JUST KILLING THEM ISN'T ENOUGH.
THAT'S RIGHT-- THE RATRI CLAN, THE DEMONS...
...CAN ALL EXPERIENCE WHAT WE DID.

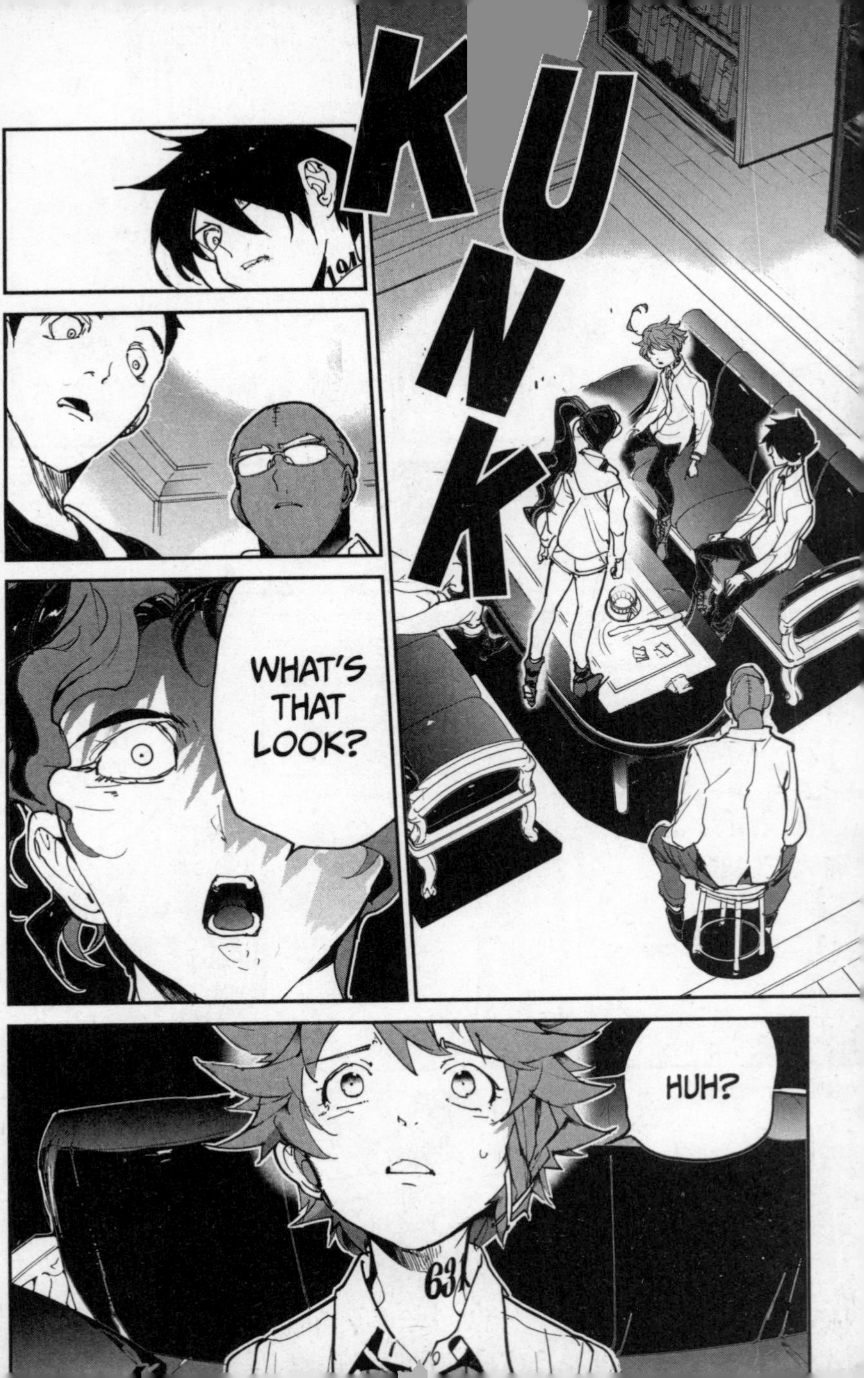
KUNK
WHAT'S THAT LOOK?
HUH?

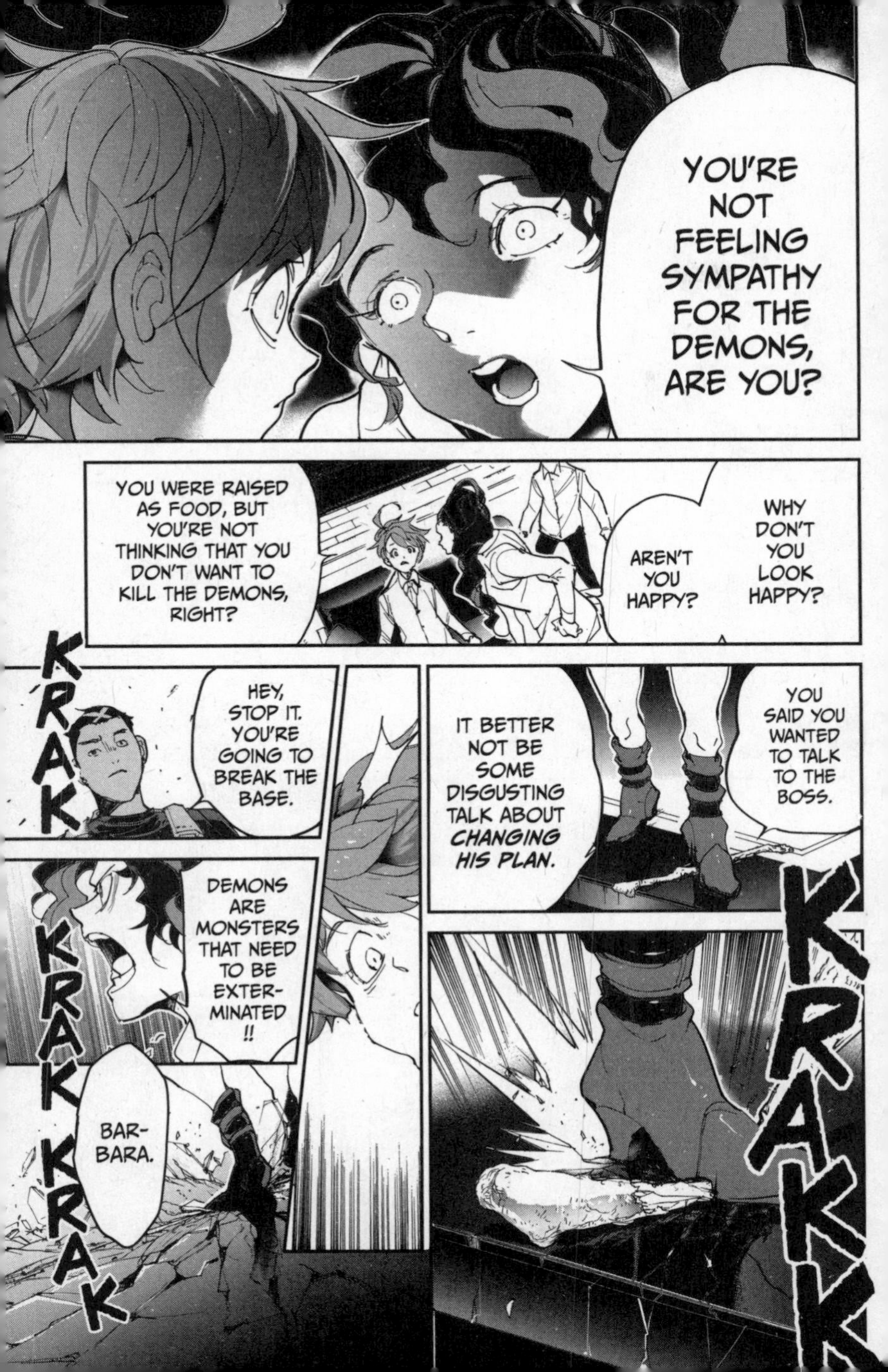
YOU'RE NOT FEELING SYMPATHY FOR THE DEMONS, ARE YOU?
WHY DON'T YOU LOOK HAPPY?
AREN'T YOU HAPPY?
YOU WERE RAISED AS FOOD, BUT YOU'RE NOT THINKING THAT YOU DON'T WANT TO KILL THE DEMONS, RIGHT?
YOU SAID YOU WANTED TO TALK TO THE BOSS.
IT BETTER NOT BE SOME DISGUSTING TALK ABOUT *CHANGING HIS PLAN.*
KRAK
KRAK
HEY, STOP IT. YOU'RE GOING TO BREAK THE BASE.
KRAK
DEMONS ARE MONSTERS THAT NEED TO BE EXTER-MINATED!!
BAR-BARA.
KRAK KRAK KRAK

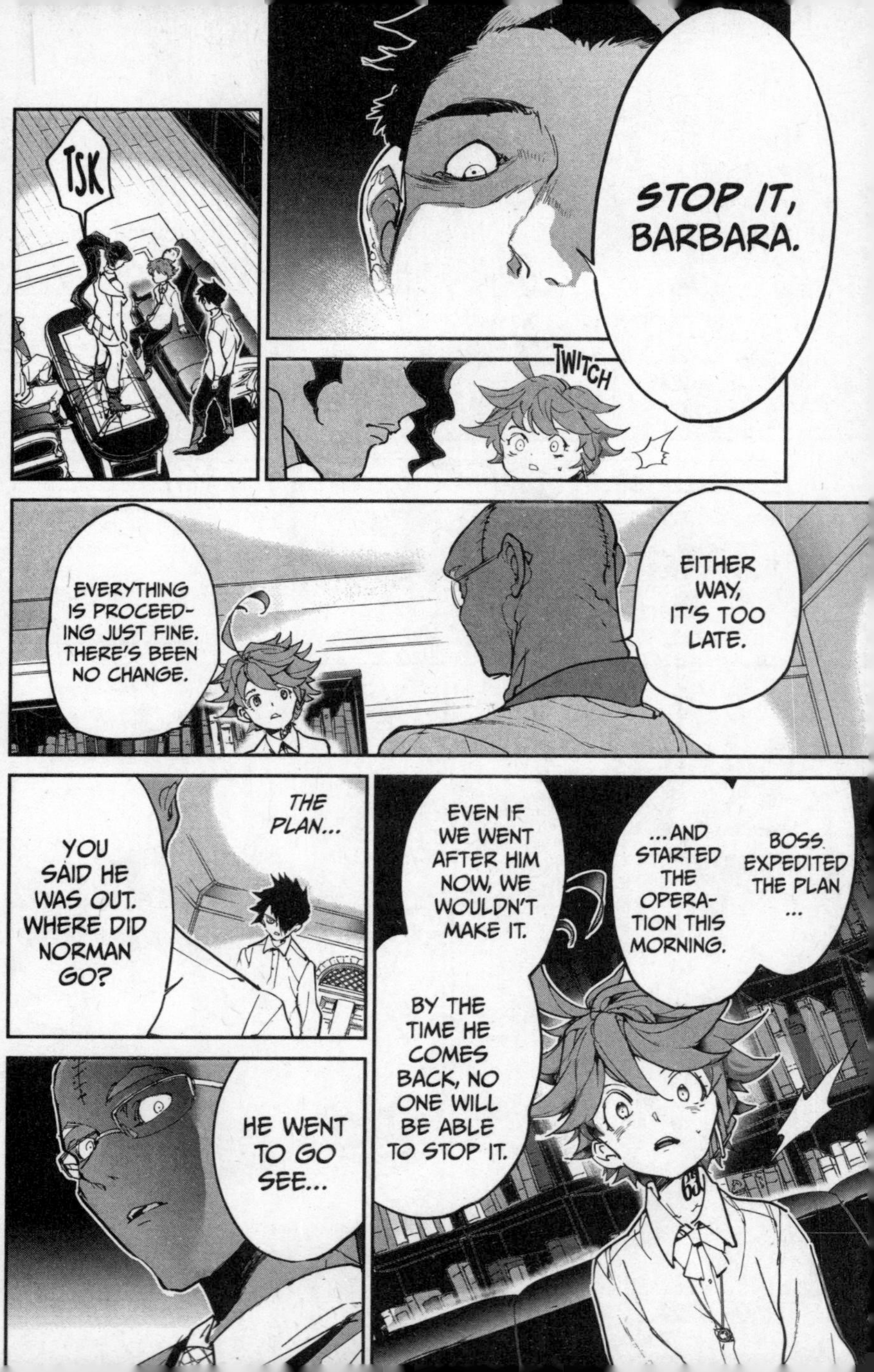
STOP IT, BARBARA.
TWITCH
TSK
EITHER WAY, IT'S TOO LATE.
EVERYTHING IS PROCEEDING JUST FINE. THERE'S BEEN NO CHANGE.
BOSS EXPEDITED THE PLAN ...
...AND STARTED THE OPERATION THIS MORNING.
EVEN IF WE WENT AFTER HIM NOW, WE WOULDN'T MAKE IT.
BY THE TIME HE COMES BACK, NO ONE WILL BE ABLE TO STOP IT.
THE PLAN...
YOU SAID HE WAS OUT. WHERE DID NORMAN GO?
HE WENT TO GO SEE...

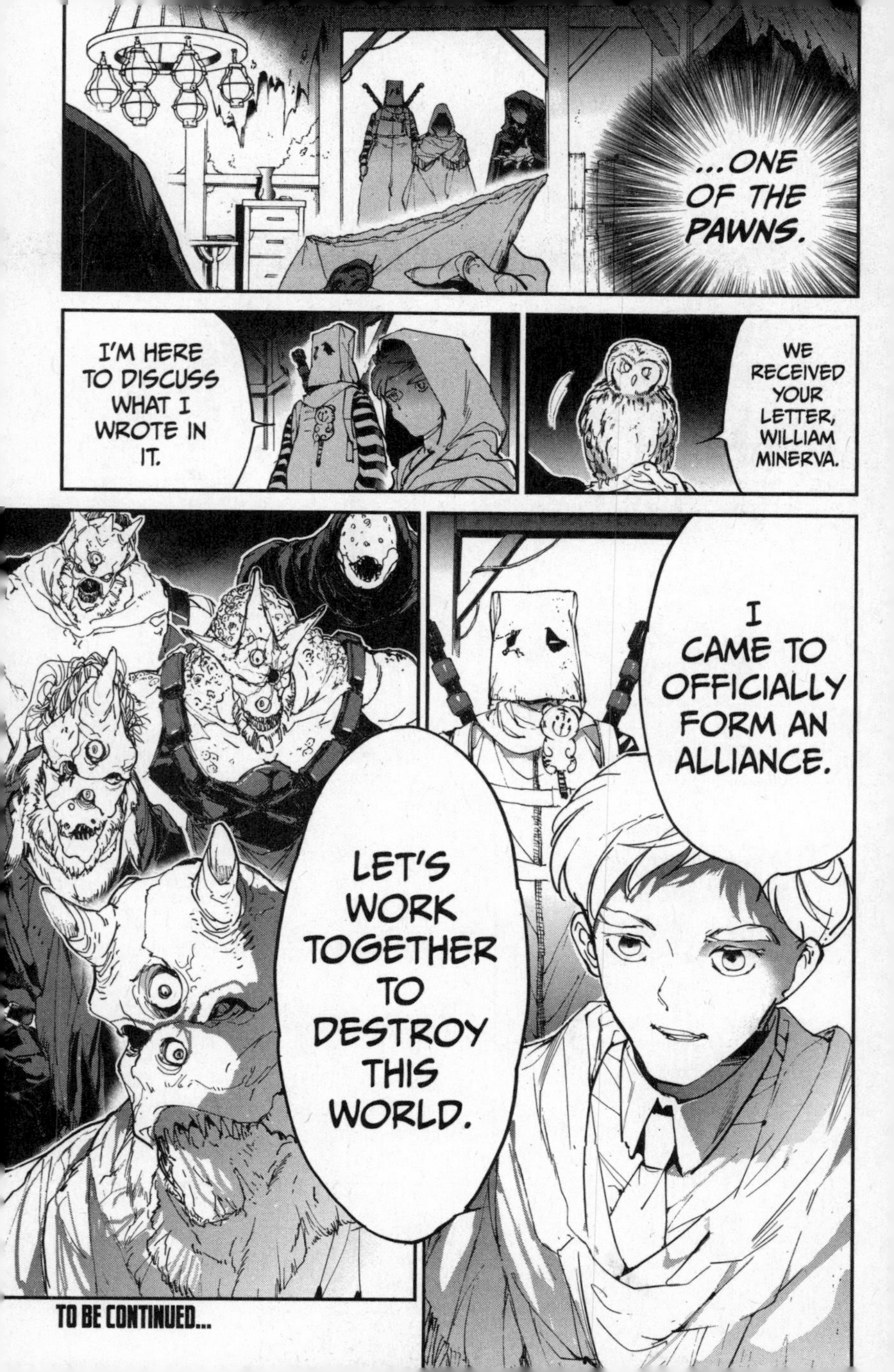
...ONE OF THE PAWNS.
WE RECEIVED YOUR LETTER, WILLIAM MINERVA.
I'M HERE TO DISCUSS WHAT I WROTE IN IT.
I CAME TO OFFICIALLY FORM AN ALLIANCE.
LET'S WORK TOGETHER TO DESTROY THIS WORLD.
TO BE CONTINUED...

YOU'RE READING THE **WRONG WAY!**

The Promised Neverland reads from right to left, starting in the upper-right corner. Japanese is read from right to left, meaning that action, sound effects and word-balloon order are completely reversed from English order.